B. Feintuch

The British Traditional Ballad
in North America

BIBLIOGRAPHICAL AND SPECIAL SERIES
PUBLISHED THROUGH THE COOPERATION OF
THE AMERICAN FOLKLORE SOCIETY

The British Traditional Ballad
in North America

REVISED EDITION

by Tristram Potter Coffin

With a Supplement by Roger deV. Renwick

University of Texas Press, Austin & London

Library of Congress Cataloging in Publication Data

Coffin, Tristram Potter, 1922–
    The British traditional ballad in North America.

    (Publications of the American Folklore Society,
bibliographical and special series)
    Bibliography: p.
    Discography: p.
    Includes index.
    1. Ballads, English—United States—History
and criticism. 2. Ballads, American—History
and criticism. I. Renwick, Roger deV., 1941–
II. Title. III. Series: American Folklore
Society. Bibliographical and special series.
ML3553.C6 1977   784.4'973   76-52476
ISBN 0-292-70719-3

To the memory

of my father:

Tristram Roberts Coffin

Contents

Introduction to the Revised Edition   xi

A Description of Variation in the Traditional Ballad of America   1

A Bibliographical Guide to Story Variation in the Traditional
Ballad in America   22

The Traditional Ballad as an Art Form   164

General Bibliography of Titles Abbreviated in the Study of
Story Variation   174

Index to Ballads Discussed   184

SUPPLEMENT   187

Preface   189

A Note on Variation in the British Traditional Ballad in
North America   195

A Bibliographical Guide to Story Variation in the British
Traditional Ballad in North America   209

Bibliography   287

Discography   294

Index to Standard Titles of Ballads and Songs   295

Introduction To The Revised Edition

The 1950 edition of *The British Traditional Ballad in North America* opened with the following statement:

> The purpose of this book . . . is to offer the ballad scholar, and particularly the student of ballad variation, a key to the published material on the Child ballad[1] in America. The task has been approached with the study of change and development in mind, although the actual presentation is one of bibliography, reference, and description.

But one learns rapidly that it is the province of the reader and the reviewer, not the author, to conclude what a particular book is all about. Thus, *The British Traditional Ballad in North America* has come to be identified as an index, while its real purpose has remained pretty well unrecognized. Amazingly, no review, no citation of the 1950 edition ever mentioned the fact that this book was before all else a guide to *story variation* in the traditional song.

It is too much to hope to change the ways of the world. But I do want to stress with particular vehemence in the introduction to this revised edition, that *The British Traditional Ballad in North America* was conceived and executed by the author as a guide to *ballad story variation*. The division of the songs into story types, the essays describing variation and the ballad as an art form, and the bibliographical material itself—all are designed to give the reader an introduction to a side of ballad scholarship that until 1950, at least, had been almost totally ignored. Moreover, should this second edition prove convenient, and I suppose the first did, as a classification, as a summary, as an index, such virtues must be seen to be incidental to its main purpose.

Variation is one of the most rewarding and important subjects that the American folk song scholar can investigate. In the alterations and modifications that are to be found in the New World versions and variants of traditional British ballad texts are probably hidden the answers to three of folklore's seemingly insolvable questions: how did folk poetry originate, what are the methods by which successions of ignorant and semi-ignorant people produce art, and what is the history of the arrival and subsequent spread of British songs in America? That the answers to these questions can ever be conclusively learned is doubtful. That they never can be conclusively learned from the studies so far completed is certain.

Two major steps are to be taken in assembling the evidence which may eventually bring us closer to the solution of these problems: the collection of texts, and the detailed study and correlation of the material collected. The first step is nearly completed in this country. Under the impetus supplied by the great students of yesterday and today: Child himself, Kittredge, Barry, John and Alan Lomax, Belden, Hudson, Flanders, Leach, Halpert, and their fellows, the surviving songs of American and Anglo-American balladry are nearly all in print, on records, or in the various archives in a large variety of forms. Although further collection will and should continue, its hey-day is past. In the words of a Tennessee informant,

> We don't sing many of the old songs now. Radio has come in and we have to keep up with *Flat Foot Floogie* . . .[2]

Of necessity, folk students of this and the next generation must attempt to complete the second step. Pioneer work in the field of textual and melodic study and correlation has been going on for some time, and though great strides have been made by Barry, Bronson, Charles Seeger, Bayard, Davis, Laws, and the rest, the task stretches on and on toward what may well be infinity. For working in the field of folksong variation is a discouraging task, if only because of the tedium and difficulty involved in locating texts and tunes. American folksongs lie scattered through a thousand books, archives, and record libraries.

The British Traditional Ballad in North America is designed to simplify the task of the textual scholar. It argues no particular thesis of how ballads originated, of how ballads vary, or of what ballads are. Rather, it presents the published scholarship on the Child ballad in the New World and centers it around the central theme of story variation. My hope is that the second edition, like the first, will do its share in opening the way for more and more scholars to produce the many detailed studies and analyses of small areas that are needed to reveal the secrets that lie locked in ballad and folk history.

The author makes no claim that his work is complete, particularly in the bibliographical sense. However, I do hope that the book does its job extensively enough to serve the same ends as completeness. I have, of course, limited *The British Traditional Ballad in North America* to certain arbitrary boundaries. For better or for worse, my definitions have been made in the interests of efficiency and compactness. 1.) I have not surveyed traditional ballads on records. Actually, such a survey involves special treatment, as there has been much doctoring and sophisticated tampering with songs that appear on records, and I have left this material to Ed Cray and Ken Goldstein who are better equipped to handle it than I. 2.) I have not surveyed archive and manuscript collections. The main reason for this omission involves space, time, and money. However, it would be desirable if some scholar could get a grant to canvass the vast store of unpublished material that lies in libraries and private collections across the land. For instance, in Ohio, the private collections of Anne Grimes and Harry Ridenour alone are larger than all the published material from that state. 3.) My coverage of unpublished master's and Ph.D. theses and the offset-mimeographed minor folklore journals is bound to be erratic, though I have made sincere efforts to do well in this line.[3] 4.) I have seen fit to ignore a whole host of books designed for singers, piano-players, and guitar-strummers. Such volumes, the product of the recent interest in folk material, are like records in that songs appearing in them are frequently doctored by the editors. My decisions in relation to such books are arbitrary and, in some cases, made on instinct or intuition. And, finally, it should be noted that I have included as a service some references to broadside and songbook texts, although no effort has been made to make a complete list of references of this sort.

Thus, *The British Traditional Ballad in North America* surveys thoroughly only that material which has been published by reliable collectors from oral tradition. The survey consists of four parts: a descriptive essay on ballad variation in general, a bibliographical guide to story variation, a treatment of the development of the traditional ballad into an art form, and a general bibliography of titles abbreviated in the guide. I have decided to drop the chart of inter-ballad corruption, as I am no longer convinced that one can reduce such matters to diagrams.

In using the bibliographies, five points should be kept in mind. 1.) The titles of the books are abbreviated in such a way that their identification in the General Bibliography at the end, where dates of editions and places of publication are given, is easily made. 2.) As a series of versions or variants of a ballad is often published in a periodical and later only one or two texts from such a series are reprinted in a book or different magazine, I have found it very misleading to indicate the separate bibliographical references that cite identical texts. Consequently, I have avoided making such indications. Nevertheless, even though most editors indicate when and where their texts have previously appeared, the student working with the individual bibliographies should keep overlapping in mind, particularly with reference to material collected by Barry, Belden, Brewster, Cox, Eddy, Flanders, Henry, MacKenzie, Tolman, and the other consistent workers, some of whom have printed texts two or three times over. Likewise, it should be remembered that the Child ballads in early books by a certain scholar often are reprinted in later works by the same man or in later, larger editions of the same book. 3.) References to obscure newspapers and privately printed works are not given when the songs included in them have been reprinted in easily obtainable sources. 4.) No references are given to British or European versions of the songs, unless such references are pertinent to the American tradition. However, Phillips Barry, H. M. Belden, Paul Brewster, J. Harrington Cox, and Cecil Sharp have placed such lists in their collections and, between them, include Old World bibliographies to most of the Child ballads that appear in this country. 5.) It may be noted by a reader that certain references included in previously published bibliographies of individual ballads have been omitted from my lists. These references will prove to be to ballad titles or tunes and not to texts. My bibliographies confine themselves to texts, with a few obvious and notable exceptions such as the Michigan list of Bertrand Jones, the Shearin & Combs Kentucky Syllabus, and the Louise Pound Nebraska Syllabus.

In connection with the local titles under which the various ballads appear, I have had to trust the various editors in my attempts to distinguish labels from actual names.

The "story types" into which I have divided the American versions and variants are arbitrary classes based on differences in plot and mood. Of course, any such division has to be somewhat subjective. However, I have tried to divide the American texts of the traditional ballad according to changes that affect the basic plot or action of the story. The story of a folksong exists only at the length and with the dramatic mood at which that song is recalled or sung at a particular time. What it once was, even what it is to become, are unimportant at the moment of performance. Thus, new ballads, new stories, are born from the old, just as *Clerk Colvill* and *Lady Alice* were evidently born from an early *Johnny Collins* or as *Edward* may have been born from *The Twa Brothers* or some similar song. Within the story types that I have created, I have made no attempt to distinguish minor variations that do not affect plot. Such a task is too particular for a work of this sort. In many cases, insights along these lines can be had by consulting the comments of the original collectors and editors.[4] Wherever possible, the representative examples of the story types have been cited from easily obtainable and extensive works in order to facilitate the task of the reader who wishes to look at an actual text. And versions that borrow material from other songs have been considered to create new story types only where I feel that the borrowing has affected the mood or plot of the original song.

A lot has happened in the field of folksong since 1950. Today the scholars are on the whole better informed about anthropology, musicology, and psychology than they were 13 years ago. In addition, their tools have improved. When *The British Traditional Ballad in North America* and G. Malcolm Laws, Jr.'s *Native American Balladry* first appeared they were pioneer works. Now, they can be used in conjunction with a number of fine studies and classifications, such as Laws' *American Balladry from British Broadsides* and Bertrand H. Bronson's *The Traditional Tunes of the Child Ballads.* The reader will note I have made frequent use of the former, but perhaps the latter volumes are of even greater significance in relation to my book. As Bronson's volumes survey the melodies of the Child ballads in Great Britain and America, they continually develop and polish those patterns my textual studies reveal. Because ballads are stories in song, *The British Traditional Ballad in North America* should be used with the continual awareness of Bronson and his work.[5]

Also, since 1950, there has been an explosion of interest in singing and mass-distributing ballads and folksongs. When this book first appeared, I was quite certain that no one but scholars and *littérateurs* would see it. Now, 13 years later, I can't be so sure. Today, all sorts of popular singers, "tune-smiths", Madison Avenuers, and bearded "types" sing, study, and discuss ballads. This book may well find its way into as many "pads" as it does libraries. Thus, I feel it important that I stress the scholarly purpose of the volume. *The British Traditional Ballad in North America* is not a handbook for singers, a musicological index, or a guide to the performance of ballads. I trust the reader will recognize these facts and not be frustrated by using it as such. The book is, I repeat, a guide to story variation in those traditional ballads that have been published by reliable collectors from oral sources.

In 1950, I expressed my appreciation of the assistance and cooperation extended me by the various libraries which I worked in, corresponded with, or had access to through the inter-library loan service, and, in particular, I thanked the staffs of the Bryn Mawr College Library, the Brown University Library, the Free Library of Philadelphia, the Harvard University Library, and the University of Pennsylvania Library. I was indebted to Dr. H. M. Belden, who wrote me willingly in connection with the F. C. Brown Collection; to Dr. W. Edson Richmond, whose project some of my work has overlapped; to Dr. Horace P. Beck, for bringing to my attention two interesting variants; and to Dr. E. Sculley Bradley, Dr. Joseph Carriere, Dr. Malcolm Laws, Mr. Lynn Hummel, Dr. Samuel P. Bayard, Mrs. Tristram R. Coffin, Miss Ruth Robinson, Mr. Thomas P. Crolius, Mrs. James A. Schnaars, and Mr. William L. Hedges for their various services and courtesies. Most of all, I stated my gratitude to Dr. MacEdward Leach, who conceived and directed my thesis, and to my wife, who did some laborious work throughout its preparation.

Now, I would like to express my gratitude to others who have helped me in revising the 1950 edition: to Dr. Roger Abrahams, Dr. Kenneth Goldstein, Joseph Hickerson, Dr. D. K. Wilgus, Dr. Robert Seager, Frederick Turner, and my brother, Peter R. Coffin. I am also indebted to Dr. Richmond again and to Dr. Herbert Halpert for the review of the 1950 edition that appeared in *Midwest Folklore*[6] and that helped guide my revisions, and to the American Council of Learned Societies and the University of Pennsylvania for granting me funds to aid in my work.

Wakefield, Rhode Island
August 1963

FOOTNOTES

[1] The "traditional" or "Child" ballads are those songs that are included in Francis J. Child's *The English and Scottish Popular Ballads*. His system of numbering has been observed.

[2] Robert Mason, *Folk Songs and Folk Tales of Cannon County*, 14.

[3] I have not been able to study these two collections of American folk songs at all: Lucy Cobb, *Traditional Ballads and Songs of East North Carolina*, Doctoral Dissertation, University of North Carolina, 1927 and Bess Owens, *Some Unpublished Folk Songs of the Cumberlands*, Master's Thesis, George Peabody College, 1930.

[4] A. K. Davis, *Traditional Ballads of Virginia*; Barry's *BESSNE* articles and his *British Ballads from Maine*; J. H. Cox, *Folk Songs of the South*; H. M. Belden, *Folk Songs of Missouri*; W. R. MacKenzie, *Ballads and Sea Songs from Nova Scotia*; A. P. Hudson, *Folk Songs of Mississippi*; P. J. Brewster, *Ballads and Songs of Indiana*; V. Randolph, *Ozark Folk Songs*; and H. H. Flanders, *New Green Mountain Songster* are particularly good in including such correlation.

[5] Bertrand H. Bronson, *The Traditional Tunes of the Child Ballads*, Princeton University Press, I (1959), II (1962), III and IV to be published, is particularly helpful to the textual scholar in that it includes, in conjunction with the tunes, many hitherto unprinted texts from both manuscript collections (Sharp, Barry, Wilkinson, etc.) and recordings. It also is a fine source for listings of the local titles various ballads go under.

[6] See 1951, 72-77.

The British Traditional Ballad
in North America

A Description of Variation
In The Traditional Ballad of America

Any description of ballad variation, and particularly a description concerning the Child ballad in America[7], must deal with three interwoven forces: personal factors, general trends of folk art, and print. Of the three, perhaps the personal factors are the most interesting. Certainly they have by far the most widespread influence. Forgetting, contamination of one ballad by stanzas from another, use of a cliche to fill in forgotten material, desire for more dramatic effects, tendency to rationalize unbelievable situations, use of localisms, invention of new story matter, misunderstanding in the oral transmission of a phrase, and the adaptation of old words to a modified or new tune, are all means by which the individual singer may change a ballad.[8]

Whether such changes are ever done consciously is a matter of some dispute. A. K. Davis, in the introductory remarks to his Virginia collection[9], prints a statement that many singers do purposefully vary their material. Quoting a Miss Flauntleroy, he notes,

> Some ballad singers, probably most ballad singers, . . . would regard the slightest deviation in words or tune hardly short a crime, while others, of less exact memories or less strict ideals, sometimes sing unimportant words or lines differently, and even vary the melodies, which is even more confusing.

MacKenzie, however, offers a passage in opposition in his *Quest of the Ballad.*

> I have laid constant stress on my belief that no ballad-singer ever makes a conscious or deliberate change in the phraseology of his song and so far, at least, as my own experience goes, there is not a shred of evidence against this belief.[10]

That Miss Flauntleroy is almost certainly correct is not of paramount importance here. The point is that variation does occur. And, with respect to this variation the general nature of folk narrative art is somewhat paradoxical. There are constants, and there are definite trends. The central or climactic dramatic situation, the outline of the plot, the stanzas with particularly vivid passages, the figures of speech, the imbedded cliche, all tend to hold the story and the text firm. While an inclination to move away from diffuseness toward concentration upon a single part of a single incident and the desire to universalize the material often opposes these factors.[11] Thus, where the trends can operate with aid from personal factors, masses of detail, archaic phraseology, commonly recurring situations, and the excess material sometimes found at the beginning and end of the songs, the constants are frequently overridden. However, it must not be forgotten that such over-

1

riding does not invariably, nor even consistently happen.

The force of print on the ballad is difficult to estimate.[12] In the first place, printed broadsides, chapbook texts, songster versions, etc. are no longer ballads to be safely studied as a part of folklore. For even if the editor has been careful to retain the language and phraseology of a text received by him from oral tradition, a fact seldom likely and almost never ascertainable, one of the essential ingredients of the ballad has been eliminated when the song is circulated on paper.[13] In the second place, the question "Can a ballad be reborn from print?" must be answered. That is, can a song that has gone from oral tradition into print return to oral tradition and be considered a folk song? There seems no reason that it cannot. Almost all collectors[14] have taken this stand. In addition, there is ample evidence that a number of folk songs have not only been reborn from print, but have had their origin on paper.[15] In the third place, although a ballad that enters print were never reborn, it may still influence oral versions of the story through any one of the personal factors. A singer reading or hearing recited or sung a printed version of a text he knows in fragmentary form may "fill" or vary his text accordingly. And, in the last place, the poet who adapts a specific popular ballad to his sophisticated ends, as did Burns, Hamilton, Scott, Swinburne,[16] and others, may find his song reentering oral tradition[17] and perhaps influencing the original song that has continued on in oral tradition.

Keeping all these points in mind, then, one can easily see that the press can mould the history of traditional texts to a great extent. A song and its story may be preserved from the normal forces of folk art for many years before it reenters oral tradition. What become unusual events and expressions are retained intact, while the new version in turn gives birth to a series of strikingly similar texts.[18] Editorial modifications, such as sentimentalized endings and moralizing, may be inserted and return with the song to the folk. Sometimes such an interim in print will be the only thing to preserve the song from complete extinction. *Barbara Allen* is not nearly so well known in Britain as it is in this country because of its popularity in nineteenth century American songbooks.

Perhaps Phillips Barry's rediscovery[19] of the Child Ad version of *Riddles Wisely Expounded* summarizes the whole subject the most graphically. Here a British broadside was freely translated into German by Herder, used by Goethe in an opera,[20] re-translated into English, and thence went back into oral tradition to be picked up a half-century or more later in Maine.

Variation itself is not a simple subject, and, especially in America, there are a great many types of ballad alteration. It seems best to divide my discussion into two parts: textual variation and story change. The former, which shall be taken first, involves those changes that do not affect the story, either as to plot or mood, but rather create the minor differences that distinguish the variants, and often the versions, of individual ballads.[21] This partition of the subject can then be carried further to distinguish verbal variations, refrain movement and degeneration, phrase-idea movement, stanza changes, in addition to corruption by means of lines, phrases, names, cliches, motifs and the like.

The most obvious sort of ballad change centers about the simple alterations of words and phrases. Any composition travelling from mouth to mouth, from generation to generation, from country to country is bound to suffer from a certain amount of verbal corruption and degeneration. This is particularly true when the word or phrase is slightly strange or out of the ordinary. The church, St. Pancras, in *Lord Lovel* can be found as St. Pancreas, Pancry, Pancridge, Panthry, Pankers, Patrick, Bankers, Peter, Varney, Varner, Vernoys, Vincent, Rebecca, Francis, King Patsybells, etc.[22] The place to which James Harris asks the carpenter's wife to go in Child 243 varies from Sweet Willie, sweet tralee, and Tennessee to Italy, the deep blue sea, and calvaree.[23] The brown girl becomes the Brown girl, merry green lea becomes Merry Green Lea, the "burial in the choir" becomes "burial in Ohio", Beelzebub becomes belchy bub, a cuckold becomes a cockle-comber, virgins become Virginnins, "so bonny O" becomes "siboney-o", colleens become golis, etc., etc. And in one puritanical text of *Sir Lionel*[24] Old Bangum "swore by blank (sic) he had won the shoes".

These variations on the word level can be traced to a number of sources besides the obvious one of oral degeneration. Rationalization and localization also exercises influence in such situations. The former process, which I shall discuss later on the story level, is simply the means of transporting an unbelievable, illogical, or outmoded phrase or situation to something more plausible. Barry in connection with the "plant burden" of *The Wife Wrapped in Wether's Skin*[25] points out that the old charm against the devil "juniper, gentian and rosemary" has been made "more sensible" so that the names of the plants have become the names of persons in American texts: "Jennifer June and the rosymaree",[26] "Jinny, come gentle, Rose Marie", "Gentle Jinny, fair Rose Marie", etc.[27]

Localization is the process of adapting the vocabulary and material of a song to a certain locality. In Earl Beck's lumberjack version of *The Farmer's Curst Wife*[28] the husband is a woodsman instead of a farmer, while the Yorkshire bite has become a New Hampshire bite in Maine.[29] With respect to this characteristic method of varying words and phrases, names of local heroes are frequently inserted into the stories in the place of men long dead and long unknown. Lord Randal becomes Johnnie Randolph in Virginia and West Virginia where the illustrious Randolph family lived,[30] and Captain Charles Stewart, U.S.N. sets out to capture Andy Barton in a large number of northern American texts.[31] Barbara Allen is made a poor blacksmith's daughter and her lover the richest man in the world in one New York village,[32] while the whole scene of this same ballad shifts to a prairie locale in another cowboy version.[33]

The meanings of individual words often suffer in transmission to the extent that the result is pure nonsense. It is not unusual to find singers standing loyally by such phrases as "he buckled his belt down by his side and away they went bluding (bleeding) away",[34] "up spoke a pretty little parrot exceeding (sitting) on a willow tree",[35] and "he mounted a roan (her on), she a milk-white steed, whilst himself upon a dapple gray".[36] However, some of the variations manage to remain within the limits of sense, even if they give at best a ludicrous picture. Lord Thomas in a Virginia text of Child 73 cut off the brown girl's head and "stowed (stoved) it against the wall",[37] while he "rattled low (loud) on the rein (ring)" before Eleanor's house in an Indiana version.[38] A few times the corrupted text will make almost as good sense as what we know as the original. For example, when in Child 84 "all her friends cried out amen (amain) unworthy Barbara Allen"[39] or when Lord Randal drinks poisoned ale (eels)[40] little is lost to the person who does not know the original.

It is true, however, that such word and phrase changes do frequently destroy rimes.

> Down she sank and away she swam,
> First place she found herself was in the mill pond (dam).[41]

Rime is never sacred to the folk, but, oddly enough, destruction of it seems to occur most often when the whim of some singer has overridden a cliche or set phrase. In a West Virginia text of *Lord Thomas and Fair Annet.*

> He called together his merry men all
> And dressed himself in black (white),
> And every town that he rode through
> They took him to be some knight.[42]

Artistically, of course, black is a more satisfactory color than white, but it is an obvious superimposition. A similar change occurs in a text of *Fair Margaret and Sweet William.*

> Lady Margaret died for pure love,
> Sweet William he died for sorrow.
> Lady Margaret was buried on the east of the church
> And Sweet William on the west.

Here the last two lines have been altered completely and the east-west arrangement has replaced the obvious today-tomorrow motif.[43] Examples similar to these can be found by the dozens in any collection of American folk songs. However, before dropping the subject, it might be worthwhile to note the representative rationalization made, in all likelihood, by a printer unfamiliar with the ballad commonplace "weep for gold and fee" that is to be found in the deMarsan broadside of *James Harris.*

> Says he, "Are ye weeping for gold, my love,
> Or are you weeping for fear (fee),
> Or are you weeping for your House Carpenter
> That you left and followed me?[44]

A part of the ballad frequently affected by such verbal variations is the refrain. Often long since antiquated, in garbled Latin, or bordering on nonsense to begin with, refrains are ripe for the forces of variation to work upon. The "juniper, gentian, and rosemary" line mentioned earlier is illustrative, as is the simple "the bough was bent to me" portion of *The Twa Sisters* which can be found as "the bough were given to me", "bow down you bittern to me", "and a bow 'twas unto me", "bow your bends to me", and any number of other similar lines. "Rosemary and thyme" becomes "rivers and seas are merry in time", "every rose grows merry in time", "every rose grows merry and fine", and so forth. Changes seem to increase in direct proportion to the amount of meaning that is lacking to the lines.

Refrains cross from one song to another with a certain regularity, and the reasons for such transposition are not hard to understand. As refrains generally carry none of the story and at most set the mood for the song in which they appear, exchange and substitution come naturally. The "juniper, gentian, and rosemary" line occurs in a Michigan *Farmer's Curst Wife*[45] and in a Maine *Captain Wedderburn's Courtship*[46]; while Belden expresses the opinion that the whole "rosemary and thyme" series found in *The Elfin Knight* and in a few texts of *The Twa Sisters* may belong to the same original burden.[47] *Riddles Wisely Expounded* can also be seen with a plant refrain in the Child Collection.[48]

But crossing over is not confined to the refrains alone. Perhaps the most important body of ballad variation falls under this heading. Names, phrases, lines, cliches, whole stanzas and motifs wander from song to song when the dramatic situations are approximately similar.[49] Sometimes this infiltration from one ballad to another is so complete and of such long standing that we cannot tell in which song a specific line, etc. originated. Thus Fair Ellen or Fair Eleanor may be the heroine of almost any song, and if she is most commonly found in *Lord Thomas and Fair Annet* she also appears frequently in *James Harris* and in *Earl Brand*.[50] Lord Barnard, Barbara (Allen), Sweet William, and Lady Margaret are always possible names for any ballad character, and it should cause no more than moderate surprise to find Lord Thomas called Jimmie Randolph in some Virginia texts.[51]

In the same fashion certain lines and expressions (although not standard cliches) will travel from one song to another. One southern text of *Little Musgrave and Lady Barnet* tells how Lord Barnard "cut off her (his wife's) head and threw it against the wall", just as Lord Thomas invariably does in Child 73.[52] A Tennessee ballad relates that Lord Thomas "rose one morning and dressed himself in blue" in the usual manner of Sweet William in Child 74.[53] And the remark of the murderess to Young Hunting's body in a Virginia text: "your clothes are not a bit too fine to rot in the salt sea" is reminiscent of *Lady Isabel and the Elf-Knight*.[54]

The cliche itself is even more likely to cross from ballad to ballad. Stock lines, phrases and even stanzas crop up in similar situations regardless of story, often serving as a means for the singer to cover his lagging memory. Gerould has discussed this characteristic of folk poetry in some detail in *The Ballad of Tradition*[55] so that the listing of a few typical American examples will suffice here. A person who goes on a journey dresses in red and green or gold and white (see Child 73, 99, 243, and others); a man receiving a letter smiles at the first line and weeps at the next (see Child 58, 65, 84, 208, 209); roses and briars grow from lover's graves (see Child 7, 73, 74, 75, 76, 84, 85); a person tirls the pin at a door, and no one is so ready as the King, etc. to let him in (see Child 7, 53, 73, 74, 81); a story begins with people playing ball (see Child 20, 49, 81, 95, 155); etc. These and many similar and soon recognizable lines crop up in every part of the country and appear in almost any song with the proper story situations. Some of them derive from ancient folk beliefs, and usually they are strong enough to control the plot, in such cases being retained even in the face of common sense.[56]

At the same time whole stanzas cross under much the same circumstances as do cliches. When Lady Isabel tells a cock not to crow too soon as she is being courted by the elf-knight, we know that somewhere this song and Child 248 have come together.[57] Similar corruptions result in the *Edward*-ending on the Vermont *Twa Brothers*[58] and on the Appalachian *Lizie Wan*.[59] *The Lass of Roch Royal* and its familiar "who will shoe my pretty little feet" lines is undoubtedly the greatest traveller of all. Stanzas from this ballad can be found in twenty-odd American songs in which someone parts from his or her love.[60]

Motifs, too, are exchanged among the ballads. Many of these are almost common enough to be considered cliches, while others are unique to one ballad although they have entered similar songs and often trace back to some particular folk custom. With the former class can be included such situations as the lover's interrupting his love's funeral (see Child 65, 75, 84, 85, 87); the lover's opening the casket to kiss his love (see Child 74, 75, 84, 85); a man's taking a girl on his knee to hear an explanation, etc. (see Child 54, 73, 81); a lover's ignoring his parents' advice to stay home (see Child 73, 99, 114); a lover's remarking he or she loves one person's finger better than another's whole body (see Child 73, 81, 88); a man's answering a call last, although he is usually the first one down (see Child 100 and 110); the use of a palmer as a source of information (see Child 114 and 141); and a man's changing clothes with a beggar (see Child 17 and 140). These motifs occur almost universally throughout the American versions of the respective ballads, and the contamination, if it occurred as we suppose it did, must have taken place far back in history.

Certain motifs can be traced back to the tradition of one ballad alone, however. When these dramatic patterns appear in a new story we know in what direction the contamination has moved. In this general group go such motifs as the bowl in which the murderer plans to place his victim's blood (from *Lamkin,* but also found in *Sir Hugh* in Virginia, North Carolina, Missouri, and other southern states and perhaps in Maine and Michigan where it may have degenerated into the "dish of heart's blood" that occurs in some texts of *Barbara Allen.*);[61] the leaning against a tree to bear a child (from *Cruel Mother,* but also found in a Maine song that contains a trace of *Jamie Douglas*);[62] as well as the "clothes being too fine to rot in the sea" and "the cutting off a head and throwing it against the wall" themes that have been discussed earlier.

Even when lines, phrases, and dramatic patterns do not cross from song to song they can often be found to change position within the versions and variants of an individual ballad. Much of this shifting is incidental, but once in a while it assumes some importance with respect to dramatic mood. For example, the fact that William rises and dresses himself in blue the morning after the dream rather than the morning of the wedding[63] makes little difference to the *Fair Margaret and Sweet William* story. However, the dramatic emphases of *Barbara Allen* and *Sir Hugh* are definitely changed when the first stanza tells of the slighting toast or contains the request of the boy to be buried with his Bible at his feet in the manner of certain North Carolina texts.[64]

As a final consideration, stanza change should be inspected as an important part of ballad variation. Almost all ballads have one of two basic types of stanza: the four-line A4B3C4B3 structure or the A4 (refrain) A4 (refrain structure). Modifications of these main classes occur and occur frequently (for example, the A4B4A4B4 form), but they are really no more than modifications. However, memory may cause the four-line structure of the ballad stanza to vary substantially. Barry points out that,

> ... there are three common forms of the ballad-type of melody. In the first the rhythmical scheme provides for the repetition, twice, of the final syllable of the fourth line of each stanza, followed by the repetition of the last line entire. In the second . . . the scheme requires that the final syllable of the fourth line be repeated but once, before being followed by the repetition of the whole line. The third form calls for the repetition of the last two lines of each stanza. The irregularity of the ballad stanza, imitated by Coleridge on the precedent of examples in *Percy's Reliques,* is a minor accident, not of folk tradition, but of literary tradition. The early collectors did not record the music. Now it is well known that, though music will carry a singer over spots where his memory of the text is weak, the attempt to recite will leave gaps, due to the loss of occasional lines, gaps which the reciter or the collector will try to bridge by running parts of two stanzas into one. The result will be the intrusion into the text of stanzas of five or six lines, instead of four, of the sort so common in the early records of popular ballads.[65]

Concrete illustration of such variation can be provided from a Virginia version of *Young Beichan*. Here the stanza:

> Then up stept the brisk young porter.
> "There's a lady standing at your gate,
> And oh! she is so fair to see.
> She got more gold about her clothing
> Than your new bride and all her kin.[66]

appears and in five lines covers material that usually, and with full detail, takes twelve.

> The porter went unto his master,
> And bowed low upon his knees.
> "Arise, arise, my brisk young porter,
> And tell me what the matter is".
>
> "There's a lady standing at your door,
> And she does weep most bitterly.
> I think she is as fair a lady
> As I would wish my eyes to see.
>
> "She has more gold on her forefinger,
> Around her waist is diamonds strung,
> She has more gold upon her clothing
> Than your new bride and all her kin ...."[67]

The same process without the change of stanza length occurs in the second of the following stanzas from *The Twa Sisters*. Here repetition is replaced by additional narrative; the first stanza is typical of the song.

> The millier picked up his drab hook,
>   Bow down,
> The millier picked up his drab book,
>   The bow has been to me.
> The millier picked up his drab book
> And fished her out of the brook.
>   True to my love, my love be true to thee.
>
> The millier got her a golden ring,
>   Bow down,
> The millier pushed her back,
>   The bow has been to me.
> The millier was hung by his mill gate,
> For drowning my poor sister Kate.
>   True to my love, my love be true to thee.[68]

The second part into which I have divided my discussion of ballad variation deals with story change. Story change, that is the alteration of the actual plot or basic mood of the ballad, is an extremely important, interesting, and oddly neglected field. Moreover, as new songs are often created and as the ways of folk art are very graphically revealed through this process, a study of ballad story change is extremely rewarding.

As was the case with textual variation the subject can be discussed under major headings based on the forces that operate to change the story of a folk song. Such headings would include the elimination of action, development toward lyric, loss of detail through forgetting; fragmentation; convention and cliche; localization; the effect of literalness; rationalization; sentimentalization; moralization; manner of use; secondary growth; new ballads which rise from the old; and mergers. I will discuss them separately. Nevertheless, the close relationship of all these forces (and in particular the first three) cannot be overemphasized. They tend to work together and supplement one another, and in my discussions of individual ballads under the respective headings the fact that the other forces are also at work should not be forgotten.

As has already been stated, the folk song in its travels from mouth to mouth always tends to concentrate more and more on the climax[69] of its story and to focus on but one unstable situation. A trend of this sort means that in the more recent versions, as so many of the American texts are, the real story will become confused and some of the remaining details baffling to even the singer himself. Then the way has been made easier, of course, for all the other forces of variation so that in some cases the thing will "snowball". Good examples of such concentration upon climax with the subsequent omission of antecedent and sometimes postcedent events are extremely numerous in the Child as well as the American collections. *The Hunting of the Cheviot, The Twa Brothers, Fair Annie, The Broomfield Hill, Mary Hamilton, Lizzie Lindsay, Lady Alice,*[70] *Edward,* and *Sir Lionel,* among others, offer fine illustrations.

Child 18, *Sir Lionel,* originally relates the following event.

> A knight finds a lady sitting in (or under) a tree, who tells him a wild boar has slain (or worried) her lord and killed (or wounded) thirty of his men. The knight kills the boar, and seems to have received bad wounds in the process. The boar belonged to a giant, or to a wild woman. The knight is required to forfeit his hawks and leash and the little finger of his right hand (or his horse, his hound, and his lady). He refuses to submit to such disgrace, though in no condition to resist; the giant allows him time to heal his wounds, and he is to leave his lady as security for his return. At the end of the time the knight comes back sound and well, and kills the giant as he has killed the boar . . . The last quarter of the Percy copy would, no doubt, reveal what became of the lady who was sitting in the tree, as to which the traditional copies give no light.[71]

In America the narrative, at best, retains the ride in the forest, a brief proposal, and the all-important fight with the boar. The more conventional and unbelievable, and so less dramatic, action has been forgotten. In this particular example, the loss of the rest of the story has contributed to a change of mood in the song, so that *Old Bangum and the Boar* is a rather jovial offspring of a dignified romance.

The Hunting of the Cheviot, that long and complicated poem of poaching, reprisal, individual combat, and general battle has become no more than a two-stanza narration of a brutal struggle between two great earls in Tennessee.[72] And, in truth, that is the essence of the entire story. It is interesting to note in this connection how much of the compression is artistically satisfying. By passing off the less dramatic elements and concentrating on the essentials, the folk frequently unconsciously increase the poignancy and unity of effect in their stories. Davis notes, in speaking of *Fair Annie,* that

> . . . the thirty-one stanzas of the Child text have been reduced to thirteen in the Virginia version without the loss of a single essential detail.[73]

The development of the New World Child ballads toward lyric is often the result of the elimination of action. Such elimination of action may eventually cause lyric poetry to evolve.[74] The Maine version of *Mary Hamilton*[75] offers an adequate illustration of the point, which is discussed in great detail in the chapter that concludes this volume.[76] Here the story of the illicit love affair, birth and murder of the baby, the Queen's subsequent anger, and the burning at the stake of the guilty girl has become a lyrical lament by the dying Mary Hamilton in which she rues her life and lot. No story is told, but one is in evidence, nevertheless; and a good deal of narrative is implied. Of the same general lyric-narrative sort are the southern text of *The Death of Queen Jane*[77] with its touching refrain "the Red Rose of England shall flourish no more"; the versions of *The Elfin Knight* where only the statement of tasks, first by the man and then by the girl, remains;[78] the texts of the *Cherry Tree Carol* that are little more than heavenly prophecies of the life of Jesus,[79] and the *Lizzie Lindsay* fragments that are merely lover's requests to "go to the highlands with me".[80]

The Maine *Rantin Laddie,* however, represents a slightly different change of the same general nature, as does the West Virginia *Braes of Yarrow.* In the former, a story of a girl who bears a nobleman an illegitimate child and is eventually rescued by him from her family, only the situation is retained

and the song has become a sort of lullaby through the addition of two
"hush-a-by" stanzas.

> Aft hae I played at the cards an' dice
> For the love o' a rantin' laddie, O,
> But noo I maun sit in the ingle neuk,
> An' by-lo a bastard babbie O.
>
> Sing hush-a-by, an' hush-a-by,
> An' hush-a-by-lo babbie, O,
> O hush-a-by, an' hush-a-by,
> An' hush-a-by, wee babbie O.
>
> Sing hush-a-by, an' hush-a-by,
> An' hush-a-by-lo babbie, O,
> O had your tongue, ma ain wee wean,
> An A gae a sook o' the pappie, O.[81]

In the latter, we find a poem based on the traditional ballad returning to
popular circulation. The lyrical embellishments and sophisticated versifica-
tion superimposed by the individual poet upon the folk song are still very
much in evidence, and stanzas such as the following are heard in oral
tradition:

> Fair was thy love, fair, fair indeed thy love,
> In flowery bands thou didst him fetter;
> Tho' he was fair and well beloved again,
> Than me he did not love thee better.[82]

Such a sophistication represents more than a development toward lyric, of
course, but the influence of the poet on folk song in both textual and narrative aspects is a separate study and can not be given more than passing
attention here.

Closely related to the elimination of action and this development toward
lyric is loss of detail, Loss of detail differs, as a force in ballad variation,
from these two other processes in that it does not derive from concentration
on the climax of the story, but rather is a result of forgetting and omission.
Even when a song does not compress the particular action or event, frequently the story will change because of lapses of memory which occur at
key points. In this way a ballad may eventually degenerate to nonsense or
become so vague that the story is impossible to follow.

The *Queen of Elfan's Nourice* tells of a girl who is abducted by fairies
that she may wet-nurse an elf-baby just after her own child is born. In
keeping with the usual practice, she can expect to be returned as soon as
this elfbairn can use his legs. In the Wisconsin text of the song,[83] we are told
of the cow-like elf-call asking the girl to come below the sea and nurse the
baby, and we are given the dialogue in which the elf-king asks her why she
mourns. But the speakers are not clear, the change in setting is not revealed,
and the details of the story cannot be followed unless the plot is previously
known. The result, to the untutored, thus becomes a series of confusing lines
on the general subject of fairy abduction. Certainly the singer who knows
only the American lines has no idea of the traditional tale, and were a
suitable explanation to present itself the story might easily be resolved into

a new form. This occurrence can be seen in a text of *Lamkin*[84] in which the story has become so abbreviated that only the baby is slain, and so it is his blood that is caught in the silver bowl.

The most graphic examples of loss of detail result when the ending of a ballad is forgotten. In a Virginia version of *James Harris* the ballad concludes without the shipwreck, although the wife does rue her decision to run away. The reason for this finish is obviously nothing but the omission of the sinking and Hell stanzas. However, the fact remains that the new form of the story with the indefinite ending has become as real as the original forms and in its indefiniteness is ready to be sentimentalized or even localized. In *The Twa Sisters* texts from the south printed by Henry, Perry and Cox[85] the omission of the robbery of the miller causes the story to end in a rescue of the girl. Whether the happy endings sometimes found in this song owe their existence to a similar fragment or not is a matter of conjecture. Nevertheless, there is the possibility. For, along similar lines, in connection with this same song, the earlier omission of the harp motif has caused a series of changes and developments that have resulted directly or indirectly in more than a dozen American plot arrangements.

It is not uncommon, moreover, to find a fragment of a ballad existing as a song in its own right. The "shoe my foot" lines of *The Lass of Roch Royal* are often sung by themselves,[86] and the common American form of *Bessy Bell and Mary Gray* is but one stanza long and appears without story as a nonsense rime.

> O Betsey Bell and Mary Gray,
> They were two bonnie lasses;
> They biggit a brig on yonder brae
> And thichet it o'er with rashes.[87]

Such fragments are usually the most catchy and melodic portions of the ballad and stay in the mind easily and long after the story has disappeared.

Sometimes loss of detail combines with the other forces of degeneration to produce extremely corrupt and nonsensical songs much as the Texas Negro *Boberick Allen* and the "sea-captain" text of the American *Brown Girl*. In the former instance the old love tale has not only become fragmentary, but Boberick is a man. In this version the girls can't see why "I" (the singer) follow him. He goes to town and back attempting to see "me" follow him, but he can't because "I was away somewhere". In the latter, a sea-captain, Pretty Polly, and Miss Betsy are involved in a unique triangle love affair in which the lovers, the story, and the dialogue are only clear in their utter confusion. Such abortionate offspring are unusual, but they do graphically illustrate the "road downhill".[88]

Alterations of the ballad story also result from the forces of convention and cliche working independently or together on the plot—usually, however, after loss of detail has served to make the story incomplete. It is, perhaps, difficult to realize the power that convention and cliche have in folk narrative unless we keep reminding ourselves of the manner in which they have often overcome common sense within the text itself. In a Newfoundland version of *Fair Margaret and Sweet William* Lady Margaret goes to her family after seeing William and his bride on the street below her window and asks her mother and sister to make her bed and bind her head because she feels ill. These are conventional lines and yet add a scene to the story that other texts do not have. In the Canadian *Andrew Lammie*, because the same sort of cliche:

> O mother dear, make my bed,
> And make it soft and bonny,
> My true love died for me today,
> I'll die for him tomorrow.[89]

entered the song the lover dies before the girl, although much of the drama of the original story depends on the fact that she dies first.[90] And, finally, the ending on the southern Appalachian *Lady Maisry*, in which the hero is so late that he can only stop the girl's funeral, kiss the corpse, and die himself, is in direct contradiction of the dramatic failure in the final few seconds of the rescue in the other texts.[91] In both these last two cases it is almost certain the cliche ending became attached after the regular conclusion had dropped off.

Somewhat similar story changes occur where literalness and localization are given the opportunity to function. In the North Carolina and Georgia versions of the American *Brown Girl* a literal interpretation of the famous,

> Oh am I the doctor that you sent for me?
> Or am I the young man whom you wanted to see?

has resulted in the lover's becoming a physician.

> There was a young doctor, from London he came,
> He courted a damsel called Sarah by name.[92]

And when a particular ballad story is closely paralleled by a local event or series of events, new names, new localities, new dramatic situations, and even new endings are likely to enter the old song. *Barbara Allen* and *Lord Randal* have already been used to illustrate the first two points, and a West Virginia *Gypsie Laddie*[93] will serve the same purpose for the last two. The traditional story of the noble lady who forsakes all comforts to flee with her gypsy lover has become a tale about "Billy Harman whose wife had gone off with Tim Wallace, Harman's brother-in-law. Wallace was very ugly and the wife very pretty. She never came back; he did". The new story mentions the local streams the "War" and the "Barranshee", and the woman's name is Melindy. Although the singer of this text could not recall the final stanza, we are told the husband in pursuit inquired if the wife "had gone that road", but on receiving a negative reply returned home. Thus, the meeting with the elopers and the subsequent scorning of the husband were left out because in the local event the lovers were not overtaken.

Rationalization is one of the most powerful of all the forces that work on ballads. In Britain and America as belief in ghosts, fairies, and other spiritual characters dwindles, everyday substitutes are provided, so that an elfin knight becomes a gypsy lover and later an illicit lover or even the lodger, while a mermaid is replaced by a mortal, if mysterious, sweetheart. So strong is such rationalization that most of our modern versions of the old ghost, witch, etc. ballads have lost all or nearly all traces of the supernatural.[94] Thus *James Harris* generally appears today as a triangle love tale between three mortals, the harp motif has nearly vanished from *The Twa Sisters,* and Sir Hugh's body seldom speaks miraculously from the well.[95] Of course, certain ballads are still completely retained in their supernatural form, but these are usually out and out ghost stories or religious tales like *The Suffolk Miracle* or *The Cherry Tree Carol* that would not survive if rationalized. But, on the whole, the devil, the elf, the mermaid, and the like have left or are leaving the songs. Barry's explanation of the *Croodlin Doo* evolution of *Lord Randal* demonstrates the trend.

> The secondary form of "Lord Randal", that is, "The Croodlin Doo" (Child J, Kc, L, M, N, O), presents the situation of a child, questioned by the mother, telling how his step-mother has poisoned him with "wee fishes", or "a four footed fish". There is no absurdity, from the point of view of folklore, of mother and stepmother appearing in the same ballad. "The Croodlin Doo" furnishes a unique example in English of *the spirit of a dead mother* returning to comfort a child abused by a cruel stepmother. . . . As the belief in ghosts faded, or perhaps for other reasons, the apparent absurdity of the situation in the ballad made necessary the finding of a villain who would not have to wait for the mother's death. Child Ka, Kb . . . and R . . . give folk rationalization . . . and have introduced the grandmother in place of the stepmother.[96]

The attitudes held by individuals toward the material often shape ballad stories with respect to mood. Morality, sentimentality, and comedy are inserted under individual circumstances by individual singers, printers, and other persons who contact folk material. Not infrequently their revisions and additions survive. A conventional stanza will often appear at the finish of *Barbara Allen* or *James Harris* warning "ye virgins all" to "shun the fate I fell in", and sometimes a whole song will be revised to point a moral. In a Wisconsin version of *The Twa Corbies,* two crows plan to eat a newly-born lambkin that lies by a rock. A passing bird, overhearing the scheme, hurries to warn the helpless animal to flee, and the song closes with the following last lines:

> God grant that each lambkin that is in our flock
> Be told of his danger as he lies by the rock.[97]

Other variations are closely allied to such moralizing. For example, Belden points out that the "naked woman" lines have been left out of a Missouri text of *Lady Isabel and the Elf-Knight* and two misplaced verses inserted instead.[98] Squeamishness and religious scruples continually haunt the American folk singer. The incest themes of *The Cruel Brother, The Twa Brothers,* and *Lizie Wan* have vanished or are rapidly vanishing. Vance Randolph and Ruby Duncan both report informants who were reluctant to sing *Our Goodman.*[99] And many a collector has been hindered by the fact that the "old love songs" are too frivolous. Likewise, the desire for justice, reflected in the ending of *The Sweet Trinity* in which the enraged crew throws the captain overboard[100] seems to show a Christian dissatisfaction with some of the stories of the traditional songs.

The sentimentalization of narrative material is common too. The lover who reforms and apologizes in the American *Brown Girl,* the trooper in *The Trooper and the Maid* who promises to return and marry the girl, the gallant refusal of the cabin boy in *The Sweet Trinity* to sink either his mates or the girl he loves no matter how treacherous the captain, the husband in *The Farmer's Curst Wife* who welcomes his shrewish mate back from Hell, the girl who turns against her lover after he slays her father in *Earl Brand*, and the other incidents of the same sort are typical of what can happen to many objective and cold Child ballads in America.

Not all ballad versions are taken as seriously as those that become sentimentalized. *Sir Lionel,* as already noted, has become a jocular jingle from an originally elaborate romance, and *The Three Ravens* has lost all the beauty of the cynical Scotch and moving English texts. Print is, of course, a frequent cause of such degenerations. In *The Soldier's Wooing* series (the American *Erlinton*[101]) the callousness of the girl who, as her father and lover battle, refuses the former's offers to permit the marriage and to give the couple a £10,000 dowry and holds out for more money has been traced by Barry to an English broadside.[102] But print is not the only factor. The following comment was made about the conclusion of *Lord Thomas and Fair Annet* in Newfoundland.

> Just imagine when they were all laying in one grave, and the trump sounded for the Judgment Day, and they was all scrabbling for their bones, if Lord Thomas should get one of the brown girl's legs.[103]

When the situations in a traditional song become ludicrous to the singers, the story cannot resist for long, and if parodies do not provide an outlet, as in the case of *Lord Lovel,*[104] the original text must suffer.[105]

The purpose for which a song is sung may also serve to modify the story and mood of a particular ballad. The use of traditional texts in dramatic presentations, in children's games, as lullabies, and as play-party or dance accompaniments has shaped and fashioned a large number of texts. *The Maid Freed from the Gallows* is given detailed consideration in this respect by Reed Smith in his *South Carolina Ballads* where he traces the development of this story through Virginia Negro dramas, New York children's games, and West Indian cante-fable revisions.[106] William Newell and Botkin both discuss *Barbara Allen* as an evening dance song,[107] and Arthur Hudson notes that a Mississippi version of *Sir Hugh* that was used to sing children to sleep was rendered with the bloody stanzas omitted.[108]

The secondary ballad[109] offers a problem in story change different from any of those we have faced so far. Usually the direct result of a broadside, a sophisticated poet's tamperings, or a printer's text, these songs share a mutual ancestry with the Child texts, but are at the same time no longer versions of the traditional ballad. *The Rich Irish Lady* (see Child 295) and *The Yorkshire Bite* (see Child 283) are the most graphic American illustrations, although *The Squire of Edinburgh Town* (see Child 221), *The Half-Hitch* (see Child 31), *High Barbaree* (see Child 285), and *The Soldier's Wooing* (see Child 8) are also popular.[110]

The *Brown Girl,* in Child, is the story of a young man who becomes attached to a girl, but sends her a letter saying he will not marry her because she is so brown. She becomes proud. Later, he is sick or lovesick and sends for her to cure him with affection. She takes her time in going and mocks him when she arrives. Revengefully she returns his troth by stroking his breast with a white wand and promises to dance on his grave. The American stories, in which the sexes are reversed, the brown color and the white wand lost, and the "Are you the doctor?" stanzas found, derive indirectly from the Child tale through a broadside adaptation that was popular in England under such titles as *The Bold Soldier* and *Sally and Billy*. *The Yorkshire Bite* goes back, not to the Child *Crafty Farmer* story, but to one of a number of parallel traditions[111] that existed in Britain during the eighteenth century. Child, in speaking of the latter song, states that,

> This very ordinary ballad has enjoyed great popularity and is given for that reason as a specimen of its class. There is an entirely similar one in which a Norfolk . . . farmer's daughter going to market to sell corn is substituted for the farmer going to pay his rent. . . . Another variety is of a Yorkshire boy sent to a fair to sell a cow.[112]

He also mentions ballads about "a country girl beset by an amorous gentleman" who mounts the villain's horse and makes off with his valise" and about "a gentleman, who, having been robbed by five highwaymen that then purpose to shoot him, tells them that he is the Pretender, and is taken by them as such to a justice".

In a somewhat like way the broadside alterations of *Geordie* have largely supplanted the older texts of the ballad and become what may be considered the primary form of the song in popular circulation. Most American versions of the story derive from *The Life and Death of George of Oxford*, a broadside undoubtedly based on a local situation in which the hero was hung. The happier finish of the traditional story is not common today.[113]

However, it is not necessary to go to broadsides and parallel traditions to find new ballads growing out of an older series of songs. One of the most important things about the study of story change is the light such pursuits throw on the birth of new works. If enough forces operate or a force of sufficient strength operates, on a tradition, a story may be created that will begin a ballad sequence in its own right. Thus, *Henry Martin* has risen from *Sir Andrew Barton* and *Giles Collins* and *Clerk Colvill* have come from the older *Johnny Collins* story of Child 85.[114] *Henry Martin* appears to be the result of the omission of the chase and capture from *Sir Andrew Barton*, while *Giles Collins* and *Clerk Colvill* show the *Johnny Collins* ballad split into two parts, each of which has become a separate story.

If subtraction and division create new narratives, so does addition. Child has noted that the entire *Edward* ballad is frequently added to other songs,

> More or less of *Edward* will be found in four versions of the *Twa Brothers* and two of *Lizie Wan*. . . . [115]

And the same junction, probably brought over from England already complete, was discovered by Mrs. Flanders in Vermont.[116] In like fashion *The Death of Queen Jane* lends its funeral to the *Duke of Bedford*[117] and *The Maid Freed from the Gallows* enters numerous badman tales.[118]

Thus we have a description of the major forces of variation that work upon the Child ballad in America. From the facts few, very few, conclusions can be drawn, because any attempt to go beyond extreme generalities is bound to cause trouble. Every word, line, phrase, stanza, and story that circulates creates its own individual history.

With this warning in mind, then, we had best merely say that variation is most likely to occur where vagueness and confusion exist, that in America the change in society and the distance in history of so many ballad events has presented ideal circumstances for change, and that new versions and variants arise from a combination of factors and processes and seldom from one force of variation operating alone. But where we speak more specifically and say that the traditional ballad entering America tends to become more sentimental and moral, we must recall that in a Texas variant of Child 95 the prisoner is hung on rather than freed from the gallows[119] and that Captain Wedderburn is not said to marry the girl he seduces in the New England versions of Child 46. When we note that these British songs become more compact and often more generalized in meaning, we cannot forget the mergers and additions that have served to expand certain texts. Rationalizations and localizations do occur in America with greater frequency than ever before, but at the same time supernatural figures, archaic customs, unknown places, and unknown characters are retained faithfully in many texts. It is true that sometimes there is a striving for artistic effect and often an overlapping of motifs and even lines in the New World, but many more times the traditional simplicity and integrity is retained. And if forgetting, merging, and loss of detail work with their customary power, songs can also be found that are word for word like their British ancestors. A few are even longer[120]

To say more than this seems to be foolhardy. It becomes an attempt to define human nature.

FOOTNOTES

[7] All Child versions are not older than their American parallels. See Barry's discussions of this point (at every opportunity) in *British Ballads from Maine,* especially 100 f. in connection with Child 49.

[8] Jane Zielonko, *op. cit.,* discusses much of this material in her "Conclusion" and gives some very helpful lists on 115 and 117.

[9] A. K. Davis, *op. cit.,* 36.

[10] W. R. MacKenzie, *Quest of the Ballad,* 189.

[11] A comparison of the Child A version of *James Harris* (243) with any of the American *House Carpenter* texts will demonstrate these points.

[12] See H. M. Belden, *op. cit.,* Headnotes for references to the influence of print on the Child ballads. Belden makes a great deal of this point and often hypothesizes on the subject. See also my discussion of *Erlinton* (8).

[13] A traditional ballad is usually considered to have the following qualities, the lack of any of which destroys the form: a narrative of plotted action with only the climax event or events given; a tendency to focus on one climax of one unstable situation; absolute impersonality; and an oral, folk tradition.

[14] See the arguments by Barry and Henry concerning this point in *JAF,* 1932, 8. *Lord Lovel* and *Barbara Allen* (see my discussions under Child 75 and 84) also support such a stand.

[15] For example, see *James Bird,* which was written by Charles Miner and printed in his paper *The Gleaner* at Wilkes-Barre, Pa. in 1814. Refer to Belden, *op. cit.,* 296,

as well as Mary O. Eddy, *Ballads and Songs from Ohio,* 267 and Franz Rickaby, *Ballads and Songs of the Shanty-Boy,* 221. Another example is *Young Charlotte,* which was written by Seba Smith and published by him in *The Rover,* II, #15, 225 under the title *A Corpse Going to a Ball.* See Barry, *BFSSNE,* XII, 27.

[16] Robert Burns' *Red, Red Rose;* William Hamilton's *Braes of Yarrow;* Sir Walter Scott's *Lochinvar;* and Swinburne's experiments (see C. Hyder's article in *PMLA,* XLIX, 295 f.) are cases in point. Note should also be made of *The Twa Corbies* text from Indiana (*JAF,* 1932, 8) which traces back to *Cleveland's Compendium,* 1859, and Allan Cunningham. Check also the discussion of Burns' use of folk song in *MLR,* VI, 514 f.

[17] William Hamilton's *Braes of Yarrow* was found in West Virginia by Cox, *op. cit.,* 137. It is almost identical textually to the poem, but quite abbreviated.

[18] These new versions are, of course, quite subject to the forces of variation in their archaisms, strangeness, etc.

[19] *BFSSNE,* XII, 9 and my discussion of Story Type C under Child 1.

[20] *Die Fischerin.* See the song sung by Vater, Nicklas, and Dortchen.

[21] With respect to this point Zielonko, *op. cit.; HFLQ,* IV, #3, 41 f.; Barry's work in *JAF, BFSSNE,* and *British Ballads from Maine; SFQ,* 1937, #4, 25 f.; and the other books and articles cited in Footnote 3 should be consulted.

[22] For additional information concerning this sort of change and the reactions of individual singers to specific word alterations, see Shearin's article in *Sewanee Review,* XIX, 317. See also *JAF,* 1946, 263 f. There is a doctoral dissertation, *Place Names in the English and Scottish Popular Ballads and Their American Variants,* done at Ohio State in 1947 by W. Edson Richmond.

[23] See Reed Smith, *South Carolina Ballads,* 57 f. and *JAF,* 1934, 338 for further examples.

[24] Davis, *op. cit.,* 130.

[25] Barry, *British Ballads from Maine,* 324.

[26] Belden, *op. cit.,* Child 277 B.

[27] Barry, *British Ballads from Maine,* Child 277A—B. For further information, see Randolph, *op. cit.,* I, 75.

[28] Earl Beck, *Songs of the Michigan Lumberjacks,* 107.

[29] Barry, *British Ballads from Maine,* 412.

[30] Davis, *op. cit.,* 105 and Cox, *op. cit.,* 24.

[31] Barry, *British Ballads from Maine,* 256.

[32] Harold Thompson, *Body, Boots, and Britches,* 379.

[33] Jules Allen, *Cowboy Lore,* 74.

[34] Davis, *op. cit.,* 90. See also *W. Va. School Journal and Educator,* XLVI, 83.

[35] *Ibid.,* 188.

[36] Cox, *op. cit.,* 18.

[37] Davis, *op. cit.,* 216.

[38] Brewster, *op. cit.,* 44.

[39] Cox, *op. cit.,* 97.

[40] *JAF,* 1903, 259.

[41] Brewster, *op. cit.,* 44.

[42] Cox, *op. cit.,* 48.

[43] Brewster, *op. cit.,* 77 and the footnote on that page.

[44] Broadside (imprint: de Marsan, List 5, #90) in the Alfred Harris Collection, John Hay Library, Brown University. Reprinted by Barry, *British Ballads from Maine,* p. 380 f.

[45] Gardner and Chickering, *Ballads and Songs of Southern Michigan,* 373.

[46] Barry, *British Ballads from Maine,* 322.

[47] Belden, *op. cit.,* 16 and 92.

[48] F. J. Child, *The English and Scottish Popular Ballads,* I B.

[49] See "An Index to Borrowing in the Child Ballads of America" which was affixed to the end of the 1950 edition of this study.

[50] For example, see the Sharp-Karpeles, *English Folk Songs from the Southern Appalachians*, 14 f. and Davis, *op. cit.*, 440 f.

[51] See Sharp-Karpeles, *op. cit.*, 17; Davis, *op. cit.*, 182; among others for illustrations. Also check the discussion in the Zielonko Master's Thesis under Child 68.

[52] Quotation from Davis, *op. cit.*, 301. Refer also to Cox, *op. cit.*, 95 and Sharp-Karpeles, *op. cit.*, 170.

[53] Mellinger Henry, *29 Beech Mt. Folk Songs*, 16.

[54] Davis, *op. cit.*, 189.

[55] Gordon Gerould, *The Ballad of Tradition*, 114 f.

[56] This point is discussed later in this paper. See p.

[57] See Brown, *NC Flklre*, II, 15.

[58] Flanders, *Ancient Blds.*, I, 318.

[59] Sharp-Karpeles, *op cit.*, 89.

[60] See my discussion under Child 76.

[61] See Barry's explanation of this motif in *JAF*, 1939, 74 which is reconstructed in the discussion of Child 93 in this paper. Also refer to Davis, *op. cit.*, 405; Belden, *op. cit.*, 71; and Sharp-Karpeles, *op. cit.*, 224 for *Sir Hugh* examples, and to Gardner and Chickering, *op. cit.*, 51 and Barry, *British Ballads from Maine*, 198 for *Barbara Allen* examples.

[62] See Barry, *British Ballads from Maine*, 470.

[63] Sharp-Karpeles, *op. cit.*, 135.

[64] *Ibid.*, 187 and 222.

[65] Barry, *British Ballads from Maine*, 128.

[66] Davis, *op. cit.*, 160.

[67] *Ibid.*, 164.

[68] *Ibid.*, 102.

[69] See Zielonko, *op. cit.*, 117 for a discussion.

[70] See the discussions referred to in Footnote 3 by Bayard and by Parker, and summarized under Child 85 in this paper, for information on the *Clerk Colvill* and *Johnny Collins* ballads.

[71] See Child, *op. cit.*, I, 208.

[72] Mason, *op. cit.*, 15. In connection with his J version of Child 293, Davis reveals similar compression.

[73] Davis, *op. cit.*, 177.

[74] Compare the remarks of L. K. Goetz in *Volkslied und Volksleben der Kroaten und Serben* on the same subject.

[75] It should be noted that Barry, *British Ballads from Maine*, 259 and Child, *op. cit.*, V, 299 both state that this tradition of Child 173 has been subject to sophisticated corruption. However, the Maine text used here is pure.

[76] See pp.   in this book.

[77] Scarborough, *A Songcatcher in the Southern Mountains*, 254. See my Story Type B under Child 170.

[78] See Sharp-Karpeles, *op. cit.*, i.

[79] *JAF*, 1932, 13. See my Story Type E under Child 54.

[80] Barry, *British Ballads from Maine*, 297. See my Story Type B under Child 226.

[81] *Ibid.*, 303—4.

[82] Cox, *op. cit.*, 138.

[83] *JAF*, 1907, 155.

[84] *JAF*, 1900, 117.

[85] Henry Perry, *A Sampling of the Folk Lore of Carter County*, 98 and Cox, *Traditional Ballads Mainly from West Virginia*, 6.

[86] See, for example, Davis, *op. cit.*, 263 f.

[87] *Ibid.*, 434.

[88] See *PTFS*, X, 149 or VII, 111 for the *Barbara Allen* text and *JAF*, 1932, 54 for the *Brown Girl* text. Also see Reed Smith, *op. cit.*, 64 where he discusses the "Poor Anzo" *Lord Randal* in his chapter *The Road Downhill*.

[89] See MacKenzie, *Ballads and Sea-Songs from Nova Scotia*, 60 and 124.

[90] See Child, *op. cit.*, 233. Note also that the fragmentary nature of the text has undoubtedly been a factor here.

[91] Scarborough, *op. cit.*, 137.

[92] Sharp-Karpeles, *op. cit.*, Child 295, texts A and F, on 295 and 298. The quotation is from text F, stanza I.

[93] Cox, *Folk Songs of the South*, p. 133 (Child 200, the D text). This song was said to have been composed by Henry Mitchell. However, at best, he adapted *The Gypsy Laddie*.

[94] On the other hand, however, the mysterious disappearance of the wife that is implied by the West Virginia account is left out of the West Virginia song because the ballad does not (at least in the text used) go beyond the husband's pursuit.

[95] See the Story Types in this study for examples of supernatural material surviving in these and other ballads.

[96] Barry, *British Ballads from Maine*, 71. See also his discussion of *Lamkin* cited in Footnote 61.

[97] *JAF*, 1907, 154.

[98] Belden, *op. cit.*, 7.

[99] Randolph, *op. cit.*, I, 183 and Ruby Duncan, *Ballads and Folk Songs in North Hamilton County*, 102.

[100] Shoemaker, *Mountain Minstrelsy*, 132.

[101] See my discussions under Child 7 and 8 in this study.

[102] *JAF*, 1910, 447.

[103] Gardner and Chickering, *op. cit.*, 20.

[104] See Davis, *op. cit.*, 258; Cox, *Folk Songs of the South*, 78; Belden, *op. cit.*, 54; and Cox, *Traditional Ballads Mainly from West Virginia*, 28.

[105] The refrain is an excellent indicator of this change in mood. Compare the American "dillum, down, dillum, kimmy ko" with the Child "blow thy horne, good hunter" in *Sir Lionel*.

[106] See Reed Smith, *op. cit.*, Chapter VIII.

[107] William Newell, *Games and Songs of American Children*, 78 and Benjamin Botkin, *American Play-Party Song*, 58.

[108] Hudson, *op. cit.*, 116.

[109] This expression has not been fully accepted by folk scholars. However, meaning "songs directly derived from Child ballads", the term has the value of definiteness for a discussion of this sort. But I do realize that exact classifications on the derivative level are almost impossible to make.

[110] These are representative titles. The songs appear under many other names.

[111] See the discussion under Child 283.

[112] Child, *op. cit.*, V, 128—9.

[113] However, see discussion under Child 209 in this work. For the discussion of a somewhat similar tradition see Barry's essay on *Sir James Ross/Rose* in *British Ballads from Maine*, 290.

[114] See the discussions of Child 167 and 85 respectively in this work for the scholarship that uncovered these facts.

[115] Child, *op. cit.*, I, 167.

[116] Flanders, *Ancient Blds.*, I, 318.

[117] See Flanders, *Vermont Folk Songs and Ballads*, 219 and Barry *BFSSNE*, II, 7.

[118] See Hudson, *op. cit.*, 113 and John Lomax, *Cowboy Songs and Other Frontier Ballads*, 159.

[119] See Child 95 in this work, Story Type D.

[120] See *The Whummil Bore* (*JAF*, 1907, 155), Child 27.

A BIBLIOGRAPHICAL GUIDE TO STORY VARIATION
IN THE TRADITIONAL BALLAD OF AMERICA

A Bibliographical Guide To Story Variation
In The Traditional Ballad in America

1. RIDDLES WISELY EXPOUNDED

Texts: Barry, *Brit Blds Me,* 429 / Botkin, *Treasury So Flklre,* 717 / Bronson, I, 3 / *BFSSNE,* X, 8; XII, 8 / Chase, *Sgs All Time,* 11, 52 / R.P.T. Coffin, *Lost Paradise,* 199 / Davis, *Fsg Va,* 3 / Davis, *More Trd Blds Va,* 1 / Davis, *Trd Bld Va,* 59 / Flanders, *Ancient Blds,* I, 45 / *Folkways Monthly,* May '62, 16 / Ives, *BI Sg Bk,* 38 / *JAF,* 1899, 129 / Jeckyll, *Jamaican Sg & Stry,* 26 / Jones, *Flklre Mich,* 5 / Leach, *Fsgs Labr Cst* (as Child 46) / A. Lomax, *Fsgs No Am,* 180 / Niles, *Blds Crls Tgc Lgds,* 2 / *Va FLS Bull,* #10, 5 / Wells, *Bld Tree,* 169.

Local Titles: The Devil and the Blessed Virgin Mary, The Devil and the Nine Questions, The Devil's Nine Questions, The Nine Questions, Riddles Wisely Expounded, There Was A Man Lived in the West, The Three Riddles.

Story Types: A dialogue with the speakers named. The Devil, sometimes rationalized as a Knight, on the threat of removing a girl to Hell, asks her what is whiter than milk, louder than a horn, higher than a tree, more innocent than a lamb, etc. The maid answers snow, thunder, Heaven, a babe, etc. and names the Devil. The latter then admits defeat.

Examples: Davis, *Trd Bld Va.*

B: The same sort of motif as that of Type A is used, but when the girl answers the questions and names the Devil, he says he will take her to Hell regardless.   Examples: Niles.

C: A lesson in the way to get a lover. The Devil has become a cavalier, and there are three pretty maids in search of a man. The youngest, who knows the answers, wins the cavalier.

Examples: *BFSSNE,* X, 8.

Discussion: The Type A and Type B American texts, which are extremely rare, are closest to the Child*, C, and D versions in their obvious concern with the Devil. (See Davis, *Trd Bld Va,* 59 for a comparison of the Virginia texts with Child.) The song seems to have originally been a battle of wits between the Devil and a girl (cf. Child A*) which was first secularized and then rationalized. It was discovered late in America, first by Alfreda Peel, and printed by Davis with the Virginia Collection. (See Davis, *Trd Bld Va,* 46—7 for an account of the discovery.)

The Type C text uncovered by Barry in New England traces back to Child Ad indirectly. See *BFSSNE,* XII, 9 where the history of the "cavalier" form of the ballad is given from d'Urfey's *Pills to Purge Melancholy* through the German translation by Herder (cf. Goethe's opera *die Fischerin*) back to an English re-translation by William Aytoun in *Blackwood's Magazine,* LVII, 173—5. Comparative texts and a discussion of this re-emergence of a folk song are given here.

Also check *BFSSNE,* X, 9 where the romantic and homeletic forms of this song are briefly discussed. The idea that the Child F; Jones, *Flklre Mich,* 5; and Flanders, *Ancient Blds,* I, 45 texts are related to *Captain Wedderburn's Courtship* (46) are treated in *BFSSNE* and in the headnotes to the Flanders songs. See also the discussion in Leach, *Fsgs Labr Cst,* under Child 46.

Elizabeth Cooke (*JAF,* 1899, 129) incorporates the riddle portion of the ballad in a story, *The Bride of the Evil One,* told her by a Martinique Negro from New Orleans. The girl in this story confounds Satan much as she does in the ballad. See also the cante fable in Jeckyll, *Jamaican Sg & Stry,* 26.

The common American refrain is the "ninety-nine and ninety-weavers bonny" burden.

2. THE ELFIN KNIGHT

Texts: Jane G. Austin, *Dr. LeBaron and his Daughter,* 314 / Barry, *Brit Blds Me,* 3 / Belden, *Mo Fsgs,* 1 / Brewster, *Blds Sgs Ind,* 23 / Bronson, I, 9 / Brown, *NC Flklre,* II, 12 / Carlisle, *50 Sgs & Blds NW Ark,* 12 / Cazden, *Abelard Fsg Bk,* I, 98 / Chappell, *Fsg Rnke Alb,* 11 / Chase, *Am Ftales & Sgs,* 112 / Child, I, 19; V, 284 / Davis, *Fsgs Va,* 3 / Davis, *More Trd Blds Va,* 8 / Eddy, *Blds Sgs Ohio,* 3 / Flanders, *Ancient Blds,* I, 51 / Flanders, *Garl Gn Mt Sg,* 58 / Flanders, *New Gn Mt Sgstr,* 8 / Flanders, *Vt Fsgs Blds,* 194 / Fowke and Johnston, *Fsgs Canada,* 138 / Gardner and Chickering, *Blds Sgs So Mich,* 137 / Gray, *Sgs Blds Me Lmbrjks,* 78 / Henry, *Fsgs So Hghlds,* 31 / *JAF,* 1894, 228; 1900, 120; 1905, 49, 212; 1906, 130; 1910, 430; 1913, 174; 1917, 284; 1939, 15 / Jones, *Flklre Mich,* 5 / Linscott, *Fsgs Old NE,* 169 / A. Lomax, *Fsgs No Am,* 17 / "Love Letter and Answer" (broadside in Harris Coll., Brown Univ.), Hunts and Shaw, Boston / Morris, *Fsgs Fla,* 235 / Musick, *Flklre Kirksville,* 1 / Pound, *Nebr Syllabus,* 10 / *PTFS,* X, 137 / Randolph, *Oz Fsgs,* I, 38 / Ring, *NE Fsgs,* 12 / SharpK, *Eng Fsgs So Aplchns,* I, 1 / Shoemaker, *Mt. Mnstly,* 134 / Shoemaker, *No Pa Mnstly,* 129 / Songs for the Million (c. 1844): "Love's Impossibility" / *SFQ,* 1944, 135 / Thompson, *Bdy Bts Brtchs,* 423 / Vincent, *Lmbrjck Sgs,* 19 / Wells, *Bld Tree,* 172 / Worthington, *9 Rare Trd Blds Va,* 1.

Local Titles: Are You Going to the Fair?, Blow Ye Winds Blow, (The) Cambric Shirt, Every Grove Is Merry in Time, Go and Make Me a Cambric Shirt, Go Marry in Time, I Want You to Make Me a Cambric Shirt, Mother Make Me a Cambric Shirt, Oh Say Do You Know the Way to Salin?, Oh, Where Are You Going? I'm Going to Lynn, Petticoat Lane, Redio-Tedio, Rose de Marian Time, Rosemary, Scarborough Fair, Strawberry Lane, (A) True Lover of Mine, (The) Two Lovers.

Story Types: A: A man imposes tasks centering about the making of a cambric shirt upon a girl. She is to be acquitted of them and get her lover if she can answer with ones no less difficult. Hers usually deal with an acre of land. The elf, a carry-over in Child from some other ballad, is properly a mortal suitor.

Examples: Barry (B); Belden (A); Brewster (C); Flanders, *Ancient Blds,* (A); Gardner and Chickering.

B: The story of Type A seems completely forgotten, and only a coy question-and-answer game between two lovers remains.

Examples: Linscott; Randolph (A);
Shoemaker, *Mt Mnstly;* SharpK (A, B).

C: A nonsense song, carrying the degeneration a step further than Type B, exists. Here, the Mother is told to make "me" a cambric shirt.

Examples: Brewster (D).

Discussion: This ballad is the best remembered of the Child riddle songs both in America and Europe. However, in this country, the elf, an interloper in Britain, has been universally rationalized to a mortal lover. Frequently, nothing remains but the riddle, sometimes even the love affair being absent. (See Child, J, K, L, and my Types B and C.)

The common American refrains, as in Child, are the "rosemary and thyme-she will be a true lover of mine" and the "blow winds blow" types, though the New York (Thompson, *Bdy Bts Brtchs,* 423), the Texas (*PTFS,* X, 137), and other versions have choruses of nonsense words. For a discussion of the "rosemary and thyme" burden see *JAF,* 1894, 232; Brown, *NC Flklre,* I, 13-15; and Cazden's notes in the *Abelard Fsg Bk,* 119.

Riddles and riddle ballads in general, as well as the specific riddles in this song are discussed in *JAF,* 1894, 230 and in the headnotes in Flanders, *Ancient Blds,* 31-32. See also Worthington, *9 Rare Trd Blds Va,* 1—25. Of interest, too, is Jean B. Saunders' discussion (*MWF,* 1958, 195—196) of the nursery song "My father left me three acres of land / Sing ivy, sing ivy", some versions of which follow the riddles of Child 2. She feels both the nursery rime and the American texts of the ballad derive from the 17th Century broadside texts of the ballad. The whole riddling situation is similar to the ones in Aarne-Thompson, Mt. 875.

See Barry (*JAF,* 1917, 284) for a review of the American songbook versions.

3. THE FALSE KNIGHT UPON THE ROAD

Texts: American Songster (Cozzens, N. Y.) / Barry, *Brit Blds Me,* 11 / Belden, *Mo Fsgs,* 8 / Brewster, *Blds Sgs Ind,* 29 / Bronson, I, 34 / *BFSSNE,* XI, 8 / *Charley Fox's Minstrel's Companion* (Turner and Fisher, Philadelphia): "Tell-Tale Polly" / Creighton, *Sgs Blds N Sc,* I / Creighton and Senior, *Trd Sgs N Sc,* 1 / Davis, *Fsgs Va,* 4 / Davis, *More Trd Blds Va,* 14 / Davis, *Trd Bld Va,* 61 / Flanders, *Blds Migrant NE,* 46 / *JAF,* 1911, 344; 1917, 285 / *The Only True Mother Goose Melodies* (Monroe and Francis, Boston, 1833), 6 / Pound, *Am Blds Sg,* 48 / SharpC, *Eng Fsgs So Aplchns,* #1 / SharpK, *Eng Fsgs So Aplchns,* I, 3 / *Va FLS Bull,* #7, 4.

Local Titles: The Boy and the Devil, False Fidee, The False Knight, The False Knight on the Road, Fause Knicht and the Wee Boy.

Story Types: A: A child, sometimes a boy and sometimes a girl, is detained by the Devil or a "false knight". A number of questions are asked, but the child is ready with witty answers and eventually names the questioner. Little of the situation or setting is revealed in the dialogue.

Examples: Brewster; Davis, *Trd Bld Va;* SharpK (A).

B: The question-and-answer sequence is similar to that of Type A, but the child throws the questioner in a well at the end.

Examples: Belden, Pound

Discussion: American texts of this song are quite rare, and it is Davis' opinion that the southern and western texts emanate from Virginia. The New England and Maritime versions are Scotch-Irish in background and follow Child A closely, as do the Type A texts in general. See, however, Gerould (*MLN,* LIII, 596—7), who advances the idea that the Davis, *Trd Bld Va* and the SharpK (from N.C.) versions may be of Irish origin, although he does not feel this to be the case with the northern and western texts. The Type B songs, where the boy throws the questioner in the well, show a dramatic flourish which stretches logic to make "right" triumph fully.

The Nova Scotia (Creighton) version has a long and unique nonsense refrain added to an incomplete text, and Sharp (SharpK, *Eng F-S Aplchns,* I, 411) points out that the introduction "A Knight met a child in the road . ." in his Tennessee version is unusual. The Maine (*BFSSNE,* XI, 8) version is interesting in its fiddle sequence and the boy's wish that the fiddle bow will stick in his questioner's throat.

Barry (*BFSSNE,* XI, 8-9) discusses the song as a homily and treats its European affiliations. The central situation is similar to the tales classified under Mt. 921-922 by Aarne-Thompson.

Although the ballad has appeared in a number of American songbooks, such circulation has not helped its popularity greatly.

4. LADY ISABEL AND THE ELF-KNIGHT

Texts: Adventure, 11-30-'23, 191 / *American Songster* (Cozzens, N.Y.), 212 / *American Speech,* III, 114 / Arnold, *Fsgs Ala,* 54 / Barbeau, *Fsgs Fr Canada,* 22 (in French) / Barbour, *6 Blds Mo Oz Mts,* #4 / Barry, *Brit Blds Me,* 14 / Belden, *Mo Fsgs,* 5 / Brewster, *Blds Sgs Ind,* 31 / Bronson, I, 39 / *NC Flklre,* II, 15 / *BFSSNE,* I, 3 / *Bull Tenn FLS,* VIII, #3, 65; XVII, #4, 86 / *Bull U SC,* #162, #1 / Chappell, *Fsgs Rnke Alb,* 12 / *Charley Fox's Minstrel's Companion* (Turner and Fisher, Philadelphia), 52 / Child, III, 496 / Child Ms., XXI, 4 / *Colorado Fsg Bull,* I, #3, 2 / Cox, *Fsgs South,* 3 / Cox, *Trd Bld W Va,* 1 / Cox, *W Va School Journal & Educator,* XLIV, 269; XLV, 240 / Creighton and Senior, *Trd Sgs N Sc,* 2 / Cutting, *Adirondack Cnty,* 61 / Davis, *Fsgs Va,* 4 / Davis, *More Trd Blds Va,* 16 / Davis, *Trd Bld Va,* 62 / Duncan, *No Hamilton Cnty,* 36 / Eddy, *Blds Sgs Ohio,* 6 / Fauset, *Flklre N Sc,* 109 / Flanders, *Ancient Blds,* I, 82 / Flanders, *Ballads Migrant NE,* 4, 129 / Flanders, *Vt Fsgs Blds,* 190 / *Focus,* IV, 161, 212 / *Folk Lore Journal,* VII, 28 / Gardner and Chickering, *Blds Sgs So Mich,* 31 / Gordon, *Fsgs Am,* 68 / Greenleaf and Mansfield, *Blds Sea Sgs Newfdld,* 3 / Henry, *Fsgs So Hghlds,* 32 / High, *Old Old Fsgs,* 10 / Hubbard, *Blds Sgs Utah,* 1 / Hudson, *Fsgs Miss,* 61 / Hudson, *Ftunes Miss,* 10 / Hudson, *Spec Miss Flklre,* #1 / Hummel, *Oz Fsgs* / Jones, *Flklre Mich,* 5 / *JAF,* 1905, 132; 1906, 232; 1909, 65, 374; 1910, 374; 1911, 333, 344; 1914, 90; 1915, 148; 1916, 156; 1922, 338; 1929, 254; 1935, 305; 1936, 213; 1939, 20; 1951, 38; 1957, 247 / *Journal of Ill State Hist Soc,* XXXI, 301 / Korson, *Pa Sgs Lgds,* 30 / A. Lomax, *Fsgs No Am,* 18 / MacIntosh, *So Ill Fsgs,* 4 / MacKenzie, *Blds Sea Sgs N Sc,* 3 / MacKenzie, *Quest Bld,* 93 / McDowell, *Memory Mel,* 6 / Morris, *Fsgs Fla,* 237 / *Narragansett Times,* 12-22-'44 / *NY Times Mgz,* 10-9-'27 / Niles, *Blds Lv Sgs Tgc Lgds,* 4 / Owens, *Texas Fsgs,* 35 / Parsons, *Flklre Sea Is SC,* 128 / Perry, *Carter Cnty,* 198 / *PTFS,* X, 138

Randolph, *Oz Fsgs*, I, 41 / Randolph, *Oz Mt Flk*, 216 / *Red, White and Blue Songster* (N.Y., 1861), 212 / Sandburg, *Am Sgbag*, 60 / Scarborough, *On Trail Negro Fsg*, 43 / Scarborough, *Sgctchr So Mts*, 126 / SharpC, *Eng Fsgs So Aplchns*, #2 / SharpK, *Eng Fsgs So Aplchns*, I, 6 / Shearin and Combs, *Ky Syllabus*, 7 / Reed Smith, *SC Blds*, 97 / *Summer School News* (Summer School of the South), 7-31-'14 / *Va FLS Bull*, #s 2-4, 6-12 / Wyman and Brockway, *Lnsme Tunes*, 82.

Local Titles: Billy (Willy) Came Over the Main White Ocean, The Cage of Ivory and Gold, Castle By the Sea, The Dapple Gray, The Daughter of Old England, The Errant Knight, The False-Hearted Knight, The False Lover, The False Knight, The False Sir John, Go Steal To Me Your Father's Gold, He Followed Me Up (and) He Followed Me Down, If I Take Off My Silken Stay, Lady Isabel and the Elfin Knight, Little Golden, The King's Daughter Fair, The Knight of the Northland, A Man in the Land, Miss Mary's Parrot, My Pretty Colinn, The Ocean Wave, The Outlandish Knight, Pretty Cold Rain, Pretty Colendee, Pretty Collee, The Pretty Gold Leaf, Pretty Golden Queen, Pretty Nancy, Pretty Polly (Pie), The Salt Water Sea, The Seven (Six) King's Daughters (Dear), Seven Sisters, The Seventh King's Daughter, Six Fair Maids, Sweet Nellie, Sweet William, Willie Came Over the Ocean, Wilson, Young Jimmie.

Story Types: A: A knight, or other deceiver, convinces the seventh daughter to rob her family and elope with him. He leads her to the water where he has drowned her six sisters. When he requests her to remove her valuable robe (other objects may be added or substituted) before she dies, she makes him turn around that he may not see her naked. (Sometimes she asks him to clear brambles or give her an opportunity to pray.) He complies, and she pushes him in the stream to drown. After she returns home and puts the money back, a parrot questions her concerning her activities. By the promise of an elaborate cage, she convinces him not to tell on her. Thus, when the king asks the parrot what the fuss is, he replies a cat has been around his cage.

Examples: Barry (A), Belden (C), Davis, *Trd Bld Va,* (A), SharpK (F).

B: The same story as that of Type A is told, but the supernatural nature of the knight is still clear.

Examples: Greenleaf and Mansfield (B).

C: The usual story is told, but the parrot accuses the girl of the murder because of stanzas borrowed from *Young Hunting* (68).

Examples: *JAF,* 1936, 213.

D: The usual story is told, but the parrot fails to deceive the girl's father, and the old man reminds the daughter that he had said she would rue her going away.   Examples: *JAF,* 1909, 374.

E: The usual story is told, but after the girl removes her cloak, the suitor drags her into the water—first up to her ankles, then her knees, waist, and eventually neck. She grabs the horse's tail and somehow (a stanza is forgotten) the lover drowns. She escapes and returns home, where her mother and the parrot have the usual conversation about the cat.

Examples: Scarborough, *On Trail N F-S.*

F: The usual story is told, though the parrot is missing. However, the song closes with the father's congratulating his daughter for her bravery and offering to line her skirt with silk.

Examples: Creighton and Senior, *Trd Sgs N Sc* (D).

Discussion: The story seems to be part of a large body of European tales. Child (I, 54) sets forth the hypothesis

> . . . that an independent European tradition existed of a half-human, half-demonaic being, who possessed an irresistible power of decoying away young maids, and was wont to kill them after he got them into his hands, but who at last found one who was more than his match, and lost his own life through her craft and courage. A modification of this story is afforded by the large class of Bluebeard tales.

Although Child rejects the idea (I, 53), the ballad may be an off-shoot of the Judith-Holofernes story. Foreign versions frequently include a conversation in which the girl asks her brother's permission to go with the lover who has sung irresistible melodies; a choice of deaths given to the maid; remarks by the head of the decapitated lover; and so forth.

The ballad is still known all over Europe. Holger Nygard's *The Ballad of Heer Halewijn* (Knoxville, 1958) is a classic study of all facets of the song's tradition. See also the excerpts from this book in *JAF*, 1952, 1-12; *JAF*, 1955, 141-152; and *MWF*, 1955, 141-151. Other detailed studies are Grundtvig's work in *Danmarks gamle Folkeviser*, IV (Copenhagen, 1853-1890); Child's introduction, I, 22f.; and Iivar Kemppinen's *The Ballad of Lady Isabel and the False Knight* (Helsinki, 1954). Kemppinen traces the false knight back to an ancient demon king of the "Wild Hunt", dating from the 12th Century in the Lower Rhine region.

In 19th Century England there were many stall versions. Belden, *Mo Fsgs* 5, divides the song into three scenes, as they were presented in these stall prints; the seducer cajoling the girl, the waterside, the parrot. Parodies of the song are also not uncommon. Barry, *Brit Blds Me*, 33 reports one from Maine containing the May Collin or Colvin name found in Child C, H, etc. and included in the printed *Charley Fox's Minstrel's Companion*, Philadelphia, 1861.

Barry argues (*Brit Blds Me*, 34) that the song must have been an early arrival in America. The versions are invariably closer to Child C—G than to A—B, with the exception of Type E which is nearest, but not exactly like, Child B. In America, certain characteristics can be noted: 1. The girl and the parrot often have the same names in the ballad (Polly), which tends to confuse the story. (MacIntosh, *Ill State Hist. Journal*, XXXI, 302, prints a text that has "my pretty golin—colleen—" and not a parrot bribed to silence. This is another and similar confusion, although the informant refused to admit a parrot has a thing to do with the song. See p. 300.) 2. The supernatural character of the lover has completely vanished. (Niles, *Blds Lv Sgs Tgc Lgds*, 4 prints a version under the local title the *Elfin Knight*, although there is nothing in the text to indicate supernaturalism in the lover's character.) See also Cox, *W. Va. School Journal and Educator*, XLIV, 269. Wimberly, *American Speech*, III, 114f., discusses this ballad with respect to this point. 3. The girl is often a very vigorous person. She throws a rock at the drowning knight in SharpK, *Eng Fsgs So Aplchns,* B and threatens, rather than cajoles, the parrot in the Niles version just cited. 4. Substitutes for the "naked girl" excuse are often given in the form of "clearing the briars", "saying prayers", etc. These reveal a change for what may well have been, in certain early American cases, puritanical reasons. The *JAF,* 1911, 334 version from Illinois-Missouri is notable in this respect, not only for the religious note in the request by the girl for a chance to pray, but also for her seeking the Lord's support in the murder she commits.

Zielonko, *Some American Variants of Child Ballads,* p. 3f. can be consulted for a detailed comparison of selected American texts. Brewster, *Blds Sgs Ind,* 31, discusses the Indiana versions in some detail. He suggests that the name William, used for the seducer in some texts, may be derived from *villain.* See also the interesting Arnold, *Fsgs Ala,* text, which is called "Billy Came Over the Main White Ocean" and in which the girl is told to "choose . . . a pot of her father's bees". The slightly corrupt Duncan, *No Hamilton Cnty,* text is also worth study. And particularly unusual is the intrusion of the warning for the cock not to crow early (see *Grey Cock,* 248) which can be seen in Brown, *NC Flklre,* II (A). This corruption was no doubt encouraged by the parrot stanzas. The Flanders A text in *Ancient Blds,* I, 84, is notable because the incremental stanzas of Child C, D, and particularly E, in which the girl removes a series of garments, are retained. In this Rhode Island song, the maid takes off her gown, shoes, stockings, and smock at her lover's commands.

The story occurs as a prose tale and cante fable as well. Elsie Clews Parsons collected a version part in song and part in prose from the South Carolina Sea Island Negroes. Isabel Carter, *JAF,* 1925, 373, prints a mountain white version, "Old Notchy Road", from the southern Blue Ridge which employs the stripping and pushing motifs in relation to a pit and an habitual murderer. See also the folk songs *The Jealous Lover, Pearl Bryan,* etc.

Note should be taken of the French-Canadian version (Barbeau, *Fsgs French Canada,* 22) which is different in story from the English-American versions. However, it derives from France and was brought over to Quebec by Frenchmen. Here Jeanneton kicks the man in the stream as he pulls off her stocking and cuts a limb off a tree to keep him under. He repents as he dies. This story has had no effect on American tradition to my knowledge.

6. WILLIE'S LADY

Willie's Lady, which is common in Denmark, has not been collected from oral tradition in the New World, although it has been found in Great Britain. The text that appears in Flanders, *Ancient Blds,* I, 124 is from *The Charms of Melody,* printed by J. & J. Carrick, Dublin. This book had wide circulation in New England.

7. EARL BRAND

Note: References to secondary versions—songs about a bold soldier and with a happy ending—can be found under *Erlinton,* Child 8.

Texts: Barry, *Brit Blds Me,* 35 / Brewster, *Blds Sgs Ind,* 37 / Bronson, I, 106 / Brown, *NC Flklre,* II, 27 / *BFSSNE,* I, 4 / *Bull Tenn FLS,* VIII, #3, 64 / Cox, *Fsgs South,* 18 / Cox, *W. Va. School Journal and Educator,* XLVI, 83 / Davis, *Fsgs Va,* 5 / Davis, *More Trd Blds Va,* 26 / Davis, *Trd Bld Va,* 86 / Flanders, *Blds Migrant NE,* 228 / Flanders, *Ancient Blds,* I, 128 / Greenleaf and Mansfield, *Blds Sea Sgs Newfdld,* 7 / Henry, *Beech Mt Fsgs,* 10 / Henry, *Fsgs So Hghlds,* 36 / Henry, *Sgs Sng Aplchns,* 45 / Hudson, *Fsgs Miss,* 66 / Hudson, *Ftunes Miss,* 22 / Hudson, *Spec Miss Flklre,* #2 / Hummel, *Oz Fsgs* / *JAF,* 1915, 152; 1929, 256; 1935, 307; 1947. 241 / *Keystone FQ,* 1957, 20 / Lomax & Lomax, *Our Sng Cntry,* 154 / MacKenzie, *Blds Sea Sgs N Sc,* 9 / MacKenzie, *Quest Bld,* 26, 60 / Morris, *Fsgs Fla,* 241 / *MLN,* XXV, #4, 104 / Perry, *Carter Cnty,* 191 / Randolph, *Oz Fsgs,* I, 48 / Randolph, *Oz Mt Flk,* 221 / Scarborough, *Sgctchr So Mts,* 114 / SharpC, *Eng Fsgs So Aplchns,* #3 / SharpK, *Eng Fsgs So Aplchns,* I, 14 / Shearin and Combs, *Ky Syllabus,* 7 / *SFQ,* 1944, 136 / *Va FLS Bull* #s, 2, 4-6, 10 / Wells, *Bld Tree,* 147.

Local Titles: As He Rode Up to the Old Man's Gate, As I Was A-going to Nothingham Fair, The Child of Ell, Fair Ellender, Lady Margaret, Lord Loving, Lord Robert, Lord William, Lord William and Lady Margaret, Rise Ye Up, The Seven Brethren, The Seven Brothers, Seven Horsemen, The Seven King's Sons, The Seven(th) Sleeper(s), Sweet William, Sweet William and Fair Eleanor, Sweet Willie.

Story Types: A: A girl is carried off by her lover who, in some songs, spends the night with her first. Her father and seven brothers pursue them. The lover halts his flight and slays all eight. After the damage has been done, the girl tells him to hold his hand, and then, desperate and crushed, she continues on with him. Often a scene in which they stop to drink at a river and the fatal bleeding of the lover stains the water is included. The song ends at his mother's house where they both die, he of wounds, she of heartbreak.

Examples: Barry (A), Brewster (A), Davis, *Trd Bld Va* (A), SharpK (A), *SFQ,* 1944, 137.

B: The usual story has a stanza (perhaps from Barbara Allen) inserted so that the mother dies as well as the lovers.

Examples: Cox, *W. Va. School Journal and Educator,* XLVI, 83; SharpK (B).

C: The usual story is told as far as the fight. Then, on the death of her father, the girl turns against her lover and wishes him in the middle of the sea.   Examples: Hudson, *Fsgs Miss.*

D: This text is similar to that of Type C, except that the lover becomes harsh with the girl after the fight and tells her if she does not like what he has done she can get another suitor. He tells her he wishes that she were back in her mother's room and he somewhere else. This ending is very abrupt.

Examples: Henry, *Sgs Sng So Aplchns.*

Discussion: The Type A ballads follow the story of Child B, Scott's *The Douglas Tragedy,* a song that may well be based on a real Selkirkshire event as far as its detail goes. (See Davis, *Trd Bld Va,* 86 and Child, I, 99.) *The*

Douglas Tragedy contains the rose-briar ending, although this feature is lacking in a large percentage of the American versions. None of Davis' Virginia collection has this motif, though SharpK, *Eng Fsgs So Aplchns,* A, C contain it. Also, in the SharpK southern texts can be found the names Fair Ellender, Lord Thomas, in addition to the *Barbara Allen* stanza (see Type B). These points indicate that Child 73 and 84 have both contacted this song.

Other American story types derive from varying causes. The girl's turning against her lover in Type C seems to be a combination of forgetting and sentimentality, while both this and the Type D versions tend to substitute a more active and less powerful dramatic scene for the pathos of the Type A ending. In Type D the change in tone after the father's death may well have come from the loss of a few key phrases somewhere in oral transmission. Compare the very similar lines as they exist in a Type A story (*JAF,* 1915, 153) also from North Carolina, and check the Brown, *NC Flklre,* II, 27 text, where contact with the stall ballad *The Orphan Gypsy Girl* is suspected.

In the American versions of the ballad the girl seldom, if ever, speaks before her father is slain. Also, the Brewster, *Blds Sgs Ind,* A text is worth noting because of its extreme beauty and the interesting condensation of the end. The lovers never reach home, and the rose-briar lines are compressed. The A. C. Morris (*SFQ,* 1944, 136) text differs from most American versions in that the hanging of the bugle about William's neck is repeated. (See Child B). For a complete description of the American tradition, see Doris C. Powers' detailed analysis of *Earl Brand* in *WF,* 1958, 77-96 and Zielonko, *Some American Variants of Child Ballads,* 21.

The tale is not an uncommon one. Child's remarks (I, 88f.) concerning the Scandinavian counterpart *Ribold and Guldborg* are important in this respect.

Reference should also be made to Child 8 (Erlinton) for the ballads called *The Soldier's Wooing,* etc. that are often printed as American secondary versions of *Earl Brand* or *Erlinton.* See Child 8 in this study.

Once in a while a collector will list *Locks and Bolts* as related to Child 7 (See, for example, Arnold, *Fsgs Ala,* 62). Such a connection is derived through some sort of wishful thinking.

8. ERLINTON

Note: There is no American text that can be for certain be called a derivative of *Erlinton.* The various *Bold Soldier* songs (Laws M27) may possibly be related to either *Earl Brand* (Child 8) or *Erlinton.*

"Bold Soldier" Texts: Barry, *Brit Blds Me,* 377 / Belden, *Mo Fsgs,* 103 / *Boston Evening Transcript, Notes and Queries,* 11-26-'21 / Brewster, *Blds Sgs Ind,* 40 / Bronson, I, 128 / Brown, *NC Flklre,* II, 287 / Bull *Tenn FLS,* II, #1, 1 / Cazden, *Abelard Fsg Bk,* I, 42 / Chappell, *Fsgs Rnke Alb,* 88 / Cox, *Fsgs South,* 375 / Creighton, *Sgs Blds N Sc,* 25 / Davis, *Trd Bld Va,* 92 / Eddy, *Blds Sgs Ohio,* 14 / Flanders, *Ancient Blds,* I, 131 / Flanders, *Garl Gn Mt Sg,* 55 / Flanders, *Vt Fsgs Blds,* 232 / Gardner and Chickering, *Blds Sgs So Mich,* 380 / Henry, *Fsgs So Hghlds,* 185 / Ives, *BI Sg Bk,* 70 / *JAF,* 1908, 57; 1910, 447; 1916, 188; 1917, 363; 1922, 414; 1932, 114; 1947, 215; 1955, 202 / *Ky Folklore and Poetry Magazine,* II, #4, 5 / Pound, *Am Blds Sgs,* 68 / Randolph, *Oz Fsgs,* 303 / SharpC, *Eng*

Fsgs So Aplchns, #41 / SharpK, *Eng Fsgs So Aplchns,* I, 333 / *West Va Folklore,* IX, #2 (1959), 18.

Local Titles: The Bold Soldier, The Gallant Soldier, I'll Tell You of a Soldier, The Poor Soldier, The Soldier, The Soldier's Wooing, The Valiant Soldier, The Yankee Soldier.

Story Types: A: A soldier returns from war and courts a rich, fair lady against her father's wishes. The father and seven men attack them as they go to get married. The soldier fights bravely and is routing the assailants when the father offers to give up his daughter and a large sum of money. However, the girl refuses to let her lover stop the fight until the old man offers all his wealth. She reasons that the fortune will be hers anyway if her father is slain. The father capitulates and takes the soldier home as his heir, more out of fear than agreement.

Examples: Belden; Randolph (A, B).

Discussion: There are a number of secondary versions of this ballad in circulation under the various "soldier" titles. However, the mood of these songs has become gay and humorous from tragic. Note the cold-bloodedness of the lady who willingly endangers her father's life in order to get the best bargain. This scene originates in the broadside texts. See *The Masterpiece of Love-Songs,* in John Ashton's *A Century of Ballads,* 164 and the *Roxburghe Ballads,* VI, 229, cited by Barry, *JAF,* 1910, 447. The outline of the tale, the elopement, and the lady who holds the horses and watches does, nevertheless, ally the American texts with *Erlinton,* or possibly *Earl Brand.* See Gardner and Chickering, *Blds Sgs So Mich,* 380; Eddy, *Blds Sgs Ohio,* 14; and Brewster, *Blds Sgs Ind,* 40. Also check Child (I, 88, 106) who finds it difficult to separate the British forms of the two traditional ballads. There is a similar "sailor" song in the English broadsides. See *Roxburghe Ballads,* VII, 559.

David M. Greene (*JAF,* 1957, 221-230) has demonstrated in a definitive article, *"The Lady and the Dragoon": A Broadside Ballad in Oral Tradition* that the "soldier" texts are related to "the ballads of the *Earl Brand* family" as a "result of conscious imitation and not . . . of traditional variation." He also traces the broadside history of the "soldier" songs in Britain and America to demonstrate what variations occur between the 17th Century broadside "original" and the present forms of the song. He sees all oral American texts as rising from the "Bold Soldier" broadside printed by Nathaniel Coverly, Jr. of Boston between 1806 and 1819. This version, he believes, was a re-working of a now lost English broadside.

These "soldier" songs offer a classic example of an American oral tradition that has sprung from British stall forms of an old ballad. The situation is not uncommon. See also *The Brown Girl* (295) and the majority of the *Katherine Jaffray* (221) texts.

Norman Cazden (*JAF,* 1955, 201-209) uses *The Bold Soldier* and *The Braes of Yarrow* (214) to demonstrate his thesis concerning the relationship of ballads and their social environment.

See Brown, *NC Flklre,* II, 289 for an interesting Civil War adaptation called *The Yankee Soldier.*

10. THE TWA SISTERS

Texts: Adventure, 9-10-'23, 191 / Barry, *Brit Blds Me,* 40 / Beard, *Personal Fsg Coll Lunsford,* 43 / Belden, *Mo Fsgs,* 16 / Botkin, *Am Play-Party Sg,* 59, 337 / Brewster, *Blds Sgs Ind,* 42 / Bronson, I, 143 / Brown, *NC Flklre,* II, 32 / *BFSSNE,* VI, 5; IX, 4; X, 10; XI, 16; XII, 10 / *Bull Tenn FLS,* IV, #3, 74; VIII, #3, 71 / Chappell, *Fsgs Rnke Alb,* 13 / Chase, *Sgs All Times,* 20 / Child, I, 137; II, 508 / Child Ms., XXI, 10 / *Christian Science Monitor,* 12-2-'37 / Cox, *Fsgs South,* 20 / Cox, *Trd Bld W Va,* 6 / Cox, *W Va School Journal and Educator,* XLIV, 428, 441 / Davis, *Fsgs Va,* 6 / Davis, *More Trd Blds Va,* 35 / Davis, *Trd Bld Va,* 93 / Eddy, *Blds Sgs Ohio,* 17 / Flanders, *Ancient Blds,* I, 150 / Flanders, *Blds Migrant NE,* 209 / Flanders, *New Gn Mt Sgstr,* 3 / *Folkways Monthly,* May '62, 19 / Garrison, *Searcy Cnty,* 19 / Gray, *Sgs Blds Me Lmbrjks,* 75 / Gardner and Chickering, *Blds Sgs So Mich,* 32 / Greenleaf and Mansfield, *Blds Sea Sgs Newfdld,* 9 / Haun, *Cocke Cnty,* 106 / Henry, *Fsgs So Hghlds,* 39 / Hubbard, *Blds Sgs Utah,* 5 / Hudson, *Fsgs Miss,* 68 / Hudson, *Ftunes Miss,* 25 / Hudson, *Spec Miss Flklre,* #3 / *JAF,* 1905, 130; 1906, 233; 1917, 287; 1929, 238; 1931, 295; 1932, 1; 1935, 306; 1951, 347; 1957, 249 / *Ky Folklore Record,* 1958, 116 / Kincaid, *Fav Mt Blds,* 22 / A. Lomax, *Fsgs No Am,* 184 / Morris, *Fsgs Fla,* 243 / Neal, *Brown Cnty,* 60 / *N.Y. Times Mgz,* 10—9—'27 / Niles, *More Sgs Hill-Flk,* 8 / Niles, *Anglo-Am Bld Stdy Bk,* 36 / Perry, *Carter Cnty,* 98 / Pound, *Am Blds Sgs,* 11 / Pound, *Nebr Syllabus,* 9 / *PTFS,* X, 141 / Raine, *Land Sddle Bags,* 118 / Randolph, *Oz Fsgs,* I, 50 / Randolph, *Oz Mt Flk,* 211 / Richardson, *Am Mt Sgs,* 27 / Scarborough, *Sgctchr So Mts,* 164 / SharpC, *Eng Fsgs So Aplchns,* #4 / SharpK, *Eng Fsgs So Aplchns,* I, 26 / Smith and Rufty, *Am Anth Old Wrld Blds,* 2 / *SFL,* 1944, 138 / Stout, *Flklre Ia,* 1 / Thomas, *Blue Ridge Cntry,* 152 / Thomas, *Devil's Ditties,* 70 / Thomas, *Sngin Gathrn,* 76 / Thompson, *Bdy Bts Brtchs,* 393 / *Va FLS Bull* #s 2—8, 12 / Vincent, *Lmbrjk Sgs,* 27.

Local Titles: All Bow Down, Bow Ye Down, The Fair Sisters, I'll Be True to My Love, Lord of the Old Country, The Miller and the Mayor's Daughter, The Miller's Two Daughters, The Old Farmer in the Countree, The Old Lord by the Northern Sea, The Old Man of (in) the North (Old) Countree, Sister Kate, The Swim Swom Bonny, There Was an Old Farmer (Joyner), There Was an Old Man Lived in a Gum Tree, (There Was an) Old Woman (Who) Lived on the Seashore (in the West), The Two (Three) (Little) Sisters, The Two Young Daughters, West Countree, The Youngest Daughter.

Story Types: A: A girl, jealous that a gentleman has courted her younger sister, invites the latter on a walk and pushes her in the water to drown. A miller robs the struggling girl, rather than rescuing her, and is punished by death for his crime. Capital punishment for the elder girl may or may not be mentioned.

Examples: Barry (A); Belden (C); Davis, *Trd Bld Va,* (A); SharpK (B).

B: Two princesses are playing by the water. The elder pushes the younger in. A miller finds the dead girl and makes a musical instrument from her body. The instrument reveals the murderer.

Examples: Barry (E), SharpK (K).

C: The usual story is started, but the musical instrument is made from the younger sister's body by the elder sister, and the instrument then names the murderer. This version has three-quarters of each stanza as refrain.

Examples: *JAF,* 1932, 7.

D: A combination of Types A and B is sometimes found in which the instrument is made from the body, and both the miller and the elder girl are executed.   Examples: SharpK (A).

E: The usual story is started, but the drowned girl appears to make a harp of herself and reveal her murderer.
Examples: Henry, *Fsgs So Hghlds* (C).

F: The usual story is told, but the miller is left out. The girl in the water may plead with her sister to pull her from the "sea-sand" (quicksand?) and be refused.   Examples: Brewster (B, C), Neal.

G: An amazing version found in Newfoundland tells of the younger sister's shoving the elder sister in the water, although the younger has received more attention from the suitor. The body is fished out with a fishing pan, the face covered with lace and the hair full of golden lumps. A ghost tells the lover how his sweetheart was killed.
Examples: Greenleaf-Mansfield

H: The usual story is told, except the elder sister bribes the miller to push the girl back into the water. Both the sister and the miller (sometimes only the miller) are hung.
Examples: Randolph, *Oz Fsgs* (D); Lomax, *Fsgs No Am,* 184.

I: The story is like that of Type A, except the miller is the father of the two girls and pushes his own daughter into the water.
Examples: Cox, *Fsgs South* (A).

J: The usual story is told, but the miller is the lover of the girls and seems to rescue the younger one after she has been pushed in.
Examples: *JAF,* 1905, 131.

K: A story similar to Type J is told, but after the rescue all go to church and "now they're (which two is not clear) married I suppose".
Examples: Thompson.

L: The story is like that of Type J, except that a prince courts the girls. The miller rescues the elder sister. She falls in love with him, and they marry.
Examples: Haun.

M: The usual story is told. However, the "fisherman", who has no previous connection with the girls, seems to rescue the drowning maid.
Examples: Cox, *Trd Blds W Va* (B); Perry.

N: Two little girls float down a stream in a boat. Charles Miller comes out with his hook and pulls one out by the hair and makes a fiddle of her body.
Examples: *BFSSNE,* XII, 10 .

O: The story is like that of Type L, except the miller rescues the younger sister after she promises to marry him. The tone is comic.
Examples: Brown (A).

P: The story is similar to Type A, except the sisters (it is not clear whether this includes the one pushed back in the water), flee "beyond the seas and died old maids among black savagees".

Examples: Flanders, *Ancient Blds* (C).

Q: The usual opening of the Type A story is followed. However, the miller's son sees the younger sister's body in the dam. The miller drains the dam and removes the body of the girl. A passing harper makes an instrument of the bones and the murder is revealed as he plays and sings.

Examples: Davis, *More Trd Blds Va* (AA).

Discussion: This song and the similar tale (see Aarne-Thompson, Mt. 780) still have current traditions in Europe. The ballad is also current in Britain (Child, I, 118) and has more American story variations than any other song. Thus, it makes an excellent subject for study. Paul Brewster has done a very complete survey of both the song and the tale in *FFC*, #147 (1953) and included a useful bibliography to both in *Blds Sgs Ind*, 42-43. He feels the song began in Norway before 1600, spread through Scandinavia, and then to Britain and the West. However, he thinks the tale is of Slavic origin. This thesis (see also his article *The Geographical Distribution of "The Twa Sisters"* in *Annuario de la Sociedad Folklorica de Mexico*, 1944, 49-54), along with Harbison Parker's *"The Twa Sisters"—Going Which Way?* in *JAF*, 1951, 347-360), re-evaluates Knut Leistøl's belief that the ballad was first composed in Britain, split into two versions, both of which came to Scandinavia, one to Norway and one to Denmark. Parker believes the ballad to have originated in Western Scandinavia, and the British versions to stem from Faroe or Norwegian texts. See also Lutz MacKenson's study in *FFC*, #49 (1923) and Child, I, 124-125. Archer Taylor (*JAF*, 1929, 238f.) discusses the American, English, and Scottish versions of the ballad. He concludes that the American texts follow the English tradition (see p. 243)exclusively. The beaver hat, the failure to call the hair yellow, and the introductory stanza are all English traits. For the Scottish traits (not common to America) see pp. 238—40.

The extremely wide variation of story types in America can probably be traced to forgetting of details combined with attempts to rationalize either the presence or absence of the "harp" motif with the rest of the narrative. Certainly there has been no printed text that has frozen the story, as is the case in other songs. Note should be made, in connection with this point, of the Gardner and Chickering, *Blds Sgs So Mich*, B version ("Peter and Paul went down the lane") which is scarcely recognizable as the same song.

Perversions of the original such as my Types C, E, and G (cf. Child B and my Type C in connection with G) are the results of small changes in some detail of the narrative. However, they reveal the sort of change that might easily create a new story if enough momentum were gained. For example, the Type A version in North Carolina and Kentucky (see *Ky Folklore Record*, 1958, 116) is ready to give birth to a new plot. Here the tale is told in the first person, first by the younger, then by the elder, sister. After the elder girl pushes the younger in the river, the miller pulls the younger girl out and is executed for the crime. The elder sister goes scot free. No mention is made of the miller's robbing the drowning girl. Type I has been melodramatized through similar alterations of detail, probably with the aid of forgetting. Types F and M are undoubtedly the results of omission of the ending in one of the other classes, though check the Cox, *Trd Blds W Va*, B text in which the miller is hung for pulling the girl to shore. Types J, K, and L have all been sentimentalized. J and K are certainly related to Child M, while K and L may echo the marriage feast that is present in the Norse forms of the story. Types D and H refer to texts that are well-known, D combining Types A and B, while H is paralleled by Child S. (Under Type J, see Garrison, *Searcy Cnty*, 20 who quotes his informant as saying "that they (some forgotten lines) told how the miller and the cruel sister, who had together plotted the younger girl's drowning in an attempt to get possession of property that had been left to her by her sweetheart, were hanged".) Type N resembles Type B in the use of the instrument motif, but seems quite corrupt at the start. Barry, *BFSSNE*, XII, 10 theorizes on this text. Type Q, from Virginia, is one of the finest texts collected in America. It resembles Child B, although it includes the "bow down" refrain of the Child R-S, U-V, Z series.

In general, the miller is present in American versions, although the gruesome musical instrument portion is lacking. (See Child Y and the whole Rf. group.) The elimination of such a supernatural motif is in keeping with the usual American practice, and the New World mood is on the whole lighter than the Old. Flanders, *New Gn Mt Sgstr*, 4 points out that texts where the girl gets capital punishment are less likely to degenerate into comedy than those where the miller is hung.

The refrains of the ballad have been given a great deal of attention. For discussions of them see Barry, *BFSSNE*, III, II; Belden, *Mo Fsgs*, 16; Henry, *Fsgs So Hghlds*, 38; *JAF*, 1932, 2 ("bow down" refrain) ; and Taylor, *JAF*, 1929, 238. The usual American refrains are the "juniper, gentian, and rosemary" corruption, or a "bow down, etc.—I'll be true to my love, if my love'll be true to me" variation. Nonsense lines ("sing i dum", "hey ho, my Nannie") are also found, and Randolph prints a refrain "bonnery-O" which seems to come from "Binnorie, O, Binnorie" (Child C). See also *BFSSNE*, IX, 4 and X, 10 and the Morris, *Fsgs Fla*, texts. The latter songs feature the word "rolling" in various combinations.

Botkin in his *Am Play Party Sg*, 59f. discusses the refrain of the song and its use in the dance-game versions, and Thomas, *Sngin Gathrn*, 79 describes the ballad as a Kentucky dance.

The song is often found utilizing the "bowed her head and swam" cliché so common to Child 286.

For a detailed discussion of a number of American texts, see Zielonko, *Some American Variants of Child Ballads*, 30. Refer also to Barry, *BFSSNE*, III, 2 and XII, 10 for detailed treatments of the tradition of the song, especially in connection with Type N.

Helen Flanders and Phillips Barry (see *Ancient Blds*, 163, G1, G2) discovered a remarkable Polish text in Springfield, Vermont. In this song, the younger sister is murdered during a raspberrying contest and a flute is made from reeds at the grave. It seems to be a folk variant of the ballad *Maliny*, written in 1829 by Alexander Chodzko (1804-1891). Barry discusses this text in detail in *BFSSNE*, X, 2-5 and XI, 2-4. See also Jonas Balys, *Lithuanian Narrative Folksongs* (Washington, D.C., 1954), G7, 119-120.

Jeckyll, *Jamaican Sg Stry*, 14 prints a cante fable called *King Daniel* that follows the outline of *The Twa Sisters* and that includes a talking parrot.

11. THE CRUEL BROTHER

Texts: Barry, *Brit Blds Me*, 431 (trace) / Bronson, I, 185 / Brown, *NC Flklre*, 36 / Flanders, *Ancient Blds*, I, 171 / Haun, *Cocke Cnty*, 87 / *JAF*, 1915, 300 / Pound, *Am Blds Sgs*, 21 / SharpC, *Eng Fsgs So Aplchns*, #20 / SharpK, *Eng Fsgs So Aplchns*, I, 36.

Local Titles: The Cruel Brother, (O) Lily O, The Stabbed Sister, Three Lads Played at Ball.

Story Types: A: Three landlords woo a girl. The third wins her. He asks her father and mother for permission to marry her, but forgets the brother. As a result, the brother, John, stabs her to death as she mounts her horse to go to the wedding. The ending, like that of *Edward*, is a testament in which John is cursed.

Examples: Haun, SharpK (A).

B: The story is similar to that of Type A, except that the brother's permission seems to be obtained, and the murder to be instigated by the brother's wife.   Examples: Pound.

Discussion: Both story types appear in Child (See A, B, etc.), but as is usually the case the American texts are shorter. Sharp (SharpK, *Eng Fsgs So Aplchns*, I, 412) points out that his North Carolina version originated in the west of England.

For a treatment of the intrafamily murder ballads and the place of the brother in the house, see Flanders, *New Gn Mt Sgstr*, 94. The suggestion of incest (Type B) may well be behind this song, *The Twa Brothers* (49), and a few other Child stories.

The most common American refrain, "rose smells sweet and gay", is probably a derivative of one of the British "rose" burdens (See Child A, F, I—K).

12. LORD RANDAL

Texts: Barry, *Brit Blds Me*, 46 / Belden, *Mo Fsgs*, 24 / Brewster, *Blds Sgs Ind*, 51 / Bronson, I, 191 / Brown, *NC Flklre*, II, 39 / *BFSSNE*, I, 4 / *Bull U SC*, #162, #2 / Chappell, *Fsgs Rnke Alb*, 14 / Child, I, 163 / *Colorado Fsg Bull*, I, #3, 3; II, 2 / Cox, *Fsgs South*, 23 / Cox, *Trd Bld W Va*, 9 / Cox, *W Va School Journal and Educator*, XLV, 266 / Creighton and Senior, *Trd Sgs N Sc*, 9 / *The Crimson Rambler* (Tonkawa, Okla.), VIII, #4 / Davis, *Fsgs Va*, 8 / Davis, *More Trd Blds Va*, 51 / Davis, *Trd Bld Va*, 105 / *Decennial Publication*, Univ. of Chicago, 1903, VII, 140 / Eddy, *Blds Sgs Ohio*, 21 / Flanders, *Blds Migrant NE*, 37, 200 / Flanders, *Ancient Blds*, I, 175 / Flanders, *Vt Fsgs Blds*, 197 / Focus, III, 399; IV, 31, 100 / Gardner and Chickering, *Blds Sgs So Mich*, 35 / Garrison, *Searcy Cnty*, 30 / *Harper's*

Mgz (May 1915), 908 / Haufrecht, *Folk Sing*, 78 / Haun, *Cocke Cnty*, 72 / Henry, *Fsgs So Hghlds*, 45 / Hubbard, *Blds Sgs Utah*, 6 / Hudson, *Fsgs Miss*, 69 / Hudson, *Spec Miss Flklre*, #4 / Hummel, *Oz Fsgs* / Ives, *BI Sg BK*, 58 / *JAF*, 1900, 115; 1903, 258; 1905, 195, 303; 1909, 376; 1911, 345; 1913, 353; 1916, 157; 1917, 289; 1922, 339; 1926, 81; 1929, 257; 1931, 302; 1957, 250 / Johnson, *Early Am Sgs*, 29 / *Ky Folklore Record*, 1956, 56 / Kolb, *Treasury Fsg*, 14 / Linscott, *Fsgs Old NE*, 191 / MacIntosh, *So Ill Fsgs*, 26 / Mason, *Cannon Cnty*, 13 / McGill, *Fsgs Ky Mts*, 19 / *MLN*, XIV, 211 / *Mod Phil*, XXIX, 105 / Morris, *Fsgs Fla*, 247 / *Musical Quarterly*, II, 127 / *Narragansett Times*, 2-2-'45 / Niles, *Anglo-Am Bld Study Bk*, 6 / Niles, *Blds Lv Sgs Tgc Lgds*, 14 / Pound, *Am Blds Sgs*, 3 / Pound, *Nebr Syllabus*, 9 / *Promenade*, IV, #3, 2 / *Outlook*, LXIII, 121 / Randolph, *Oz Fsgs*, I, 63 / Randolph, *Oz Mt Flk*, 215 / Scarborough, *Sgctchr So Mts*, 178 / *Sewanee Review*, XIX, 317 / SharpC, *Eng Fsgs So Aplchns*, #6 / SharpK, *Eng Fsgs So Aplchns*, I, 38 / Shoemaker, *Mt Mnstly*, 144 / Shoemaker, *No Pa Mnstly*, 139 / Shearin and Combs, *Ky Syllabus*, 7 / Reed Smith, *SC Blds*, 101 / *Va FLS Bull*, #s 2-5, 7-11 / Wells, *Bld Tree*, 101 / *West Va Folklore*, 1955, 22.

Local Titles: A Rope and Gallows, Billy Randall, Croodin Doo, The Cup of Cold Poison, Dear Willie, Durango, Fair Nelson My Son, Fileander My Son, Henry My Son, The Jealous Lover, Jeems Randal, Jimmie Randall (Randolph, etc.), John Elzie, Johnny Randall (Rilla, Reeler, Ramsay, Ransom, Riller, Reynolds, Ramble, Rillus, Randolph, etc.), Johnnie Randolph My Son, John Willow My Son, Lord Henry, Lord Lantoun, Lord Nelson, Lord Ronald My Son, McDonald, Mother Make My Bed Soon, The Poisoned Child, Poor Anzo (Randall, Ransell, etc.), Sweet Nelson My Son, Sweet William, Terence, Three Cups of Cold Poison, Tyranty, Tyranty My Son, Uriar My Son, Where Have You Been (to My Dear Son)?, Willy Ransome, Willie Where Have You Been?, Wooing and Death of John Randal.

Story Types: A: A man, through a dialogue with his mother, tells that he has spent the night with his sweetheart, eaten a poisoned supper, and is now sick. His dogs usually are revealed to have died from the leavings. In his last "bequests" the sweetheart is cursed and shown to be the murderer.

Examples: Belden (C); Cox, *Fsgs South* (A); Davis, *Trd Bld Va* (A); Reed Smith (A).

B: The story is the same as that of Type A, except that the hero forgives his sweetheart and seems to remain faithful to her although he knows she has poisoned him.

Examples: Davis, *Trd Bld Va* (L).

C: Some versions name other persons than the sweetheart as the murderer. Henry (Randal's brother), grandmother, sister, stepmother, wife, grandpa, and even Randal himself has this role.

Examples: Barry (K, O); Cox, *Fsgs South* (E); Davis, p. 118—9; Eddy (B, C); Gardner and Chickering; *JAF*, 1905, 201f.; Linscott.

D: There is a Massachusetts version in which Randal goes fishing and catches an eel which he cooks and eats by mistake. The dialogue consists of his mother's discovery of the fatal error.

Examples: Barry (N).

E: The same story as that of Type A, except the sister and the sweetheart have conspired to kill Randal.

Examples: Shoemaker, *Mt. Mnstly*.

F: The same story as that of Type A is told, except that a moral couplet saying that Randal is buried in the churchyard and "his wicked love" has been hanged has been added.

Examples: Davis, *More Trd Blds Va* (AA).

Discussion: This ballad has extremely long and varied European, British, and American traditions (See Child, I, 151 f. and Barry, *Brit Blds Me,* 64f.). It is said to be the most popular purely traditional song in America, for there have been no pocket songster versions to aid its spread as has been the case of *Barbara Allen* and *Lord Thomas* and *Fair Annet* (See Barry, *Brit Blds Me,* 65). In the texts, there are any number of detail variations, but the story itself has remained quite constant.

This song has been the subject of a large amount of study and research, most of it connected with the names given the hero (See Zielonko, *Some American Variants of Child Ballads,* 47 and Reed Smith, *SC Blds,* 56). The alliance of the Randolph family of Virginia and West Virginia with the story has been noted by Davis, *Trd Bld Va,* 105, although Vance Randolph, *Oz Fsgs* I, 63 points out that the ballad was aligned with the Randolphs in the Old World as well. Check, too, Scott, *Minstrelsy of the Scottish Border* (1902 ed.), III, 51. Scott also indicates in the same work the similarity of the story to that of King John's death. See the Child C "King Henry" type, retained in Cox, *Fsgs South,* E.

The poison used by the true-love is generally considered to be snakes, served as eels or fish (Child, I, 155), although frequently she may serve simply poison or some such corruption as "ale" (eel), or even the cold cakes and coffee of Cox, *Fsgs South,* H. (See *JAF,* 1903, 259.) Toads and reptiles of other sorts are also used, and Barry, *Brit Blds Me,* 61 points out that newts were, by many people, considered poisonous when eaten.

The death wished for the true-love is by "hell-fire and brimstone" (Cox, *op. cit.,* A) in most American versions, while the death of the hawks and dogs is often omitted.

The story groups do not vary in general character, although they change in mood and motive. The Type C ballads in which the grandmother is the villain are probably the results of influence by the Scottish *Croodlin Doo* texts (Barry, *Brit Blds Me,* 66) and in New England frequently refer to the man as Tyranti (See Brown, *NC Flklre,* II, 39 for a NC "Tyranti" text). Barry, *op. cit.,* 71—2 deftly explains this grandmother intrusion into the American texts. He believes the Child J-O series tells a story in which a stepmother poisons a boy with small fish, and the dying youth is questioned by the ghost of his natural mother. This incident became rationalized as people ceased to believe in ghosts, and the grandmother and the natural mother herself were substituted into the narrative. Once this had happened, other members of the family might have slipped in. Type D he feels was "communally recreated" from Type C.

Reed Smith in his chapter "The Road Downhill" in *SC Blds,* 64 prints a *Poor Anzo* version that is unbelievably corrupt and that should be studied carefully as the extreme of transmission degeneration. Besides the new name of the hero, the mother's questions mean little: "What did you leave your father (etc.) for, Anzo, my son?" 'His reply that he has this or that is equally pointless. When asked why he left his sweetheart Anzo says, "Here is a red hot iron will broil a bone". Finally the mother wants to know what he'll have for supper, and his reply, "Make me a little breely broth soup" is a consistent close. No mention is made of Anzo's having been poisoned.

Other deviations and corruptions of note are: 1. Shoemaker, *Mt Mnstly,* 145 prints a footnote indicating that the Type E version from Pennsylvania has a funeral and a bequest for an unborn child. 2. The Flanders, *Ancient Blds,* H text has the lad give nothing at all to his mother and "hell, etc." to the sweetheart, which might possibly be a transfer of the *Edward* theme of maternal instigation through the similarity of endings. However, it is just as likely not. 3. Niles, *Blds Lv Sgs Tgc Lgds,* 14 prints a version that has the final request of "Randal" that he be laid at his grandfather's son (probably uncle here)'s side. 4. The moral ending on Type F is definite, though not especially artistic. Also, of some interest is the Flanders, *Ancient Blds,* A text that has a "derry-down" refrain.

Taylor, *Mod Phil,* XXIX, 105 attempts to explain the greenwood meeting by relating the song to *The King's Dochter Lady Jean* (Child 52), and the testament ending has been associated with incest (see *WF,* 1949, 314—319.

For remarks on the relationship of this ballad to *Billy Boy* see Linscott, *Fsgs Old NE,* 166 and Sharp, *100 English Folk-Songs,* XXXIV. For an analysis of a South Atlantic States "poor buckra" text, see C. E. Means, *Outlook,* Sept. 1899, 121. Jane Zielonko, *Some Variants of Child Ballads,* 41f. discusses a number of American texts in detail. See also Flanders, *Ancient Blds,* where a great variety of texts are collected in one spot.

13. EDWARD

Texts: Barry, *Brit Blds Me,* 433 (trace) / Bronson, I, 236 / Brown, *NC Flklre,* II, 41 / *CFQ,* V, 300 / Cox, *Trd Blds W Va,* 11 / Davis, *Fsgs Va,* 9 / Davis, *More Trd Blds Va,* 61 / Davis, *Trd Bld Va,* 120 / Eddy, *Blds Sgs Ohio,* 23 / Flanders, *Ancient Blds,* I, 208, 318 / Flanders, *Blds Migrant NE,* 96, 100 / *Focus,* III, 398, 399 / Gordon, *Fsgs Am,* 56 / Haun, *Cocke Cnty,* 89 / Hudson, *Fsgs Miss,* 70 / Hudson, *Spec Miss Flklre,* #5 / Hummel, *Oz Fsgs* / Ives, *BI Sg Bk,* 48 / *JAF,* 1926, 93 / A. Lomax, *Fsgs No Am,* 25 / Morris, *Fsgs Fla,* 248 / Niles, *Anglo-Am Study Bk,* 10 / *N.Y. Times Mgz,* 10-9-'27 / Owens, *SW Sings,* n.p. (2 texts) / Owens, *Studies Texas Fsgs,* 16 / Owens, *Texas Fsgs,* 59 / Pound, *Am Blds Sgs,* 23 / *PTFS,* XXVI, 137 / Randolph, *Oz Fsgs,* I, 67 / Randolph, *Oz Mt Flk,* 207 / Scarborough, *Sgctchr So Mts,* 180 / *Sewanee Review,* XIX, 313 / SharpC, *Eng Fsgs So Aplchns,* #7 / SharpK, *Eng Fsgs So Aplchns,* I, 47 / Shearin and Combs, *Ky Syllabus,* 7 / *SFQ,* 1940, 13 / Taylor, *Edward and Sven I Rosengard,* 80 / *Vt. Historical Society Proceedings,* N.S., VII, 1939, 102 / *Va FLS Bull* #s 2-4 6, 9-10 / Wells, *Bld Tree,* 103.

Local Titles: Blood on the Lily-White Shirt, The Cruel Brother, Dear Son, Edward, How Come (What Is) That Blood on Your Shirt Sleeve?, How Come That Red Blood on Your Coat?, The Little Yellow Dog, The Murdered Brother, Percy What's on Your Sword?, Ronald, What Blood on the Point of Your Knife?, What is That on the End of Your Sword?, What is That on Your Sword So Red?

Story Types: A: A man has committed fratricide (sometimes patricide or killed his brother-in-law), and his mother by steady questioning eventually

gets from him the facts of the crime along with a statement that he is fleeing the land never to return. No implication of the mother herself is indicated.
Examples: *CFQ,* V, 300; Davis, *Trd Bld Va* (A); Scarborough (A).

B: In the version that is half *The Twa Brothers* and half *Edward* (see Type E of Child 49), the mother is implicated. However, the implication makes little sense in this "new" story, as we are told earlier that the killing is the result of spontaneous anger and frustration during the fight.
Examples: Flanders, *Ancient Blds,* I, 318 (#49, A).

C: This text involves fratricide resulting from an argument over "the cutting of an elm tree" and implicates the mother in the crime.
Examples: Davis, *More Trd Blds Va* (AA).

Discussion: Unlike Child A, B the American texts (excepting the unusual Types B and C) do not implicate the mother in the crime. This characteristic and the New World emphasis on fratricide (Child A) rather than patricide (Child B) reveals a close relationship to what Taylor (see *Edward and Sven I Rosengard*) feels is the original form of the song. Taylor's work is the definitive study of the ballad. He feels the song began in Britain and then travelled to Scandinavia, but that the Scandinavian texts are closer to the now-extinct British original than modern British texts are. He also feels the story was originally one of fratricide (patricide being a chance substitution) and that the mother was not originally an accomplice in the crime. Because incest is a theme that might well vanish from such a story, an intrafamily fixation is probably the cause of the crime in the older, now lost, texts. See *WF,* VIII, 314—19. See Zielonko, *Some American Variants of Child Ballads,* 52 for a discussion of a few American texts and Taylor, *op. cit.,* for a definitive treatment of the whole tradition of the song. Taylor includes a large number of American, British and, translated Scandinavian variants, pp. 59—111. There is also an article by Margaret M. Blom (*SFQ,* 1956, 131-142) which discusses the famous Percy *Edward* (Child B), emphasizing that this variant has no folk tradition and is a truly literary ballad.

Helen H. Flanders (*Ancient Blds,* I, 318, under Child 49) prints a song under the title *Edward.* This text is actually a version of *The Twa Brothers* which has been corrupted by *Edward.* Child, I, 167 discusses the habits of *Edward* with respect to other songs.

Eddy, *Blds Sgs Ohio,* 24 notes that this song was frequently used as a children's game in nineteenth century Missouri.

One of the oddest changes in the American forms of the song occurs in the SharpK, *Eng Fsgs So Aplchns,* E text where the name Edward has become attached to the murdered brother. See footnote, I, 49.

14. BABYLON

Texts: Barry, *Brit Blds Me,* 72 / Bronson, I, 248 / Brown, *NC Flklre,* II, 44 / *BFSSNE,* VII, 6 / *Bull Tenn FLS,* VIII, #3, 69 / *Caravan,* Feb. '58, 22 / Child, III, 5 / Davis, *Fsgs Va,* 9 / Davis, *More Trd Blds Va,* 68 / Flanders, *Ancient Blds,*

I, 213 / Flanders, *Blds Migrant NE*, 61 / Greenleaf and Mansfield, *Blds Sea Sgs Newfdld*, 10 / Karpeles, *Fsg Newfdld*, 78 / Wells, *Bld Tree*, 104 / Worthington, *Nine Rare Trd Blds Va*, 26.

Local Titles: Baby Lon, The Bonny Banks of the Virgie-O, The Burly, Burly Banks of Barbary-O, Hecky-Hi Si-Bernio, On the Pretty Bonny Banks of the Barbaree-O, The Three Sisters.

Story Types: A: Three girls go out to walk or to "pull flowers", and on their way they meet a robber. He kills two of them, and, when the third wishes her brothers were there or says her brother is near-by, he questions her and finds out he has slain two of his sisters. After the discovery, he kills himself.   Examples: *Bull Tenn FLS*, VIII, #3, 70; Greenleaf and Mansfield.

B: The same situation occurs. The man seizes the eldest of the three girls and asks her to be "a robber's" or "young Robey's" wife. When she refuses, he stabs her to death. After he has done the same to the second girl, the third kills him.
   Examples: *Caravan;* Flanders, *Ancient Blds* (A).

Discussion: This ballad is quite rare in America. The Type A versions follow the Child A story, although the Barry text from Maine (a fragment) seems to belong to Child F and may have been preserved through the singing of tinkers and gypsies. Also, the Newfoundland text, besides condensing twelve stanzas into four so that the number of girls is not clear, mentions two brothers (Child F) instead of one. In Tennessee, the brother's name is Baby Lon, and the "pulling flowers" for a talisman is retained at the start (see Child A).

The Type B ballad is not even as common as Type A. The *Caravan*, Feb. '58, 22 text was brought to this country from Scotland, where it had served as a game song. See Child 14 F and #4 (SharpK, *Eng Fsgs So Aplchns*, B).

The refrains vary. Two that give the title to the song (see Child A) are the Newfoundland "too ra lee and a lonely O-On the bonny, bonny banks of Virgie, O" and the New York (*BFSSNE*) "hecky-hi Si Bernio-On the bonny, bonny banks of Bernio".

MacKenzie (*JAF*, 1912, 184) prints a song called *Donald Munro* in which a father unknowingly kills his sons and which MacKenzie feels is "vaguely reminiscent" of *Babylon*.

The Brown, *NC Flklre*, II, 44 text ends with the confused lines "He's taken his keen, sharp knife / An enticed his heart to be nobody's wife"— which seems to mean the robber kills himself.

See Paul C. Worthington's remarks in *Nine Rare Trd Blds Va*, 26-47.

17. HIND HORN

Texts: Barry, *Brit Blds Me*, 73 / Bronson, I, 254 / Creighton, *Maritime Fsgs*, 5 / Creighton and Senior, *Trd Sgs N Sc*, 11 / Flanders, *Blds Migrant NE*, 47 / Flanders, *Ancient Blds*, I, 223 / Greenleaf and Mansfield, *Blds Sea Sgs Newfdld*, 12 / Karpeles, *Fsgs Newfdld*, 99.

Local Titles: The Beggarman, The Jolly Beggar, The Old Beggar Man.

Story Types: A: Horn gives his love a watch and in return is given a ring that will shine when she is true and turn pale when she is in love with another. He sets sail for foreign shores. On arriving abroad, he notices the ring to be pale, and so he returns home at once. He meets a beggar who tells him his sweetheart is to be married on the morrow. Then he borrows the beggar's clothes and listens to instructions on how to act in his disguise. (He can beg from Peter or Paul, but need not take anything from anybody except his bride.) After gaining admittance to the wedding feast, he gets a glass of wine from the bride and slips the ring into it. She, of course, wants to know where he got it. He tells her the truth, and she swears to be his forevermore, even though he is a beggar. They flee, and he reveals his disguise.

Examples: Barry (A), Greenleaf and Mansfield.

B: (from recollection, but no text) The story follows the narrative outline of Type A, but Horn takes the beggar with him and sends him on errands Horn does not wish to handle himself. Horn finds his lady married and kills her husband in a duel. She goes abroad to forget her sorrows and dies there.

Examples: Barry, p. 79 (no text).

Discussion: The Type A texts represent an unusual form of Child G, a ballad of Scottish origin that is well-known in Ireland. Type B is noted without text in Barry, *Brit Blds Me,* 79 as an extended version recalled by a sea-captain as having been sung by his men. If his memory is reliable, there seems to be both corruption from an outside source and degeneration present. This man also claims to have heard another, and now lost, ballad based on a different portion of the Horn legend and called *The Beggar Man.* See Barry, *op. cit.,* 479.

Note Walter R. Nelles (*JAF,* 1909, 42 f.) for a critical study of the *Hind Horn* story in balladry. This article also deals with *Kitchie-Boy* (252) on p. 59 f. Child and Nelles both consider the latter to be an offshoot of the Horn legend. Check the chart on p. 59.

18. SIR LIONEL

Texts: Barry, *Brit Blds Me,* 434 (trace) / Belden, *Mo Fsgs,* 29 / *Boletin Latino Americano de Musica,* V, 278 / Bronson, I, 265 / Chase, *Am Ftales Sgs,* 126 / Davis, *Fsgs Va,* 9 / Davis, *More Trd Blds Va,* 72 / Davis, *Trd Bld Va,* 125 / Flanders, *Ancient Blds,* I, 226 / Flanders, *Blds Migrant NE,* 60 / *Focus,* IV, 48 / *JAF,* 1906, 235; 1912, 175; 1917, 291; 1941, 84; 1957, 344 / *Ky Folklore Record,* 1956, 57 / A. Lomax, *Fsgs No Am,* 510 / Lomax and Lomax, *Our Sngng Cntry,* 149 / McGill, *Fsgs Ky Mts,* 79 / *MLR,* XI, 396 / *NC Folklore,* II, #1 (1954), 5 / Randolph, *Oz Fsgs,* I, 72 / Elizabeth M. Roberts, *The Great Meadow* (N.Y., 1930), 151, 281, 298 / Scarborough, *On Trail N Fsg,* 51 / Scarborough, *Sgctchr So Mts,* 191 / SharpC, *Eng Fsgs So Aplchns,* #8 / SharpK, *Eng Fsgs So Aplchns,* I, 55 / Smith and Rufty, *Am Anth Old Wrld Blds,* 4 / *Va FLS Bull,* #s 3-5, 9 / *W Va Folklore,* IV, #2 (1954), 18.

Local Titles: (Old) Bangum and the Boar, Bingham, Brangywell, Jason and the Wild Boar, Old Bangum (Bang'em), Rach's Spinning Song, The Wild Hog.

Story Types: A: Bangum and his lady are in a forest. Bangum mentions a man-eating hog known to the vicinity and sometimes blows his horn to attract the beast. The boar comes rushing out, and Bangum slays him with a knife, usually wooden. The mood of the adventure is mock serious. Some versions do not mention the lady; some have the boar kill a number of Bangum's retinue; others have the boar run away after a long battle; and still others tell of a cave in which lie the bones of many slain men. In a number of these texts the winning or losing of "shoes" is mentioned by Bangum.

> Examples: Davis, *Trd Bld Va* (A); Roberts, p. 281;
> Scarborough, *Sgctchr So Mts.*

B: Bangum rides into a wood and meets a maid. He proposes to her, but she refuses him. He then tells her of a man-eating boar in the forest and sets out to kill it. After a successful fight, he returns to the girl. She accepts a second proposal.   Examples: Lomax and Lomax.

C: The King goes in to fight the boar in his den, where the bones of earlier victims lie scattered. The Queen wrings her hands. The King never comes out, and all mourn, for there is no king in all the land.

> Examples: *JAF*, 1957, 344.

Discussion: All the American texts show a great deal of variation from the Child versions of the story. In the history of *Sir Lionel* one can see the complete degeneration of a romance into a burlesqued backwoods song. The original form of the story was probably *Sir Eglamour of Artois* (See Child, I, 209), and the British ballads retain much of the mood of this and other like works. The composite story of the British texts as given by Davis, *Trd Bld Va*, 125 from Child, I, 208 appears in the introductory description of variation at the beginning of this work.

The American versions (see Zielonko, *Some American Variants of Child Ballads*, 57 f.) reduce the story to little more than a fight with a boar, in Type A with mere mention of the lady. The whole mood is changed. The pageantry is gone. The details of the old tale are forgotten. And the song that survives is, at most dignified, mock serious in tone. Perhaps the change of the refrain best illustrates this, the typical Child A lines "blow thy horne good hunter—as I am a gentle hunter" becoming "cubbi ki, cuddle dum, killi quo quam", etc. Similar refrains are paralleled in English versions collected since Child's day, however. Check *JAF*, 1917, 292.

It is notable that the Type B text retains a great deal more of the original story, if not any more of the original spirit, than do those of Type A. In addition, Barry, *Brit Blds Me*, 134, notes that a Maine sea-captain recognized thirteen stanzas of Child A. The Type C Text, from Negro West Virginia, has little to do with the original tale, although it has restored a certain "courtly" atmosphere. The Flanders text from Vermont (see *Ancient Blds*, I, 227) has appropriately substituted "bear" for boar".

Kenneth W. Porter (*JAF*, 1941, 84) states that the "wooden knife" is a corruption of the "wood-knife" used by huntsmen to carve game, etc. The misinterpretation of course came as the implement passed from use.

Belden, *Mo Fsgs*, 29 suggests that there may be a broadside original for the Missouri (at least) texts, but he has no proof.

For a treatment of the influence of *A Frog Went a-Courtin'* on *Sir Lionel* in America read Zielonko, *op. cit.*, p. 57 f.

19. KING ORFEO

Davis, *Fsgs Va*, 10; Branford P. Millar, *SFQ*, 1953, 165; and Reed Smith, *SFQ*, 1937, #2, 9-11 list this ballad among the Child texts surviving in the New World. However, the text cited by Davis is a version of Child 27, *The Whummil Bore*, in which the hero serves a King named Orfeo. (See *SFQ*, 1957, 190, Footnote 7.) Millar and Smith were thinking of this text, also. The song does not seem to have survived in the New World. Davis, *More Trd Blds Va*, 79-80 has written definitive remarks on the confusion.

In an article on *The Whummil Bore* (Child 27) in *SFQ*, 1957, 187-193, Davis and Paul C. Worthington suggest that Child 27 may be connected with an incident in the *King Orfeo* ballad.

Also see Judith Ann Knoblock (*WF*, 1960, 35-45), where Child 19 is discussed in connection with Child 200 (*The Gypsy Laddie*) which is seen to be a parody of the Orfeo romance.

20. THE CRUEL MOTHER

Texts: Barry, *Brit Blds Me*, 80/ *Boletin Latino Americano de Musica*, V, 279 / Bronson, I, 276 / *BFSSNE*, VIII, 7 / Cazden, *Abelard Fsg Bk*, II, 104 / Creighton, *Sgs Blds N Sc*, 3 / Creighton and Senior, *Trd Sgs N Sc*, 17 / Cox, *Fsgs South*, 29 / Cox, *W Va School Journal and Educator*, XLVI, 64 / Davis, *Fsgs Va*, 10 / Davis, *More Trd Blds Va*, 81 / Davis, *Trd Bld Va*, 133 / Eddy, *Blds Sgs Ohio*, 24 / Flanders, *Ancient Blds*, I, 230 / Flanders, *Blds Migrant NE*, 66 / Greenleaf and Mansfield *Blds Sea Sgs Newfdld* 15 / Henry, *Fsgs So Hghlds*, 47 / Jones, *Flklre Mich*, 5 / *JAF*, 1912, 183; 1919, 503 / *JFSS*, II, 109 / Karpeles, *Fsgs Newfdld*, 8 / Korson, *Pa Sgs Lgds*, 38 / Kennedy, *Cultural Effects*, 320 / MacKenzie, *Blds Sea Sgs N Sc*, 12 / MacKenzie, *Quest Bld*, 104 / McGill, *Fsgs Ky Mts*, 83 / Morris, *Fsgs Fla*, 250 / *NYFQ*, 1948, #1, 36 / *NC Folklore*, V, #1 (1957), 20 / Niles, *Blds Crls Tgc Lgds*, 18 / Randolph, *Oz Fsgs*, I, 73 / Randolph, *The Ozarks*, 185 / Scarborough, *Sgctchr So Mts*, 169 / SharpC, *Eng Fsgs So Aplchns*, #9 / SharpK, *Eng Fsgs So Aplchns*, I, 57 / Shearin and Combs, *Ky Syllabus*, 7 / *SFQ*, 1944, 139 / Smith and Rufty, *Am Anth Old Wrld Blds*, 6/ Thompson, *Bdy Bts Brtchs*, 447 / *Va FLS Bull*, #s 3-5 / Wells, *Bld Tree*, 150.

Local Titles: The Cruel Mother, Down by the Greenwood Side (Shady, Sideo), Fair Flowers of Helio, Green Woods of Siboney-O, Greenwood Side (Siding, Society), The Lady Gay, The Lady of York, There Was a Lady Lived in York, The Three Little Babes.

Story Types: A: "Leaning her back against a thorn", a woman bears her father's clerk two (or more) illegitimate children. These babies she murders with a pen-knife, buries, and deserts. Later, she sees some children playing ball. She tells them that if they were hers she would treat them in fine style. However, they inform her that they are the children she bore and murdered and usually tell her she is fated to dwell in Hell.

Examples: Barry (A); Cox, *Fsgs South* (A);
Davis, *Trd Bld Va* (A).

B: Sometimes an additional group of stanzas is found on a Type A version in which the mother is told the penance she must do for her crime. She must spend twenty-one years ringing a bell and existing in various bestial forms. In some texts the mother expresses a preference for such a fate over that of going to Hell.

Examples: Creighton; MacKenzie, *Blds Sea Sgs N Sc;* Thompson.

Discussion: The full story of this song frequently appears in American texts, although there are many that omit the antecedent action which reveals who the girl's lover is and the details of the birth and crime. Those that are wholly dialogue are clear enough if the original story is known. Type A stories are similar to the Child A—H texts, while Type B versions follow Child I—L.

There is a great deal of folk superstition included in the various American texts of the ballad. The binding of the children's feet to keep the ghosts from walking is discussed in L. C. Wimberly's *Folk-Lore in the English and Scottish Ballads,* 254. (See Child H; Cox, *Fsgs South,* B; SharpK, F; and *SFL,* 1944, 139 for examples). Many versions contain a "MacBethian" attempt to wash the blood from the knife after the crime, and there is an attempt to throw the knife away which results in its coming nearer and nearer in Newfoundland and Nova Scotia. (See Creighton and MacKenzie, *Blds Sea Sgs N Sc.*) The idea that the mother can gain redemption by being a fish, a beast, and a belltoller, etc. for seven years has come into this song from *The Maid and the Palmer* (Child 21). See Child, I, 218 and my Type B.

Zielonko, *Some American Variants of Child Ballads,* 90f. discusses the minor variations and distribution (check particularly in this connection the "garter" discussion by Barry in *Brit Blds Me,* 91f.) in American versions, while Davis, *Trd Bld Va,* and Cox, *Fsgs South,* carefully relate their texts to those in Child. SharpK, *Eng Fsgs So Aplchns,* B seems to take its initial stanza from *The Wife of Usher's Well* (79) and, with his L and *BFSSNE,* VIII, 7 contains the names Peter and Paul. The Thompson, *Bdy Bts Brtchs* text implies that poverty is one of the reasons for the killing of the children.

Zielonko, *op. cit.,* 63, in her discussion of 20, notes that the American methods of telling the story are three in number, as is the case with the Child texts: direct narrative (Child A—C, F—I and Barry A, C, F); indirect narrative (Child K—L and Davis A—B); and a combination of the two methods (Child D, E, J, N and Barry B). See also Barry's discussion in *BFSSNE,* VIII, 7 concerning the number of children and the saints, traits which may reveal influence from *Dives and Lazarus* (56).

22. SAINT STEPHEN AND HEROD

Texts: Bronson, I, 297 / Flanders, *Ancient Blds,* I, 239 / Flanders, *Blds Migrant NE,* 217 / *Vt Historical Society, Proceedings,* NS., VII, 73-98.

Local Titles: Saint Stephen and Herod.

Discussion: This ballad is so rare in Britain and America that Mrs. Flanders' text from Vermont is the only one taken from oral tradition to-date. Child's version is from the Sloane Ms. (15th Century). The Vermont text follows Child's first four stanzas with modernizations of phraseology and vocabulary. There is little doubt that it was learned from print.

The story tradition from which this ballad has arisen has been traced back into the 1200's by R.C.A. Prior in *Ancient Danish Ballads* (Edinburgh, 1860), but the motif is common to pseudo-Biblical lore. See also Child's comments on #55. Similar stories exist in Germanic folksongs.

24. BONNIE ANNIE

Barry, (*BFSSNE*, X, 11 and XI, 9) printed two Maine fragments which he believed belong to Child 24, *Bonnie Annie*. The two lines that follow:

> Captain take gold, and captain take money
> Captain take gold, but leave me my honey.
>
> —X, 11.

cannot be found in the Child texts, but may well be from an American version of the Jonah-like story about the girl who elopes with her lover, only to be cast off the floundering ship in a storm. However, the second set of lines,

> He kissed her cold lips a thousand times o'er
> And called her his darling though she was no more.
>
> —XI, 9.

belong to the Robson-Colwell comic ballad, *Villikins and his Dinah*. The informant did place them in the same song with the first two lines, and Barry (XI, 9—10) attempts to rationalize this as corruption. My opinion is that such fragments are too brief to prove much.

25. WILLIE'S LYKE-WAKE

Nothing that can be called a text of Child 25 has been collected from oral tradition in America. Flanders (see *Ancient Blds*, I, 242 and *JAF*, 1951, 130) did obtain a two-line fragment from Vermont. The second line, "He laid himself down as if he were dead" has direct counterparts in Child A and C, but whether or not the line is from a now lost American *Willie's Lyke-Wake* can be neither proved nor disproved. See *Ancient Blds*, I, 242 for a discussion. The fragment was also noted in *Vt Historical Society, Proceedings*, N.S., VII, 73-98.

26. THE THREE RAVENS (THE TWA CORBIES)

Texts: Barry, *Brit Blds Me*, 435 (trace) / Belden, *Mo Fsgs*, 31 / Botkin, *Am Play-Party Sg*, 63 / Brewster, *Blds Sgs Ind*, 53 / Bronson, I, 308 / Brown, *NC Flkre*, II, 26 / *Bull Tenn FLS*, VIII, #3, 76 / *Caravan*, Oct. '57, 14 / Carlisle, *Fifty Blds Sgs NW Ark*, 15 / Chappell, *Fsgs Rnke Alb*, 15 / Chase, *Am Ftales Sgs*, 114 / *Chelsea Song Book*, 31 / Christy's *New Songster and Black Joker* (cop. 1863), 58 / Cleveland's *Compendium* (Philadelphia, 1859) / Cox, *Fsgs South*, 31 / Creighton and Senior, *Trd Sgs N Sc*, 21 / Davis, *Fsgs Va*, 10 / Davis, *More Trd Blds Va*, 84 / Davis, *Trd Bld Va*, 137 / Doerflinger, *Shntymen and Shntybys*, 21 / Flanders, *Ancient Blds*, I, 243 / Flanders, *Vt Fsgs Blds*, 198 / *Focus*, V, 279, 281 / Frank Brower's *Black Diamond Songster*, 30 / Frank Converse's *Old Cremona Songster* (cop. 1863), 56 / Haun, *Cocke Cnty*, 102 / *Heart Songs*, 485 / Henry, *Fsgs So Hghlds*, 48 / Hudson, *Fsgs Miss*, 72 / Hudson, *Ftunes Miss*, 1 / Hudson, *Spec Miss Flkre*, #6 / Jones, *Flklre Mich*, 5 / *JAF*, 1907, 154; 1918, 273; 1932, 8 / *Ky Folklore Record*, 1960, 127 / *Keystone Folklore Qtly*, 1956, 4 / Leach,

Fsgs Labr Cst / Linscott, *Fsgs Old NE*, 289 / McGill *University Song Book* (Montreal, 1921), 94 / Morris, *Fsgs Fla*, 254 / *NYFQ*, 1953, 274 / Niles, *Blds Crls Tgc Lgds*, 7 / Owens, *Studies Tex Fsg*, 23 / Owens, *Texas Fsgs*, 42 / *PTFS*, VII, 110 / Randolph, *Oz Fsgs*, I, 74 / Scarborough, *Sgctchr So Mts*, 194 / *Scottish Student's Song Book*, 268 / *Singer's Journal*, I, 239 / SharpC, *Eng Fsgs So Aplchns*, #10 / SharpK, *Eng Fsgs So Aplchns*, I, 63 / Shoemaker, *Mt Mnstly*, 276 / *Stout, Flklre Iowa*, 2 / *Va FLS Bull*, #s 4, 5, 7-10 / Waite's *Carmina Collegensia* (Boston, cop. 1868), 26 / Wells, *Bld Tree*, 151 / Wetmore and Bartholomew, *Mt Sgs NC*, 10.

Local Titles: Bally-Way-Wiggle-Dum-Daw, The Crow Song, Three (Two) (Black) Crows (Blackbirds, Corbies, Ravens).

Story Types: A: Two or three carefree crows wonder what they will have for supper. The corpse of a horse, or some other animal, is spied in a near-by field, and in the spirit of revelry they fly down for a feast. .

Examples: Brewster (A), Davis, *Trd Bld Va* (A), Stout (A).

B: Two birds on a tree wonder where they can dine. One remarks that a ship went down by the seashore and that he plans to go there. The other says he knows of a sweeter meal—a knight who has been slain. Only the knight's hawk, hound, and lady know the man is lying there. All three are away, the lady with another lover. The birds plan their feast, while the last six lines tell of the cold bare grave of the knight in Anglo-Saxon style. This is the original *Twa Corbies* type.

Examples: *JAF*, 1932, 10; Shoemaker.

C: The Type B story is told, except that the English *Three Ravens* text is followed in that the hawks and true-love remain faithful. The girl dies at dawn.   Examples: Flanders, *Ancient Blds* (A), Stout (E).

D: The two crows decide to eat a newly-born lambkin lying by a rock. A bird overhears the plan, goes to rouse the lamb, and tells him to flee. There is a moralistic, sentimental close.

Examples: *JAF*, 1907, 154.

E: A lyric song is sung by a girl of a lover who went to war in the Lowlands and now lies there known only to his horse and his "Lady Marie". He will sleep there, but she must grieve. There is no crow dialogue, and the mood is tragic.   Examples: Niles

Discussion: The American versions of this song lack, in general, the dignity and feeling or cynicism of the English and Scottish versions. Except for the few texts in Types B and C, and the corrupted Type E, there are no human actors in the New World. The ballad has become an animal song, degenerated and parodied. (For its relations to the minstrel stage refer to Kittredge, *JAF*, 1915, 273. Also check Davis, *Trd Bld Va*, 145 and Cox, *Fsgs South*, 31 for notes on the comic degeneration of the ballad.)

Keys to the general spirit of almost all the American texts are the refrains ("Billy Magee Magaw"; "Caw, Caw, Caw"; "Skubaugh"; etc. in place of the "hey down, hey derry day" and "sing lay doo and la doo and day" of Child B); endings such as the stock lines "Oh maybe you think there's another verse, but there isn't" on Brewster, *Bld Sgs Ind*, A; the interpolations of cures, "cracker-barrel philosophy," and politics (See Davis, *Trd Bld Va,* C, G; Haun, *Cocke Cnty,* 102); and the sentimentality of Type D. The rationalization that the horse has been slain by a butcher (Randolph, *Oz Fsgs,* A) carries the whole thing one step further. See Davis, *op. cit,* F, M where the horse becomes a "pig with a glass eye" and where a "quack, quack" refrain can be found, as well as Carlisle, *Fifty Blds Sgs NW Ark,* 15 where the song opens with the phrase "Said the blackbird to the crow / What makes the white folks hate us so?" Flanders, *Ancient Blds,* I (J) is another extreme burlesque: the locale is a farmyard and the song concerns itself with a man named Jeems who goes out to saw wood and a horse named Ned who dies. Owens' (*Tex Fsgs*) text is sung by Negroes to the tune of *Johnny Comes Marching Home.*

There are a few texts in existence in America that retain the spirit of the Child versions. Particularly remarkable in this respect is Flanders, *Ancient Blds,* I (A) which is dignified and concludes with a "rose and lily" cliché. See also Flanders, *op. cit.,* B and Stout, *Flklre Iowa,* E. These songs all follow the tradition of the faithful girl. Type B, with the unfaithful hounds and lover, owes its American forms to the inclusion of a *Twa Corbies* text in Cleveland's *Compendium* (1859). Shoemaker and Chase found this form in Pennsylvania and the Appalachians respectively, and Barry spoke to a sea-captain in Maine who claimed to recognize seven of the ten Child stanzas. However, this man remembered a rescue of the knight directed by the ravens and a subsequent return to health of the warrior.

The forms of the song that I have used as Types D and E are not related to anything in Child. The sentimental rescue of the lambkin in D reminds one of the ending Barry's sea-captain claimed for the song. The absence of the crows and the confused story of Type E seem to indicate corruption, though there is a moving lyric-tragic tone to this text.

Mention should be made of the extensive study of the ballad and its English and Scottish variants in Hermann Tardel's *Zwei Liedstudien, I. Die englisch schottische Roben Ballade,* Beilage zum Jahresheit des Realgymnasiums zu Bremen. See also Zielonko, *Some American Variants of Child Ballads,* 71 f.

For a description of the ballad as a play-party game see Botkin, *Am Play-Party Sg,* 63. Doerflinger, *Shntymen and Shntybys,* 21 reports it in use as a sea-chanty, sung to the tune of *Blow the Man Down.*

27. THE WHUMMIL BORE

Texts: Barry, *Brit Blds Me,* 437 (trace) / Davis, *Fsgs Va* 10 (listed as Child 19) / Davis, *More Trd Blds Va,* 89 / *JAF,* 1907, 155 / *SFQ,* 1957, 193 / Worthington, *Nine Rare Trd Blds Va,* 48.

Local Titles: King Orfeo.

Story Types: A: A servant of the King tells of the only time he has seen the princess nude. He looked at her through a small hole while her maids were dressing her. Among other things, he tells how sad she looked, of the "tike" that was biting her shoe, and of the beauty of her hair, the rings on her hands, and her bosom. In a wistful close, he remarks that he can never know more of this lady.

Examples: *JAF*, 1907, 155; Davis, *More Trd Blds Va*.

Discussion: The Virginia version is briefer than the *JAF* text (from a Scotswoman visiting in Wisconsin) and does not mention the nudity of the girl. However, it is from a truly American oral heritage, not from an informant visiting in this country. Its affinities to Child 19 (see the *King Orfeo* local title) have caused it to be mistaken for Child 19. See the discussion under *King Orfeo* in this volume; in *SFQ*, 1957, 190f.; in Davis, *More Trd Blds Va*, 79-80, 89-90; and in Worthington, *Nine Rare Trd Blds Va*, 48-59.

29. THE BOY AND THE MANTLE

The Boy and the Mantle is not known in the oral tradition of the New World. The text that appears in Flanders, *Ancient Blds*, I, 257 is from *The Charms of Melody*, printed by J. & J. Carrick, Dublin. *The Charms of Melody* circulated widely in New England. Its text of Child 29 is longer and more detailed than the Percy Ms. version.

31. THE MARRIAGE OF SIR GAWAIN

There are no texts of Child 31 in American oral tradition. There is a song, usually called *The Half-Hitch* or *The Loathly Bride* (See Flanders, *Ancient Blds*, I, 265 and Barry, *Brit Blds Me*, 382) that some scholars have seen as derived from *The Marriage of Sir Gawain*. This song, which Laws classified as N 23, alters the story considerably. In the Child ballad the girl suffers under a hex that keeps her ugly until she can find a man who will treat her with courtesy despite her looks. In Laws N 23 she purposely disguises herself as a hag to test a silly vow her lover has made. In a rash moment, he has sworn to marry the first woman he meets. The mood is no longer romantic, but comic; there is no riddle to answer in exchange for King Arthur's life; and the sacrifice of Gawain to the hag is lacking.

See Flanders, *Ancient Blds*, I, 265-266 and Laws, *Am Bldry Brit Brdsdes*, 214-215 for bibliography and discussion, as well as Bronson, I, 317.

36. THE LAILY WORM AND THE MACHREL OF THE SEA

Reed Smith claimed this ballad to be in the F. C. Brown collection (see *NCFlklre*) from North Carolina. As far as anyone can tell (see Branford Millar's remarks in *SFQ*, 1953, 159, Footnote 4), the song has not been collected in America.

37. THOMAS RYMER

Texts: Brown, *NC Flklre*, 46.
Local Titles: True Thomas.

Story Types: A: True Thomas is lying on a hill when a lovely lady in grass green clothes rides up. She takes him up behind her on her horse, and they speed off. Eventually they come to a garden, where Thomas eats of some fruit. The woman then promises to show him "fairies three", and after dressing him in green and silver she takes him away to elf-land for seven long years.   Examples: Brown.

Discussion: This North Carolina text is unique to America. The ballad itself (See Child, I, 317f.) goes back to a fifteenth century romance concerning a thirteenth century seer who was given prophetic power by the Queen of the Elves. In North Carolina, the story follows Child A without too much deviation. The first four stanzas of the American version parallel Child A, stanzas, 1, 2, 6, and 8. Two lines of North Carolina Stanza 5 are almost exactly like Child A, Stanza 11, while North Carolina Stanza 6 parallels Child A, Stanza 16.

38. THE WEE, WEE MAN

Texts: Brown, *NC Flklre,* 47.
Local Titles: None given.

Story Types: A: A man out walking encounters a little fairy, no bigger than his ear, but strong "as any buck". The man picks the elf up, and, after watching him throw a huge stone far away, goes along a lane with the little fellow until they come to a castle. Here a lovely lady comes out and wishes to "rassle". They go to bed, and after a night of sport the man awakes to find both his love and the elf-man gone.
                    Examples: Brown.

Discussion: This North Carolina version of Child 38 does not follow any of the texts given by Child in his collection, although its first five stanzas are generally the same as the corresponding parts of all seven British stories. North Carolina Stanzas 6, 7, 8, and 9 are, however, a vulgarization and rationalization of the fairy-lore found in the final lines of the Child texts. In fact, Stanza 6 was so crude that the informant refused to sing it to the collector. (A note on the manuscript reads, "One stanza Mr. S. censored here, a description of the girl's physical qualities. He didn't know me well enough".) There is a great deal of localization and modernization of the old lines in this unique American version.

39. TAM LIN

Texts: Bronson, I, 327 / Child Ms. / Scarborough, *Sgctchr So Mts,* 250.
Local Titles: Tam Lane.

Story Types: A: Tam Lane (who has been wooed away to the land of the fairies as a lover of the Queen of Elves) appears to Lady Margaret while she is pulling roses in Cartershay (Carterhaugh). He seduces her. When she wishes to know if he is a "Christian knight" he tells her of his plight and that, because the fairies pay a tithe to Hell every seven years, he wants to return. In order to bring him back to be a father to her child, Lady Margaret is to go to the crossroad and pull the rider from the white steed as the fairy folk ride by. She does this and wins the knight, though the Fairy Queen is extremely irritated and tells Tam Lane what would have happened to him had she known his plans. (The holding of the knight through various horrible shapes that the fairies cause him to take and the throwing him in the well are lacking, while the fatherhood of Tam in respect to the girl's baby is not clear.)   Examples: Scarborough.

Discussion: The Child Ms. text, from Margaret Reburn, an Irishwoman living in Iowa, can not be considered to be taken from American oral tradition. Neither can anything except the melody and the first stanza of the Scarborough text. Scarborough got these from Elinor Wylie. See *Sgctchr So Mts*, 250-251. The story in Scarborough's text follows Child closely.

See Child, I, 335f. for a discussion of the folklore centering about the well, Carterhaugh, the fairies and earth-maiden, as well as the crossroads. He also traces the history of the Rymer story.

Allison White (*SFQ*, 1955, 156-163) notes that the Little Tommy Green of the nursery rime *Pussy's in the Well* was once Little Tom O'Lynne. This point and related matters are discussed by Jean B. Saunders, in *MWF*, 1958, 190-191.

40. THE QUEEN OF ELFAN'S NOURICE

Texts: JAF, 1907, 155.
Local Titles: None given.

Story Types: A: This text is almost a lyric and concerns a girl who hears an elf-call in the form of a cow lowing. This call tells her to come and nurse an elf-child under the sea. When asked by the elf-king why she moans, she says not for breakfast, but for her lover whom she will never more see.

Examples: *JAF*, 1907, 155.

Discussion: The story and the speakers in this text do not become clear until one reads Child's discussion (I, 358). Here it is explained that the girl has been abducted by water-sprites a few days after she has had a baby in order that she may suckle an elf bairn. The girl is told she can expect to be returned to her Christian home as soon as the young elf is able to walk.

The American text is not far from Child's version, but it is not close either. It certainly is abbreviated.

W. E. Richmond and Herbert Halpert pointed out in a review of *The British Traditional Ballad in North America* (see *MWF*, 1951, 76) that Arthur Beatty collected this ballad from a Wisconsin University student, Charles H. Eldred, who had learned it from a Mrs. MacLeod of Dumfries, Scotland. There are, thus, no real grounds for claiming an American oral tradition for Child 40.

42. CLERK COLVILL

See the discussion of *Lady Alice* (Child 85).

43. THE BROOMFIELD HILL

Texts: Barry, *Brit Blds Me*, 438 (trace) / Bronson, I, 336 / Child, I, 390, ftnte / Combs, *Fsgs États-Unis*, 127 / Flanders, *Ancient Blds*, I, 276 / Henry, *Fsgs So Hghlds*, 53 / Hubbard, *Blds Sgs Utah*, 8 / *JAF*, 1911, 14; 1951, 40.
Local Titles: The Broomfield Hill, Green-broom, Green Broom Field, The Hard-Hearted Young Man, The Merry Green Fields.

Story Types: A: Wagering that she can go to a tryst with a knight in the broomfield a maid and return a maid still, a girl sets out to meet her lover. In the field she finds him asleep beside his hawk. She scatters broom over his head and feet to insure his remaining asleep and hides to see what he will do upon waking. He soon rises and scolds his hawk for not letting him know that his sweetheart was near, saying that had he known he would have had his will of her. He then starts to pursue the girl, but is told she has fled too swiftly to be caught.

Examples: Combs.

B: This type differs from Type A in that the bet is actually made by the girl and her lover in the ballad. The man tells his parrot to wake him should he be asleep in the field when his love arrives. When he learns that he has been duped he is willing that "all the birds in the broomfield feast on her heart's blood".   Examples: Henry.

C: The Type C texts are variations of Type B. The parrot is omitted, and the girl upbraids the lover for his desire to kill her when he learns he has been tricked.   Examples: *JAF,* 1951, 40.

Discussion: The story is not clear in the Type A version. In the Child British texts the girl has a rendezvous with a knight which she is afraid to keep for fear of being seduced and afraid to miss because of her lover's wrath. A witch offers a solution by pointing out that she will find her lover asleep, can prolong this state by spreading blossoms on him, and leave her ring as a token she has been there. In Child the deceived knight scolds his horse and hawk, and they defend themselves.

The bet, made in the Type B version, also appears in the Child C-F series, and the story is clear in this American form, but the lines are less lyric than the Combs text. Type C is much like Type B, although the ending, involving the girl's reaction to her lover's wrath, is different.

For a discussion of the means used by the girl to prolong her lover's sleep, as well as for a treatment of the use of drugs and runes in European stories, see Child, I, 391 f.

MacKenzie, *Bld Sea Sgs N Sc,* 74 prints a song called *The Sea Captain* which is, as he states, rather closely related to *The Broomfield Hill.* See also *BFSSNE,* VII, 12.

44. THE TWA MAGICIANS

Barry, *Brit Blds Me,* 442 reports that an Islesford, Maine woman recognized, but could not repeat, the Child Buchan Mss. text. See also the Barry Mss. in the Harvard University Library.

45. KING JOHN AND THE BISHOP

Texts: Barry, *Brit Blds Me,* 445 (trace) / Bronson, I, 354 / Flanders, *Ancient Blds,* I, 280 / Flanders, *Blds Migrant NE,* 111 / Flanders, *Garl Gn Mt Sg,* 58 / Flanders, *Vt Fsgs Blds,* 200 / Gardner and Chickering, *Blds Sgs So Mich,* 379 / Hubbard, *Blds Sgs Utah,* 10 / *JAF,* 1908, 54, 57; 1951, 42 / Leach, *Fsgs Labr*

Cst / NYFQ, 1945, #1, 45 / Parsons, *Flklre Cape Verde Is,* 94 (prose) / Smith and Rufty, *Am Anth Old Wrld Blds,* 8 / Thompson and Cutting, *Pioneer Sgstr,* 4.

Local Titles: The Bishop of Canterbury, King John and the Abbot, King John and the Bishop, The King's Three Questions.

Story Types: A: Mighty King John sends for the Archbishop of Canterbury and tells the churchman that he is a greater scholar than this king (or makes some such accusation) and that if he doesn't answer three questions correctly he will be beheaded. The questions are how much the King is worth mounted in all his state, how long the King will be travelling this world about, and what the King is thinking. The bishop goes homeward. On the way he meets a shepherd who offers to disguise himself as the churchman and answer the riddles. The shepherd tells King John that he is worth a piece less than Jesus, may go with the sun and circle the world in twenty-four hours, and thinks the man before him is the Archbishop of Canterbury. The King is amused by the wit of the man and excuses both.

Examples: Flanders, *Ancient Blds* (A^1, A^2); *JAF,* 1908, 54.

Discussion: The American versions, all from the North, seem to be closely related to Child B. See Gardner and Chickering, *Blds Sgs So Mich,* 379 and Flanders, *Ancient Blds,* I, 281f., A^1, A^2. The story is varied in a number of minor details, such as the shepherd's reward and the reason for the riddles being asked. However, even the refrain "derry down" is retained in the Vermont texts. See Flanders, *op. cit.* Five of the Flanders texts, the A and B series, are worth study in that they form unusual sequences. A^1 and A^2 were learned by two informants from a mutual grandmother; B^1 was sung for Flanders in 1933 word for word the same by a brother and sister, but was re-collected from the brother in 1939 (B^2) and again in 1951 (B^3). See Flanders, *op. cit.,* 280-281 for further details.

The riddles of the ballad are not unusual, of course. The ballad is little but a song version of a widely known folktale (Aarne-Thompson, Mt. 922) that has been traced back to at least the 9th Century. The story has been studied in detail by Walter Anderson in *FFC,* #42 (1923). Also see Parsons, *Flklre Cape Verde Is (MAFS,* 1923), 94; Dean S. Fansler, *Filipino Popular Tales (MAFS,* 1921), 287; *JAF,* 1908, 58 (from N.J. via Mo.); Leach, *Fsgs Labr Cst;* and Child, I, 405f.

The Thompson and Cutting text from the mid-19th Century Stevens-Douglass Ms. notes that King John has "Built up great wrongs, / "Tore down great rights."

46. CAPTAIN WEDDERBURN'S COURTSHIP

Texts: Barry, *Brit Blds Me,* 93 / Bronson, I, 362 / Cazden, *Abelard Fsg Bk,* II, 20 / Creighton, *Maritime Fsgs,* 6 / Creighton, *Sgs Blds N Sc,* 6 / Creighton and Senior, *Trd Sgs N Sc,* 21 / Flanders, *Ancient Blds,* I, 299 / Flanders, *Blds Migrant NE,* 43 / Gardner and Chickering, *Blds Sgs So Mich,* 139 / *JAF,* 1910, 377; 1911, 335; 1916, 157 / Korson, *Pa Sgs Lgds,* 35 / Leach, *Fsgs Labr Cst* / MacKenzie, *Blds Sea Sgs N Sc,* 14 / MacKenzie, *Quest Bld,* 108.

Local Titles: Bold Robbington, Buff the Quilt, Captain Wedderburn (Walker, Washburn)'s Courtship, Captain Woodstock, A Gentle Young Lady, Mr. Woodstock's Courtship, Six Questions, A Strange Proposal.

Story Types: A: A keeper of the game wishes to sleep with a certain girl. She coyly refuses until he has answered six (or some other number) questions. When he replies to those asked, he claims his right to sleep with her and not lie "next to the wall". She, however, asks three more questions. When he answers these, she asks no more and soon yields to his wishes. They may or may not marry first.

Examples: Barry (A); Flanders, *Ancient Blds* (A,B);
Creighton, *Sgs Blds N Sc.*

Discussion: The American texts of *Captain Wedderburn's Courtship* are rare and, it seems, concentrated in the northeastern portions of the United States and the Maritime regions of Canada. Where the ballad is found, it is close to the Child versions, although usually condensed and frequently without mention of the marriage of the couple (See Child A,B). The song has mixed with *Riddles Wisely Expounded* (Child 1) in a number of cases (See Barry, *Brit Blds Me*, 95-98 and Flanders, *Ancient Blds*, I, 45-46, 310-311). In fact, the riddles have caused a great deal of confusion in connection with the identification of Child 46.

Riddle ballads are extremely old (see Child, I, 415—6), and it is likely that the actual questions and answers that are used by the coy maid and her lover have become attached to this song from a tradition of their own. Throughout the United States it is common to find the riddles existing alone as a song known under the title *I Gave My Love a Cherry.* For representative examples consult Bronson, I, 376; Brown, *NC Flklre*, II, 48; Chase, *Am Ftales Sgs,* 156; Alberta P. Hannum, *Thursday April,* 204; Henry, *Fsgs So Hghlds,* 141; Henry, *Sgs Sng So Aplchns,* 25; Kincaid, *Fav Mt Blds,* 15; Kolb, *Treasry Fsgs,* 30; Leach, *Bld Bk,* 162; A. Lomax, *Fsgs No Am,* 27; Scarborough, *Sgctchr So Mts,* 230; Scott, *Sing of Am,* 54; and SharpK, *Eng Fsgs So Aplchns,* II, 190.

Child, I, 415 refers to a number of nursery songs which also use these riddles. See Halliwell's *Popular Rhymes and Nursery Tales,* 150. Such texts are common to America under such titles as the *Four Brothers* or *Peri Meri Dictum* and make use of the motif that four brothers (three cousins) have sent a series of presents, the first a "cherry without a stone", etc. The gifts are subsequently explained. Representative texts can be found in the following works: Bronson, I, 380; Eddy, *Blds Sgs Ohio,* 25; *Franklin Square Song Collection* (N. Y., 1881), 66; *JAF,* 1916, 157; Linscott, *Fsgs Old NE,* 267; *Mother Goose's Melodies* (N. Y., 1877), 53, 82; Niles, *More Sgs Hill Flk,* 12; *NYFQ,* 1953, 273; and Randolph, *Oz F-S,* II, 432. The garbled Latin refrain "perry merry dictum, dominee" is characteristic of these songs. See Jean B. Saunders discussion in *MWF,* 1958, 196-197.

Two points of note concerning the American versions of Child 46 are that the Gardner and Chickering, *Blds Sgs So Mich,* text is told in the first person and that the "next to the wall" theme has caused a large amount of textual confusion.

For a discussion of the American ramifications of the Child ballad and the riddles see Henry, *F-S So Hghlds,* 140.

47. PROUD LADY MARGARET

Reed Smith, *SC Blds*, 171—4 lists this ballad among the American survivals of Child songs. I have been unable to find any printed record of its existence in oral tradition. However, as the song is not on Smith's subsequent list (*SFQ*, 1937, #2, 9—11), I believe the first entry to be a mistake. See the local titles for *Young Hunting* (68).

49. THE TWA BROTHERS

Texts: Barry, *Brit Blds Me*, 99 / Belden, *Mo Fsgs*, 33 / Brewster, *Blds Sgs Ind*, 55 / Bronson, I, 384 / Brown, *NC Flklre*, 49 / BFSSNE, V, 6 / Carlisle, *Fifty Sgs Blds NW Ark*, 17 / Chappell, *Fsgs Rnke Alb*, 17 / Child, I, 443 / Cox, *Fsgs South*, 33 / Cox, *Trd Blds W Va*, 15 / Creighton and Senior, *Trd Sgs N Sc*, 25 / Davis, *Fsgs Va*, 11 / Davis, *More Trd Blds Va*, 92 / Davis, *Trd Bld Va*, 146 / Eddy, *Blds Sgs Ohio*, 26 / Flanders, *Ancient Blds*, I, 316 / Flanders, *Blds Migrant NE*, 96, 230 / Haun, *Cocke Cnty*, 97 / High, *Old, Old Fsgs*, 47 / Hudson, *Fsgs Miss*, 73 / Hudson, *Spec Miss Flklre*, #7 / *JAF*, 1913, 353, 361; 1915, 300; 1916, 158; 1917, 293; 1935, 298; 1939, 35; 1957, 251 / JFSS, VI, 87 / Linscott, *Fsgs Old NE*, 278 / McGill, *Fsgs Ky Mts*, 55 / Morris, *Fla Fsgs*, 254 / *North American Review*, CCXXVIII, 223 / Pound, *Am Blds Sgs*, 45 / Pound, *Nebr Syllabus*, 10 / Powell, *5 Va Fsgs*, 15 / Randolph, *Oz Fsgs*, I, 76 / Scarborough, *Sgctchr So Mts*, 166 / SharpC, *Eng Fsgs So Aplchns*, #11 / SharpK, *Eng Fsgs So Aplchns*, I, 69 / Shearin and Combs, *Ky Syllabus*, 7 / *SFQ*, 1938, 65; 1944, 141 / *Vt Historical Society, Proceedings*, N.S., VIII, 1939, 102 / *Va FLS Bull*, #s 3—5, 7, 9, 10.

Local Titles: As Two Little Schoolboys Were Going to School, Billy Murdered John, Brother's Murder, The Dying Soldier, Jessel Town, John and William, Little Willie, The Rolling of the Stones, Said Billie to Jimmie, Take My Fine Shirt, The Two Brothers, Two Born Brothers, Two Little Boys (Going to School), Two Little Schoolmates, Two School Boys.

Story Types: A: Two brothers wrestle (or fight in some way), and, because of jealousy over a mutual sweetheart (though this is often not clear), one pulls a knife and kills the other. Sometimes the older is the murderer; sometimes the younger. After the crime, there is a dying dialogue in which the killer asks his brother what he is to tell the family and the true-love. In some versions the dying lad's replies are actually repeated by the killer to the persons involved. Regardless, when the girl hears of the murder she charms the dead lover from his grave and requests a last kiss. The request is refused, and in a few texts the grief of the maid is revealed.

Examples: Davis, *Trd Bld Va* (A); Belden; *SFQ*, 1944, 141.

B: The story is the same as that of Type A, except the crime is accidental, rather than being the result of jealousy, passion, or the like.

Examples: Linscott; *JAF*, 1913, 361;
1916, 158; SharpK (C).

C: The story is the same as that of Type A, except that all traces of the love affair and the jealousy have vanished.

Examples: Brewster (A, B); Davis, *Trd Bld Va* (J);
Randolph, *Oz Fsgs* (A, B, C).

D: From *The Dying Soldier* title and the absence of the murder, the story seems to have assumed a battlefield locale. It has become a plea for Willie to wrap "his" wound, carry him to the church, and bury him.

Examples: *SFQ*, 1938, 66.

E: The murder happens as the result of spontaneous anger during a day-long test of strength between two brothers in the woods. The whole Type A story is included. Additional *Edward* stanzas occur at the end and serve to add most the Type A of that ballad, as well as to implicate the mother in the crime. This last feature is in direct contradiction of *The Twa Brothers* reason for the crime.

Examples: Flanders, *Ancient Blds* (A).

Discussion: The American texts of this ballad may well be older than the Child B version which is the parallel of so many of them. Barry, *Brit Blds Me*, 100, in relating his own texts with the SharpC, *Eng Fsgs So Aplchns*, and McGill, *Fsgs Ky Mts*, Southern versions expresses this view and points to the marked similarities in the widely separated texts, as well as to the fact that no songbook copies exist.

Child B has major points in common with most New World versions (See Type A). The stabbing is on purpose and not accidental, the *Edward*-ending is not present, and the kissing of the ghost motif (from *Sweet William's Ghost*, 77) appears. Generally, American versions name the girl Susie and not Margaret as in Child, though the boy's names, John and William, are retained. Usually, the brothers of Child become small boys whose age is incompatible with the events of the story.

Barry (*BFSSNE*, V, 6f.) suggests the rivalry was originally for the incestuous love of the sister. Belden, *Mo Fsgs*, 33 and SharpK, *Eng Fsgs So Aplchns*, K lend support to this idea. Incestuous love is not uncommon to the ballad, as is indicated by Flanders, *New Gn Mt Sgstr*, 94. See also Child 11 and 51.

Other American texts follow Child A (my Type B) and the Child D-G series (my Type E). Type B simply has the accidental death, which is a well-established mitigation of the tragedy. Type E adds the *Edward*-ending. With this addition, the Flanders, *Ancient Blds* (A), text goes even farther than the Child D-G series in modelling a new story about 49 by means of 13. The implication of the mother is utterly out of place here because we are told earlier that the murder is the result of anger and frustration caused by the even struggle. For further study of this unique (to America) combination, Child G (the children's game); Cox, *Fsgs South*, 33; and Powell, 5 *Va Fsgs* (for similar start) should be investigated. See, as well, Morris (*SFQ*, 1944, 140) who points out the relationships of *The Twa Brothers* to *Edward*, *Sir Orfeo*, and *Sir Hugh* in its theme, harping, and nursery language.

Type C stories reflect the process of forgetting. Randolph, *Oz Fsgs*, I, 79 prints a comment in a headnote that is revealing. " 'It was originally a long piece', she (his informant) said, 'about a fool boy who murdered his brother with a pocket-knife, just because he did not feel like playing baseball!"

Type D may well relate to this same group, although the battlefield locale seems to indicate localization. The Kirklands (*SFQ*, 1938, 65) state that the singer believed the ballad to be a Civil War song. See also the last stanza of the Hudson, *Spec Miss Flklre*, 7 text.

Two other American deviations worth note are the Chappell, *Fsgs Rnke Alb*, 17 version which is unusual in that the older boy throws the younger on a pit of stones before killing him and is told to inform the parents as well as the true-love where the body is buried; and the Haun, *Cocke Cnty*, 97 text which has a number of lines directed at mean school-teachers and has the dying boy ask to have his teacher told he is going where he can get some peace. This latter song was collected from a little girl at school, which may account for the change. The Cox, *Trd Blds W Va*, 15 version is remarkable in that it opens with "girls a-rolling stone" as well as the usual boys playing ball.

Zielonko, *Some American Variants of Child Ballads*, 76f. discusses a selected group of texts quite thoroughly.

51. LIZIE WAN

Texts: Bronson, I, 403 / *BFSSNE*, VII, 6 / Flanders, *Ancient Blds*, I, 332 / Flanders, *Blds Migrant NE*, 143 / Morris, *Fsgs Fla*, 257 / SharpK, *Eng Fsgs So Aplchns*, I, 89 / *SFQ*, 1944, 142.

Local Titles: Fair Lucy.

Story Types: A: Lucy is with child by a lover (that her plight is the result of incest is not clear). Her brother, James, kills her and takes her head to her mother. There follows a question and answer (see *Edward*) motif of the "what will you do when your father comes home?" sort. The brother, of course, says he will leave and never return.

Examples: SharpK.

B: Lucy is pregnant and her own brother is the lover. Her mother, sister, and brother each hear her crying, ask the cause, and are told the reason. The brother takes her to a wood and kills her. There is the *Edward*-ending.

Examples: *BFSSNE*, VII, 7 (I); *SFQ*, 1944, 142.

Discussion: The story is not clear in the Type A version. The plight of Lucy, the brother's entrance, and the dialogue with the mother are all that remain. In the Type B texts, where the story is clearer, the trip to the wood is found, a feature not in Child. See Flanders, *Ancient Blds*, I, A[1] and A[2] for an interesting sequence of texts. In actuality, the two texts printed by Flanders form a pattern of five descending from one Vermont informant. Barry even felt a Kentucky version of the song descended from this same man. See his ms. notes and SharpK, *Eng Fsgs So Aplchns*, I, 89. Check also Flanders, *op. cit.*, 332-338.

It is certain that an interchange between this song and *Edward* took place sometime early in British tradition.

The song is rare in America, although there is a re-working of the story in *The Forget-me-not Songster* (Nafis & Cornish, N. Y., c. 1845), p. 247 called *The Bloody Brother*.

53. YOUNG BEICHAN

Texts: Barry, *Brit Blds Me,* 106 / *Berea Quarterly,* XVIII, 12 / Bronson, I, 409 / Brown, *NC Flklre,* II, 50 / *Bull Tenn FLS,* VIII, #3, 68 / Carlisle, *Fifty Sgs Blds NW Ark,* 20 / Chappell, *Fsgs Rnke Alb,* 18 / Cox, *Fsgs South,* 36 / Cox, *Trd Blds W Va,* 16 / Cox, *W Va School Journal and Educator,* XLVI, 20 / Creighton, *Maritime Fsgs,* 7 / Creighton and Senior, *Trd Sgs N Sc,* 53 / Davis, *Fsgs Va,* 12 / Davis, *More Trd Blds Va,* 102 / Davis, *Trd Bld Va,* 158 / Duncan, *No Hamilton Cnty,* 38 / Eddy, *Blds Sgs Ohio,* 28 / Edward Eggleston, *Transit of Civilization,* 137 / Flanders, *Ancient Blds,* II, 9 / Flanders, *Blds Migrant NE,* 54 / Flanders, *Vt Fsgs Blds,* 204 / Gardner and Chickering, *Blds Sgs So Mich,* 143 / Garrison, *Searcy Cnty,* 16 / Greenleaf and Mansfield, *Blds Sea Sgs Newfdld,* 17 / *Harper's Mgz* (May, 1915), 903 / Henry, *Fsgs So Hghlds,* 58 / High, *Old Old Fsgs,* 14 / Hudson, *Fsgs Miss,* 75 / Hudson, *Spec Miss Flklre,* #8 / Hummel, *Oz Fsgs* / *JAF,* 1905, 209; 1907, 251; 1909, 64; 1910, 449; 1913, 353; 1915, 149; 1917, 294; 1928, 585; 1929, 259; 1957, 251 / *Ky Folklore Record,* 1960, 127 / Kincaid, *Fav Mt Blds,* 26 / MacKenzie, *Blds Sea Sgs N Sc,* 16 / MacKenzie, *Quest Bld,* 115 / Morris, *Fsgs Fla,* 259 / Pound, *Am Bld Sgs,* 33 / Pound, *Nebr Syllabus,* 9 / Musick, *Flklre Kirksville,* 2 / Raine, *Land Sddle Bags,* 109 / Randolph, *Oz Fsgs,* I, 80 / Randolph, *Oz Mt Flk,* 197 / Ritchie, *Sgng Family,* 109 / Elizabeth M. Roberts, *The Great Meadow* (N.Y., 1930), 64-65 / Scarborough, *Sgtchr So Mts,* 210 / Scott, *Sing of Am,* 40 / *Sewanee Review,* XIX, 316 / SharpC, *Eng Fsgs So Aplchns,* #12 / SharpK, *Eng Fsgs So Aplchns,* I, 81 / Shearin and Combs, *Ky Syllabus,* 7 / *SFQ,* 1944, 144 / Reed Smith, *SC Blds,* 104 / Thomas, *Devil's Ditties,* 86 / *Va FLS Bull.* #s, 2, 3, 5-9, 12 / *W Va Folklore,* III, #2 (1953) 18 / Wheeler, *Ky Mt Fsgs,* 89 / Wyman, and Brockway, *Lnsme Tunes,* 58.

Local Titles: A Gentleman of the Court of England, The Jailer's Daughter, Lord Bateman (Ateman, Bakeman, Baitsman, Batesman, Baton, Behan, etc.), Lord Bateman and the Turkish Lady, Lord Bateman's Castle, Lord Darker, Lord Wetram, The Noble Lord, The Turkish Lady, Young Behan.

Story Types: A: Lord Bateman, an English nobleman, is captured by the Turks while on a sea voyage. Put in prison, he wins the heart of a Turkish maid who sees him there. She frees him, after a mutual pact that neither will marry for seven years is agreed upon. At the end of that time, having no word from her lover, she sets out to find him. In England, Lord Bateman has just brought home a bride, but when he learns that his true-love has appeared on the scene he sends the bride home again (none the worse for him) and plans a marriage with the Turkish girl.

Examples: Barry (A); Davis, *Trd Bld Va* (A); Randolph, *Oz Fsgs* (A).

B: The story is basically the same as that of Type A. However, the girl's father builds her a ship to sail after her lover, Lord Bateman attempts to marry the Turkish girl to his elder and younger brothers when she appears in England, and she continually reminds the Lord of a £ 90,000 forfeit he must pay if he doesn't marry her.

Examples: Henry (A).

Discussion: Most American versions of this song compare closely with Child L as to length, detail, and story outline. Some of the minor points vary: for example, the mention of the hole bored in the hero's shoulder (see Child H, etc.), the lady's desire for the Lord's body rather than material reward, and a home such as India, etc. for the hero. The miraculous voyage

(Child C, etc.) has been excluded in America, as is generally the case with such matter, and no traces of the supernatural Billy Blin remain.

Kittredge (JAF, 1917, 295) used "the hole bored in the hero's shoulder" as a means of distinguishing the texts akin to Child L from those of the Coverly broadside (Isaiah Thomas Collection, Worcester, Mass.) group. It is possible the Indian home of Beichan comes from this broadside, although Barry (*Brit Blds Me*, 109) is doubtful. It is also noteworthy that the great majority of the New World texts use a variation of the English Bateman name, rather than the Scottish Beichan. The "tree" to which Young Beichan is attached (literally a "draught-tree") and the American misunderstandings of it are discussed in Brown, *NC Flklre*, II, 51, as is the reference to the heroine's baptism (see Child A) which is retained in some American texts.

The name of the hero is subject to a great number of spellings in America: Bacon, Ateman, and Beechman being particularly unusual. The girl, as in Child, always has a singularly un-Turkish name such as Suzanne, Sophia, Honey, Silky, Friar, Susie Free, Susie Pines, Susanna Spicer, etc.

SharpK, *Eng Fsgs So Aplchns* (F) prints an interesting American ending that relates how the Turkish girl "was put on the house enrolment, Lord Beechman's landlady", which seems unbelievable in view of the fact that one stanza before he has returned the bride to her mother. The Wyman and Brockway (*Lnsme Tunes*, 58 and *JAF*, 1909, 64) Kentucky texts do not include the return of the bride, but in them the Lord swears he'll give up all his lands and dwellings for his Turkish love. See also Scott, *Sing of Am*, 40. The Henry (*JAF*, 1929, 259) text finds Behan (note the Scottish name) living in Glasgow and the jilted bride a brown girl. In the Cox, *Trd Blds W Va*, *Lord Wetram* version the length of time is four rather than seven years and the bride's father and not her mother takes the daughter home.

The story has been subject to confusion and corruption in America. Thomas (*Devil's Ditties*, 86) prints a text that is obscured as to narrative through the misplacement of a stanza. In addition, there is a large group of derivative songs that go under the name of *The Turkish Lady* in this country. Creighton, *Sgs Blds N Sc*, 26 and MacKenzie, *Blds Sea Sgs N Sc*, 66 and *Quest Bld*, 130 publish examples, while Barry reprints a *Forget-me-not Songster* (Nafis and Cornish, N. Y., c. 1845) 169 text in *JAF*, 1910, 450. Other illustrative examples of the derivatives of this song can be seen in the *Forget-me-not Songster* (Turner and Fisher, Philadelphia and N. Y.), 248; *Marsh's Book of a Thousand Songs for the Million*, 171; *The Old Forget-me-not Songster* (Locke & Dubin, Boston), 171; and the *Washington Songster* (Turner and Fisher, Philadelphia and N. Y.), 131. The *JAF* list (1917, 296f.) cited in the note includes the "Lord Bateman" broadsides in the Harvard University Library and some *Turkish Lady* references. The song also appears in children's book form. See Mc Loughlin, N. Y., c. 1877.

Child (I, 455f.) discusses the affinities of this song and the *Hind Horn* romance and the Gilbert a Becket legend. For remarks on the seven-year pact and the traditional common law on presumption of death see Wheeler, *Ky Mt Fsgs*, 89, headnote. The version printed here is one of the more complete of the American texts. Zielonko, *Some American Variants of Child Ballads,* 83f. treats the whole American tradition through an extensive study of selected texts.

54. THE CHERRY-TREE CAROL

Texts: Barry, *Brit Blds Me,* 446 (trace) / Botkin, *Trsry So Flklre,* 758 / Bronson, II, 3 / Brown, *NC Flklre,* II, 61 / *BFSSNE,* VI, 14 / Bull *Tenn FLS,* VIII, #3, 78 / Chase, *Sgs All Times,* 25 / Creighton and Senior, *Trd Sgs N Sc,* 34 / Davis, *Fsgs Va,* 12 / Davis, *Trd Bld Va,* 172 / Flanders, *Ancient Blds,* II, 70 / Flanders, *Cntry Sgs Vt,* 48 / *Folkways Monthly,* May '62, 17 / Fowke and Johnston, *Fsgs Canada,* 128 / Henry, *Fsgs So Hghlds,* 59 / Jackson, *Down East Spirituals,* 60 / *JAF,* 1916, 293, 417; 1932, 13; 1938, 15 / McGill, *Fsgs Ky Mts,* 60 / Morris, *Fsgs Fla,* 262 / *NYFQ,* 1945, 48 / Niles, 7 *Ky Mt Tunes,* 4 / Pound, *Am Blds Sgs,* 47 / Randolph, *Oz Fsgs,* I, 88 / Scarborough, *On Trail Negro Fsg,* 60 / *SFQ,* 1944, 145 / SharpC, *Eng Fsgs So Aplchns,* #13 / SharpK, *Eng Fsgs So Aplchns,* I, 54 / Silber, *Reprints People's Sgs,* 43 / Smith and Rufty, *Am Anth Old Wrld Blds,* 12 / *Theatre Arts Mnthly,* Dec. '32, 1018 / Thomas, *Bld Makin' Mts Ky,* 223f. / *Va FLS Bull,* #s 4-5 / Wells, *Bld Tree,* 187 / Wheeler, *Ky Mt Fsgs,* 3.

Local Titles: Cherry-Tree Carol, The Cherry Tree, Joseph and Mary, The Sixth of January, Sweet Mary, Sweet Mary and Joseph.

Story Types: A: Mary accompanies Joseph to Jerusalem. On the way she requests her husband to pull some cherries down from a tree, as she thinks she is pregnant and desires them. Angered, Joseph tells her to get the father of her child to pull them down. Christ then speaks from the womb (or the Lord speaks from Heaven) to the tree which bends to the ground miraculously. Generally, it is implied that Joseph is abashed.

Examples: Davis, *Trd Bld Va* (A).

B: The Type A story is sometimes continued to the extent that Joseph takes Mary on his knees, begs forgiveness, and asks the child when his birthday will be. The child speaks from the womb and names Old Christmas Day as his birthday. Some texts have an additional description of the birth.

Examples: McGill, SharpK (A, B); Thomas, p. 229 C.

C: Mary asks for cherries and orders the tree to bow herself. There is no remark about the father. Heavenly voices, rather than the Christ-child, tell Joseph of his son's birth and of the manger.

Examples: Thomas, p. 226 B; Wheeler.

D. The usual story is presented but a number of stanzas are added telling where and how the Saviour was born and reviewing, when the Christ-child speaks, the main events of His life.

Examples: Flanders, *Ancient Blds,* II.

E: A lyric derived from the above story which reveals how, as Joseph and Mary walked in the cherry garden, they heard angel voices prophesying the birth of Jesus in a stall.

Examples: *JAF,* 1932, 13; *NYFQ,* 1945, 48.

F: Joseph takes Mary on his knees and asks her when the child will come. She says on "Old Christmas Night". Then she walks in the garden and requests the cherries. Joseph's refusal to get them for her and the bowing of the tree complete the song.

Examples: Creighton and Senior (A), Fowke and Johnston.

Discussion: Child (II, 1) discusses the origin of the story in the Pseudo-Matthew-Gospel. See also Migne, *Patrologia Graeca,* LXVII, 1281. Here the tree is a palm, and the baby does not speak from the womb. In England, the tree became a cherry, Jesus is in the womb, and Joseph suspects infidelity when he hears of his wife's pregnancy. There are also further stanzas added in which an angel of the Nativity speaks to Joseph. The story has a wide-spread history, Child (II, 1) noting its occurrence in the Coventry Mystery Cycle and Davis (*Trd Bld Va,* 172) finding it in the sermon of a Negro preacher. See also *JAF,* 1917, 297.

The ballad was not found in America until 1915 (see *JAF,* 1916, 293—4). It is not extremely rare, however. The American texts located have six story types, all of which show affinities with the Child texts. Certain American variations usually can be found: Joseph generally takes Mary on his knees; Jesus more consistently speaks from the womb; Type A lacks the "angel" stanzas; and Old Christmas Day is named as the child's birthday.

This last feature, which does not occur in the Child texts, is the subject of an interesting discussion in SharpK, *Eng Fsgs So Aplchns,* I, 415. Here it is pointed out that the B and C texts give January 5 as the date of Old Christmas as it was in 1752—99 after eleven days were dropped from the calendar (1751). In 1800 another day was taken away, and still another in 1900, so that January 7 is now Old Christmas Day. The McGill, *Fsgs KyMts,* 60 text prints January 6 as the date.

Child (II, 1) points out that "in Catalan and Provencal the tree is an apple". Barry, *Brit Blds Me,* 446 reports that a number of Maine people were familiar with this song and one individual with an Irish "apple-tree and Virgin (not Mary)" text. Also note the natural phenomena (stones crying from the street in praise of Mary, stars trembling with glee) that are present in versions such as those in Brown, *NC Flklre,* A, B. See Child A, B for the use of the stones as a mourning symbol.

The song is sometimes given humorous treatment in America. See Niles, *7 Ky Mt Tunes,* 5 (footnote) and the text itself.

56. DIVES AND LAZARUS

Texts: Bronson, II, 17 / Brown, *NC Flklre,* II, 210 (see also 211) / Davis, *Fsgs Va,* 12 / Davis, *Trd Bld Va,* 175 / Flanders, *Ancient Blds,* II, 74 / Jackson, *Down East Spirituals,* 27 / SharpC, *Eng Fsgs So Aplchns,* 253 / SharpK, *Eng Fsgs So Aplchns,* II, 29 / *SFQ,* 1938, 68 / *Va FLS Bull,* #12.

Local Titles: Dives and Lazarus, Lazarus, Lazarus and Dives, The Rich Man and Lazarus, The Rich Man Dives.

Story Types: A: Lazarus begs the crumbs from rich Dives' table. The latter scorns him, although the dogs take pity on him and lick his sores. After death, when Dives has gone to Hell and Lazarus to Heaven, the situation is reversed, and Dives begs Abraham to send Lazarus to him with water. Abraham reminds the sinner of his actions while on earth and of the great gulf between Heaven and Hell. In the complete Virginia text, Dives then repents and requests that Lazarus be sent to warn Dives' brethren who are headed for ruin too.

Examples: Davis, *Trd Bld Va.*

Discussion: The texts of *Dives and Lazarus* that have been collected in the New World are not, as Barry pointed out (*BFSSNE*, I, 12), texts of the old English carol, Child 56. What they seem to be is a fresh telling of the same tale. Typical of the changes wrought in the Child story is the incident of the dogs. In Child, Dives sends men with whips and dogs out to mangle Lazarus, but they find they have no power to hurt him. In the American texts, the dogs are restrained by pity alone. Sharp does not include his *Lazarus* ballad with his Child texts; neither does the Brown, *NC Flklre,* collection.

Brown, *NC Flklre,* 211 prints another telling of the Dives and Lazarus story, which is very moral and homiletic. It is "avowedly the production of a local ballad-maker".

For a discussion of a possible Gaelic introduction of this song into America, see George P. Jackson, *Down East Spirituals,* 27. His text is reprinted from Davis, *Trd Bld Va.*

Generally, the song is known only to the Southeast. The Flanders, *Ancient Blds,* fragment from Vermont is unusual.

58. SIR PATRICK SPENS

Texts: Bronson, II, 29 / Brown, *NC Flklre,* 63 / *SFQ,* 1937, #1, 10; #4, 1.
Local Titles: Sir Patrick Spens.

Story Types: A: The king needs a skipper to sail his ship to Norway and "bring home" Queen Margaret's lass. On a counsellor's advice, he writes Sir Patrick Spens. Spens rues the assignment because of the season, but sets out anyway. After a number of insults thrown at him and his crew in Norway, Spens from pride sets sail in the face of an impending storm. The gale strikes, and in spite of cloth wrapped about its sides the ship flounders. The ladies may sit and wait, but Sir Patrick Spens will never come home.

Examples: *SFQ,* 1937, #1, 10; #4, 1.

Discussion: For a discussion of the discovery of this ballad in America see *SFQ,* 1937, #1, 1. The text given in that issue is excellent, with the famous "old moon" and closing stanzas intact.

Child, II, 19-20 cites events that are possible historical bases for the story. The most likely of his hypotheses are the voyages centering about the marriage of Margaret and Eric of Norway in 1281 and the subsequent events, which culminated in a proposed marriage of their daughter and the eldest son of Edward I of England but nine years later. However, G. Ellis Burcaw, Curator of the Commercial Museum in Philadelphia, offers convincing corrections to most of Child's remarks. In a paper read before the American Folklore Society in Philadelphia in 1960, Burcaw pointed out:

1.) Aberdour is most certainly Aberdour, a small town near Dumferling in the south of Scotland, and not Aberdeen. 2.) All the place names in the various versions of the ballad are near this Aberdour. 3.) The King of Scotland sat at Dumferling until c. 1400. 4.) Spens was a clan name of the MacDuffs in the Aberdour region. 5.) Spens was sent on the voyage of the ballad by rival clansmen or political enemies. 6.) The coast off Aberdour is known for its deep. The story, in the light of Burcaw's remarks, seems almost certainly to be a tale of political and clan feuding, in which Spens was disposed of in the rather ingenious fashion of the song. See also the paper read by Norman L. McNeil of the Texas College of Arts and Industries at the April, 1963 meetings of the Texas Folklore Society. The paper reviews the ideas of Buchan, Scott, and T. F. Henderson on the historical Sir Patrick Spens.

The American story follows the Child G-J series. The Tennessee-North Carolina text (see *SFQ*, 1937, #4, 1; reprinted in Brown, *NC Flklre*, 63) is abbreviated, and leaves out the "moon" stanza, the "wrapping" of the ship during the storm, and the poetic end. The reasons for Spens' leaving Norway and for his being sent have been obscured, and the King is looking for a new sailor in the end. The mood is cold and objective.

62. FAIR ANNIE

Texts: Barry, *Brit Blds Me*, 446 / *Boston Sunday Globe*, 4-18-'20 / Bronson, II, 40 / Child Ms. / Combs, *Fsgs États-Unis*, 129 / Davis, *Fsgs Va*, 12 / Davis, *Trd Bld Va*, 177 / Hubbard, *Blds Sgs Utah*, 13 / *JAF*, 1951, 44 / SharpC, *Eng Fsgs So Aplchns*, #14 / SharpK, *Eng Fsgs So Aplchns*, I, 95.

Local Titles: Fair Annie, Lady Eleanor, Rosanna, The Sister's Husband.

Story Types: A: Lord Thomas tells his poor and stolen love, Fair Annie, by whom he has had six sons and is expecting another, that he is bringing a rich bride home. She is crushed, but waits for his return and even serves at the wedding. Later she and the bride learn that they are sisters. (Traditionally this discovery originates in a song sung by the heroine. In America the song is just unexplained fluting.) The bride offers her riches to this sister and sends her back to the home from which Thomas had stolen her. In some songs a condition that Thomas be hung is made.

Examples: Davis, *Trd Bld Va*.

B: The added information is presented at the start of the story that Annie was stolen by Indians and ransomed from them by the Lord.

Examples: Combs.

Discussion: A summary of the Child stories (See Davis, *Trd Bld Va*, 177) is as follows: Annie was stolen in her childhood by a knight from over the sea, to whom she has born seven sons out of wedlock. Her consort bids her prepare to welcome a bride, with whom he shall get gowd and gear; with her he got none. She must look like a maid, comb down her yellow locks, and braid her hair. Annie meekly assents, as she loves the knight. Suppressing her tears, Annie serves at the wedding and makes the bride comfortable. When the married couple go to bed, Annie in a room by herself bewails her lot in a sad song to her harp or her virginals. The bride hears the song and goes to Annie's chamber to see what is wrong. There, she inquires of Annie's parentage and learns they are sisters. The bride, who had come with many well-loaded ships, gives most of her wealth to Annie and goes home a virgin.

The American versions are invariably compressed and take a lot for granted even if the story is already known—a fact that reveals clearly how material becomes unexplainable in transmission. The Type A story follows Child A most closely and retains the names Annie and Thomas (probably borrowed in Britain from 73). The Child Mss. version printed by Barry in *Brit Blds Me,* 446 (See *JAF,* 1915, 57) is from Massachusetts and differs textually from the southern American versions. The SharpK, *Eng Fsgs So Aplchns,* North Carolina text has lost the fluting and is very hard to follow. So is the sentimentalized text from Utah (see Hubbard, *Blds Sgs Utah,* 13). In this text the heroine is named Rosanna, and both her father and the hero are named King Henry. The ending is abbreviated.

Combs, *Fsgs États-Unis,* 129 attributes the presence of Indians in his version to the currency of the ballad on the frontier. See Type B.

63. CHILD WATERS

Texts: Bronson, II, 44 / Brown, *NC Flklre,* II, 65 / Randolph, Oz *Fsgs,* I, 69.
Local Titles: Fair Ellen, The Little Page Boy.

Story Types: A: A young man deserts a poor girl to court a rich lady. The girl disguises herself as a page and accompanies him to the castle. She cares for his horse and even rides behind him unrecognized. Eventually her sex becomes known through pregnancy. She gives birth to a son in a stable, and the lover, hearing this, comes to her and decides to marry her.

Examples: Brown.

Discussion: The American texts follow the Child B tradition, although the version from Arkansas (see Randolph, *Oz Fsgs,* I, 69) is fragmentary. In the North Carolina text, the Mother, hearing moans from the stable, is astute enough to refer to the "page" as "she".

Flanders, *Ancient Blds,* II, 76 reprints a text from *The Charms of Melody,* a song collection that circulated in New England, but was printed in Dublin by J. & J. Carrick. The text is interesting in that it can be read in comparison to Child's *Child Waters,* which he felt was a ballad with "no superior in English and if not in English perhaps nowhere". *The Charms of Melody* version shows most graphically what the city presses did to traditional songs. Of course, *Child Waters* has not appeared in New England oral tradition.

65. LADY MAISRY

Texts: Barry, *Brit Blds Me,* 448 (trace) / Bronson, II, 50 / Davis, *Fsgs Va,* 12 / Davis, *Trd Bld Va,* 180 / Scarborough, *Sgctchr So Mts,* 137 / SharpK, *Eng Fsgs So Aplchns,* I, 97 / *Va FLS Bull,* #11.
Local Titles: Lady Maisry.

Story Types: A: A girl is with child, and her parents are planning to burn her at the stake. She sends her oldest brother's son to tell her lover what has happened and to get him to attend the burial. The boy goes and informs the lover who hurries to the girl's house blowing his bugle. The girl, hearing, is tied to the stake unafraid. The hero rushes up just in time to tear her dying form from the flames and kiss her. He then wills his land to the oldest brother's son.

Examples: SharpK (A).

B: The same story is told. However, it is abbreviated and has a cliché ending added so that the man is late and can only stop the funeral, kiss the corpse, and die himself.

Examples: Scarborough.

Discussion: The American versions remain pretty close to the Child story, although the complete tale does not exist over here. Child (II, 112)'s summary of the story, as quoted by Davis, *Trd Bld Va,* 180, gives the action as follows: It is discovered that Maisry goes with child. Her brother or father demands that she renounce the lord who is the English lover, but she refuses. Her father offers her the choice of marrying an old man or burning at the stake. In some versions the family (in keeping with romance practice) begins preparations to burn her without mention of choice. Maisry is warned of her fate and sends a devoted young messenger to carry word to her lord. The English lord, on learning what has happened, saddles his best steeds and hurries off. Maisry, in the flames, hears the bugle. She scorns her family's efforts. In some texts she cries out to her lover that she would cast his son from the fire if her hands were free. He leaps into the blaze for a last kiss as her body crumbles. On seeing her dead, the Englishman threatens cruel retaliation on the family, deeds to be followed by his suicide.

The Type A text seems to substitute the will-writing for the revenge threats, though one can not be sure. Certainly the ending of this incomplete version is less severe. The Type B story is not in Child and is quite conventional (See *Lord Lovel* and *Barbara Allen*).

66. LORD INGRAM AND CHIEL WYET

Reed Smith claimed that Phillips Barry had found this song in Kentucky. It does not, however, seem to have been collected from American oral tradition. See Branford Millar's remarks in *SFQ,* 1953, 159, Footnote 4.

67. GLASGERION

On Page II of *BFSSNE,* III there is a text printed by Phillips Barry of *Jack the Jolly Tar* which he terms a secondary form of Child 67. This song is a comic work concerning a sailor who gets a place to sleep for the night by anticipating the lover of a girl. However, such stories are extremely old and common. Laws, *Am Bldry Brit Bdsdes,* 161 lists this song as K40 and gives an Anglo-American bibliography to it. See also Child, II, 137 and the article on the "night-visit" by C. R. Baskerville in *PMLA,* XXXV, 565f. Flanders, *Ancient Blds,* II, 82-86 prints texts and discussion of *Jack the Jolly Tar. Glasgerion* has not been collected in the New World.

68. YOUNG HUNTING

Texts: American Speech, III, 117 / Arnold, *Fsgs Ala,* 60 / Barry, *Brit Blds Me,* 122 / Belden, *Mo Fsgs,* 34 / Brewster, *Blds Sgs Ind,* 166 / Bronson, II, 60 / Brown, *NC Flklre,* II, 67 / *Bull Tenn FLS,* VIII, #3, 72 / *Bull U SC,* #162, #4 / Cambiaire, *Ea Tenn Wstn Va Mt Blds,* 28 / Chappell, *Fsgs Rnke Alb,* 21 / Cox, *Fsgs South,* 42 / Crabtree, *Overton Cnty,* 283 / Creighton and Senior, *Trd Sgs N Sc,* 36 / Davis, *Fsgs Va,* 13 / Davis, *More Trd Blds Va,* 111 / Davis, *Trd Bld Va,* 182 / Delaney's *Scotch Song Book* (N.Y., 1910) / Duncan, *Hamilton Cnty,* 44 / *Focus,* V, 280 / Garrison, *Searcy Cnty,* 22 / Gordon, *Fsgs Am,* 66 / *Harper's Mgz* (May '15), 909 / Henry, *Fsgs So Hghlds,* 145 / Hudson, *Fsgs Miss,* 77 / Hudson, *Spec Miss Flklre,* #9 / Hummel, *Oz Fsgs / JAF,* 1907, 252; 1917, 297; 1931, 67; 1939, 30 / Jeckyll, *Jamaican Sg Stry,* 96 / *Ky Cnties Ms.* / Lunsford and Stringfield, *30 & 1 Fsgs So Mts,* 22 / McDonald, *Selctd Fsgs Mo,* 20 / Morris, *Fsgs Fla,* 263 / *N.Y. Times Mgz,* 10-9-'27 / *NC Folklore,* III, #1 (1955), 7 / Owens, *SW Sings* / Owens, *Studies Tex Fsgs,* 24 / Owens, *Texas Fsgs,* 44 / *PTFS,* X, 143 / Randolph, *Oz Fsgs,* I, 90 / Randolph, *Oz Mt Flk,* 203 / Sandburg, *Am Sgbag,* 64 / Scarborough, *Sgctchr So Mts,* 134, / SharpC, *Eng Fsgs So Aplchns,* #15 / SharpK, *Eng Fsgs So Aplchns,* I, 101 / Reed Smith, *SC Blds,* 107 / Smith and Rufty, *Am Anth Old Wrld Blds,* 15 / *Va FLS Bull,* #s 5—7, 10 / *William and Mary Literary Mgz,* XXIX, 664 / Wells, *Bld Tree,* 152..

Local Titles: The Faulse Lady, Little Scottie (Scotchee), Lord Banyan, Lord Barnet, Lord Barnet and Fair Eleonder, Lord Bonnie, Lord Henry, Love Henry (Henery), Loving Henry, The Old Scotch Well, Pretty Polly, Proud Lady Margaret, Scot Eals, The Scotland Man, Sir Henry, Sir Henry and Lady Margaret, Sweet William and Fair Ellender.

Story Types: A: Lord Henry returns from a hunt and is invited to spend the night with his mistress Margaret. He refuses, saying a lady he loves far better (in SharpK, *Eng Fsgs So Aplchns,* N it is his wife) is waiting for him. About to depart, he leans over his horse's neck, her pillow, or the fence to kiss Margaret good-bye, and she stabs him. Henry then reveals he loves Lady Margaret and dies. She, with or without the aid of maids, sisters, etc., throws his body in a well. A bird accuses her of the crime; she attempts to bribe him and then threatens him, all to no avail. In most versions, the bird reveals her guilt.

Examples: Belden, Davis, *Trd Bld Va* (A), SharpK (A).

B: The story is like that of Type A, but the motive for the killing has been obliterated. Henry refuses to stay for the night as he wishes to see his parents.

Examples: Barry (B), Randolph, *Oz Fsgs* (A).

C: A Ky.-Miss. version begins with the girl's walking in the garden where she meets her father-in-law. He asks for his son, and she says her husband is out hunting, but is expected back soon. The bird then speaks up and reveals that the lover is dead and his body in the well. The girl tries to bribe the bird, but the bird refuses to cease his accusations. Men dig in the well and find the body, and the girl, as well as her maid, is hung.

Examples: Hudson, *Fsgs Miss* (A).

D: The usual story is told. However, the regretful girl commits suicide that night. She leaves her ring on Henry's finger or a letter pinned to her breast in some versions.

Examples: Davis, *More Trd Blds Va* (FF), Scarborough.

E: A corrupted version (*The Forsaken Girl* series) exists. In it Henry gives the girl's faithlessness as an excuse for his leaving her. She then upbraids him for forsaking her, wishes she were dead, and rues her lot of bearing him a child.

Examples: Henry

F: A confused and corrupt version exists in which the murder occurs outside a barroom. The body is thrown in a well, and the girl announces to all what she has done. The bird sequence has lost its purpose.

Examples: SharpK (H).

G: A lyric has developed from the final stanzas of dialogue between the bird and the girl in which the murder is only mentioned.

Examples: Morris.

Discussion: The original story of this ballad (Child A, C, H, K) frequently mentions the king's duckers, who find the body after a hint from the bird. The lady then swears she is innocent and tries to blame her maid. However, a trial by fire leaves the maid unscathed, but consumes the guilty one. Such material, except for traces in Type C, is not in America.

In general, the ballad is far more common in the South than in the North. In fact, the song is extremely rare in British North America, though Barry (*JAF*, 1905, 295) gives a melody without text. Belden, *Mo Fsgs*, 35 suspects the presence of a stall copy to have perpetuated the song over here. The similarity of the American versions backs up his opinion. As usual, these versions are compressed, and they lack the dressing up of the dead man and the mounting of him on his horse (Child A-D, G, H, J-K), the recovery of the drowned body (Child A-D, G, H, J-K), and the intoxication of the hero before the murder (Child A, J, K). It may be possible, nevertheless (see Belden, *loc. cit.*), that remnants of the drinking may be in Davis, *Trd Bld Va*, C, D; SharpK, *Eng Fsgs So Aplchns*, D; *JAF*, 1917, 301; Cambiaire, *Ea Tenn Wstn Va Mt Blds;* and Brewster, *Blds Sgs Ind.*

The American Type A stories lack the fire ending and the duckers. Type B reveals how a ballad story can change. With some singer's (or publisher's) caprice the motive for the crime has been obliterated (see *Bull Tenn FLS,* VIII, #3, 72), although Barry, *Brit Blds Me,* 126 shows, through a later stanza in his B version, that this group is actually the same as Type A. Type C seems to be an adaption of the Child A, C, H, K series, although the lover is more properly married and the father of the youth is present. The revelation of the crime by a bird is in Child J-K.

The song has been subjected to much corruption. (See Zielonko, *Some American Variants of Child Ballads,* 93f.) The parrot stanzas of *Lady Isabel and the Elf-Knight* (Child 4) have attached themselves to it both here and in Great Britain (Child I and Davis, *op. cit.,* A), while it has also mingled with its own derivative, *The False Young Man* (SharpC, *Eng Fsgs So Aplchns*, 333, note, and #94) ; Henry, *Fsgs So Hghlds*, 146; *JAF*, 1931, 67; and my Type E.) Types D and F are almost self-explanatory. The former is either a rationalization of the antiquated "fire" judgment or a localization, while the latter is one of those hybrids that is certain to occur if any song wanders long enough.

The confusion of the Scarborough, *Sgctchr So Mts*, B text should be noted. The parrot and the girl, who are so often both named Polly, become completely confused, and the story vanishes in nonsense. In addition, Brewster, *op. cit.*, 166 prints a version of *The Trooper and the Maid* (299) that is about half *Young Hunting*. See Type C under 299.

See Zielonko, *op. cit.*, 93f. for study of selected New World texts.

Jeckyll, *Jamaican Sg Stry*, 96 prints a cante-fable version.

73. LORD THOMAS AND FAIR ANNET

Texts: Arnold, *Fsgs Ala*, 108 / *Berea Quarterly*, IX, #3, 10; XIV, #3, 27; XVIII, #4, 14 / Barry, *Brit Blds Me*, 128 / Beard, *Personal Fsg Coll Lunsford*, 47 / Belden, *Mo Fsgs*, 37 / *Boletin Latino Americano de Musica*, V, 279 / Brewster, *Blds Sgs Ind*, 58 / Bronson, II, 88 / Brown, *NC Flklre*, II, 69 / *Bull U SC*, #162, #5 / *CFQ*, V, 211 / Cambiaire, *Ea Tenn Wstn Va Mt Blds*, 34, 115 / Carlisle, *Fifty Sgs Blds NW Ark*, 23 / Chappell, *Fsgs Rnke Alb*, 23 / Child, III, 509 / Child Ms., XIII, #73, / Cox, *W Va School Journal and Educator*, XLV, 186 / Creighton, *Maritime Fsgs*, 9 / Creighton, *Sgs Blds N Sc*, 8 / Creighton and Senior, *Trd Sgs N Sc*, 40 / Cutting, *Adirondack Cnty*, 65 / Davis, *Fsgs Va*, 13 / Davis, *More Trd Blds Va*, 123 / Davis, *Trd Bld Va*, 191 / *Decennial Publication*, U. of Chicago, VII, 140 / Duncan, *No Hamilton Cnty*, 48 / Eddy, *Blds Sgs Ohio*, 29 / Flanders, *Ancient Blds*, II, 89 / Flanders, *Garl Gn Mt Sg*, 61 / Flanders, *Vt Fsgs Blds*, 209 / *Focus*, III, 204; IV, 162 / *Folk Lore Journal*, VII, 33 / *The Forget-me-not Songster* (Nafis & Cornish, N.Y.), 236 / Fuson, *Blds Ky Hghlds*, 49 / Gardner and Chickering, *Blds Sgs So Mich*, 37 / Garrison, *Searcy Cnty*, 7 / Greenleaf and Mansfield, *Blds Sea Sgs Newfdld*, 18 / Haufrecht, *Wayfarin' Stranger*, 10 / Haun, *Cocke Cnty*, 74 / Henry, *Beech Mt Fsgs*, 16 / Henry, *Fsgs So Hghlds*, 60 / Henry, *Sgs Sng So Aplchns*, 41 / *HFQ*, III, #1, 10 / Hubbard, *Blds Sgs Utah*, 16 / Hudson, *Fsgs Miss*, 78 / Hudson, *Ftunes Miss*, 13, 21 / Hudson, *Spec Miss Flklre*, #10 / Hummel, *Oz Fsgs* / Ives, *BI Sg Bk*, 55 / *JAF*, 1905, 128; 1906, 235; 1907, 254; 1915, 152; 1916, 159; 1926, 94; 1929, 262; 1935, 314; 1939, 75; 1950, 261; 1957, 254 / *Ky Cnties Ms.* / Kincaid, *Fav Mt Blds*, 36 / Luther, *Amcns Their Sgs*, 23 / MacKenzie, *Blds Sea Sgs N Sc*, 20 / MacKenzie, *Quest Bld*, 97 / Mason, *Cannon Cnty*, 14 / C.H. Matschat, *Suwannee River*, 63 / McDowell, *Memory Mel*, 10 / McGill, *Fsgs Ky Mts*, 28 / Morris, *Fsgs Fla*, 265 / Neely and Spargo, *Tales Sgs So Ill*, 136 / Niles, *Blds Crls Tgc Lgds*, 20 / Niles, *7 Ky Mt Tunes*, 12 / *North American Review*, CCXXVIII, 221 / *Outlook*, LXIII, 120 / Owens, *Studies Tex Fsgs*, 20 / Owens, *Texas Fsgs*, 39 / Perry, *Carter Cnty*, 177 / Pound, *Am Blds Sgs*, 27 / Pound, *Nebr Syllabus*, 11 / *PTFS*, X, 144 / Raine, *Land Sddle Bags*, 112 / Randolph, *Oz Fsgs*, I, 93 / Ritchie, *Sgng Family*, 18 / Sandburg, *Am Sgbag*, 157 / Scarborough, *Sgctchr So Mts*, 105 / SharpC, *Eng Fsgs So Aplchns*, #16 / SharpK, *Eng Fsgs So Aplchns*, I, 115 / Shearin and Combs, *Ky Syllabus*, 8 / Sheppard, *Cabins in the Laurel*, 285 / Shoemaker, *Mt Mnstly*, 160 / Shoemaker, *No Pa Mnstly*, 155 / Reed Smith, *SC Blds*, 109 / Smith and Rufty, *Am Anth Old Wrld Blds*, 17 / *SFQ*, 1938, 69; 1944, 147 / Stout, *Flklre Iowa*, 5 / *The Survey*, XXXIII, 374 / Thomas, *Devil's Ditties*, 88 / *Va FLS Bull*, #s 2, 3, 5-10 / Wells, *Bld Tree*, 106 / *W Va Folklore*, II, #2 (1952), 3; II, #4 (1952), 8; VII, #1, (1957), 54 / Wyman and Brockway, *20 Ky Mt Sgs*, 14 / *Wyman Ms.*, #9.

Local Titles: The Brown Bride, The Brown Girl, The Legend of Fair Eleanor and the Brown Girl, Fair Eleanor (Ellender, etc., etc), Fair Ellen, Fair Eleanor and the Brown Girl, Fy Ellinore, Lord Thomas, Lord Thomas and Fair Annet, Lord Thomas and Fair Eleanor, Lord Thomas and Fair Ellen, Lord Thomas and the Brown Girl, Lord Thomas's Wedding, The Three Lovers, The Three True Lovers.

Story Types: A: Lord Thomas, in love with poor but fair Eleanor, is persuaded to marry the rich brown girl. Dressed in scarlet and green, Eleanor, who has been personally informed of her misfortune by Lord Thomas, attends the wedding. She outshines the bride, and the latter stabs her to death in a fit of jealous rage. Lord Thomas then kills the bride, usually by chopping off her head, and commits suicide.

Examples: Davis, *Trd Bld Va,* (A); SharpK (L); Smith (B).

B: The story is identical to that of Type A, except the youth is advised to marry the brown girl because she is poor and Fair Eleanor rich. In an Iowa text Lord Thomas' name has become attached to Eleanor's father.

Examples: *JAF,* 1939, 75; Scarborough (E).

Discussion: Child 73, 74, and 75 are very closely related, and they are frequently found blended. See, for example, Stanza 1 in the otherwise pure version of 73 in Henry, *Beech Mt Fsgs,* 16. Davis, *Trd Bld Va,* 191 cites the distinguishing marks. (See also Child, II, 180.) In 73 there is a triangle with three violent deaths; in 74, a triangle and two remorseful deaths; in 75 there is no triangle and two remorseful deaths. All three make use of the rose-briar motif, although 73 uses this theme far less than the other two.

The majority of the American versions of this ballad are related to Child D, an English text. The Scottish form, with the contamination from 74 and the remarks by the brown girl on how Annet got her fair complexion, are not common in any of the more modern versions. Belden, *Mo Fsgs,* 37 feels that those ballads in which Lord Thomas is a bold forester show a close relationship to print. Check the bibliography with respect to Barry, Davis (*Trd Bld Va*), SharpK, Shoemaker, and *The Forget-Me-not Songster.* This "bold forester" beginning is the most common form in America and has generally replaced the scene of the lovers on the hill which is common to both 73 and 74 in Child.

There are two recent articles on Child 73 in which the British and American texts of the ballad are studied comparatively. One, by Anne Beard (*SFQ,* 1955, 257f.), concludes that the American texts derive from a broadside that Child did not see and that this broadside possessed certain details lacking in Child D. The other, by Richard Harris (*MWF,* 1955, 79-94), concludes that the American variants of Child 73 may well be more artistic examples of oral tradition than the Old World variants. Harris feels that the American singers have improved the compactness and unity of the ballad.

In America, Lord Thomas invariably goes to tell Eleanor of his decision himself and does not send a messenger as in Child C, E, F, H, and I. The lovers always consult their parents, never their sisters, as in Child A, B, F, G, and H. Gardner and Chickering, *Blds Sgs So Mich,* 37 contains the added injury of Thomas' seating Annet at his right, while Hudson, *Fsgs Miss,* E has a unique repetition of lines. The names of the heroine may vary all the way from Eleanor to Fairrellater and Fair Ellington, and the hero is called Jimmie Randolph in Virginia. Note that Cutting, *Adirondack Cnty,* 67 mentions "Dunny's Well" running black. See Child E.

For a very detailed discussion of the verbal variations in this song see *SFQ,* 1937, #4, 25f. Reed Smith, *SC Blds,* 110 treats the history of the song, and Belden, *MLN,* XXII, 263, reviews the methods by which the counsel is asked. For a comparison of Percy's text and a South Atlantic States "poor buckra" version see C. E. Means in *Outlook,* September 1899, 120f. Tolman, *JAF,* 1916, 159 publishes a parody (many of which exist), and Mabel Minor, *PTFS,* X, 144 notes that the song is used as a play-party game in Texas.

74. FAIR MARGARET AND SWEET WILLIAM

Texts: Barry, *Brit Blds Me,* 134 / Beard, *Personal Fsg Coll Lunsford,* 53 / Belden, *Mo Fsgs,* 48 / Brewster, *Blds Sgs Ind,* 71 / Bronson, II, 155 / Brown, *NC Flklre,* II, 79 / Bull Tenn FLS, VIII, #3, 66 / Chappell, *Fsgs Rnke Alb,* 25 / Child, V, 293 / Cox, *Fsgs South,* 65 / Cox, *W Va School Journal and Educator,* XLV, 378 / Cutting, *Adirondack Cnty,* 64 / Davis, *Fsgs Va,* 15 / Davis, *More Trd Blds,* 138 / Davis, *Trd Bld Va,* 221 / Eddy, *Blds Sgs Ohio,* 34 / Flanders, *Ancient Blds,* II, 122 / Flanders, *Blds Migrant NE,* 80, 83 / Flanders, *Vt Fsgs Blds,* 213 / *Focus,* IV, 426 / Gardner and Chickering, *Blds Sgs So Mich,* 40 / *Harper's Mgz* (June 1903), 272 / Haun, *Cocke Cnty,* 94 / Hudson, *Fsgs Miss,* 87 / Hudson, *Spec Miss Flklre,* #11 / Hummel, *Oz Fsgs* / *JAF,* 1906, 281; 1910, 381; 1915, 154; 1916, 160; 1917, 302; 1918, 74; 1922, 340; 1935, 301; 1950, 262; 1957, 256 / Karpeles, *Fsgs Newfdld,* 95 / *Ky Folklore Record,* 1957, 89; 1960, 127 / Lunsford and Stringfield, *30 & 1 Fsgs So Mts,* 2 / Luther, *Amcns Their Sgs,* 20 / MacKenzie, *Blds Sea Sgs N Sc,* 25 / MacKenzie, *Quest Bld,* 124 / McGill, *Fsgs Ky Mts,* 71 / *Musical Quarterly,* II, 126 / Neely and Spargo, *Tales Sgs So Ill,* 141 / *North American Review,* CCXXVIII, 221 / Pound, *Am Blds Sgs,* 40 / Randolph, *Oz Fsgs,* I, 108 / Randolph, *The Ozarks,* 181 / Scarborough, *Sgctchr So Mts,* 103 / SharpC, *Eng Fsgs So Aplchns,* #17 / Sharp K, *Eng Fsgs So Aplchns,* I, 139 / Shearin and Combs, *Ky Syllabus,* 8 / *SFQ,* 1938, 69 / *Va FLS Bull,* #s 2—6, 8—10 / Wells, *Bld Tree,* 106 / *W Va Folklore* II, #4 (1952), 11 / Wyman and Brockway, *Lnsme Tunes,* 94.

Local Titles: Fair Margaret and Sweet William, False William, Lady Margaret (Marget, Maggie, Margot, etc., etc.), Lady Margaret's Ghost, Lady Maud's Ghost, Little Marget, Lyddy Margot, Lydia Marget, Pretty Polly and Sweet William, Sweet William, Sweet William's Bride, Sweet (King, Prince) William and Lady Margaret, Sweet Willie, William and Margaret, William Hall.

Story Types: A: Sweet William, rising and dressing in blue, denies that he and Lady Margaret are in love and states that she will see his bride the next day. Margaret, after watching the wedding procession past her window, throws down her comb, leaves the room, and is never more seen alive. That night William sees Margaret's ghost at the foot of his bed in a dreamlike vision. (In some texts he also dreams of swine and blood.) The ghost asks how he likes his bride, and he replies that he loves the person at the foot of his bed far better. When William awakes, he tells his wife of the vision and goes to see Margaret. Her family shows him her body, and he kisses the corpse before dying himself.

Examples: Belden (A); Davis, *Trd Bld Va* (A); Gardner and Chickering.

B: The story is the same as that of Type A, except that Margaret commits suicide by throwing herself from the window (or by some such means). The death is on-stage, instead of off-stage.

Examples: Barry (A); Belden (B); Randolph, *Oz Fsgs* (A).

C: The story is the same as that of Type A, except that it is William's bride who has the dream. She tells it to William.

Examples: Barry (B), Haun.

D: The usual story is told, but the off-stage actions of Margaret after she leaves the window are described. She has her mother and sister make her bed and bind her head because she feels ill. She then dies of a broken heart.

Examples: MacKenzie, *Blds Sea Sgs N Sc.*

E: The usual story is told, except that Margaret is still alive when she comes to the foot of William's bed.

Examples: *JAF,* 1910, 381.

F: This type follows the usual opening for the story, but there is no ghost. William goes by daylight to see Margaret. She has died, however. The ending is normal, though the "rose-briar" cliché is distorted so that nothing grows from William's grave, and the rose from Margaret's grave dies after it reaches William's breast, but before it can tie in a lover's knot. The love is unrequited, even after death.

Examples: *JAF,* 1950, 261.

G: For the most part, this type follows the usual story. However, the ghost appears at the foot of the bed and blesses the lovers before going to the grave, and the song ends with Lady Margaret's seven brothers telling William to "go home and kiss your nut-brown bride and leave our sister alone."

Examples: Brown (D-F).

Discussion: This song is very popular in America, but the New World texts are not really close to any Child version. Generally (see Davis, *Trd Bld Va,* 221), they follow Child A in the "such dreams" stanza; Child B in the conversation of William and Margaret's ghost (but see Barry, *Brit Blds Me,* B and Haun, *Cocke Cnty*); and Child C in the fact the bride is not brown (a corruption from 73 when it does occur). The puzzling opening scene of Child A (the talking on the hill) is generally dropped in America (but see Haun, *Cocke Cnty,* 94), and usually a scene of William rising and dressing in blue replaces it. The phrase "with the leave of my (wedded) lady" of the Child texts is frequently expanded (see Cox, *Fsgs South,* G and SharpK, *Eng Fsgs So Aplchns,* A) to a formal asking of the wife's permission to visit the dead Margaret.

Type B texts show the frequent trend toward the spectacular in the American ballad, and Type D is even more specific in the details of the death, at the same time revealing a change in narrative through the influence of convention. Types E and F are excellent examples of the American tendency to rationalize supernatural material. Type G, with the blessing given by the ghost and the seven brothers, is an unusual find.

The SharpK, *op. cit.*, versions are exceptionally interesting. A, a Type A story, has a confused beginning and a ghost which appears to both William and the bride. In B, also Type A, the wife goes with William to see Margaret the next morning. In addition, the Flanders, *Ancient Blds* (F), version opens with two stanzas that begin, "If you're no woman for me, and I'm no man for you". And the whole Eddy text (*JAF*, 1922, 340) is worth note.

This song has affinities with 73, other than those mentioned above. See Child, II, 200. In the Brewster, *Blds Sgs Ind*, 76, C text Margaret attends the wedding against the advice of her mother, as does Annet or Eleanor in 73. The rest of the narrative of this version is the usual Type A sort.

75. LORD LOVEL

Texts: Allan's *Lone Star Ballads* (Galveston, 1874), 31 / Anderson, *Coll Blds Sgs,* 27 / Arnold, *Fsgs Ala,* 124 / Barry, *Brit Blds Me,* 139 / Beadle's *Dime Songs of the Olden Tradition* (N.Y., 1863), 13 / Beard, *Personal Fsg Coll Lunsford,* 57 / Belden, *Mo Fsgs,* 52 / Brewster, *Blds Sgs Ind,* 79 / Bronson, II, 189 / Brown, *NC Flklre,* II, 84 / BFSSNE, I, 4 / *Bull Tenn FLS,* III, 92; VIII, #3, 61 / *Bull U SC,* #162, #6 / *CFQ,* V, 210 / Chappell, *Fsgs Rnke Alb,* 27 / Chase, *Sgs All Times,* 58 / Child, V, 294 / Child Ms. / *"Celebrated Lord Lovel and Lady Nancy Bell", Comic Ballad argd by J.C.J.* (Oliver Ditson, Boston, 1857) / Cox, *Fsgs South,* 78 / Cox, *Trd Bld W Va,* 24 / Cox, *W Va School Journal and Educator,* XLIV, 358 / Creighton and Senior, *Trd Sgs N Sc,* 41 / Cutting, *Adirondack Cnty,* 69 / Davis, *Fsgs Va,* 16 / Davis, *More Trd Blds Va,* 146 / Davis, *Trd Bld Va,* 240 / Eddy, *Blds Sgs Ohio,* 39 / *Everybody's Songster* (Sanford & Lott, Cleveland, 1839) / Flanders, *Ancient Blds,* II, 148 / Flanders, *Vt Fsgs Blds,* 215 / *Focus,* IV, 215 / Frank Converse's *Old Cremona Songster* (N.Y., 1868), 16 / Gardner, *Flklre Schoharie Hills,* 203 / Gardner and Chickering, *Blds Sgs So Mich,* 43 / *Guiding Song Songster* (N.Y., 1865), 84 / Hadaway's *Select Songster* (Portsmouth, N.H., 1832), 86 / Haun, *Cocke Cnty,* 91 / Hubbard, *Blds Sgs Utah,* 17 / Hudson, *Fsgs Miss,* 90 / Hudson, *Ftunes Miss,* 16 / Hummel, *Oz Fsgs* / Clifton Johnson, *What They Say in New England* (Boston, 1897), 225 / M. and T. Johnson, *Early Am Sgs,* 19 / Jones, *Flklre Mich,* 5 / *JAF,* 1905, 291; 1906, 283; 1910, 381; 1913, 352; 1916, 160; 1922, 342; 1935, 303; 1954, 252 / Linscott, *Fsgs Old NE,* 233 / A. Lomax, *Fsgs No Am,* 401 / Mason, *Cannon Cnty,* 16 / McDonald, *Selcted Mo Fsgs,* 23 / McDowell, *Memory Mel,* 8 / McGill, *Fsgs Ky Mts,* 10 / Frank Moore's *Personal and Political Ballads* (N.Y., 1864), 321 / Frank Moore's *Songs of the Soldiers* (N.Y., 1864), 174 / Morris, *Fsgs Fla,* 273 / Musick, *Flklre Kirksville,* 4 / *New Pocket Song Book* (N.Y., c. 1860), 20 / New York broadsides: c. 1855, J. Andrews; c. 1860, H. deMarsan / *North American Review,* CCXXVIII, 220 / Tony Pastor's *New Union Song Book* (cop. 1862), 66 / Pound, *Am Blds Sgs,* 4 / Pound, *Nebr Syllabus,* 9 / Randolph, *Oz Fsgs,* I, 112 / Randolph, *Oz Mt Flk,* 193 / Sandburg, *Am Sgbag,* 70 / Scarborough, *On Trail N Fsgs,* 55 / Scarborough, *Sgctchr So Mts,* 99 / SharpC, *Eng Fsgs So Aplchns,* #18 / SharpK, *Eng Fsgs So Aplchns,* I, 146 / Shay, *Drawn from the Wood,* 134 / Shoemaker, *Mt Mnstly,* 146 / Shoemaker, *No Pa Mnstly,* 140 / Shearin and Combs, *Ky Syllabus,* 8 / *Singer's Own Song Book* (Woodstock, Vt., 1838, 9 / Bob Smith's *Clown Song Book,* 51 / SFQ, 1938, 70; 1944, 150 / Reed Smith, *SC Blds,* 121 / Smith and Rufty, *Am Anth Old Wrld Blds,* 20 / Thompson, *Bdy Bts Brtchs,* 379 / Thomas, *Sngin Gathrn,* 38 / *Va FLS Bull* #s 2—10 / Carolyn Wells, *A Parody Anthology,* 326 / Evelyn Wells, *Bld Tree,* 108 / *W Va Folklore,* V, #2 (1955), 23; IX, #2 (1959), 19 / R.G. White's *Poetry, Lyrical Narrative and Satires of the Civil War* (N.Y., 1866), 115.

Local Titles: Lady Nancy, Lady Nancy Bell, Lord Lovel (Lovell, Lowell, Lovinder, Leven, Lover, etc.), Lord Lovel and (Lady) Nancy (Nancibell), Lord Lovel and Lady Nancy, Nancy Bell and Lord Lover.

Story Types: A: Lord Lovel tends his horse while Lady Nancy wishes him "good speed". He tells her he is going to see strange countries and says how long he will be gone. Sometimes, he says he is going for "too long" and that she will be dead when he gets back. Lovel leaves. He misses Nancy and comes home early. However, on arriving, he hears funeral bells and discovers his love has died. Dying of grief, he kisses the corpse. Usually, the rose-briar motif follows.

Examples: Barry (A); Belden (C); Davis, *Trd Bld Va,* (A).

B: The story is the same as that of Type A, except that Lord Lovel returns after only two or three miles of travel when the ring on his finger "busts off" and his nose begins to bleed. Nancy's church-knell is underway before he is halfway back!

Examples: Cox, *Fsgs South* (B).

Discussion: Barry, *Brit Blds Me,* 146 prints a brief history of this ballad. It is very common in America, and practically all the versions that are over here follow Child H, a London broadside. Most of them agree with each other. This similarity of texts and the song's popularity is undoubtedly due to its frequent inclusion in pre-Civil War songbooks and broadsides. See the bibliography.

Belden, *Mo Fsgs,* 52 states that the church name (St. Pancras) can be used to judge how close to print a version from oral tradition is. The name has taken a great number of forms, many of which are listed in the introductory, descriptive essay in this study.

Reed Smith has remarked that "the difference between reading it (Lord Lovel) as a poem and singing it is the difference between tragedy and comedy". (See *SC Blds,* 121). Davis, *Trd Bld Va,* 240—1 also points out that the melodies are too light for the story matter and mitigate the tragedy. For this reason, the song has often been subject to parody. Typical burlesques appear in Barry, *op. cit.,* 145; Belden, *Mo Fsgs,* 54; Cox, *Fsgs South,* 78; Cox, *Trd Bld W Va,* 28; and Davis, *Trd Bld Va,* 258 (on Abe Lincoln).

The conventional ending in Haun, *Cocke Cnty,* 91 finds one lover buried under an oak and the other under a pine. Their hands touch with the leaves. The Type A, Cox, *Fsgs South,* C text implies that Lovel has been false to Nancy and thus gives a more substantial reason for her death. (See also Brown, *NC Flklre,* II, 87 (D).) The Type B text reflects the effect a cliche can have on the story of a ballad. The result is, of course, preposterous with respect to time. For a song with similarities see *BFSSNE,* I, 4.

76. THE LASS OF ROCH ROYAL

Texts: The Lass of Roch Royal: Bronson, II, 218 / Brown, *NC Flklre,* II, 88 / Combs, *Fsgs États-Unis,* 134 / Cox, *Fsgs South,* 83 / Cox, *W Va School Journal and Educator,* XLV, 347 / Flanders, *Ancient Blds,* II, 174 / Haun, *Cocke Cnty,* 107.
Examples of *Shoe My Foot* Stanzas: Anderson, *Coll Blds Sgs,* 29 / Arnold, *Fsgs*

Ala, 14, 33 / Barry, *Brit Blds Me,* 149 / Belden, *Mo Fsgs,* 480f. / Brewster, *Blds Sgs Ind,* 92 / Bronson, II, 218 / Brown, *NC Flklre,* III, #s 250, 253, 254, 302, 307 / *Bull Tenn FLS,* II, #1, 23 / Cambiaire, *Ea Tenn Wstn Va Mt Blds,* 72 / Chappell, *Fsgs Rnke Alb,* 128 / Child, III, 511 / Cox, *Fsgs South,* 87 / Davis, *Fsgs Va,* 17 / Davis, *Trd Bld Va,* 260 / Flanders, *Ancient Blds,* II, 176 / *Focus,* III, 275; IV, 49 / *Folk Lore Journal,* VII, 31 / Fuson, *Blds Ky Hghlds,* 131 / Garrison, *Searcy Cnty,* 33 / Haufrecht, *Folk Sing,* 155 / Henry, *Fsgs So Hghlds,* 69 / Henry, *Sgs Sng So Aplchns,* 24, 175-176 / Hudson, *Fsgs Miss,* 91 / Hudson, *Ftunes Miss,* 21 / Hummel, *Oz Fsgs* / Guy B. Johnson, *John Henry,* 98f. / *JAF,* 1891, 156; 1909, 240; 1913, 181; 1915, 147; 1933, 50; 1947, 236 / Kolb, *Treasury Fsg,* 40 / A. Lomax, *Fsgs No Am,* 214f. / Mason, *Cannon Cnty,* 17 / Morris, *Fsgs Fla,* 278 / Niles, *Blds Crls Tgc Lgds,* 6 / *NC Booklet,* XI, 29 / Owens, *Texas Fsgs,* 58 / Randolph, *Oz Fsgs,* I, 115 / Richardson, *Am Mt Sgs,* 37 / Sandburg, *Am Sgbag,* 3—7, 98, 126—7 / Scarborough, *Sgctchr So Mts,* 123 / Seeger, *Am Fav Blds,* 65 / SharpC, *Eng Fsgs So Aplchns,* #s 56A, 61A, 87, 94C / SharpK, *Eng Fsgs So Aplchns,* II, #s 87, 94C, 109A, 114A / Shearin and Combs, *Ky Syllabus,* 8 / Spaeth, *Weep Some More My Lady,* 134—5 / Reed Smith, *SC Blds,* 152—3 / *Va FLS Bull,* #s 2—10.

Local Titles: Fair Annie and Gregory, Lass of Roch Royal, Love Gregor, My Lady's Slipper, An Old Love Song, The Storms Are on the Ocean, Sweet Annie of Roch Royal, Who Will Shoe My Pretty Little Feet? (See also the list at the end of the *Discussion.*)

Story Types: **A:** A girl with a new-born child goes to find her true love in a boat given her for the purpose by her father. A month later, when she reaches her lover's land and door, his mother answers her knock. The old woman accuses the girl of being a witch, etc., and, although the baby is freezing to death, will not believe that this is her son's sweetheart. She demands the love tokens, but, upon seeing them, says Gregory has another love now and slams the door. (At this point there is a mix-up of person, for the sleeping lover seems to be talking to the girl.) When Gregory awakes from his sleep, he tells his mother he has dreamed that his sweetheart was at the door. The mother relates what really happened. The lover curses her and races to the shore just in time to see his love's ship split in two drowning both her and their child. He then pulls the girl's body ashore and, after much mourning, dies of a broken heart. The "shoe my foot" sequence is at the start.

Examples: Combs, Cox (A).

B: The "shoe my foot" stanzas or stanza is often used as a song by itself, frequently with foreign material attached.

Examples: Davis, *Trd Bld Va* (A); Henry, *Fsgs So Hghlds* (A); Sandburg (B).

C: These "shoe my foot" stanzas, divorced from the story, are put in the mouth of a man in Maine.

Examples: Barry (A).

D: This type is a combination of "careless love" lines, the ship and voyage vestiges of the story, the "shoe my foot" stanzas, and the refrain from Child 10. A girl's lover leaves her. She has her father build her a ship, follows him, and reaches the door of his home. His mother casts her out. It seems, she then finds her love dead in the sea.

Examples: Haun.

Discussion: There are few versions of this ballad in America, if the widely sung "shoe my foot" stanzas are discounted. The Type A texts follow Child D in story and detail, although the Flanders, *Ancient Blds,* II (A) fragment is unique to the New World in that it follows Child A. However, there is a good chance the informant (or someone in his family) was familiar with the Child volumes. See also Arthur Scouten's remarks on the fidelity of source materials in *JAF,* 1951, 131. The Type D text is a degeneration of what was probably a Type A ballad. Other lines seem to have entered the song, and the ending has been turned about.

David C. Fowler (*JAF,* 1958, 553-563) has made it clear that *The Lass of Roch Royal* was originally a variant of the *Accused Queen* story (see Aarne-Thompson, 706-707 and Chaucer's *The Man of Laws' Tale*). See also the discussion of European analogues, *"Handjeris and Lioyenneti"* and *Child 76 and* 110 by Paul Brewster and Georgia Taasouli in *FFC,* #183, 3-17.

"Shoe my foot" stanzas are common all over the country. Whether they can be fairly considered native to Child 76 is questionable. They stand alone as songs (Davis, *Trd Bld Va,* A-U; Sandburg, *Am Sgbag,* B); stand in conjunction with foreign matter (Davis, *op. cit.,* Appendix A-I, Cox, *Fsgs South,* 413; Cambiaire, *Ea Tenn Wstn Va Mt Blds,* 72; SharpC, *Eng Fsgs So Aplchns,* 270); and infiltrate into all sorts of places. Belden, *Mo Fsgs,* 55, 480f.; Davis, *op. cit.,* 260; and Henry, *Fsgs So Hghlds,* 67f. discuss these lines in America. For Americanization of the material, Scarborough, *Sgctchr So Mts,* 124 (*Honey Babe*) and Odum and Johnson, *Negro Workaday Songs* (*Who's Going to Buy Your Whiskey?*) should be consulted, along with *The Blue-eyed Boy* printed in Belden, *op. cit.,* 478. Of all the varied combinations of these stanzas with other material, perhaps the Chappell, *Fsgs Rnke Alb,* 128 text is the most interesting. Here "shoe my foot" lines, the "dove" stanzas from *Lady Alice* (85), and the "my love is like a rose" stanzas that Burns adopted (See *MLR,* VI, 514) are combined into one song. Also check Davis, *op. cit.,* Appendix D, p. 272.

A list of songs frequently using "shoe my foot" lines is: *Kitty Kline, The False True Lover, John Henry, John Hardy, Wild Bill Jones, The Gamblin' Man, Lord Randal, James Harris, I Truly Understand, Careless Love, The Foolish Girl, My Dearest Dear, The Storms Are on the Ocean, The True Lover's Farewell, The Rejected Lover, Cold Winter's Night, The False Young Man, The Irish Girl, Turtle Dove, Mother's Girl, He's Gone Away, Bright Day, Hush o Hush You'll Break My Heart, Carolina Mountains,* a Negro Dancing Song. There are others.

77. SWEET WILLIAM'S GHOST

Texts: Bronson, II, 229 / Brown, *NC Flklre,* II, 92 / Davis, *Fsgs Va,* 17 / Davis, *More Trd Blds Va,* 152 / Flanders, *Ancient Blds,* II, 178 / Flanders, *Vt Blds Fsgs,*

240 / *Green Mountain Songster,* 34 / Greenleaf and Mansfield, *Blds Sea Sgs Newfdld,* 21 / Karpeles, *Fsgs Newfdld,* 3 / Leach, *Fsgs Labr Cst* / *North American Review,* CCXXVIII, 222 / Worthington, *Nine Rare Trd Blds Va,* 60.

Local Titles: Lady Margaret, Lady Margaret and Sweet William, Margaret and Willie, Sweet Willie's Ghost, Sweet Willy.

Story Types: A: Lady Margaret in her bower hears a sound and learns it is her true love William. She asks what token he has brought her, and he replies only his winding-sheet. He then leads her to his grave and shows her where he lies. She wishes to lie with him, but his parents are at his head and feet and three hell-hounds at his side. The hounds stand for drunkeness, pride, and the deluding of a maid. He embraces her, bids her goodnight, and wishes her good rest. The return of the troth is not mentioned.

Examples: Greenleaf and Mansfield.

B: The story is the same as that of Type A, except the girl does not seem to wish to lie with her ghost-lover and the parents and hounds are replaced by three deceived sweethearts, three bastards, and three maids to guide his soul. He is seeking the return of his unfulfilled troth, and she refuses to give it back until he takes her to Scotland and kisses or weds her. When he reveals he is a ghost, she accepts the separation and gives him her troth.

Examples: Flanders, *Ancient Blds* (A).

C: The usual story is told as far as the request for the kiss, but the lover frankly states that he is a ghost and is given his troth back so he can "go above". When the girl asks if she can lie with him, he says there is no room at his head or feet, but she can lie in his arms. The rooster then crows, and she knows that her hour to die has come.

Examples: Brown.

D: In a fragmentary text from Virginia, the ghost requests the girl to follow him. Later, at the grave, he requests her to kiss him. He, rather than she, is the aggressor.

Examples: Davis, *More Trd Blds Va.*

Discussion: The Type A and B American versions follow Child C in general story outline, though Type A seems to have lost the reason for the ghost's return. Type C is a new interpretation of the story, though similarities to Child A and Child D (in the place for Margaret to lie) can be noted. The quick return of the troth and the use of the rooster at the end of the tale (Child G) are notable. Type D is fragmentary and is not really close to any Child text. Davis, *More Trd Blds Va,* 154 suggests that it may have been corrupted by *The Cruel Ship's Carpenter.* For a discussion of such variation, of variation in the Child texts, and the folklore behind the song, see Child, II, 226-229 and Paul C. Worthington, *Nine Rare Trd Blds Va,* 60-88.

The *North American Review,* CCXXVIII, 222 fragments are cited as lines from *Clerk Saunders* (69). This may be explainable in that some British texts of the latter have *Sweet William's Ghost* as an ending. See Child, II, 156.

78. THE UNQUIET GRAVE

Texts: Bronson, II, 234 / Brown, *NC Flklre,* II, 94 / Davis, *Fsgs Va.* 17 / Davis, *More Trd Blds Va,* 157 / *English Studies in Honor of James Southall Wilson,* 99 / Flanders, *Ancient Blds,* II, 184 / Flanders, *Blds Migrant NE,* 232 / Greenleaf and Mansfield, *Blds Sea Sgs Newfdld,* 23 / *JAF,* 1939, 53; 1956, 74 / Niles, *More Sgs Hill-Folk,* #9 / Wells, *Bld Tree,* 154.

Local Titles: The Auld Song from the Cow Head, The Broken Hearted Lover, Cold Blows the Winter's Winds, The Restless Grave, Shakespeare's Ghost, The Unquiet Grave.

Story Types: A: A girl loses her lover who is slain. She mourns on his grave. After a year and a day the lad's ghost rises and asks her why she refuses to let him be. She requests one kiss. However, he reminds her that a kiss would be fatal and tells her not to mourn for him, that he must leave her and all the world for the grave.

Examples: Greenleaf and Mansfield; *JAF,* 1939, 53.

B: The usual story is told, except the dead person is a girl and the mourner a man.

Examples: Davis, *More Trd Blds Va;* Flanders, *Ancient Blds.*

Discussion: This song is not common in America. Most the New World texts (Type A) follow Child B and C in the sex of the mourner, although the American ending is not in those British texts. Similar endings are on Child A and D. Type B texts, with the sexes reversed, are close to Child A. Davis, *More Trd Blds Va,* 157-159 gives a thorough discussion of the Anglo-American tradition of the song.

The *JAF,* 1956, 74 text collected by Herbert Halpert from New Jersey is unusual in that it is partly a prose narrative and partly a sung dialogue. Called *Shakespeare's Ghost,* it supposedly tells of an incident in the poet's life. After he had been married two or three years another man fell in love with his wife. She spurned the new lover, but he persisted. Finally, he hired thugs to kidnap and castrate Shakespeare. The wife, however, remained loyal to Shakespeare and said his condition made no difference to her. But the poet felt differently and coaxed his wife to enter a convent. Soon Shakespeare died. The wife then left the convent and would go to his grave to beg for a kiss. Halpert cites the parallel between this story and the Héloise-Abélard legend.

79. THE WIFE OF USHER'S WELL

Texts: Arnold, *Fsgs Ala,* 56 / Barry, *Brit Blds Me,* 449 (trace) / Beard, *Personal Fsg Coll Lunsford,* 62 / Belden, *Mo Fsgs,* 55 / Bronson, II, 246 / Brown, *NC Flklre,* II, 95 / Cambiaire, *Ea Tenn Wstn Va Mt Blds,* 121 / Chase, *Am Ftales Sgs,* 116 / Child, V, 294 / Cox, *Fsgs South,* 88 / Cox, *W Va School Journal and Educator,* XLIV, 388; XLV, 11 / Davis, *Fsgs Va,* 17 / Davis, *More Trd Blds Va,* 161 / Davis, *Trd Bld Va,* 279 / Duncan, *No Hamilton Cnty,* 58 / Eddy, *Blds Sgs Ohio,* 46 / Flanders, *Blds Migrant NE,* 64 / Flanders, *Ancient Blds,* II, 187 / Fuson, *Blds Ky Hghlds,* 59 / *Grapurchat,* East Radford (Va.) State Teachers College, 8-25-'32 / *Harper's Mgz* (June, 1904), 121 / Haun, *Cocke Cnty,* 104 / Henry, *Fsgs So Hghlds,* 71 / High, *Old Old Fsgs,* 48 / *History and Encyclopedia of Country, Western, and Gospel Music* / Hudson, *Fsgs Miss,* 93 / Hudson, *Ftunes Miss,* 17 / Hudson,

Spec Miss Flklre, #12 / Hummel, *Oz Fsgs* / *JAF,* 1900, 119; 1910, 429; 1917, 305; 1926, 96; 1931, 63 / A. Lomax, *Fsgs No Am,* 185 / McDonald, *Slctd Mo Fsgs,* 25 / McGill, *Fsgs Ky Mts,* 5 / Morris, *Fsgs Fla,* 279 / Niles, *Anglo-Am Bld Stdy Bk,* 14/ Niles, *Blds Crls Tgc Lgds,* 4 / Owens, *Texas Fsgs,* 33 / Pound, *Am Bld Sgs,* 18 / Pound, *Nebr Syllabus,* 10 / Randolph, *Oz Fsgs,* I, 122 / Randolph, *The Ozarks,* 180 / Scarborough, *Sgctchr So Mts,* 167 / SharpC, *Eng Fsgs So Aplchns,* #19 / SharpK, *Eng Fsgs So Aplchns,* I, 150 / Shearin and Combs, *Ky Syllabus,* 9 / *SFQ,* 1944, 152 / Smith and Rufty, *Am Anth Old Wrld Blds,* 23 / *Va FLS Bull,* #s 3—5, 9 / Wells, *Bld Tree,* 155 / *W Va Folklore,* II, #2 (1952), 10; III, #4 (1953), 61 / Wheeler, *Ky Mt Fsgs,* 14 / Wyman Ms. #16.

Local Titles: The Beautiful Bride, Children's Song, Cruel Mother, The Ladie Bright, The Lady and the Children Three, The Lady Gay (Gains), The Lone Widow, A Moravian Song, The Three Babies, The Three (Poor) (Little) Babes, The Wife at Usher's Well, A Woman Lived in a Far Country.

Story Types: A: A mother sends her three children away to school in the north. They die there. Usually she grieves and prays for their return. At Christmas time they do come back. However, when she prepares a feast and a fine bed for them, they refuse her efforts to please them saying that such things are worldly pride and that the Saviour forbids such indulgence. At dawn or on the summons of the Saviour they leave, telling the mother her tears but wet their winding sheets.

Examples: Cox (A); Davis, *Trd Bld Va* (E); McGill.

B: The story is identical to that of Type A, but the inference is made by the children that it was the mother's "proud heart" that caused their deaths.

Examples: SharpK (A, B).

C: The old woman has three sons who sail the sea. They appear to be lost, but return. The fact they are ghosts is almost completely obscured. The mother is so pleased she offers each a gift. Malcolm asks for the family coat-of-arms; Jock wants the house and lands; but Dan requests the hand of the maid who "daily lights your fire". The mother is so delighted she plans a wedding. By this time, any feeling the boys are ghosts has vanished.

Examples: Flanders, *Ancient Blds* (B).

Discussion: Zielonko, *Some American Variants of Child Ballads,* 104f. and Belden, *Mo Fsgs,* 55—6 discuss the American variations of this song in some detail. The latter lists six points in which the most common American texts differ from the Child A, B, C series: 1. The revenants are children, often girls, and not grown boys; 2. there is no cursing of the waters, but the mother usually prays for the children's return; 3. the ghosts refuse earthly pleasures in some cases because the Saviour stands yonder; 4. the recall of the ghosts at the crowing of the cocks is omitted or occurs when the "chickens" crow, except in Irish texts; 5. the children leave home to learn their gramarye; 6. the folk idea that tears for the dead wet the winding sheets and disturb the peace is present. In addition, the fact that the ghostly nature of the children is frequently assumed in America without being definitely stated (see Davis, *Trd Bld Va,* A) is an interesting proof of the belief in the "flesh and blood" reality of spirits. See Wimberly, *Folklore in English and Scottish Popular Ballads*, 226. Zielonko, *op. cit.*, 109 notes in connection with these points that there are three narrative elements interwoven into the American texts: the *Unquiet Grave* theme of the corpse disturbed by the mourning of the living; the moralistic punishment of pride theme from Child C; and the theme of the transformation of one dead man into three children.

The Type B texts seem to represent a confusion of the story, so that the new end contradicts the opening stanza in a way somewhat similar to the *Edward-Twa Brothers* fusion noted under Child 13 and 49. The Type C text, from New Hampshire, is a remarkable find. Here the story has become a sentimental love tale. The text seems near print, and is perhaps related to Child C where the boys are named Joe, Peter, and John. Other variations worthy of note are the Flanders, *Ancient Blds* (A) text, which is close to Child A; the Shearin and Combs, *Ky Syllabus*, 9 text where the children are sent to America and die on shipboard; the George P. Jackson's *Spiritual Folk Songs of Early America*, 28 text where it is pointed out that *The Romish Lady* has had an influence on the SharpK, *Eng Fsgs So Aplchns*, O version; the incremental Haun, *Cocke Cnty*, 104 text; the Cox, *Fsgs South*, A text where the children return at New Year's time rather than Christmas time; and the Brown, *NC Flklre* (F) text where the children tell the mother her tears will not wet their winding-sheets.

Belden, *op. cit.*, 56 suspects a printed source for the American texts because of their marked similarities.

81. LITTLE MUSGRAVE AND LADY BARNARD

Texts: Adams, *Nigger to Nigger*, 145 / *The American Songster* (Cozzens, N.Y.) / Barry, *Brit Blds Me*, 150 / Beard, *Personal Fsg Coll Lunsford*, 66 / Belden, *Mo Fsgs*, 57 / Bronson, II, 267 / Brown, *NC Flklre*, II, 101 / *BFSSNE*, III, 6; IV, 12; VII, 9 / Bull Tenn FLS, III, 95 / *Bull U SC*, #162, #7 / Cambiaire, *Ea Tenn Wstn Va Mt Blds*, 50 / Chappell, *Fsgs Rnke Alb*, 29 / Cox, *Fsgs South*, 94 / Creighton, *Maritime Fsgs*, 11 / Creighton, *Sgs Blds N Sc*, 11 / Creighton and Senior, *Trd Sgs N Sc*, 43 / Davis, *Fsgs Va*, 19 / Davis, *More Trd Blds Va*, 170 / Davis, *Trd Bld Va*, 289 / Duncan, *No Hamilton Cnty*, 63 / Eddy, *Blds Sgs Ohio*, 48 / Flanders, *Ancient Blds*, II, 195 / Flanders, *Blds Migrant NE*, 86 / Flanders, *New Gn Mt Sgstr*, 135 / Fuson, *Blds Ky Hghlds*, 52 / Gardner and Chickering, *Blds Sgs So Mich*, 46 / *Grapurchat*, East Radford (Va.) State Teachers College, 8-25-'32 / Henry, *Fsgs So Hghlds*, 73 / Henry, *Sgs Sng So Aplchns*, 65 / *JAF*, 1910, 371; 1912, 182; 1917, 309; 1929, 265; 1957, 255, 336; 1963, 190 / Korson, *Pa Sgs Lgds*, 32 / Leach, *Fsgs Labr Cst* / A. Lomax, *Fsgs No Am*, 316 / MacKenzie, *Blds Sea Sgs N Sc*, 27 / MacKenzie, *Quest Bld*, 14, 88 / *Notes from the Pine Mt. Settlement School*, Harlan County, Ky., 1935, VII, #1 / Perry, *Carter Cnty*, 105 / *PMLA*, XXXIX, 470 / Randolph, *Oz Fsgs*, I, 124 / Ritchie, *Sgng Family*, 135 / Scarborough, *Sgctchr So Mts*, 143 / SharpC, *Eng Fsgs So Aplchns*, #20 / SharpK, *Eng Fsgs So Aplchns*, I, 161 / Shearin and Combs, *Ky Syllabus*, 8 / Reed Smith, *SC Blds*, 125 / Smith and Rufty, *Am Anth Old Wrld Blds*, 26 / *Va FLS Bull* #s, 3, 6, 7, 9, 11 / *Univ. West Virginia Studies*, III (*Philological Papers*, II), 14 / Wells, *Bld Tree*, 110 / *WF*, 1959, 44 / Wyman and Brockway, *20 Ky Mt Sgs*, 22, 62.

Local Titles: Lord Banner (Barney), Lord Daniel, Lord Darnell, Lord Darnold, Lord Valley, Lord Vanover, Lord Arnold (Banner, Daniel, Donald, Orland, Vanner)'s Wife, Little (Young) Matthew (Mathy, Matha, Matly, Mose) Grove(s), Little Mosie

(Massey) Grove (Grew), Little Musgrave and Lady Barnswell, The Red Rover, Tomper's Song.

Story Types: A: Matthew Groves attends church or a ball and catches the eye of Lord Arnold's wife who, even though pregnant in some versions, makes advances toward him and asks him to sleep with her that night. When he sees by the ring on her finger that she is the Lord's wife, he refuses, but consents when she assures him her husband is away. A page overhears their plans and hurries off to inform the Lord. After blowing on his bugle (sometimes it is a friend of Matthew's in the Lord's retinue who blows the bugle against orders), Lord Arnold surprises the sleeping lover in bed. He offers Matthew the best sword and then kills him in a fair fight. In some texts he regrets his act. However, he then slays his wife when she tells him she loves Groves better than she loves him. In a group of texts the Lord plans suicide or says he will die in the near future.

Examples: Barry (Aa); Belden; Davis, *Trd Bld Va* (A); Fuson.

B: The story is the same as that of Type A, but it is mentioned at the end that the Lord shall "be hanged tomorrow".

Examples: Chappell, Creighton, Smith (A).

C: The story is the same as that of Type A, but there is no cajoling of the lover by the lady or refusal by Matthew at the start. He embraces her at once, when she makes advances toward him. The page, seeing this, departs.

Examples: Henry, *Fsgs So Hghlds* (A).

Discussion: This ballad, as it has a pure oral tradition in America, offers the scholar an excellent subject for study. Several of the texts are outstanding, and identical versions have been found as far apart as Maine and Missouri (See Barry, *Brit Blds Me*, 177f. and *JAF*, 1917, 315). Barry, *op. cit.*, 180f. prints a long discussion of the ballad as a means of revealing how folk songs develop. His contention is that there are two versions (the Banner and the Arnold or Daniel: one containing the bugle blowing and the "away, Musgrave, away" refrain, the other mentioning King Henry) which split in Britain and developed independently in America. In connection with this argument, he points out (p. 182) that the American texts are more vivid and incisive than Child's and probably older and decides that the song has been in this country over three hundred years.

The idea of a pre-American split is attacked point-blank by Helen Pettigrew (*Univ. of West Virginia Studies* III, *Philological Papers* II, 8f.) She also disagrees with Barry's interpretation of the trip of the husband and discusses the American versions and variants farther. She indicates how few New World texts have the lady pregnant and that none (as do eight Child texts) have Musgrave blame the lady for the compromising situation when the lovers are discovered. In addition, she points out that the horn-blowing is still frequently retained over here (See MacKenzie, *Blds Sea Sgs N Sc*, A, C; Gardner and Chickering, *Blds Sgs So Mich;* Scarborough, *Sgctchr So Mts,* A; SharpK, *Eng Fsgs So Aplchns*, F) and attributes the visit to King Henry to American romanticization. Marie Campbell, *A Study of 25 Versions of "Little Musgrave and Lady Barnard" in Ballad Collections of North America* (*Bull Tenn FLS,* XXI, 14-19) also treats the song in detail. See also Davis, *More Trd Blds Va,* 170-172, who discusses the discussions.

The American texts vary somewhat in their inclusion and exclusion of material, as do those in Child. See particularly the remarks in Brown, *NC Flklre,* II, 101 where the expression "cost me deep in purse" is discussed as a mark of the American tradition. Type A stories may begin at church (Child A, C, H), at a ball (*BFSSNE,* III, 6), or playing ball (Child D, E, K, L), although the letter-writing (Child G) does not seem to be in America. (Belden, *Mo Fsgs,* 58 points out that the church-beginning characterizes southern American texts, while the playing at ball, the northern.) The attempts to bribe the page are missing (Child C-F, H-L, O), though not in the unusual Flanders, *Ancient Blds* (A) text. The bugle-blowing scenes are faulty and, if included, disagree as to whether the Lord himself or a friend of Musgrave's warns the lover against orders. The Lord may or may not regret his act, and a few times, as in Child C and G, he commits suicide. Musgrave's wife is omitted, but the pregnancy of Lady Barnard is frequently retained. The Cambiaire, *Ea Tenn Wstn Va Mt Blds,* 50 version finds a close friend of the family taking the page's role.

Type B follows the ending of Child E, while Type C is perhaps closer to the spirit of the British texts than the other American versions. The lady is never as aggressive in England as she is on this side of the ocean. Nevertheless, no American song that I have seen contains the barbaric torture to be found in Child A, nor do any indicate clearly a past affair between the lovers. However, see Type C. Check also the texts, such as the one in *WF,* 1959, 44, which end with the lord taking the lady "down the lane" where he slays her. Leach, *Fsgs Labr Cst,* collected a version divided into stanzas of unequal lengths based on story units.

There is a Negro text which goes under the name *Tomper's Song.* This ballad consists of an argument between the lovers about how close the husband is. In it, the warning is given by a sparrow, as well as by the "footspeed".

For a discussion of this ballad in Jamaica see *PMLA,* XXXIX, 455f. and *JAF,* 1963, 190.

The song is generally considered "dirty" by folk-singers. Check the headnotes in Randolph, *Oz Fsgs,* I, 124f.

83. CHILD MAURICE

Texts: Greenleaf and Mansfield, *Blds Sea Sgs Newfdld,* 25.

Local Titles: Gil Morissy.

Story Types: A: A lady receives a letter from Gil Morissy and is so pleased her husband gets very jealous. He goes outside and finds the youth combing his yellow hair, challenges him to a battle, and kills him. The lady, who was the boy's mother, laments over the grave. The husband regrets his rash act on hearing the lament.

Examples: Greenleaf and Mansfield.

Discussion: The Canadian version, which was recited and not sung, is condensed, but fairly inclusive in its coverage of the story outline.

Flanders, *Ancient Blds,* II, 238 also includes a text of *Child Maurice.* This version is reprinted from the *Charms of Melody,* a book of songs that was known in New England, but which was printed in Dublin by J. & J. Carrick. This text, which is very close to one in Gavin Greig's *Last Leaves of Traditional Ballads* (Aberdeen, 1925), 64-67 is, of course, not from American oral tradition.

84. BONNY BARBARA ALLEN

Texts: Adventure Mgz, 4-10-'25, 4-10-'26 / Allen, *Cowboy Lore,* 74 / *American Songster* (Kenedy, Baltimore, 1836) / Anderson, *Coll Blds Sgs,* 33 / Arnold, *Fsgs Ala,* 8 / Barry, *Brit Blds Me,* 195 / Beadle's *Dime Songs of the Olden Times* (N.Y., 1863), 38 / Beard, *Personal Fsg Coll Lunsford,* 73 / Beck, *Down-east Blds Fsgs,* 30 / Belden, *Mo Fsgs,* 60 / *Berea Quarterly,* XVIII, 12 / *Boletin Latino Americano de Musica,* V, 280 / Boni, *Fireside Bk Fav Am Sgs,* 316 / Botkin, *Treasury Am Flklre,* 820 / Botsford, *Sgs of Amcas,* 26 / Brewster, *Blds Sgs Ind,* 99 / Bronson, II, 322 / Brown, *NC Flklre,* II, 111 / *Bull Tenn FLS,* II, #1, 23; III, 92; IV, #3, 73 / *Bull U SC,* #162, #8 / Cambiaire, *Ea Tenn Wstn Va Mt Blds,* 66 / Carlisle, *Fifty Sgs Blds NW Ark,* 27 / Chappell, *Fsgs Rnke Alb,* 32 / Charley Fox's *Minstrel's Companion* (Turner & Fisher, Philadelphia) / *Colorado Fsg Bull,* I, #3, 4; II, 4-5 / Cox, *Fsgs South,* 96 / Cox, *W Va School Journal and Educator,* XLIV, 305 / Crabtree, *Overton Cnty,* 204 / Creighton, *Maritime Fsgs,* 13 / Creighton and Senior, *Trd Sgs N Sc,* 49 / Davis, *Fsgs Va,* 19 / Davis, *More Trd Blds Va,* 182 / Davis, *Trd Bld Va,* 302 / Downes and Siegmeister, *Treasury Am Sg,* 34 / Duncan, *No Hamilton Cnty,* 69/ Eddy, *Blds Sgs Ohio,* 53 / *Everybody's Songster* (Sanford and Lott, Cleveland, 1839) / *Farm Life,* March, 1927 / Fauset, *Flklre N Sc,* 113 / Flanders, *Ancient Blds,* II, 246 / Flanders, *Blds Migrant NE,* 197 / *Focus,* III, 445; IV, 101, 160; V, 282 / *The Forget-me-not Songster* (Turner & Fisher, Philadelphia), 129 / Fuson, *Blds Ky Hghlds,* 47 / Gardner and Chickering, *Blds Sgs So Mich,* 50 / Gordon, *Fsgs Am,* 69 / *Grapurchat,* East Radford (Va.) State Teachers College, 8—25—'32 / Green-leaf and Mansfield, *Blds Sea Sgs Newfdld,* 26 / *Harper's Mgz* (June 1888), 35; (May 1915), 907 / Haufrecht, *Folk Sing,* 150 / Haun, *Cocke Cnty,* 62 / *Heart Songs,* 247 / Henry, *Beech Mt Fsgs,* 12 / Henry, *Fsgs So Hghlds,* 82 / Henry, *Sgs Sng So Aplchns,* 248 / Hubbard, *Blds Sgs Utah,* 20 / Hudson, *Fsgs Miss,* 95 / Hudson, *Ftunes Miss,* 14 / Hudson, *Spec Miss Flklre,* #13 / Hummel, *Oz Fsgs* / Ives, *BI Sg Bk,* 50 / Johnson, *Early Am Sgs,* 8 / Jones, *Flklre Mich,* 5 / *JAF,* 1893, 132; 1906, 286; 1907, 256; 1909, 63; 1913, 352; 1915, 144; 1916, 160, 198; 1922, 343; 1926, 97, 211; 1929, 268, 303; 1932, 13; 1933, 28; 1935, 310; 1936, 207; 1939, 22, 77; 1941, 40; 1947, 210; 1950, 264; 1957, 338 / C. Kennedy, *Treasury Am Blds,* 25 / C. Kennedy and Jordan, *Am Blds,* 155 / T. Kennedy, *Effects Isolation,* 320 / *Ky Cnties Ms.* / Kincaid, *Fav Mt Blds,* 14 / Kolb, *Treasury Fsgs,* 2 / Linscott, *Fsgs Old NE,* 163 / A. Lomax, *Fsgs No Am,* 183 / J. Lomax, *Adv Bld Hunter,* 243 / Luther, *Amcns Their Sgs,* 15 / MacIntosh, *So Ill Fsgs,* 7 MacKenzie, *Blds Sea Sgs N Sc,* 35 / MacKenzie, *Quest Bld,* 100 / Mason, *Cannon Cnty,* 23 / McDon-ald, *Selctd Mo Fsgs,* 30 / McDowell, *Memory Mel,* 15 / McGill, *Fsgs Ky Mts,* 40 / *Musical Quarterly,* II, 121; IV, 296 / Morris, *Fsg Fla,* 283 / Musick, *Flklre Kirksville,* 6 / Neal, *Brown Cnty,* 52 / Neely and Spargo, *Tales Sgs So Ill,* 137 / *N.J. Journal Educ.,* XVI, #6, 7 / N.Y. broadside: H. J. Wehman #395, Harvard Univ. Library / *NYFQ,* 1946, 55; 1948, 179 / *N.Y. Times,* 10—9—'27 / Niles, *Anglo-Am Bld Stdy Bk,* 18 / Niles, *More Sgs Hill-Flk,* 6 / *North American Re-view,* CCXXVIII, 219—20 / *162 Popular Songs* (Vickery, Augusta, 1895) / Owens, *Studies Tex Fsgs,* 30 / Owens, *Texas Fsgs,* 49 / *Ozark Guide,* XIV, 48 / *Ozark Life,* V, #7 / *The Pearl Songster* (Huestis, N.Y., 1846), 104 / Perry, *Carter*

Cnty, 140 / Pound, *Am Blds Sgs,* 7 / Pound, *Nebr Syllabus,* 9 / *PTFS,* VII, 111; X, 146; XXV, 61 / Raine, *Land Sddle Bags,* 115 / Randolph, *Oz Fsgs,* I, 126 / Randolph, *The Ozarks,* 183 / Rayburn, *Oz Cntry,* 232 / Ritchie, *Sgng Family,* 184 / Robison, *Top Album* / Sandburg, *Am Sgbag,* 57 / Scarborough, *On Trail Negro Fsg,* 59 / Scarborough, *Sgctchr So Mts,* 83 / Scott, *Sing Am,* 56 / Seeger, *Am Fav Blds,* 79 / *Sewanee Review,* XIX, 315 / SharpC, *Eng Fsgs So Aplchns,* #21 / SharpK, *Eng Fsgs So Aplchns,* I, 191 / Shearin and Combs, *Ky Syllabus,* 8 / Shoemaker, *Mt. Mnstly,* 127 / Shoemaker, *No Pa Mnstly,* 122 / Reed Smith, *SC Blds,* 129 / Smith and Rufty, *Am Anth Old Wrld Blds,* 30 / *SFQ,* 1938, 71 / *The Southern Warbler* (Charleston 1845), 275 / Sulzer, *25 Ky Flk Blds,* I, 16 / Thomas, *Devil's Ditties,* 94 / Thomas, *Sngin Gathrn,* 6 / Thompson, *Bdy Bts Brtchs,* 377 / Thompson and Cutting, *Pioneer Songster,* 7 / Trifet's *Monthly Budget of Music,* 1892 / *Univ. of Va. Mgz* (April, 1913), 329 / *The Vagabonds, Old Cabin Sgs for Fiddle and Bow,* n.d., / *Va FLS Bull,* #s 2-10 / *The Virginia Warbler* (Richmond, 1845), 275 / Wells, *Bld Tree,* 113 / *W Va Folklore,* III, #4 (1953), 60 / Wheeler, *Ky Mt Fsgs,* 39 / Wilson, *Bckwds Am,* 99 / Wyman and Brockway, *Lnsme Tunes,* 1.

Local Titles: Ballet of Barbara Allen, Barbara Allen (both names with many variants), Barbara Allen's Cruelty, Barbara Ellen, Barbarous Ellen, Edelin, Hardhearted Barbery Ellen, (The Sad Ballet of) Little Johnnie Green, Sir John Graham, The Love of Barbara Allen, Mary Alling.

Story Types: A: A young man lies on his death-bed for the love of Barbara Allen. He requests a servant to bring her to him (the man usually delivers the message in person, though in some texts a letter is sent). She comes without too much enthusiasm and remarks that the lover looks as though he were dying. In response to his pleadings, she accuses him of slighting her in tavern-toasting or at a ball. He defends himself, but she continues to scorn him. He dies of remorse. Later, when she hears the funeral bells, she repents and dies. Sometimes the rose-briar theme is added.

Examples: Cox, *Fsgs South* (E); Davis, *Trd Bld Va* (A); SharpK (A).

B: The story is like that of Type A, but the lover accepts Barbara's scorn without offering a defense to any accusations that are stated. Not all these texts have accusations.

Examples: Belden (K); Brewster (A); Davis, *Trd Bld Va* (J).

C: The same story as that of Type A, but the lover acknowledges the justice of Barbara's charge.

Examples: *JAF,* 1907, 256.

D: The story may follow Type A or B, but the lover curses Barbara in the end.

Examples: Brewster (D); Eddy (A); Davis, *Trd Bld Va* (Q).

E: This type resembles Type D, but Barbara curses the lover in return.

Examples: Davis, *Trd Bld Va* (P).

F: The story may be of either the A or B type, but the man lavishes gifts on Barbara in direct contrast to her cruelty.

Examples: Davis (S, T); *JAFL,* 1916, 161; *NYFQ,* 1946, 55.

G: The story is like that of Type A or B, although the mother (or both parents) is usually blamed by Barbara for causing her to be cruel and the mother (or both mothers) joins the lovers in death.

Examples: Davis, *Trd Bld Va* (W); Scarborough, *Sgctchr So Mts* (F); SharpK (B, C).

H: The story is the same as that of Type A, but a view is given of the courtship where Sir James the Graeme (See Child 213) tells Barbara she will be mistress of seven ships if she marries him. He then slights her at the tavern, and the regular story ensues.

Examples: MacKenzie, *Blds Sea Sgs N Sc* (A).

I: A Negro version exists which, in its fragmentary form, reveals that "Boberick Allen" is a man. The other girls can't see why "I" follow him. He goes to town and back attempting to see "me" follow him, but he can't because "I was away somewhere".

Examples: *PTFS*, VII, III; X, 149 (C).

J: There is a fragmentary text from West Virginia which can be summarized thus: In Scarlet Town there is an "ill-famed" dwelling where men drink and toast the innocent Barbara Allen. Evidently they tell stories about her lover. When Barbara's love is dying, Barbara turns from him, thinking he is "lying". She has been told he drank a toast to Eva Baylor and so failed in his role as lover. He dies, and Barbara regrets listening to the gossip and plans to die for him on the morrow.

Examples: *JAF*, 1957, 338.

Discussion: The popularity of this song is undoubtedly due to its inclusion in ten or more early nineteenth century songbooks and on innumerable broadsides. Certainly it is extreme in its number of texts and minor variations, although the basic story outline is amazingly consistent.

In America, the girl's name seldom varies much beyond the to-be-expected spelling changes, but that of her lover takes many forms: the first name may be William, Willie, James, Jemmy, Jimmy, John, etc., and the last name, often not given, Grove, Groves, Green, Grame, Graham, Hilliard, Ryley, Rosie, etc. The rose-briar motif is frequently found, even though it is not in Child's texts, sometimes with the names Lord Thomas and Fair Eleanor (Eddy, *Blds Sgs Ohio,* F) or Sweet William being present as well. If this ending is lacking, another conventional close such as the "turtle dove and sparrow" stanza (SharpK, *Eng Fsgs Aplchns,* D) or "a warning to all virgins" (Davis, *Trd Bld Va,* M) usually is substituted. The time of year is most often May as in Child B, but Martinmas (Child A) and autumn (Gardner and Chickering, *Blds Sgs So Mich*) are not uncommon. For detailed discussions of various texts of this song, see Davis, *op. cit.,* 302—4; C. A. Smith in the *Musical Quarterly,* II, 109; and MacKenzie, *Blds Sea Sgs N Sc,* 35 in particular. However, most of the early editors devote some time to this ballad.

The important narrative changes are included in the story types above.

The main story variations center about the actions of Barbara and her lover concerning the accusation, defense, and parting. The Child story is simpler than that of most of the American versions. The curse of the lover on Barbara, the lavishing of gifts by the lover on Barbara, Barbara's curse of the lover, the lover's acknowledgement of the justice of Barbara's charges, the on-stage views of the courtship, the parental problems, and the suicide of the mother(s) are all absent in Child and enter with the broadside and songbook texts and the subsequent widespread oral tradition. The mitigation of the cruelty reflected in Types C and G is typical. Type I reflects a complete degeneration and has been discussed in my descriptive essay. Type J is quite interesting, with clear signs of localization and confusion without losing the central theme of the old texts. It is also worth noting that the color scarlet and sin have been associated in this variant. All in all, in America, Barbara is a remorseful girl, the lover denies slighting her (or all mention of the slighting is omitted), and the lover accepts his fate objectively more or less as in Child A-B.

Barbara Allen has had frequent localizations, besides the one mentioned in connection with Type J. Flanders, *Ancient Blds* (E), entitled *Mary Alling*, probably recalls some local belle. One Southwestern text opens "In Dallas town" and describes May as the month when the "cactus was a-blooming" (see *JAF*, 1941, 40). In Thompson, *Bdy Bts Brtchs*, 379 Barbara rides out of town on a white horse. She is "a poor blacksmith's daughter" and her lover "the richest man in Stonington". In Creighton, *Maritime Fsgs*, 14, Barbara proves to be David Allen's daughter and her lover "the finest man all in New York".

Other minor, but notable, variations include the attempt of the lover to embrace Barbara, who avoids him, in some texts, by "skipping all over the room" (see SharpK, *op. cit.*, B); the basin of blood or tears by the bed (see the Michigan, Maine, Newfoundland, and other Northern versions); and the shift of person in the narration. An interesting study of the use of the first and third person in Child 84 could be started by studying Davis, *Trd Bld Va* (D); Brown, *NC Flklre* (F); and Child B. There have been a number of general remarks on textual variation in *Barbara Allen*. See Davis, *Trd Bld Va*, 302-304; C. A. Smith, *Musical Quarterly*, II, 109; W. Roy MacKenzie, *Blds Sea Sgs N Sc*, 35; *PTFS*, 47-74, where Joseph Hendren treats the history of the ballad; and the soon to be published study of versions and variants by Charles Seeger and Ed Cray.

Newell, *Games and Songs of American Children*, 78 cites *Barbara Allen* as an old New England child's game and evening party dance. He gives no text. Also see Botkin, *Am Play-Party Sg*, 58.

Cambiaire, *Ea Tenn Wstn Va Mt Blds*, 68 notes that there is a very old Spanish romance with the same theme. However, the motif is a universally popular one. See *WF*, 1949, 371 for a Serbian variation and *MWF*, 1955, 105-106 for mention of *The Lovers of the Banu Ozrah* in the Near-Eastern *The 1000 Nights and a Night*. This tale resembles *Barbara Allen* to some extent.

85. LADY ALICE

Texts: Anderson, *Coll Blds Sgs,* 44 / Barry, *Brit Blds Me,* 452 (trace) / Beard, *Personal Fsg Coll Lunsford,* 78 / Bronson, II, 392 / Brown, *NC Flklre,* II, 131 / Bull *Tenn FLS,* IV, #3, 75 / Bull *U SC* #162, #9 / Cambiaire, *Ea Tenn Wstn Va Mt Blds,* 76 / Carlisle, *Fifty Sgs Blds NW Ark,* 30 / Chappell, *Fsgs Rnke Alb,* 33 / Child, II, 279 / Combs, *Fsgs Ky Hghlds,* 8 / Cox, *Fsgs South,* 110 / Cox, *W Va School Journal and Educator,* XLVI, 124 / Crabtree, *Overton Cnty,* 125 / Davis, *Fsgs Va,* 22 / Davis, *More Trd Blds Va,* 199 / Davis, *Trd Bld Va,* 346 / Focus, III, 154; IV, 50 / Gardner and Chickering, *Blds Sgs So Mich,* 53 / Haun, *Cocke Cnty,* 71 / Henry, *Beech Mt Fsgs,* 2 / Henry, *Fsgs So Hghlds,* 89 / Henry, *Sgs Sng So Aplchns,* 47 / Hudson, *Fsgs Miss,* 107 / Hudson, *Ftunes Miss,* 7 / Hudson, *Spec Miss Flklre,* #14 / *JAF,* 1915, 151; 1919, 500; 1926, 102; 1939, 47; 1945, 75 / Morris, *Fsgs Fla,* 291 / *NC Folklore,* IV, #1 (1956), 31 / N.Y. *Times Mgz,* 11—17—'40 / Perry, *Carter Cnty,* 201 / Randolph, *Oz Fsgs,* I, 139 / Scarborough, *Sgctchr So Mts,* 117 / SharpC, *Eng Fsgs So Aplchns,* #22 / SharpK, *Eng Fsgs So Aplchns,* I, 196 / Reed Smith, *SC Blds,* 142 / *The Survey,* XXXIII, 373 / *Va FLS Bull,* #s 2—10.

Local Titles: Dame Alice Was Sitting on Widow's Walk, The Dying Hobo, George Collins (Allen, Allien, Carey, Collie, Collands, Colon, Coleman, Collum, Promer, etc.), Giles Collins, Johnny (John) Collins, John Harman, The Mournful Dove, Young Collins.

Story Types: A: Johnny Collins rides out one day and meets a sweetheart washing a white marble stone. (She is his fairy love.) She warns him of his impending death. He leaps in the water and swims homeward. Convinced that he will die that night, Collins requests to be buried by the marble stone. After he dies, his mortal true-love sees the funeral coming. She halts the procession, kisses the corpse, and trims her own shroud before dying.

Examples: Cox, *Fsgs South* (A, B); *JAF,* 1945, 75; Davis, *Trd Bld Va* (A, B).

B: Giles Collins comes home one night, is taken ill, and dies. His sweetheart, upon hearing the news, goes to his grave, opens the coffin, and kisses him. Her mother tries to be philosophical about the affair, but to no avail.

Examples: Cox, *Fsgs South,* (C, D); Davis, *Trd Bld Va* (C, D); SharpK (A).

C: The story follows that of Type B at the start. However, the girl interrupts the funeral and then joins her lover in death. The lily-north wind motif (see Child B) is often in this version.

Examples: Hudson, *Fsgs Miss* (A).

D: A lyric song rises from the stanza so often found in Lady Alice about the "snow-white dove" on "yonder pine" mourning for his love. A second stanza of the "go dig my grave wide and deep" sort completes the lyric.

Examples: Gardner and Chickering.

Discussion: Samuel P. Bayard, using Barbara M. Cra'ster's article (*JFSS* IV, 106) for leads, states (*JAF,* 1945, 73f.) convincingly that Johnny Collins as it is printed by him (p. 75. See also Cox, *Fsgs South,* A and B) represents the full form of the early European *Clerk Colvill* story infiltrated by ballad conventionality and Celtic lore. The British *Clerk Colvill* (Child

42), the *Giles Collins* versions of *Lady Alice,* and the abbreviated *Johnny Collins* version of the same song can be considered to tell only portions of the original narrative. Moreover, in modern versions of *Johnny Collins* an attempt has been made by folk-singers who have forgotten the meaning of the old story to rationalize the supernatural lover and the mortal girl who mourns Johnny's death to be one person.

The original story behind *Johnny Collins, Clerk Colvill* and *Giles Collins* "fragments" then is that of a man who renounces his fairy lover for a mortal girl, meets the fairy, and learns he is to have his life exacted as revenge for his faithlessness. (Bayard conjectures that the elf-woman has been replaced by a mermaid in *Clerk Colvill* and by "a washer at the ford" in *Johnny Collins,* the latter entering the story from Gaelic lore while the ballad existed in Ireland. Harbison Parker, *JAF,* 1947, 265f., considers incorrect a belief in either the Irish tradition of the songs or the Gaelic banshee characteristics of the supernatural lover and states convincingly (and to the satisfaction of Bayard) that a Scandanavian-Shetland-Orkney-Scottish series of locales and the accompanying selkie lore accounts for the actions of the mermaid or fairy lover and, in *Clerk Colvill,* possibly even for the title itself.) In any case, after embracing his mistress the young man swims ashore and goes home, where he is, quite naturally, apprehensive that he is about to die. He requests to be buried near the stone at the foot of the fairy hill. He then dies. His mortal lover sees the funeral, stops the procession when she learns the dead person is her lover, and states that she too will die of a broken heart. See Davis, *More Trd Blds Va,* 199-202 for a more complete summary of this scholarship.

Gardner and Chickering, *Blds Sgs So Mich,* 53 print the "dove and pine" stanza that is so frequently found at the end of the American texts of *Lady Alice* and another conventional phrase as a song (see Type D) derived from *Lady Alice.* Though these conventional "dove" phrases are of the sort that might derive from any number of sources (see *JAF,* 1926, 149 and Thomas, *Sngin Gathrn,* 34), Gardner and Chickering put forth a fairly convincing defense of their stand. The "dove" stanza does appear in Child 85 in West Virginia (Cox, *Fsgs South*), Virginia (Davis, *Trd Bld Va*), Mississippi (Hudson, *Fsgs Miss*), North Carolina (Henry, *Sgs Sng So Aplchns*), etc. as well as in the *JAF,* 1926, 104 and 1915, 152 texts. See Gardner and Chickering, *op. cit.,* for other references.

Types A and B are the usual American forms of the story, while Type C follows the Child A, B story closely and utilizes the conventional ending of B. See also Child, III, 515.

There are many parodies of the song, and one version, *Giles Scroggins,* was a great favorite in early nineteenth century America. See Davis, *op. cit.,* 352; Randolph, *Oz Fsgs,* I, 140; *Heart Songs,* 246; *The New England Pocket Songster* (Woodstock, Vt.); *The Singer's Own Book* (Woodstock, Vt., 1838); *The Songster's Companion* (Brattleborough, Vt. 1815); The Isaiah Thomas Collection in Worcester, Mass., #95; and Worthington Ford, *Broadside Blds, etc. Mass.* #3126.

The Randolph, *op. cit.*, I version, though called *George Collins* and containing the "dove" stanzas like so many of the Type B stories, seems to be closer to *Johnny Collins* in narrative.

86. YOUNG BENJIE

Barry, *Brit Blds Me*, 453 reports that a Maine woman recognized this ballad as one she had heard in her childhood in Ireland.

87. PRINCE ROBERT

Texts: Barry, *Brit Blds Me*, 453 (trace) / Combs, *Fsg États-Unis*, 138.
Local Titles: Harry Saunders.

Story Types: A: A man marries against his mother's wishes. Leaving his bride at his new home, he returns to visit his mother. She poisons him. His wife, when he does not return, rides to the mother's home and interrupts the funeral. She requests her husband's watch and chain, but is perfectly willing to forfeit his money and land. The mother refuses to grant the request, and the girl falls to kissing the corpse. She collapses and dies of a broken heart.

Examples: Combs.

Discussion: The Kentucky text, although the ring is replaced by the watch and chain and the poisoned wine by tea, is similar to the Child texts in story. However, the rose-briar motif, found in Child A and B, is absent.

Barry, *Brit Blds Me*, 454 notes that a Maine woman recognized the song as one she heard in her youth in Ireland.

88. YOUNG JOHNSTONE

Texts: Bronson, II, 411 / MacKenzie, *Blds Sea Sgs N Sc*, 41.
Local Titles: Johnson and Coldwell, Johnson and the Colonel.

Story Types: A: Johnson kills the Colonel after the latter has made slurring remarks about Johnson's sister. He then flees to this sister's house, but when she says that he will surely be hanged in the morning he rides off to the home of his true-love, the Colonel's sister. His sweetheart hides him. When the King's guards come after Johnson and describe him, his hawks, and his hounds to the girl, she tells them that he passed the house earlier. After they hasten off, she goes to tell Johnson of her service, startles the sleeping man, and is stabbed. He immediately regrets his rash and unplanned act and promises her the best doctors. However, she dies, nobly.

Examples: MacKenzie (A).

B: The story is the same as that of Type A. However, Johnson goes in sequence to his mother, sister, and sweetheart. Each asks him where he has been. To each he replies "at the state house teaching young Clark to write". Each then tells him of a bloody dream she has had, and he is forced to confess the crime.

Examples: MacKenzie (B).

Discussion: MacKenzie, *Blds Sea Sgs N Sc,* 41 states that he cannot account for the variations that occur in his A text, although he points out that in the absence of the dream and of the description of the hawk it resembles Child C. Type B is like Child D.

Johnson's reply to the girl, when she asks him where he has been ("the young Clark to write" line) is also discussed by MacKenzie.

Flanders, *Ancient Blds,* II, 293 includes a text of Child 88 from the pages of the *Charms of Melody,* a book of songs that was known in New England, but was printed in Dublin by J. & J. Carrick. This text, entitled *The Cruel Knight,* is close to Child A.

90. JELLON GRAME

Texts: Davis, *Fsgs Va,* 24 / Davis, *More Trd Blds Va,* 207 / *SFQ,* 1958, 170 / Worthington, *Nine Rare Trd Blds Va,* 89.

Local Titles: Jellon Grame.

Story Types: A: Before dawn, Jellon Grame sends a servant boy to his love, Rosy Flower, to tell her to meet him in the green woods. She hurries off, eventually coming to a new grave by an oak. Jellon appears and tells her she must die, for he fears her father will hang him when he learns Rosy is pregnant. She pleads for her life, but he stabs her anyway. However, he rescues her child from "her blood" and raises it as his sister's son. One day, while Jellon and his son are hunting, the boy asks why his "mammy" keeps him in the woods all the time. Jellon tells him he killed his real mother and that she is buried near-by. The boy then shoots his father with an arrow.

Examples: Davis, *More Trd Blds Va.*

Discussion: This unique version from Virginia is related to Child A, omitting the references the girl makes to the child in her womb and the fact that Jellon used nine nurses to help him raise the boy. Arthur K. Davis and Paul C. Worthington discuss Child A; the Gavin Greig, *Last Leaves of Traditional Ballads* (Aberdeen, 1925) text; and the Virginia text in great detail in Davis, *More Trd Blds Va,* 207-211; in *SFQ,* 1958, 163-172; and in Worthington, *Nine Rare Trd Blds Va,* 89-104.

92. BONNY BEE HOM

SharpK, *Eng Fsgs So Aplchns,* I, 200 refers his readers to this ballad in connection with his version of *The Lowlands of Holland.* See also Combs, *Fsgs États-Unis,* 173 and Gray, *Sgs Blds Me Lmbrjks,* 88. Also, check Child, II, 317 (headnote) where similarities of certain stanzas in the two songs are noted and Bronson, II, 418.

93. LAMKIN

Texts: Barry, *Brit Blds Me,* 200 / Beck, *Flklre Me,* 91 / Beck, *Down-East Blds Fsgs,* 32 / Brewster, *Blds Sgs Ind,* 122 / Bronson, II, 428 / Brown, *NC Flklre,* II, 140 / Bull *Tenn FLS,* VIII, #3, 75 / Chappell, *Fsgs Rnke Alb,* 76 / Child, III, 515; V, 295 / Creighton, *Maritime Fsgs,* 20 / Davis, *Fsgs Va,* 24 / Davis, *More Trd Blds Va,* 214 / Davis, *Trd Bld Va,* 354 / Eddy, *Blds Sgs Ohio,* 59 / Flanders, *Ancient Blds,* II, 296 / Flanders, *Blds Migrant NE,* 104

/ Gardner and Chickering, *Blds Sgs So Mich,* 313 / Marion H. Gray, *The Flight of the Ballad,* Woman's Dept. Club Ballad, Terre Haute, Pt. 3, 4-10-'30, 4 / Henry, *Beech Mt Fsgs,* 20 / Henry, *Fsgs So Hghlds,* 91 / Henry, *Sgs Sng So Aplchns,* 62 / Hubbard, *Blds Sgs Utah,* 23 / Jones, *Flklre Mich,* 5 / *JAF,* 1900, 117; 1916, 162; 1922, 344; 1931, 61; 1935, 316; 1939, 70; 1957, 330 / Karpeles, *Fsgs Newfdld,* 17 / Leach, *Fsgs Labr Cst* / Linscott, *Fsgs Old NE,* 303 / E. H. McClure, *McClures and Mayers* (private), Detroit, '42, 3 / *N.J. Journal Educ.,* XIX, #1, 9 / Perry, *Carter Cnty,* 205 / Randolph, *Oz Fsgs,* I, 141 / SharpC, *Eng Fsgs So Aplchns,* #23 / SharpK, *Eng Fsgs So Aplchns,* I, 201 / *SFQ,* 1941, 137 / *Va FLS Bull,* #s, 3, 9.

Local Titles: Boab King, Bolakin, Beau (Bo, Bow) Lamkin(s), Bold Lantern (Dunkins, Hamkins), (The) False Lambkin, False Linfinn, Lamford, Lamkin (the Mason), Lampkin, Squire Relantman, Tumkin, Ward Lampkin, Young Alanthia.

Story Types: A: Lamkin, a mason, does some work for a lord and is not paid. The lord, leaving home for a time, fears trouble. He orders his house sealed to protect his family. Lamkin, seeking revenge, gets in through some opening left by accident or with the assistance of a nurse. Most of the servants are away. At the nurse's advice, he hurts the baby in order to get the mother downstairs. When the lady of the house comes, Lamkin seizes her. She offers him gold and even her daughter in marriage to save her own life. But Lamkin scorns these bribes and gloats over his plan to murder her. He makes the nurse or the servants clean a silver basin to hold the lady's blood. The lord returns to find the house red with gore and only his daughter, who was warned by the mother to stay hidden, surviving. Lamkin is hung or burned, and the nurse, burned or hung.

Examples: Davis, *Trd Bld Va* (A); Linscott; SharpK (B).

B: The story is the same as that of Type A, but Lamkin, when not paid, builds a false window in the house. He enters through this window to commit the crimes.

Examples: Gardner and Chickering (A); *JAF,* 1939, 70; Randolph.

C: The story is abbreviated so that only the baby is slain, and it is his blood that is caught in the silver bowl.

Examples: *JAF,* 1900, 117.

D: The story is the same as that of Type A, except that it is suggested that there was a love affair between Lamkin and the lady before the marriage. Thus, Lamkin had sworn revenge on the lord for winning his girl. Lamkin gets in by persuading the nurse the baby is crying, and the nurse becomes innocently suspected and punished.

Examples: Davis, *Trd Bld Va* (B).

Discussion: The American story is similar in basic outline to the Child B, C, F group (see Child, II, 320—1), although certain differences should be noted. The offer of the daughter's hand as a bribe, and the large role given the daughter (Child F, T, X) are common in America. The false window built by the mason (Child E) can also be found with some frequency (Type B), while the catching of the baby's blood in the bowl (Type C) seems to occur as a result of combined story degeneration and reconstruction. The Type D text does not appear much different from the usual Type A story. However, Davis, *Trd Bld Va,* 357 (headnote) makes clear that the singer believed that there had been a love affair between the lady and the mason, although this conception is not consistent with the normal opening line, "Why need I reward Lampkin?" The idea that the daughter, Betsy, is away at school and has to be sent for was also added as a footnote by the singer of this version. See Barry, *Brit Blds Me,* 204 for a textual study of seven American and British variants of the Child F version. Note also Karpeles, *Fsgs Newfdld,* 17, where the baby is named Sir Johnson.

Three American texts are worth particular attention. The Flanders, *Ancient Blds* (G) version is called Tumkin, supposedly meaning Tom King, who is called a companion of Dick Turpin by the informant. The fragment is confused, involving Will Turpin and an anecdote about Will's feeding his male horse, Black Bess, through a window. The Gardner and Chickering, *Blds Sgs So Mich,* 315, B version never gets as far as the murder or the hanging of Lamkin, and, although certainly not complete, is unusual as the most dramatically active portion is the forgotten portion. The Chappell, *Fsgs Rnke Alb,* 76 text contains a splice between the "spare me" lines of the lady and some love song on the general theme of the opening scene of *Young Hunting* (Child 68). The seven resultant stanzas are pointless.

Fannie Eckstrom (*JAF,* 1939, 74) offers Phillips Barry's explanation of the source of this song by means of the *False Linfinn* title. In Irish folklore, a leper (called "white" man) could be cured by the blood of an innocent person collected in a silver bowl. Barry feels that the Irish mason, who was reputed to use human blood in the mixing of his cement, was rationalized into the ballad after the fear of lepers had vanished.

For a discussion of the change in names from Bold Lamkin to Boab King, see Henry, *Fsgs So Hghlds,* 91.

Anne Gilchrist's classic, *Lambkin: A Study in Evolution* (*JEFDSS,* I, 1-17) deals with British tradition for the most part. See Davis, *More Trd Blds Va,* 215 for a summary of the Gilchrist study and for general remarks on the ballad.

95. THE MAID FREED FROM THE GALLOWS

Texts: The Alumni Bulletin (U. of Va., 1912) / *American Speech,* I, 247 / Anderson, *Coll Blds Sgs,* 48 / Arnold, *Fsgs Ala,* 68 / Barry, *Brit Blds Me,* 206, 381 / Beard, *Personal Fsg Coll Lunsford,* 82 / Belden, *Mo Fsgs,* 66 / *Boletin Latino Americano de Musica,* V, 281 / Botkin, *Treasury Am Flklre,* 822 / Bronson, II, 448 / Brown, *NC Flklre,* II, 143 / *Bull Tenn FLS,* #3, 95 / *Bull U SC,* #162, #10 / Cambiaire, *Ea Tenn Wstn Va Mt Blds,* 15 / Chappell, *Fsgs Rnke Alb,* 35 / Child, V, 296 / Cox, *Fsgs South,* 115 / Cox, *Trd Blds W Va,* 29 / Cox, *W Va School Journal and Educator,* XLV, 297 / Davis, *Fsgs Va,* 24 / Davis, *More Trd Blds Va,* 221 / Davis, *Trd Bld Va,* 360 / Downes and Siegmeister, *Treasury Am Sg,* 44 / Duncan, *No Hamilton Cnty,* 77 / Eddy, *Blds Sgs Ohio,* 62 / Flanders, *Ancient Blds,* III, 15 / Flanders, *New Gn Mt Sgstr,* 118 / Fuson, *Blds Ky Hghlds,* 113 / Gardner and Chickering, *Blds Sgs So Mich,* 146 / Grapurchat, East Radford (Va.) State Teachers College, 8-25-'32 / Haun, *Cocke Cnty,* 99 / Henry, *Beech Mt Fsgs,* 18 / Henry, *Fsgs So Hghlds,* 96 / Hudson, *Fsgs Miss,*

111 / Hudson, *Ftunes Miss*, 19 / Hudson, *Spec Miss Flklre*, #15 / Hummel, *Oz Fsgs* / Jeckyll, *Jamcn Sg Stry*, 58 / *JAF*, 1906, 22; 1908, 56; 1913, 175; 1914, 64; 1917, 319; 1926, 105; 1929, 272; 1935, 312; 1943, 242 / *JFSS*, V, 231 / *Ky Folklore Record*, 1960, 127 / Kittredge, *Child Blds* (Cambridge Ed.), xxv / Kolb, *Treasury Fsgs*, 16 / Lomax and Lomax, *Cowboy Sgs Frntr Blds*, 159 (another song) / Mason, *Cannon Cnty*, 20 / McDowell, *Memory Mel*, 21 / Morris, *Fsgs Fla*, 295 / *Musical Quarterly*, II, 114f. / *NJ Journal of Education*, XV, #6, #7 / Owens, *Studies Tex Fsgs*, 26 / Owens, *Texas Fsgs*, 45 / *Ozark Life*, VI, #2 / Parsons, *Ftales Andros Is*, 152 / Parsons, *Flklre Sea Is*, 189 / Perry, *Carter Cnty*, 154, 304 / *PMLA*, XXXIX, 475 / Randolph, *Oz Fsgs*, I, 143 / Ritchie, *Sgng Family*, 152 / Sandburg, *Am Sgbag*, 72 / Saxon, Dreyer, Tallant, *Gumbo Ya-Ya*, 444 / Scarborough, *On Trail Negro Fsgs*, 35f. / Scarborough, *Sgctchr So Mts*, 196 / SharpC, *Eng Fsgs So Aplchns*, #24 / SharpK, *Eng Fsgs So Aplchns*, I, 208 / Reed Smith, *SC Blds*, 144 (see Chapter VIII also) / Smith and Rufty, *Am Anth Old Wrld Blds*, 37 / *SFQ*, 1938, 71 / *Speculum*, XVI, #2, 236 / Thomas, *Devil's Ditties*, 164 / Thompson, *Bdy Bts Brtchs*, 397 / *Va FLS Bull*, #s 2-6, 8-10 / Wells, *Bld Tree*, 115 / *W Va Folklore*, V, #2 (1955), 24 / Wyman and Brockway, *Lnsme Tunes*, 44.

Local Titles: By a Lover Saved, Down By the Green Willow, The Gallant Tree, The Gallis Pole, The (Dreary) Gallows Tree, The Golden Ball, Hang Me Hang Me on That Tree, The Hangman (Hangerman, Hangsman), Hangman Hold Your Rope, The Hangman's Son, The Hangman's Song, The Hangman's Tree, Highway Man, Hold Your Hands Old Man, Lord James, The Maid (Girl) Freed from the Gallows, The Miller's Daughter, My Father Oh No, The Scarlet Tree, The Sycamore Tree, True Love, The True Love Freed from the Gallows, Under the Creep-O Mellow Tree, The Weep-O Mellow Tree.

Story Types: A: A girl, at the gallows, is about to be hung. She requests the hangman to stop the proceedings as she sees a member of the family (usually the father) coming. She asks her father if he has gold or fee, etc. to set her free. He says he has not; he has come to see her hung. This sequence of questions and answers goes on through the girl's relations (usually mother, brother, sister; sometimes, uncle, grandmother, cousin, etc.) until the sweetheart comes and replies that he has brought the fee to free her. In a few texts he has a knife to cut the rope.

Examples: Barry (I); Davis, *Trd Bld Va* (A); Smith (A).

B: The sequence of events is similar to that of Type A, but an offense of which the girl is guilty is hinted at. This usually connects with golden ball-virginity legend.

Examples: Barry (II); Davis, *Trd Bld Va* (K); SharpK (B).

C: The usual story is told, but the sex of the prisoner is male.

Examples: Belden; Davis, *Trd Bld Va* (E); Randolph (D).

D: Dr. Maurice Gallagher formerly of the Romance Language Department at the University of Pennsylvania recalled having heard a text sung in Texas in 1916 in which a man waited in vain for the usual rescue and was eventually hung.

No examples.

E: The story is the same as that of Type A, except the fate of the girl is uncertain and there is a touching plea to the lover in the last four lines.

Examples: Eddy (A).

F: There are a few texts of badman ballads which utilize the *Maid Freed from the Gallows* motif. Usually a few stanzas of blues clichés are present. In one text the man sees his sweetheart through a train window. He shoots her and is sentenced to hang. The story is garbled, but the rescue by the sweetheart comes in the normal fashion.

Examples: Hudson, *Fsgs Miss* (D); Henry, *Fsgs So Hghlds* (E); Davis, *More Trd Blds Va* (DD).

G: This type contains stanzas directed by the girl at the Saviour, who does not answer, complaining that her golden lands will be taken when she is in Eternity and that no one loves her. The true-love, Edward, appears. She says, and he repeats, that he has no gold; nevertheless, he loves her and will set her free. The lovers then forgive the parents, but hope the brother is hung.

Examples: Haun.

Discussion: There are detailed discussions of the history of this ballad in Reed Smith, *SC Blds,* Chapter VIII and in Scarborough, *On Trail Negre Fsg,* 35f. Consult also Erich Pohl's monograph in *FFC* #105, 1-265 and Iivar Kemppinen, *Lunastettava neito. Vertaileva balladitutkinus* (Helsinki, 1959). Child, II, 346f. and Sager, *Mod Phil,* XXVII, 129f. discuss the whole European tradition and the German parallels respectively—Child, II, 346 expressing the opinion that the English versions are all "defective and distorted". See Child, IV, 482 for further references, Also consult *NYFQ,* 1946, 139 for an Italian version beginning "Sailors do not drown me" and *SFQ,* 1941, 25 for a discussion of a Rumanian analogue; and Brewster, *Blds Sgs Ind,* 125 for a Hungarian text.

In Europe the song invariably centers about some variation of a theme concerning a girl's capture by corsairs or a hero's imprisonment. In Britain and America the antecedent action, if mentioned at all, ties up with a crime —the conventional loss of a golden ball, key, or comb, possibly representing virginity. See Broadwood, *JFSS,* V, 231; Kittredge, *JAF,* 1917, 319; Scarborough, *op. cit.,* 38. Belden, *Mo Fsgs,* 66 notes this song's importance in the study of ballad origins. Many of the forces of variation have worked on it, although its incremental repetition (see Kittredge's edition of *Child's Ballads,* xxv) has served to keep the framework intact.

The American story types, usually with a hangman (Child G) instead of a judge, are large in number, although the structure of the song has remained amazingly constant. Type A tells the usual British story, and Type B seems to illustrate the manner in which a ballad can contact popular tale (see Child G, H). The Type C "sex reversal" is most likely a sentimental mitigation of the tragedy. If so, in Duncan, *No Hamilton Cnty,* B this change in mood is carried one step farther. There the mother rescues her son, because mother love is stronger than "sweetheart love". See Duncan, *op. cit.,* 76. Such "sex reversals" are the rule in the Slavic countries and in America occur most often in the South. Type D does not follow the tradition of the story and in its failure to reverse the progression possesses a dramatically weak conclusion, while Type E (which could result in Type D if reconstructed by the folk) is simply incomplete. The Type F degeneration ally themselves with the Lomax, *Cowboy Sgs Frntr Blds,* text which is a curious adaptation of *The Maid Freed from the Gallows* motif to the life of the West called *Bow Down Your Head and Cry.* Type F is discussed in some detail by Barry and Henry in the latter's *Fsgs So Hghlds,* and by Davis in *More Trd Blds Va,* 223-224. Davis gives a good bibliography to Type F texts. Type G, which allies itself with the Scottish Child I text in the lack of gold and the curse on the brother, is treated at length by Haun in *Cocke Cnty,* 31. The Thompson, *Bdy Bts Brtchs,* 397 text shows some affinities with this story type. The Arnold, *Fsgs Ala,* 68 text, called *The Miller's Daughter,* is interesting in that the "hangman stanza" has but three lines. There is also a song called *The Streets of Derry* or *James Derry* (listed by Barry, *Brit Blds Me,* 389-393 as a derivative of Child 95) that may be connected to the Irish uprisings of 1798. It is an excellent ballad.

The story itself has taken a number of forms in America. It is, particularly with negroes, popular as a drama (Davis, *Trd Bld Va,* 361; Scarborough, *op. cit.,* 39; Reed Smith, *op. cit.,* 85f.) and is also found as a children's game (Davis, *op. cit.,* 361; *JAF,* 1917, 319; Botkin, *Am Play Party Sg,* 62; Smith, *op. cit.,* 88f. See also Child F). It exists as a prose tale in the United States and West Indies and upon occasion has been developed as a cante-fable. (See Smith, *op. cit.,* Chapter VIII). These stories vary widely. Parsons, *Ftales Andros Is,* 152 prints a cante-fable where a girl goes away to school, falls in love against her stepmother's wish, is falsely accused of theft, and is sentenced to hang. Beckwith, *PMLA,* XXXIX, 475 prints a Jamaica version in which an engaged princess breaks a family rule and is to be hung. Her future husband comes with a great chariot, smashes the gallows, and rescues her. (For more Jamaican texts, see Jeckyll, *Jamcn Sg Stry,* 58 f.) And Mary Owen, *Voodoo Tales,* 185 f. found the song material used as a part of a Missouri story of a negro girl with a magic golden ball that made her white. Barry, *Brit Blds Me,* 210—3 disputes the idea that the cante-fable and game stages are the last steps in the song's deterioration, and Russell Ames (*JAF,* 1943, 242) discusses Leadbelly's version which the latter developed from cante-fables.

Barry, *op. cit.,* 389 f. prints three secondary versions of this song from Maine. Hudson, *Fsgs Miss,* 113 maintains his E version, which contains a borrowed stanza at the end, to be a parody. The text is fragmentary, however.

For studies relating this ballad to Negro songs, see Reed Smith, *SC Blds,* Chapter VIII and *Musical Quarterly,* II, 114f.

96. THE GAY GOSHAWK

Texts: Child, II, 365 / Child Ms. / Flanders, *Ancient Blds,* III, 43 / *JAF,* 1951, 130.

Local Titles: None.

Story Types: A: The informant could recall only the opening stanza, but could summarize the story as follows. The lover, who was French, went "up to England. They took her up there in a coffin. They were to stop at the first kirk to get her across the border. There was to be a second stop. The third stop was to be their destination."

Examples: Flanders, *Ancient Blds.*

Discussion: The Flanders text from Vermont is unusual, if the informant is recalling the ballad accurately. The stanza he knew is the first stanza of Child A, but the Child texts tell of a girl "going up to Scotland" to meet a Scottish lover. In them the procession stops three times before arriving at the final kirk. Child's texts retain the basic motif of the story—that is the trick the lovers play on the girl's family by means of the mock funeral. Type A seems to have omitted this deception.

The fragment that Child prints as his F version was collected in Iowa from an Irishwoman. It is four stanzas long, and three of the stanzas deal with the witch's "boiling lead" which is to be dropped on the girl to help her feign death. The other stanza concerns her hunger upon her arrival. See also Child B. This is the text that Reed Smith was citing in his list of American survivals of Child ballads in *SFQ,* 1937, #2, 9-11. See Branford Millar's remarks on this text in *SFQ,* 1954, 159-160.

99. JOHNIE SCOT

Texts: Barry, *Brit Blds Me,* 213 / Bronson, II, 484 / Creighton, *Maritime Fsgs,* 15 / Flanders, *Ancient Blds,* III, 45 / Flanders, *Blds Migrant NE,* 101 / *Green Mountain Songster,* 41 / Haun, *Cocke Cnty,* 109 / Henry, *Fsgs So Hghlds,* 100 / *JAF,* 1929, 273 / Kennedy, *Effects Isolation,* 321 / SharpC, *Eng Fsgs So Aplchns,* #25 / SharpK, *Eng Fsgs So Aplchns,* I, 215 / Wilson, *Bckwds Am,* 94.

Local Titles: Johnie Scot, Johnny Scots.

Story Types: A: Johnie Scot, out hunting or in service at the English court, gets a princess or noble lady with child. He returns to the North, but she is locked up by her father. After he writes and asks her to join him (sometimes this is omitted), she requests or the King summons him to come to England. He sets out to rescue the girl. As Johnie approaches the castle he sees his love looking out. At the court, the King scorns the force that has accompanied Johnie from his home and sentences them to hang. Johnie, however, prefers to fight, and the King brings forth an Italian champion to duel Johnie. The Italian is slain, and the King is so impressed that he frees the girl and gives his permission for the marriage. In some texts Johnie returns to Scotland, not only married, but as King.

Examples: Barry (A, B); Haun; *JAF,* 1929, 273.

B: The story, if garbled, is like that of Type A, except that Johnie attacks the King (in this case Henry) and kills him along with his guards. He then takes the girl home with him.

Examples: SharpK (B).

Dicussion: The Type A versions are generally similar to those in Child, but the SharpK, *Eng Fsgs So Aplchns,* B, Type B text seems to be unique.

The SharpK, *op. cit.*, C text may be of the same sort, however, although it is too incomplete to tell. The idea that King Henry flees, found in some versions, is American.

Barry, *Brit Blds Me,* 222 f. breaks the Type A texts into two main divisions according to the minor details of the story, and he also notes that the Maine *Lord of Salvary* (B) is the result of contact with a similar Breton ballad, *Les Aubrays.* See also Child, II, 378.

The document of Rev. Andrew Hall (*Interesting Roman Antiquities,* etc., 1823, p. 216) which Child quotes, II, 378 and SharpK, *op. cit.,* requotes, 418, reveals a story of the court of Charles II where a Scot, James Macgill, fought a professional Italian gladiator who leaped over him as if to "swallow him" and was "spitted" in mid-air. "Italian" becomes "taveren", "taillant", and the verb "swallow", a bird.

The *Green Mountain Songster* text lacks mention of the Italian, a feature also missing in Child Q and R. See Flanders, *Ancient Blds,* III, 46.

100. WILLIE O WINSBURY

Texts: Barry, *Brit Blds Me,* 224 / Bronson, II, 495 / *BFSSNE,* IX, 6 / Combs, *Fsgs États-Unis,* 140 / Flanders, *Ancient Blds,* III, 57 / Flanders, *Blds Migrant NE,* 233 / Greenleaf and Mansfield, *Blds Sea Sgs Newfdld,* 28 / Karpeles, *Fsgs Newfdld,* 25 / Leach, *Fsgs Labr Cst.*

Local Titles: Fair Mary, John(ny) Barbour, Young Barbour.

Story Types: A: A girl is observed to be ailing by her father, the King. He suspects correctly that she is with child, although she denies it at first. The King wishes to know the man's rank, and, upon learning the lover is one of his Spanish servingmen or one of his seven sea boys, he orders the lad to be hung. The girl pleads for her lover. The lover, when brought before the King, so impresses the latter with his physical beauty that he is forgiven and offered gold, land and the girl's hand in marriage. He accepts the girl, but refuses the material wealth as he is rich himself.

Examples: Greenleaf and Mansfield (A, B);
Flanders, *Ancient Blds* (A).

Discussion: The ballad, which is quite popular in Newfoundland, enjoys limited currency in the United States. The texts in Flanders, *Ancient Blds,* III, 57 f. are unique to the States, excepting an incomplete West Virginia version which ends with the girl pleading for her lover and the questionable fragment Barry identified in his B version of Johnie Scot (99).

Both the Newfoundland and American versions follow the Child story. See Child, II, 398. Flanders, *Ancient Blds* (C¹, C²) follow Child D from the Percy Papers.

101. WILLIE O DOUGLAS DALE

Barry, *Brit Blds Me,* 454 notes that a Maine woman recognized the whole song but could not repeat any of it.

102. WILLIE AND EARL RICHARD'S DAUGHTER

Texts: Bronson, II, 509 / *JAF*, 1956, 34.

Local Titles: The Birth of Robin Hood.

Story Types: A: The Earl of Huntington's daughter is pregnant by the Earl's steward, Archibald. When she is about to give birth, the couple go off to the woods, where the lover offers to serve as mid-wife. She refuses to allow this and sends him out to slay a "nice, fat doe" while she bears the child. He kills a deer and brings it back. When he has returned he learns she has borne a child, but died. He mourns and wonders how to nurse the child. At this point, the Earl and the two men approach. Archibald flees. The Earl discovers his dead daughter and the child. He carries the child off, threatening to hang the father if he can catch him. The daughter is buried and the child is christened Robin Hood.

Examples: *JAF*, 1956, 34.

Discussion: This text, which is unique to the New World, is very close to Child B and was probably learned from Kittredge's edition of the Child ballads. The variations from Child B are minor, but interesting. John Greenway, who collected the text from Aunt Molly Jackson, discusses these changes in some detail in *JAF*, 1956, 32-36. The most important variation involves Aunt Molly's failure to see the symbolism of the "white hind". In her text, Archibald simply goes out to find a "nice, fat doe", and the fact that the animal is the spirit of his love is unrecognized.

Aunt Molly also composed two ballads on Robin Hood's life. One borrows its early framework from Child 149 (*Robin Hood's Birth, Breeding, Valor, and Marriage*) and tells again the tale of Robin Hood's birth. The other accounts for Archibald, who is found old and withered in a log cabin by his son, Robin Hood. This song concludes with a sentimental reunion. Greenway discusses both these texts on pp. 36-37 of the *JAF* article.

105. THE BAILIFF'S DAUGHTER OF ISLINGTON

Texts: Barry, *Brit Blds Me*, 225 / Belden, *Mo Fsgs*, 68 / Bronson, II, 515 / Crabtree, *Overton Cnty*, 307 / Creighton and Senior, *Trd Sgs N Sc*, 58 / Davis, *Fsgs Va*, 24 / Davis, *Trd Bld Va*, 383 / Flanders, *Ancient Blds*, III, 67 / Flanders, *Cntry Sgs Vt*, 6 / Flanders, *Garl Gn Mt Sg*, 74 / Flanders, *New Gn Mt Sgstr*, 74 / *Focus*, V, 280 / Greenleaf and Mansfield, *Blds Sea Sgs Newfdld*, 34 / Hudson, *Fsgs Miss*, 114 / Hudson, *Ftunes Miss*, 4 / Hudson, *Spec Miss Flklre*, #16 / *JAF*, 1917, 322; 1926, 106; 1939, 54 / Linscott, *Fsgs Old NE*, 160 / Morris, *Fsgs Fla*, 300 / SharpK, *Eng Fsgs So Aplchns*, I, 219 / Shearin and Combs, *Ky Syllabus*, 8 / *SFQ*, 1944, 155 / *Va FLS Bull*, #4.

Local Titles: The Bailiff's Daughter, The Bailiff's Daughter of Islington (Ireland Town), The Bailor's Daughter, The Bellyan's Daughter, The Comely Youth, There Was a Youth, True Love Requited.

Story Types: A: A loving youth and the very coy bailiff's daughter have been parted for seven years. She had scorned him because she did not feel he really loved her, and his family had sent him away from "his fond and foolish pride". Sometimes, she has been locked up, also. The girl, however, disguises herself in rags, slips off, and goes in quest of her lover. She meets him along the way. When he asks if she knows the bailiff's daughter in her town, she replies that the girl has been dead for a long while. He then says he will go away to a far-off land. On hearing this she reveals her identity and promises to marry him. Sometimes the marriage is included.

Examples: Barry; Davis, *Trd Bld Va* (A); SharpK (A).

B: The story outline is the same as that of Type A, but the girl does not disguise herself as a beggar. Rather, she dresses in fine silk and asks for a kiss instead of a penny. The lad buys the girl jewels, and they have a merry wedding.   Examples: Hudson, *Fsgs Miss.*

Discussion: The Type A stories are similar to Child, but shorter. They derive from print and are generally quite stable. Type B, however, seems to reveal a rather undramatic change that has taken place in the original narrative. However, see Alfred Williams, *Fsgs Upper Thames,* 174, (head-note).

There is a discussion of the stability and scope of this ballad in America in Flanders, *New Gn Mt Sgstr,* 63. For two unique stanzas see this article. Also see Flanders, *Ancient Blds* (B). Morris, *SFQ,* 1944, 155, remarks on some intrusions of "Cracker" language into the ballad.

It is hard to understand why Child included this ballad of separated lovers and mistaken identity in his collection, while omitting other broadside songs much like it. The motif of #105 has been used and re-used by printers for many, many years. There are a number of analogues to Child 105 in circulation here and abroad. See W. Splettstosser, *Der heimkehrende Gatte und sein Weib* (Berlin, 1899). Also note Warren Roberts' discussion of similar ballad themes in Thomas Heywood's *The Fair Maid of the West* in *JAF,* 1955, 19-23. Laws, *Am Bldry Brit Bdsdes,* 224 (N 42) gives a bibliography to *A Pretty Fair Maid,* a similar and common American ballad.

106. THE FAMOUS FLOWER OF SERVING-MEN

Texts: Barry, *Brit Blds Me,* 227 / *The Blackbird Songster* (Cozzans, N.Y., c. 1845) / Bronson, II, 530 / Creighton and Senior, *Trd Sgs N Sc,* 62 / Flanders, *Ancient Blds,* III, 106 / Flanders, *Blds Migrant NE,* 127.

Local Titles: The Famous Flower and her Serving Man, Sweet William.

Story Types: A: A noble girl marries a knight who builds her a home. The place is attacked by robbers (sent by the stepmother); the knight, slain; the others, routed. The girl escapes, dresses herself as a man, and goes to the King's court where she becomes a chamberlain. One day, when the King is out hunting, she takes a harp and sings her own true story to an old man. He later tells the tale to the King, who then marries the girl and rewards the old man.   Examples: Barry.

Discussion: This song survives only in the Northeastern portions of the New World. Its survival in this region may be due to its inclusion in *The Blackbird Songster* (N.Y., c. 1845) and other anthologies. Barry, *Brit Blds Me,* 230 reprints the "Blackbird" version, and it is clear that it is close to the fragment sent to Percy in 1776 by the Dean of Derry (see Child, II,

429). In it, the stepmother, rather than the mother, is the villain. The Barry texts, the Creighton text, and the Flanders texts (B-D²) are close to this version. Flanders A, which is from print, is close to Child A.

110. THE KNIGHT AND THE SHEPHERD'S DAUGHTER

Texts: Bronson, II, 535 / Brown, *NC Flklre*, II, 149 / *BFSSNE*, IX, 7 / Greenleaf and Mansfield, *Blds Sea Sgs Newfdld*, 35 / *JAF*, 1909, 377.

Local Titles: Sweet Willie, The Knight and the Shepherd's Daughter.

Story Types: A: A knight gets drunk and seduces a country girl. She asks his name so that she can call her baby after him. He replies that it is William, of the court, and rides away. She follows on foot. When she reaches the court, she tells the King her story, and he replies that if the man is married he shall hang; if single, shall be married to her. William is called down and bewails the revelry that has caused him to be forced into a marriage that is below him. Nevertheless, the ceremony is performed. The girl turns out to be a duke's daughter; William, a blacksmith's son.

Examples: Greenleaf and Mansfield.

B: The story is the same as that of Type A, but the bribe is retained: that is, the knight offers the girl £ 500 to maintain her child, if she will forget the marriage.   Examples: *BFSSNE*, IX, 7.

Discussion: The Newfoundland version (Type A) is close to the usual Child story, although the seduction is nearer rape as in Child E, the attempts to buy off the girl are left out, and the end is made even more dramatic in the knight's being a blacksmith's (Child K), not at least a squire's, son. The Brown, *NC Flklre* text is generally similar to the other Type A versions, although the knight is now a soldier, some of the details such as the reason for requesting the man's name, the King's decree for the married and single man, etc. are left out. In this text, the girl also indicates that she has a local suitor, and, while her rank is revealed to be that of a princess in the end, her lover's rank does not change.

Type B retains the bribe, and in the text cited above the revelation of the girl's being a princess comes in direct contradiction of the opening line's "shepherd's daughter".

Creighton's *Maritime Fsgs* text follows Type A, although the ending is abbreviated so that the reluctant knight rides off with the girl unaware she is as well-born as he. The text could well develop into a moral and relatively unhappy story type before long.

See the discussion of European analogues entitled *"Handjeris and Lioyenneti"* and *Child 76 and 110* in *FFC,* #183, 3-17.

112. THE BAFFLED KNIGHT

Texts: Barry, *Brit Blds Me,* 454 (trace) / *BFSSNE,* XII, 12 / Creighton and Senior, *Trd Sgs N Sc,* 63 / Flanders, *Ancient Blds,* III, 89 / *Green Mountain Songster,* 51 / *Ky Folklore Record,* 1957, 91.

Local Titles: Blow Ye Winds in the Morning, The Shepherd's Son.

Story Types: A: A man out walking meets a pretty girl and asks her

where she is going. She smiles and flees. He chases and catches her with the remark "pretty maid, now let us understand".
Examples: *BFSSNE,* XII, 12; *Ky Folklore Record,* 1957, 91.

B: The shepherd's son discovers a girl swimming in a brook, and, although he says he will not take her clothes, he swears to have his will of her. They mount horses and come to a meadow where he decides to have her. She asks him to wait till they get home, however, as the dew will ruin her gown. He consents. But, once home, she slips through the gates, locks him out, and mocks him. He threatens her, but leaves.
Examples: Flanders, *Ancient Blds* (A).

Discussion: Type A has the "blow ye winds" chorus of Child Db (See also IV, 495) and follows the tradition of *JFSS,* II, 18 and W. B. Whall, *Sea Sgs & Chanties,* 24.

The *Green Mountain Songster* text (reprinted in Flanders, *Ancient Blds,* III, 90) is close to Child D for the first four stanzas and to IV, 495 in the first stanza, but then it varies from the Child texts, although at many points a similarity to Child E can be seen. The parting threat of the knight is not in Child, however. The Creighton and Senior text is also close to Child D, but it is hard to follow. Here the girl even suggests a good spot where the knight can make love to her.

A ballad with a similar motif is *Katie Morey* (see Laws, *Am Bldry Brit Bdsdes,* 215 (N 24). There is a bibliography to these songs in Laws. See also Barry's remarks, *Brit Blds Me,* 455f.

114. JOHNIE COCK

Texts: Creighton, *Trd Sgs N Sc,* 65 / Davis, *Fsgs Va,* 24 / Davis, *Trd Bld Va,* 385 / *Va FLS Bull,* #8.
Local Titles: Johnie Cock, Johnie o' Cockleslee.

Story Types: A: Johnny, against his mother's warnings, goes out to poach deer. He kills an animal and feasts himself and his dogs so freely that they all fall asleep. Foresters hear him blow his horn, and an old man directs them to the poacher. They attack Johnny. He kills six of them and throws the seventh, badly wounded, over a horse that he may carry the news of the fight home. Johnny then sends a bird to Fair Eleanor asking that he be fetched back as he is wounded.
Examples: Davis, *Trd Bld Va.*

B: The story is essentially that of Type A. However, Johnie lies down to rest after outstripping his hunting companions. When the foresters attack, he kills all but three, and these run off. He wants to send a bird to tell his mother of his wounds, but evidently is unable to locate one; he blows his horn and "four and twenty knights" come to take him home. His mother quickly cures him, and he is off pursuing the three escaped foresters in three days.   Examples: Creighton and Senior

Discussion: The Type A version, from Virginia, is shorter than the Child texts, though similar to them. Minor American variations are the blast of the horn, Johnie's comments on the forester's attack, the manner in which the seventh forester is sent off, and the flight of the bird to Eleanor rather than to the mother. This text most resembles Child A or B with some traits of D and M, but it has a final stanza that seems to be the result of contact with *Lord Thomas and Fair Annet.* See Davis, *Trd Bld Va,* 385 for a discussion of this and other points in connection with the song. He notes there that the text is incomplete and spotty, although the continuity has remained intact.

Type B is most unusual and is not close to any of the Child texts. The four and twenty knights are undoubtedly borrowed from Child 138, *Robin Hood and Allan a Dale,* or another Robin Hood song. Johnie's weariness after the hunt and his determination to pursue the escapees are both remarkable. However, the informant, who was over 90, had an incomplete recollection of her text.

118. ROBIN HOOD AND GUY OF GISBORNE

Texts: Brown, *NC Flklre,* II, 151.
Local Titles: Robin Hood and Guy of Gisborne.
Story Types: A: A distorted text tells how Robin Hood lived in the forest, killed men and deer, and frightened people. One day a stranger speaks to this outlaw, saying that he is searching for one Robin Hood. As they travel together, Robin Hood reveals himself and then slays the stranger.

Examples: Brown, *NC Flklre.*

Discussion: The story given in this American ballad tells only a small fragment of the original tale. Robin Hood, having dreamed that two yeomen beat and bound him, sets out with Little John for revenge. In the greenwood they encounter a yeoman. John wishes to ask the stranger his intentions, but Robin, thinking this too bold, objects so roughly that John is hurt and goes home. At home, John finds Robin's men pressed by the sheriff, and he is captured and tied to a tree when his bow breaks. Meanwhile, Robin learns from the yeoman that he is seeking Robin Hood, but has lost his way. Robin offers to be his guide, and they go off. A shooting match is proposed, and, when Robin excels, the stranger in admiration wishes to learn his name. They identify themselves as Guy of Gisborne and Robin Hood, and a fight ensues. After stumbling and being hit, Robin kills Guy with the aid of the Virgin. He then nicks Guy's face beyond recognition, switches clothes, and blows Guy's horn. The sheriff hears in the sound tidings that Guy has slain Robin and believes it is Guy he sees approaching. Robin, as Guy, refuses a reward, but frees John. The sheriff then takes flight, but is slain by an arrow which John sends from Guy's bow:

The North Carolina text is metrically poor and almost prose in spots. Belden in his editing of the Brown Collection notes that the state of the text is likely "due to imperfect recollection on the part of the reporter".

Jay Williams (*JAF,* 1952, 304-305) uses Child 118 to argue for a myth-ritual position in opposition to William Simeone's remarks on *The May Games and the Robin Hood Legend* (*JAF,* 1951, 265-274). See also Simeone's reply in *JAF,* 1952, 418-420. Simeone has written a good many articles that touch on this and other Robin Hood ballads. See, in particular, his summary *Robin Hood Ballads in North America* (*MWF,* 1957, 197-201).

120. ROBIN HOOD'S DEATH

Texts: Davis, *Fsgs Va,* 25 / Davis, *Trd Bld Va,* 388 / *Va FLS Bull,* #2.
Local Titles: The Death of Robin Hood.

Story Types: A: Robin Hood complains to Little John that he can no longer shoot well and says he wishes to go to a cousin to be let blood. Robin sets out alone to Kirkely nunnery and is received cordially. His cousin opens a vein, locks him in a room, and lets him bleed till noon the next day. Robin is too weak to escape by a casement. He blows his horn three times, and the notes are so weak that John, on hearing them, concludes his master must be near death. He thus goes to Kirkely, breaks in, and gets to Robin. Little John wants to set fire to the hall, but Robin, who has never harmed a woman, refuses to let him. Robin asks for a bow to shoot his last shot which shall mark his grave, a grave with green grass, a bow at his side, and a tablet stating that Robin Hood lies there.

Examples: Davis, *Trd Bld Va.*

Discussion: This Virginia version follows Child B as to story, but shows definite traces of the professional ballad writer. In fact, this text seems to represent a poor broadside version that has slipped back into oral tradition.

The song, obviously incomplete in America, lacks the "blood-letting" stanzas, although it does contain the attempt to ally Robin Hood with Robert, Earl of Huntingdon (see Child Bb) at the end. There is no refrain to the Virginia version.

See Davis, *Trd Bld Va,* 388 for a detailed discussion of this text.

125. ROBIN HOOD AND LITTLE JOHN

Texts: American Speech, II, #2 / Creighton, *Maritime Fsgs,* 19 / Creighton and Senior, *Trd Sgs N Sc,* 67 / *JAF,* 1910, 432; 1956, 25 / *SFQ,* 1938, 72; 1940, 15.
Local Titles: Robin Hood and Little John, Little John Garland and Robin Hood.

Story Types: A: Robin Hood meets Little John on a narrow bridge over a river; neither will give way to let the other pass. When Robin threatens John, the latter calls him a coward as Robin has a bow and John only a staff. Robin then cuts himself a staff, and they fight. After an exchange of blows, Robin is knocked in the water. He pulls himself out and summons his men with a bugle blast. The men are going to duck Little John and pluck out his eyes, but Robin deters them and asks John to join the band. All have a feast.

Examples: *American Speech,* II; *SFQ,* 1938, 72.

Discussion: American texts are rare and the few that do exist show the influence of print. The Nebraska version is from Kentucky and the Illinois text from Virginia which points to a southern origin for the song.

For a detailed analysis of the effects of transmission on *Robin Hood and Little John* see E. C. Kirkland, *SFQ*, 1940, 15-21. He compares a Tennessee-Ohio version line by line with Child 125A to demonstrate the improvements oral tradition has made in the ballad with respect to narrative effect and diction. H. S. V. Jones (*JAFL*, 1910, 432) compares the Virginia-Illinois version with Child 125, also.

John Greenway (*JAF*, 1956, 25) discusses this ballad as one his informant, Aunt Molly Jackson, seems to have learned from the Kittredge one-volume edition of Child. He compares it to Child 125, which it follows closely, if not completely. The text borrows the opening of Child 154, *A True Tale of Robin Hood.*

The Canadian, Nova Scotia, find is fragmentary.

126. ROBIN HOOD AND THE TANNER

Texts: Davis, *Fsgs Va,* 25 / Davis, *Trd Bld Va,* 393 / A. Lomax, *Fsgs No Am,* 189 / Smith and Rufty, *Am Anth Old Wrld Blds,* 39 / *Va FLS Bull,* #2.

Local Titles: Robin Hood and Arthur O'Bland.

Story Types: A: Robin Hood goes to the forest where Arthur O'Bland, the forester, stops him. A two-hour fight ensures. Finally, Robin cries hold and asks the forester's name. (From Child we must supply the missing portion which concerns the learning of the name, the invitation extended to Arthur to join the outlaws and get some fee, and Arthur's acceptance.) Arthur then asks after his kinsman, Little John. Robin blows his horn, and in comes Little John, who wants to wrestle Arthur until all is explained. John then embraces his kinsman, and all three dance about the oak.

Examples: Davis, *Trd Bld Va.*

Discussion: Consult Davis, *Trd Bld Va,* 393 for a full treatment of the Virginia text. Except for an obviously corrupt first stanza, the Virginia version is quite similar to the Child analogue. It is, however, more compact, having twenty-four, rather than thirty-seven, stanzas.

In Child, Robin Hood is the forester and stays Arthur; a direct reversal has occurred in America.

129. ROBIN HOOD AND THE PRINCE OF ARAGON

Texts: Barry, *Brit Blds Me,* 233.

Local Titles: None given.

Story Types: A: Robin Hood, Will Scarlet, and Little John in the wood meet a girl who says a princess must marry the Prince of Aragon (Oregon) unless she and two other girls can find three champions to battle the Prince and his two serpent-crowned giants. The three adventurers plan to accept the challenge, and, when they do, the Prince is greatly annoyed. The villains are slain, and Will finds his long lost father. He also wins the princess who chooses him over the two other champions.

Examples: Barry.

Discussion: The Maine version is obviously from print and is a pretty poor specimen. The story, although more compact, is the same as that in Child, III, 147.

132. THE BOLD PEDLAR AND ROBIN HOOD

Texts: American Songster (Cozzens, N.Y.), 207 / Barry, *Brit Blds Me,* 457 (trace) / *BFSSNE,* IX, 8 / Creighton, *Sgs Blds N Sc,* 12 / Creighton and Senior, *Trd Sgs N Sc,* 12 / Flanders, *Ancient Blds,* III, 101 / Flanders, *Blds Migrant NE,* 67 / Flanders, *Vt Fsgs Blds,* 217 / Wells, *Bld Tree,* 37.

Local Titles: Bold Robin Hood and the Pedlar, Bold Robing Hood, Pedlar Bold.

Story Types: A: Robin Hood and Little John encounter a peddler, and Little John tries to force the man to share his pack with them. The peddler puts his pack on the ground and says that if Little John can move him from it he can have the whole thing. They fight, and John is forced to cry hold. Robin then tries and is also forced to quit. They ask the peddler his name, but he refuses to tell them until they name themselves. They do and learn that the peddler is Gamble Gold, Young Gamwell, etc., a cousin of Robin Hood. They all go and make merry over a bottle in a near-by tavern and dance around the oak.

Examples: Creighton, *Sgs Blds N Sc.*

Discussion: This ballad was printed in the *American Songster* in New York before 1850 in a version that is close to the one in Child. The Canadian tradition and Flanders, *Ancient Blds* (C) texts are close to this form. Flanders, *Ancient Blds* (A and B) differ slightly and may represent an older tradition of the ballad. Barry's confidence (*Brit Blds Me,* 459) that this song would turn up in New England was justified. See *BFSSNE,* IX, 8.

Child 132, which is a traditional variation of Child 128, can be traced back to the *Tale of Gamelyn.* Note the names Young Gamwell, Gamble Gold, Gammel Gay, etc. For a brief discussion of the relation of American texts of Child 132 to Child 128 and to broadside songs see *BFSSNE,* IX, 8.

133. ROBIN HOOD AND THE BEGGAR

Texts: JAF, 1956, 31.

Local Titles: Robin Hood and the Beggar.

Story Types: A: While riding to Nottingham, Robin Hood meets a beggar. They get into a fight with staves, and the beggar more than holds his own. Robin Hood is sufficiently impressed to exchange his clothes for the beggar's rags. Dressed as the beggar, he goes to town where three yeomen are to be hung for stealing deer. Robin Hood blows his horn and 300 outlaws appear to free the yeomen, who decide to join Robin Hood's band.

Examples: *JAF,* 1956, 31.

Discussion: This text is unique in America. John Greenway collected it from Aunt Molly Jackson, who he feels learned it from Kittredge's one-volume edition of Child. The Jackson version is about one-third the length of the Child text, but it covers the entire story. Greenway discusses the differences between this text and the Child material in *JAF*, 1956, 32.

135. ROBIN HOOD AND THE SHEPHERD

Barry, *Brit Blds Me*, 461 states that a Maine woman had heard this song in Ireland in her youth.

138. ROBIN HOOD AND ALLEN A DALE

Texts: JAF, 1956, 28.

Local Titles: Robin Hood and Allen a Dale.

Story Types: A: Twice, Robin Hood sees a young man in the woods. The first time he is dressed like a king. The second time he is shabby. Robin Hood has his men bring the stranger to him. The stranger tells Robin Hood that a rich old knight has stolen his true love. Robin Hood offers to get the girl back, even though the stranger can't pay him. Dressed as a harper, Robin Hood attends the wedding of the rich knight and the stolen girl. He approaches the couple, blowing his horn. Twenty-four followers appear, led by Allen a Dale. When the bishop protests, Robin Hood dresses Little John as the bishop, and Allen is married to his girl.

Examples: *JAF*, 1956, 28.

Discussion: This text, which is unique to America, was collected by John Greenway from Aunt Molly Jackson. Greenway believes she learned it from the Kittredge one-volume edition of Child and then changed the text. He analyzes these changes minutely in *JAF*, 1956, 30. For the most part, they involve the background of the incident and the motivation of the characters. Greenway feels that his informant improved the ballad.

139. ROBIN HOOD'S PROGRESS TO NOTTINGHAM

Texts: Creighton, *Sgs Blds N Sc*, 15 / Creighton, *Trd Sgs N Sc*, 69.

Local Titles: Robin Hood.

Story Types: A: The Nova Scotia fragments tell the portion of the story involving the skirmish, how Robin Hood kills fourteen or fifteen foresters with one arrow, routs ten men who come to capture him, and escapes to the greenwood.

Examples: Creighton, *Trd Sgs N Sc.*

Discussion: The story (see Child, III, 175) in full tells how Robin Hood when fifteen years old fell in with fifteen foresters who were drinking at Nottingham. He made a bet he could kill a deer at one hundred yards. However, when he did it, the men refused to pay. Robin Hood, therefore, killed them all, as well as the men who were sent from Nottingham to capture him. The story is from the Sloane Ms. 715, 7, fol. 157 and was made into a popular ballad in the 17th Century. The two Canadian fragments, printed together in Creighton, *Trd Sgs N Sc,* 69, are close to Child 139, Stanzas 12-14, 16-17.

140. ROBIN HOOD RESCUING THREE SQUIRES

Texts: American Songster (Cozzens, N.Y.), 204 / Barry, *Brit Blds Me,* 240 / Brown, *NC Flklre,* II, 152 / Chase, *Am Ftales Sgs,* 124 / Flanders, *Ancient Blds,* III, 107 / Flanders, *Blds Migrant NE,* 69.

Local Titles: Bold Robin Hood (Rescuing the Three Squires), Bold Robing, Robin Hood.

Story Types: A: Robin Hood meets a young lady who, weeping, tells him that three squires of Nottingham have been taken prisoner. Robin calls his men for council and sets out for the town. En route, he meets a beggar. He changes clothes with the man for fifty guineas. Robin then meets the sheriff and tells the officer that he would like to hang the three squires personally and to give three blasts on his horn "that their souls in heaven might be". The request is granted. Robin mounts the scaffold and gives the three blasts, which serve as a signal to his men. They come, and the sheriff gives over the three squires.

Examples: Barry.

Discussion: The New England and Southern texts follow Child C, although the lady is not the mother of the three squires. Thus, the hanging of the sheriff on his own gallows, a feature of Child B, is not included. See the *American Songster* for a different text which Barry, *Brit Blds Me,* 242 feels comes from either a poor stall copy or an oral source.

The Flanders, *Ancient Blds,* A¹ and A² texts offer an excellent study in the manner in which an informant will change a text, in this case after nine years.

Creighton, *Maritime Fsgs,* 20 notes that she has collected a fragment from New Brunswick.

141. ROBIN HOOD RESCUING WILL STUTLY

Texts: Davis, *Fsgs Va,* 251 / Davis, *Trd Bld Va,* 397 / *Musical Quarterly,* II, 4 / *Va FLS Bull,* #2.

Local Titles: The Rescue of Will Stutly.

Story Types: A: Robin Hood learns that Will Stutly has been captured and is to be hung the next day. Robin Hood and his men go to the rescue and have news of the capture confirmed by a palmer standing under the wall of the castle in which Will is confined. Stutly is brought out, and Little John asks the sheriff for permission to speak to Will. He is curtly refused. Then Little John cuts Will's bonds and gives him a sword stolen from one of the sheriff's men. Robin Hood puts the sheriff to flight with an arrow, and Will rejoices.

Examples: Davis, *Trd Bld Va.*

Discussion: The Virginia version has been abbreviated to twenty-one stanzas from the thirty-eight in Child, but is, nevertheless, very close to the Child text. There is one notable difference, however. In the latter Stutly, not Little John, addresses the sheriff, and he asks for a sword that he may die fighting rather than having to be subjected to hanging. Refused, he asks only to have his hands freed. Again he is refused. Little John then frees him.

The American and British texts of the ballad are obviously from print, and the story itself is an imitation of Child 140 in many respects. Davis, *Trd Bld Va*, 397 prints a detailed stanza comparison of his text with Child's.

143. ROBIN HOOD AND THE BISHOP

Flanders collected one-line from a Vermont informant. See *Ancient Blds*, III, 117; *JAF*, 1951, 131; and *Vt Historical Society, Proceedings*, N.S., VII, 73-98. This line is from Stanza 3 of Child's text and is a line that is repeated in varying forms in the other stanzas of the Child broadside. This is the only evidence that Child 143 has existed in American oral tradition.

149. ROBIN HOOD'S BIRTH, BREEDING, VALOR, AND MARRIAGE

John Greenway (see *JAF*, 1956, 36) has collected a recently fabricated ballad called *Robin Hood Learns of His Father*. This song uses several lines from and the early framework of Child 149. See the discussion under Child 102 in this book. Child 149 cannot be said to survive in American oral tradition on the evidence to date.

155. SIR HUGH OR THE JEW'S DAUGHTER

Texts: Altoona Tribune, 11-16-'31, 6 / Arnold, *Fsgs Ala*, 42 / Barry, *Brit Blds Me*, 461 (trace) / Belden, *Mo Fsgs*, 69 / *Berea Quarterly*, XVIII, 12 / Brewster, *Blds Sgs Ind*, 128 / Brown, *NC Flklre*, II, 155 / *BFSSNE*, V, 6 / *Bull Tenn FLS*, VIII, #3, 76 / Child, III, 248, 251 / Cox, *Fsgs South*, 120 / Creighton, *Sgs Blds N Sc*, 16 / Davis, *Fsgs Va*, 25 / Davis, *More Trd Blds Va*, 229 / Davis, *Trd Bld Va*, 400 / Eddy, *Bld Sgs Ohio*, 66 / Flanders, *Ancient Blds*, III, 119 / Flanders, *Blds Migrant NE*, 30 / Flanders, *New Gn Mt Sgstr*, 254 / *Focus, III*, 396, 399 / *Grapurchat*, Ea. Radford (Va.) State Teacher's College, 8-25-'32 / Henry, *Beech Mt Fsgs*, 22 / Henry, *Fsgs So Hghlds*, 102 / Hubbard, *Blds Sgs Utah*, 24 / Hudson, *Fsgs Miss*, 116 / Hudson, *Spec Miss Flklre*, #17 / Jones, *Flklre Mich*, 5 / *JAF*, 1902, 195; 1906, 293; 1916, 164; 1922, 344; 1926, 108, 212; 1928, 470; 1931, 64, 296; 1934, 358; 1935, 297; 1939, 43; 1951, 47, 224; 1958, 16 / *Ky Folklore Record*, 1957, 92; 1960, 127 / Korson, *Pa Sgs Lgds*, 36 / A. Lomax, *Fsgs No Am*, 511 / Morris, *Fsgs Fla*, 302 / *Musical Quarterly*, II, 124 / Newell, *Games Sgs Am Children*, 75 / *NY Tribune*, 7-27-'22; 8-4-'22 / *NC Folklore*, VII, #1 (1959), 35 / Pound, *Am Blds Sgs*, 13 / Randolph, *Oz Fsgs*, I, 148 / Scarborough, *On Trail N Fsgs*, 53 / Scarborough, *Sgctchr So Mts*, 171 / SharpC, *Eng Fsgs So Aplchns*, #26 / SharpK, *Eng Fsgs So Aplchns*, I, 222 / Shearin and Combs, *Ky Syllabus*, 8 / Reed Smith, *SC Blds*, 148 / *SFQ*, 1944, 154 / *University of Va. Mgz*, Dec. 1912, 115 / *Va FLS Bull*, #s 2—5, 7, 9, 11 / *W Va Folklore*, III, #2 (1953), 19; V, #2 (1955), 26; IX, #2 (1959), 20; XI, #2 (1961), 21.

Local Titles: Ballad, The Blue Drum Boy, Fair Scotland, Hugh of Lincoln, It Rained a Mist, The Jeweler's Daughter, The Jew's Daughter, The Jew's Garden, The Jew's Lady, Little Boy and the Ball, A Little Boy Lost His Ball, A Little Boy Threw His Ball (Boss) So High, Little Harry Hughes (Huston), Little Saloo (Sir Hugh), The Queen's Garden, Once in the Month of May, Sir Hugh (of Lincoln), The Two Playmates, Water Birch.

Story Types: A: Some little boys are playing ball, usually in the rain. One tosses the ball into the Jew's garden where no one dares go. However, the Jew's daughter invites the scared boy in. After enticing him to accept her invitation with a red apple, cherry, etc., she takes him to a remote part of the house. There she sticks him with pins, stabs him like a sheep, etc.

Sometimes, he sees his nurse inside the house picking a chicken, but she pays no attention to his plight. In some endings the "the Bible-at-the-head and prayer book-at-the-feet" motif appears, and the boy requests that his mother be told he is asleep and his playmates be told that he is dead. In certain texts, the body is thrown in a well.

Examples: Belden (A); Cox (A); Davis, *Trd Bld Va* (A).

B: The story is similar to that of Type A. However, the mother sets out to find her missing boy in the end of these ballads. She locates his body in the well, talks to him miraculously, and sometimes has his body even more miraculously returned to her.

Examples: Child (G, N); *JAF*, 1939, 43; SharpK (B,F).

C: The story is similar to that of Type A. However, the dialogue between the Jew's daughter and the boy is left out, and the youth volunteers to climb the wall. There is no woman, only "they".

Examples: Belden (B).

D: A little boy is called away from playing ball by his mother with whom he evidently does not live. Knowing her evil intentions, he goes reluctantly. She kills her son and disposes of the body in a well in an attempt to protect herself and save her family's reputation. Scheming further to protect herself, she pretends to search for her overdue son and is confounded when the corpse miraculously speaks and predicts her damnation.

Examples: *JAF*, 1958, 16.

E: The murderess is a spiteful aunt, who simply slays her nephew and throws his body in a well. There is no religious prejudice at all.

Examples: *JAF*, 1951, 47.

Discussion: This ballad is founded on an incident that may have occurred in 1255. Child, III, 235 states the story as told in the *Annals of Waverly* in this manner:

> A boy in Lincoln, named Hugh, was crucified by the Jews in contempt of Christ, with various preliminary tortures. To conceal the act from the Christians, the body, when taken from the cross, was thrown into a running stream; but the water would not endure the wrong done its maker, and immediately ejected it upon dry land. The body was then buried in the earth, but was found above dry ground the next day. The guilty parties were now very much frightened and quite at their wit's end; as a last resort they threw the corpse into a drinking well. The body was seen floating on the water, and, upon its being drawn up, the hands and feet were found to be pierced, the head had, as it were, a crown of bloody points, and there were various other wounds: from all which it was plain that this was the work of the abominable Jews. A blind woman, touching the bier on which the blessed martyr's corpse was carrying to the church, received her sight, and many other miracles followed. Eighteen Jews, convicted of the crime, and confessing it with their own mouth, were hanged.

Further references to Matthew Paris and *The Annals of Burton* are given by Child on pp. 235 and 237.

The concept of Our Lady, used by Chaucer in The Prioress's Tale, has vanished in America. Our Lady's drawwell is just a well, the mother is just a sorrowing mother, and the religious note is almost forgotten. See Morris, *Fsgs Fla*, 302, where the girl is a jeweler's daughter. Walter M. Hart, *English Popular Ballad*, 30—1 compares Chaucer and the ballad as representatives of the artistic and folk forms of one story. Summers, *The History of Witchcraft and Demonology*, 195 relates the legend with black magic. James Woodall (*SFQ*, 1955, 77-84) uses Child 155 as a means of discussing the reasons for ballad survival. He stresses that sex and mystery, not anti-Semitism, "make the ballad," allow it to survive.

The American Story Types A and B follow the Child groups K-O and A-F respectively. Type C probably results from forgetting, while Type E merely tells of a domestic crime (an aunt kills her nephew). There are no religious overtones. Type D, which was printed by William H. Jansen and Frances C. Stamper (see *JAF*, 1958, 16-22), represents a completely different version of the story. In it, Hugh is murdered by his mother. (See also SharpK, *Eng Fsgs So Aplchns*, I, D-E, where the Jewess calls Hugh her little son.) Jansen discusses this unusual Southern Appalachian tradition, expressing the belief that his text, called *Water Birch*, represents a complete re-creation of Child 155. He is impressed with how much of the wording and original detail is retained from whatever the source version was, possibly an Irish text. See, for instance, Child F, N.

Brewster (*Blds Sgs Ind*)'s A version tells of a "duke's daughter" and a "mother's maid" (nurse) in the house, while his C version takes place on a sunny day. Note also the "king's daughter" of Randolph, *Oz Fsgs*, B; the "Queen's garden" of Lomax, *Fsgs No Am;* and the "gypsy" of Henry, *Fsgs So Hghlds*, B. The Jew is a man in Hudson, *Spec Miss Flklre*, 7. And the Bahaman version, printed by Parson, *JAF*, 1928, 470, is corrupted and confused even to the extent of having the boy promise to marry Barbary Ellen when he grows up. The real story has vanished.

Hudson, *Fsgs Miss*, 116 notes that his version (with the bloody stanzas omitted) has been used as a lullaby to sing children to sleep. Newell, *Games and Sgs Am Children*, 75 prints a New York (from Ireland) version which has become a child's game. See Child N for the same text.

Reference should be made to Foster Gresham (*JAF*, 1934, 385f.) for a discussion of textual variation in action. He uses two versions of Child 155, one taken from a little girl and the other taken from her grandmother who taught the song to her.

156. QUEEN ELEANOR'S CONFESSION

Brown, *NC Flklre*, II, 160 notes that *Queen Eleanor's Confession* is not now in the F. C. Brown Collection, but it seems clear that this ballad or *Fair Rosamond* was known in Avery County, N.C. as *Fair Rosamund and Queen Eleanor*. Brown failed to record what little of the song the informant could recall. The song also may have been known in New England. Flanders, *Ancient Blds*, III, 127 contains a text from print, and Barry, *Brit Blds Me*, 462 reports meeting a Maine woman who recognized the Child A text. The

Flanders version is close to Child A also. See the Child Ms. for the report of the ballad as known by an Irishwoman living in Iowa.

Linscott, *Fsgs Old NE*, 193 prints a song, *Fair Rosamond*, which is related to Child 156. This song, usually called *Rosamond's Overthrow*, and *Queen Eleanor's Confession* were both common to 18th and 19th Century ballad collections, although *Queen Eleanor's Confession* is certainly a good bit older.

157. GUDE WALLACE

Flanders, *Ancient Blds*, III, 133 prints a fragment from Vermont that does not correlate to any Child material. The fragment seems to suggest an earlier portion of the story that is not normally found in *Gude Wallace* texts, which center on the events surrounding his sweetheart's selling him to the English, her attempts to rectify her deception, and the fight with the English troops at the inn. The fragment seems to relate to the burning of Lanark and the murder of Sheriff Hezelrig in May 1297. Wallace supposedly killed Hezelrig to revenge the death of his beloved, Marion Bradfute. The slaying of Hezelrig, incidentally, was the only specific charge levelled against Wallace in his indictment at Westminster.

Barry, *Brit Blds Me*, 465 found a sea-captain who claimed to recognize the story.

162. THE HUNTING OF THE CHEVIOT OR CHEVY CHASE

Texts: Barry, *Brit Blds Me*, 243 / Davis, *Fsgs Va*, 26 / Davis, *More Trd Blds Va*, 239 / Davis, *Trd Bld Va*, 416 / Flanders, *Ancient Blds*, III, 135 / Ford, *Broadsides, Blds, etc. Mass*, #s 3011—13 / Harvard University Library Broadside #25242.53 (312) / Mason, *Cannon Cnty*, 15.

Local Titles: The Battle of Chevy Chase, The Battle of Shiver Chase, Chevy Chase.

Story Types: A: Percy kills some deer in Scotland, and Douglas, objecting, says he will prevent future foraging. Subsequently, after a feast on slain deer, Percy and his men are attacked by Douglas and his clan. The two leaders are going to fight, but a squire steps forth and announces that he will not stand by while his earl fights. Eventually, however, Douglas and Percy do battle alone. Percy weakens, and Douglas asks him to surrender. When the Englishman refuses he is slain. An arrow from an English bow then kills Douglas, and a general fight follows. Individual deeds and men are described and named.

Examples: Barry; Davis, *Trd Bld Va.*

B: A fragment tells in two stanzas of a brutal fight between two earls.

Examples: Mason.

Discussion: The Virginia and Maine texts, both incomplete, follow Child B rather than Child A. However, the fighting has been abbreviated in Virginia, and the order of the deaths changed. See Davis, *Trd Bld Va*, 416 and Barry, *Brit Bld Me*, 247 for summaries and stanza comparisons. The Flanders text is from print.

The *Chevy Chase* tune was popular in the Revolution (see *The Cow*

Chase). For a Revolutionary War anecdote concerning the song, see Barry, *op. cit.*, 248 quoted from William Gordon, *History of the Rise . . . of the Independence of the United States of America*, London, 1788, I, 481. See also Henry N. MacCracken's remarks on Major André in *NYFQ*, 1959, 58-65. It seems André wrote a filthy attack on Anthony Wayne by parodying the song.

164. KING HENRY THE FIFTH'S CONQUEST OF FRANCE

Texts: BFSSNE, II, 5; IV, 10 / Flanders, *Ancient Blds*, III, 145 / Flanders, *Cntry Sgs Vt*, 36 / Flanders, *New Gn Mt Sgstr*, 193 / Henry, *Fsgs So Hghlds*, 108 / *JAF*, 1932, 17 / *N.J. Journal of Educ.*, XX, #s 3-4, 6-7 / *PMLA*, XLVIII, 307 / Wells, *Bld Tree*, 43.

Local Titles: King Henry the Fifth's Conquest of France.

Story Types: A: King Henry decides to collect a tribute from the King of France. He sends a page abroad, and the messenger brings back some tennis balls as the French monarch's reply. Henry then musters an army of men, none married, none sons of widows. He attacks France, and, after withstanding the first onslaught, triumphs. With a bribe of the French princess and a large amount of gold he returns to England.

Examples: Flanders, *Ancient Blds;* Henry, *Fsgs So Hghlds.*

Discussion: The American stories differ little from Child or from each other. The ballad is extremely rare in this country, although the discovered texts have been frequently reprinted.

For an analysis of the relation of this ballad to the Alexander romance see Child, III, 322 and Flanders, *New Gn Mt Sgstr*, 195. The parallel between Alexander's insult from Darius and his marriage to Roxanna to the events in the ballad is stressed. The balls and the references to the eventual victor's tender years are in both stories, as well as in a number of other hero tales.

166. THE ROSE OF ENGLAND

The subject of the ballad is a basically accurate account of the winning of the English crown by Henry VII from Richard III. In the ballad, the Red Rose of Lancaster was rooted up by a White Boar, Richard, who it was felt had murdered Henry VI and his son Edward. The Earl of Richmond, the seed of the Rose, escaped to France in 1471, only to return in 1485 to begin a campaign that was to lead him to the throne. He brought with him the Blue Boar, the Earl of Oxford, and the White Boar was defeated and the Red Rose was able to bloom once more.

Mrs. Flanders obtained an account of these events and the two stanzas that open the Child text from a Vermont informant in 1933. This find was reported in *Vt Historical Society, Proceedings*, N.S., VII, 73-98. The stanzas were printed in *Blds Migrant NE*, 91 and again in *Ancient Blds*, III, 149. This is the only report of the song from modern oral tradition, and the chances are good the stanzas were learned from print.

167. SIR ANDREW BARTON (including 250, HENRY MARTYN)

Texts: Adventure, 11-30-'23; 11-20-'24 / Barry, *Brit Blds Me*, 248 / Belden, *Mo Fsgs*, 87 / Child, IV, 395; V, 302 / *Colorado Fsg Bull*, I, #2, 2; I, #3, 5 / Creighton and Senior, *Trd Sgs N Sc*, 86 / Cox, *Fsgs South*, 150 / Davis, *Fsgs Va*, 31 / Davis, *More Trd Blds Va*, 290 / Eddy, *Blds Sgs Ohio*, 78 / Flanders, *Ancient Blds*, IV / Flanders, *Blds Migrant NE*, 72, 201 / Flanders, *Cntry Sgs Vt*, 8 / *Focus*, V, 280 / Gardner and Chickering, *Blds Sgs So Mich*, 211 / Gray, *Sgs Blds Me Lmbrjks*, 80 / Haufrecht, *Wayfarin' Stranger*, 20 / Hubbard, *Blds Sgs Utah*, 32 / Ives, *BI Sg Bk*, 46 / Ives, *Sea Sgs*, 30 / *JAF*, 1905, 135, 302; 1917, 327; 1951, 49 / Karpeles, *Fsgs Newfdld*, 104 / Kolb, *Treasury Fsg*, 19 / MacKenzie, *Blds Sea Sgs N Sc*, 61 / Randolph, *Oz Fsgs*, I, 177 / Reed Smith, *SC Blds*, 156 / *SFQ*, 1938, 205 / Thompson, *Bdy Bts Brtchs*, 37 / *WF*, 1952, 181 / Worthington, *Nine Rare Trd Blds Va*, 120.

Local Titles: Andrew (Andy) Bardeen (Barden, Batan, Battan, Bratann, etc.), Bolender Martin, Elder Bardee, Henry Martyn, The Pirate, Ronald Barton, Three Brothers of (Merrie) Scotland, The Three Scotch Brothers, Zanzibar Dream.

Story Types: A: Three Scottish brothers cast lots to see which of them shall become a pirate to support the family. The lot falls to the youngest, Andy. He attacks and robs a rich English merchant. When the King learns of this crime, he sends Captain Stewart (Howard, in England) out to catch the robbers. Stewart locates and takes Andy, and brings him back to the gallows in England. Sometimes, however, Andy is sunk and drowned instead.

Examples: Barry (under 167) (B); Belden; *SFQ*, 1938, 205.

B: The story is the same as that of Type A. However, Andy beats Stewart in the fight and continues on his way.

Examples: Barry (under 167) (A); Cox; Randolph.

C: The Barry (*Brit Blds Me*, 253f.) "Henry Martyn" type story ends with the capture of the merchant ship and the bad news reaching England. In some versions the hero receives a death-wound and dies.

Examples: Eddy (A); Haufrecht; *JAF*, 1905, 135.

Discussion: This ballad and Henry Martyn (Child 250) are closely allied (see Child, IV, 393), and Barry, *Brit Blds Me*, 253 f., argues that they are the same song. He bases his claim on the older American texts and points out that the Child *Henry Martyn* stories are all fragments of the *Andrew Barton* tale which leave the chase and the capture out. Any ballad that has a chase and capture is *Sir Andrew Barton*. The American *Henry Martyn* songs that have the hero die and fall overboard are the result of a crossing with a text of *Sir Andrew Barton* itself or of an accident of traditional change. His conclusion is that *Sir Andrew Barton* exists in two forms in America: the story in which Sir Andrew Barton is hung (Type A), and the story in which, through contact with *Captain Ward and the Rainbow* (Child 287), Sir Andrew Barton wins and escapes (Type B). There are also abbreviations of these types which do not contain the chase and the capture. Such songs should be properly considered as *Henry Martyn* versions of *Sir Andrew Barton*. See Eddy, *Blds Sgs Ohio*, 81; Cecil Sharp, *100 English Fsgs*, xvii;

and S. Baring-Gould, *Sgs of the West,* in a note to the texts for further discussion.

Davis, *More Trd Blds Va,* 290-299 writes a brilliant refutation of Barry's thesis and states that all the American references to Child 167 and 250 should be ascribed to Child 250. He sees Child 250 existing in three American forms: 1) the *Martyn* form, such as Child B (my Type C); 2) the *Ward* form, such as Davis, *More Trd Blds,* AA (my Type B); and 3) the *Bardan* form, such as Barry, *Brit Blds Me,* 252 and Belden *Mo Fsgs,* 87 (my Type A). On p. 296 he classifies all the American texts under one of these three headings. See also Worthington, *Nine Rare Trd Blds Va,* 120-151.

It is surely academic whether the American texts are perpetuated under number 167 or number 250. The confusion between the ballads is obvious. The fact that 167 or 250 (or whatever one labels the ballad) has three rather distinct American plots is clear. And it is probable that the broadside publishers, with their lack of concern over classification, had a hand in the confusion.

Henry Martyn was a popular stall ballad in the nineteenth century (see Kittredge's note in *JAF,* XXX, 327), but there is no record of *Sir Andrew Barton* being printed in America.

Barry, *ibid.,* also poses an interesting and probably accurate hypothesis that the Charles Stewart (Stuart) who replaces Howard in the ballad is Captain Charles Stewart (1778-1869), U. S. N.

169. JOHNIE ARMSTRONG

This ballad has never been collected from oral tradition in the New World. Flanders, *Ancient Blds,* III, 153 includes a text from print that is a very accurate copy of Child B, a London broadside of the 17th Century, presenting the hero in a favorable light.

170. THE DEATH OF QUEEN JANE

Texts: Barry, *Brit Blds Me,* 466 (trace) / Beard, *Personal Fsg Coll Lunsford,* 85 / *BFSSNE,* II, 6 / Davis, *Fsgs Va,* 26 / Davis, *Trd Bld Va,* 419 / Flanders, *Ancient Blds* III, 159 / Flanders, *Blds Migrant NE,* 78 / Flanders, *Vt Fsgs Blds,* 219 / Niles, *Anglo-Am Bld Stdy Bk,* 24 / Niles, *Blds Lv Sgs Tgc Lgds,* 16 / Scarborough, *Sgctchr So Mts,* 254 / SharpK, *Eng Fsgs So Aplchns,* I, 230.

Local Titles: The Death of Queen Jane.

Story Types: A: Queen Jane is in labor for more than six weeks. She tells the doctors to cut her open and save the baby. However, King Henry refuses to sacrifice her for the child. She dies, and the baby is saved, regardless. The funeral takes place, and the baby is christened.

Examples: Niles, *Blds Lv Sgs Tgc Lgds;* SharpK (A, B).

B: The story is similar to that of Type A. However, Queen Jane has become "a neighbor", and she calls for her father and mother before she calls for King Henry.

Examples: *BFSSNE,* II, 6.

C: A lyric on the theme of Queen Jane's labor survives from the ballad and contains repeated comments by her mother, her father, and Prince Henry that "the Red Rose of England shall flourish no more".
Examples: Scarborough.

D: Sally is taken sick and goes to bed. King Henry is sent for. Then the "Are you the doctor?" lines from the American *Brown Girl* (Child 295) enters (see Child 170 B), as does the gloating over the dying girl by the jilted lover. Sally's presentation of the ring and her death follow.
Examples: Davis, *Trd Bld Va*, p. 420; SharpK, p. 303.

Discussion: The full ballad is a threnody on the death of Jane Seymour, who succumbed twelve days after the birth of Prince Edward, October 12, 1537. The Queen is ill, begs for surgery to save her unborn (in the ballad) child. See Child, III, 372-3. King Henry refuses to sacrifice the mother for the child. An operation becomes necessary, and the boy lives through it, while the mother dies. The jubilation over the birth is lost in lamentation.

The Type A version follows this story rather closely. Type B is probably from a broadside (see *BFSSNE*, II, 7) and shows a variation from "in labor" to "a neighbor" that might eventually change the details of the story. The refrain has become "the red roads of England shall flourish no more". It should also be noted that Henry does not enter the song until the eighth of ten stanzas. If a singer were to forget the last three stanzas a new story would exist. For a comparison of this version to Child A, E, H, and I see *BFSSNE*, II, 7.

The Type C text is rather beautiful, but it needs little explanation. It is the result of a common American ballad tendency. The Type D stories, however, reveal the growth of a new ballad from the merger of two older ones. The entrance of the doctor into a dying woman's room has been sufficient to switch the story into the American *Brown Girl* and to change the Queen's name to Sally, although the "black and yellow" funeral stanzas are retained at the end. The result appears to be a counterpart of *Barbara Allen* with the sexes reversed. See Davis, *Trd Bld Va*, 419.

Flanders, *Ancient Blds*, A prints a song which contains the first two lines of Stanza 5 and the last two lines of Stanza 6 (the funeral description) of Child 170D. It is given as a version of *The Death of Queen Jane*, but it seems to me to be *The Duke of Bedford* which has been corrupted by Child 170. See also *BFSSNE*, II, 7 and Flanders, *Ancient Blds*, B.

172. MUSSELBURGH FIELD

In *JAF*, 1953, 74, Albert Friedman reproduced *Musselburgh Field* from *Choyce Drollery: Songs and Sonnets* (London, 1656), 78-80 and from J. W. Ebsworth's *Choyce Drollery* (Boston, 1876). The song has no American oral tradition but was reproduced at least once in American songsters.

173. MARY HAMILTON

Texts: Barry, *Brit Blds Me*, 258 / *BFSSNE*, III, 8 / Chase, *Sgs All Times*, 11 / Combs, *Fsgs États-Unis*, 141 / Creighton, *Maritime Fsgs*, 22 / Davis, *Fsgs Va*,

26 / Davis, *More Trd Blds Va*, 245 / Davis, *Trd Bld Va*, 421 / Flanders, *Ancient Blds*, III, 163 / Flanders, *Blds Migrant NE*, 79 / *Franklin Square Song Collection* (J. P. McCaskey), VI, 75 / *110 Scotch Songs*, Thomas a Becket, Jr. (Ditson, Boston) / Owens, *Texas Fsgs*, 63 / Randolph, *Oz Fsgs*, I, 151 / Silber, *Reprints People's Sgs*, 95 / Smith and Rufty, *Am Anth Old Wrld Blds*, 42 / Wells, *Bld Tree*, 48.

Local Titles: Mary Hamilton, The Four Marys.

Story Types: A: Mary Hamilton, one of Queen Mary of Scotland's four servants named Marie, is with child by a member of the court. She throws the baby in the sea when it is born, but Queen Mary suspects and discovers the truth. Mary Hamilton is condemned to burn at the stake or hang. After telling the people not to weep for her and drinking a toast or two, Mary Hamilton rues the outcome of her life before she dies.

Examples: Combs.

B: A lyric lament at the stake or gallows, with almost no trace of the story, has been found.

Examples: Barry (A); Davis, *Trd Blds Va* (A).

Although Mary Queen of Scots had four maids-in-waiting named Mary Seaton, Mary Beaton, Mary Fleming, and Mary Livingston, it is not likely any of these women is the heroine of the ballad. The ballad story seems to involve the mixing of an event that occurred in Mary's court in the mid-1560's when a French girl and the Queen's apothecary had an affair and an event that occurred in Czar Peter of Russia's court in 1718-19 when a Scotch woman, Mary Hamilton, and an officer named Orloff had an affair. No doubt an older ballad, which had already confused the French girl and the apothecary with one of the maids-in-waiting and Darnley absorbed the Mary Hamilton name when her scandal was going the rounds. See Child, III, 380f.; Tolman, *PMLA*, XLII, 422; and Andrew Lang, *Blackwoods Magazine*, September 1895 for discussion.

The Type A texts are close to Child A, though the most common American form is that of the lyric lament (Type B), which is the way the song appeared in McCaskey's *Franklin Square Song Collection* and other New World songsters (see Child BB). Flanders, *Ancient Blds* (A, B) prints two texts that resemble the song as it was sung by Marjorie Kennedy at David Kennedy's *Scottish Entertainments* in the 1880's. See Flanders, *Ancient Blds*, III, 164 for a discussion.

In *JAF*, 1951, 131-132, Arthur Scouten discusses suspicions he has about the texts that Miss Alfreda Peele collected from Mrs. Texas Gladden. For remarks designed to demonstrate through a study of *Mary Hamilton* that a ballad's "emotional core" will remain after many details of the story vanish, see *JAF*, 1957, 212-214, reprinted in revised form as the final chapter of this book.

176. NORTHUMBERLAND BETRAYED BY DOUGLAS

Flanders collected Stanza 9 from the Child text of *Northumberland Betrayed by Douglas* from a Vermont informant, George Edwards. Edwards refused to sing the rest of the song as he said it reflected dishonor upon his family. This find was noted in *Vt. Historical Society, Proceedings,* N.S., VII, 73-98; printed in *JAF,* 1951, 131; and again in *Ancient Blds,* III, 171. Otherwise, the song is not known to New World tradition.

178. CAPTAIN CAR OR EDOM O GORDON

Texts: Flanders, *Ancient Blds,* III, 173.

Local Titles: Adam Gorman.

Story Types: A: Adam Gorman attacks Towie House when only the lady and her children are there to protect it. She, seeing the troops coming, thinks her lord has returned. When she finds this is not the case, she locks the castle up and attempts to persuade Adam to go away. Adam is infuriated by her actions, even though he proposes to her. However, when she rejects him, he orders the place sacked and burned. In the confusion, the daughter requests to be thrown over the wall. This is done and she is impaled on the point of Adam's spear. As Towie House burns Adam leaves. Soon the lord of the castle arrives to find all dead. He mourns, swears to redress the wrongs, and pursues Adam till he revenges his lady with Adam's heart's blood.

Examples: Flanders.

Discussion: The A text in Flanders, which was collected in New York via Vermont, is the only version of this song taken from a New World singer. However, Flanders A, like Flanders B, is clearly from print and close to Child D, although it tells a somewhat more detailed story and has the revenge of the final stanza. The reference that Reed Smith (*SFQ,* 1937, #2, 9-11) makes to the presence of this ballad in American oral tradition is to the Child Ms. material that was collected from an Irishwoman living in Iowa.

180. KING JAMES AND BROWN

Barry, *Brit Blds Me,* 467 reports that a Maine sea-captain recognized the ballad.

181. THE BONNY EARL OF MURRAY

Texts: Barry, *Brit Blds Me,* 468 (trace) / Brown, *NC Flklre,* II, 160 / Flanders, *Ancient Blds,* III, 185 / Flanders, *Blds Migrant NE,* 133 / *JAF,* 1907, 156; 1931, 297.

Local Titles: The Earl of Murray (Morey), Highlands and Lowlands.

Story Types: A: One text is an almost lyric moan for the Earl of Murray who has been slain and laid on the green. It was ordered he be captured, not killed. He was a capable man, a favorite of the Queen, and might have become King.

Example: *JAF,* 1931, 297.

B: A similar lyric, which mourns Murray, upbraids Huntly for killing the man in his bed, reminds him his wife will rue the deed, and tells him he will not dare come into Dinnybristle town for a long time.

Examples: *JAF,* 1907, 158.

Discussion: The Type A story follows Child A closely, while Type B is an incomplete variation which resembles Child B (Stanzas 6 and 9) in its final two stanzas. In Type B the speakers and the story background are not clear. For the complete story behind the ballad and for the details of the murder of Murray by Huntly in February 1592 see Child, III, 147 and Edward D. Ives' article on the ballad as history in *MWF*, 1959, 133-138.

Flanders, *Ancient Blds* (B) prints a text that is a mixture of the two Child texts. Barry, *Brit Blds Me*, 468 found a sea-captain who recognized the song, while Elsie C. Parsons knew a Rye, N.Y. woman who had learned it from a Scotsman.

183. WILLIE MACINTOSH

Texts: Barry, *Brit Blds Me*, 264.

Local Titles: None given.

Story Types: A: Willie MacIntosh, involved in a border feud, is burning Auchendown, although he has been warned that Huntly is moving to head him off.

Examples: Barry.

Discussion: Barry, *Brit Blds Me,* text follows Child A closely. However, the ballad was taken down from recitation and appears to be no longer sung in Maine. See Barry, *op. cit.,* 265.

The ballad is based on one of a series of revenge incidents which originated in the Murray murder (see Child 181) of 1592. William MacIntosh and his men were attacked and routed by Huntly while ravaging the latter's lands. See Child, III, 465 for the complete details of the events and an explanation of the confusion of two William MacIntoshes.

185. DICK O THE COW

In *Focus* (Farmville, Va.), V, 297, Reed Smith notes that this ballad "had been found in Missouri. Johnnie Armstrong steals Dick's three cows. Dick retaliates gloriously". I have not seen a text.

187. JOCK O THE SIDE

Shoemaker, *Mt Mnstly,* 238 prints a story outline of this ballad as it was recited in Pennsylvania with a few stanzas recalled. The stanzas compare to Child B, Stanzas 1, 11, 12—14, 26—28. The long story is summarized by Child, III, 476—7. The plot (Child B) revolves about the rescue of Jock from Newcastle by a handful of men who climb the town wall, enter the jail, kill the porter, and escape, with Jock still in irons, by swimming the Tyne just ahead of the pursuing English.

188. ARCHIE O CAWFIELD

Texts: Barry, *Brit Blds Me*, 393 / BFSSNE, VI, 7 / Child, III, 494 / Gardner and Chickering, *Blds Sgs So Mich*, 217 / JAF, 1895, 256 / Linscott, *Fsgs Old NE*, 172.

Local Titles: Bold Dickie.

Story Types: A: Two brothers bewail a third brother who is in prison.

They muster forty men and, under the leadership of one brother, Dickie (Hall), cross a river and break into the jail. The inmate, Archer, is chained and pessimistic, but Dickie frees him. They ride to the river, where Archer loses courage because his horse is lame and cannot swim. However, the mount is changed, and he gets over. The sheriff then appears with one hundred men, and when Archer sees them in pursuit his courage wavers again. Dickie, however, just mocks his pursuers.

Examples: Child F, Linscott.

Discussion: The ballad resembles *Jock o the Side* (Child 187) quite closely, more so in Child A-E than in the American Child F. For a complete treatment of the English stories in comparison with F see Child, III, 484f. See also the fragment, similar to Child F, in *BFSSNE*, VI, 7.

Barry, *Brit Blds Me,* 393f., prints four Massachusetts and one Maine derivatives of Archie o Cawfield which probably reveal the Child ballad adapted to the imprisonment of a Massachusetts mint-master, John Webb, by the Government in 1800. Webb was freed by friends. Barry states that these fragments, if placed together, "would very nearly complete the ballad" and suggests a comparison to Child F, although resemblances to Child A and B are noted. The titles *John Webber* and *Billy and Johnny* are used.

Gardner and Chickering, *Blds Sgs So Mich,* print a long secondary version which was collected in Michigan and which they feel follows Child B. See also Ives, *BI Sg Bk,* 30.

199. THE BONNIE HOUSE O AIRLIE

Texts: Barry, *Brit Blds Me,* 266 / Cox, *Fsgs South,* 128 / Creighton and Senior, *Trd Sgs N Sc,* 70 / *English Journal* (April 1918), 270 / Flanders, *Ancient Blds,* III, 191 / Gardner and Chickering, *Blds Sgs So Mich,* 209.

Local Titles: Prince Charlie, The Bonnie Hoose o' Earlie, The Plundering of Arley.

Story Types: A: During the reign of Cromwell, the Duke of Argyle moves to plunder the house of the Earl of Airly. The latter is away. Lady Margaret Airly sees Argyle approach with his men. When he reaches the gates, she refuses to come down and kiss him. He seizes her, however, and eventually discovers her dowry among the planting. Then, he lays her down on the streamside while he plunders the home. The wife swears if she had seven (eleven) sons, she would give them all to Charles.

Examples: Barry (A).

B: The story is essentially like that of Type A. However, the lady of the estate is just a girl and the absent protector just a knight. In addition, she requests to be taken to the valley where she cannot see the plundering, but is instead taken to a mountain top and made to watch the destruction. The real story is lost, and the War of the Roses is used as the background.

Examples: Barry (B).

C: The story of Type C is essentially a cross between Types A and B.

The heroine is still Lady Margaret, whose husband, the Earl, is absent, but the mood, detail, and story are those of Type B.

Examples: Cox.

Discussion: The historical background of this ballad is summarized by Child, IV, 55 and centers about the 1640 commission issued to the Earl of Argyle by which he was permitted to subdue and bring to "their duty" certain political and religious undesirables. Argyle interpreted his commission rather savagely.

The Type A story follows Child A, while Type B is related to Child BB and Greig, *Last Leaves of Trd Blds,* B. The West Virginia (Type C) text, which appears to be a cross of Types A and B is closest to Child C.

A comparison should be made of the two unusual stanzas at the start of the Gardner and Chickering, *Blds Sgs So Mich,* fragment and Stanzas 10 and 12 of a Ford broadside (See Ford, *Broadsides, Blds, etc. Mass* (2nd series), 167-9). These stanzas begin, in the Gardner and Chickering book, with the line "What loo' is that, 'quoth the brave Lor' Heel".

An Illinois version, that is said to be "the work of a high school student born in Scotland, but long a resident of this country" is printed in *English Journal* for April, 1918, p. 270. This text would be a Type D story, if one could be certain that it was not partly composed by the student in question. The story begins like Type A, but after the lady refuses to come down a change occurs in the narrative events. In the next stanza, Airly returns and, finding the carnage, swears revenge. He attacks Argyle's clan (the Campbells), but fails to slay the Lord. His drummer makes light of the fray; so Airly in a rage throws him from a tower. The boy swears he will haunt his master on the latter's death-day. Later, on hearing drums playing mysteriously from the tower, Airly knows his time has come.

Russell M. Harrison found a text in Oregon (see *WF,* 1952, 182), but does not print it.

200. THE GYPSY LADDIE

Texts: Anderson, *Coll Bld Sgs,* 49 / Arlington's *Banjo Songster* (Philadelphia, 1860), 47 / Barry, *Brit Blds Me,* 269 / Beard, *Personal Fsg Coll Lunsford,* 88 / Belden, *Mo Fsgs,* 73 / Brewster, *Blds Sgs Ind,* 134 / Brown, *NC Flklre,* II, 161 / *CFQ,* V, 212 / Cambiaire, *Ea Tenn Wstn Va Mt Blds,* 59 / Chappell, *Fsgs Rnke Alb,* 37 / Chase, *Sgs All Times,* 12 / Chase, *Trd Blds Sgs Sgng Games,* 4 / Child, IV, 72 / Cox, *Fsgs South,* 130 / Cox, *Trd Blds W Va,* 31 / Cox, *W Va School Journal and Educator,* XLIV, 428 / Creighton and Senior, *Trd Sgs N Sc,* 71 / Davis, *Fsgs Va,* 27 / Davis, *More Trd Blds Va,* 253 / Davis, *Trd Bld Va,* 423 / DeWitt's *Forget-me-not Songster* (N.Y., 1872), 223 / Duncan, *No Hamilton Cnty,* 85 / Eddy, *Blds Sgs Ohio,* 67 / Flanders, *Ancient Blds,* III, 193 / Flanders, *Garl Gn Mt Sg,* 69 / Flanders, *Vt Fsgs Blds,* 220 / Garrison, *Searcy Cnty,* 10 / Gilbert, *Lost Chords,* 35 / Greenleaf and Mansfield, *Blds Sea Sgs Newfdld,* 38 / Haufrecht, *Folk Sing,* 159 / Haun, *Cocke Cnty,* 65 / Henry, *Beech Mt Fsgs,* 6 / Henry, *Fsgs So Hghlds,* 110 / Hooley's *Opera House Songster,* 46 / Hubbard, *Blds Sgs Utah,* 26 / Hudson, *Fsgs Miss,* 117 / Hudson, *Ftunes Miss,* 26 / Hudson, *Spec Miss Flklre,* #18 / *JAF,* 1905, 191; 1906, 294; 1911, 346; 1912, 173; 1913, 353; 1917, 323; 1935, 385; 1939, 79; 1957, 339 / Karpeles, *Fsgs Newfdld,* 13 / Ky Cnties Ms. / *Ky Folk-Lore and Poetry Magazine,* II, #4, 7-8 / *Ky Folklore*

Record, 1956, 58 / *Keystone Folklore Quarterly,* 1957, 21 / Kincaid, *Fav Mt Blds,* 33 / Linscott, *Fsgs Old NE,* 207 / Lomax and Lomax, *Am Blds Fsgs,* 292 / Lomax and Lomax, *Our Sgng Cntry,* 156 / Lunsford and Stringfield, *30 & 1 Fsgs So Mts,* 4 / McIntosh, *So Ill Fsgs,* 17 / Martz' *Sensational Songster,* 65 / Mason, *Cannon Cnty,* 21 / McGill, *Fsgs Ky Mts,* 15 / *MLN,* XXVII, 242 / Morris, *Fsgs Fla,* 304 / Musick, *Flklre Kirksville,* 8 / Neely and Spargo, *Tales Sgs So Ill,* 140 / NY broadside (de Marson, List #3, #28), Brown Univ. Library / *NYFQ,* 1954, 52 / Owens, *Studies Tex Fsgs,* 28 / Owens, *Texas Fsgs,* 47 / Perry, *Carter Cnty,* 86, 298 / Pound, *Nebr Syllabus,* 10 / Raine, *Land Sddle Bags,* 119 / Randolph, *Oz Fsgs,* I, 152 / Sandburg, *Am Sgbag,* 311 / Scarborough, *Sgctchr So Mts,* 215 / SharpC, *Eng Fsgs So Aplchns,* #27 / SharpK, *Eng Fsgs So Aplchns,* I, 237 / Smith and Rufty, *Am Anth Old Wrld Blds,* 44 / *SFQ,* 1944, 156 / Stout, *Flklre Iowa,* 11 / *Va FLS Bull,* #s 3, 5, 8, 9, 11 / Wells, *Bld Tree,* 116 / *W Va Folklore,* III, #2 (1953), 21 / Harry L. Wilson, *Lions of the Lord,* 376-380.

Local Titles: Bill Harman, Black-eyed (Black-jack, Black Cat) Davy (David, Daley), Cross-eyed David, The Dark-clothes Gypsy, Egyptian Davy O, Gay Little Davy, Georgia Davy, The Gyps of Davy, Gypsea Song, Gypsy Daisy, Gypsie (Gypsen, Gypso) Davy, The Gypsies, The Gypsy Laddie, The Gypsy Lover, The Gyptian Laddie, Harvey Walker, The Heartless Lady, How Old Are You My Pretty Little Miss?, It Was Late in the Night When Johnny Came Home, Johnny Fall and Lady Cassilis, The Lady's Disgrace, A Neat Young Lady, Oh Come and Go Back My Pretty Fair Miss, Seven Gypsies in a Row, The Three Gypsies, When Carnel First Came to Arkansas, When the Squire Came Home.

Story Types: A: A gypsy sings or whistles before the lord's house and charms his lady away, often after he has received gifts of such things as wine, nutmeg, rings, etc. from her. When the lord returns and finds his wife gone, he orders his horses saddled and overtakes the elopers. He asks his lady if she has forsaken him, her child, and warm bed. Mentioning, in some texts, that she married against her will in the first place, she assures him she has. Most texts include some of the following material: the husband asks his wife who will care for the children and receives the reply, "you will"; the husband tells the wife to remove her fine Spanish shoes and give him her hand in farewell; some comments are made on the comparative poverty of the woman's new station.

Examples: Barry (A); Cox, *Fsgs South* (C); Davis, *Trd Bld Va* (A); *JAF,* 1905, 191 (B); Perry (B).

B: The story is the same as that of Type A, except that the wife writes her husband a few weeks later that she is tired of her lover and wishes to come home. He writes back that he has another girl, and she can stay with her gypsy.

Examples: Davis, *Trd Bld Va* (B).

C: The story is similar to that of Type A, except that the gypsy casts the lady off in the end.

Examples: Belden (C), Garrison.

D: The story is similar to that of Type A. However, in a fashion that is reminiscent of Type B, the lord remarries inside six months.

Examples: Child (J).

E: The story resembles Type A. However, the lady repents. She may even go home to her "feather bed and baby" and her husband may offer to lock her up where "the Egyptians can't get a-nigh her".

Examples: Cox, *Fsgs South* (B); Brown, (C, E).

F: A West Virginia adaptation of the ballad to a local event has the husband follow the elopers and give up the chase when he loses their trail.

Examples: Cox, *Fsgs South* (D).

G: The sexes become reversed in some texts (though in the garbled Scarborough example the original arrangement remains in the opening stanza), and the lady runs off with another girl.

Examples: Scarborough (C); *JAF*, 1905, 194 (F).

H: The versions that have been corrupted by stanzas from the old English folksong "I'm Seventeen Come Sunday" have the "gypsy" ask the girl her age and get the "seventeen (sixteen) next Sunday" reply. He may also ask the girl whether or not she will flee with him and again get the "next Sunday" reply. She then removes her low (high) shoes of Spanish leather, puts on her high (low)-heeled ones, and rides off with her new lover. The normal pursuit of her husband, the usual scorning of him, and the "cold ground-feather bed" comparison follow.

Examples: Hudson, *Fsgs Miss* (B); Davis, *More Trd Blds Va* (AA).

I: A short lyric has been found: last night I lay in my feather bed, but tonight in the arms of a gypsy. The story is completely gone, and only the comparison of the two lives remains.

Examples: Flanders, *Ancient Blds* (W).

J: The story is the usual one, except the lord kills both his wife and the gypsy at the end.

Examples: Flanders, *Ancient Blds* (J).

Discussion: The basic outline of the traditional story (see Child, IV, 61 for detail) is as follows: Some gypsies sing at a lord's gate and entice the lady down. When she shows herself they cast a spell over her, and she gives herself over to the gypsy chief (Johnny Faa from Seanin an Faith or Johnny the Seer in Gaelic. See Linscott, *Fsgs Old NE*, 208.) without reservation. Her lord, upon returning and finding her gone, sets out to recover her. He captures and hangs fifteen gypsies.

The song is probably the rationalization of a fairy-lover story (The Randolph, *Oz Fsgs*, E text has the lady admit she is bewitched. This may, of course, be a modern reversal to the original motif, or it may be a survival of that motif.) that has later become allied with a traditional story of the love affair and subsequent elopement of one Johnny Faa and Lady Cassilis, wife of the Earl of Cassilis. See Child, IV, 63 where the name Johnny Faa is stated to be a very common one among the nomads and where the story is discussed and Judith Ann Knoblock (*WF*, 1960, 35-40) where Child 200 is seen as a parody of King Orfeo (19).

There are any number of minor variations in this story as told by the American ballads. In this country, the hanging of the gypsies and the names Faa and Cassilis are generally omitted. (However, check Flanders, *Ancient Blds*, E). The rationalization has frequently been carried further so that the gypsy becomes merely a lover and the lady becomes a landlord's wife, etc. (See Cambiaire, *Ea Tenn Wstn Va Mt Blds*. Note also Davis, *Trd Bld Va*, E, where the gypsies are on their way to becoming Indians.) For a detailed discussion of one American (Ohio) text see *MLN*, XXVII, 242—4.

In general, it may be said that American texts follow the Child H and I versions most closely. There are, however, a large number of story types, the differences centering mostly about the final outcome of the tale. Type A tells the usual American narrative, with the rejection of the secure home for the insecure nomad life seeming to appeal to the New World (See Type I). The Spanish boots so frequently mentioned are to be found in Child G as well. Types B, C, and D reveal an almost puritanical revision of the end in the interests of seeing justice done or exist because of local incidents that have attached themselves to the story as Garrison, *Searcy Cnty*, 11 suggests. Type E is pure sentimentality, and Type F shows the influence of a local event on the narrative. The West Virginia elopement of Tim Wallace, a very ugly man, with Billy Harman's wife, an exceptionally pretty woman, is retold in the framework of *The Gypsy Laddie*. Type G is an example of degeneration through transmission—in this case to the point of absurdity. (See Flanders, *Vt. Fsgs Blds*, 220 and Reed Smith, *SC Blds*, 37 for discussion.) Type H is the result of a corruption of the ballad by "I'm Seventeen Come Sunday". The amount of transfer varies to some degree within this type, but members of the group are not uncommon. See Haun, *Cocke Cnty*, 65; *JAF*, 1939, 79; Mason, *Cannon Cnty*, 21; and Neely and Spargo, *Tales Sgs So Ill*, 140; as well as others.

The jingling American refrains are not in the British texts. See Belden, *Mo Fsgs*, 74. Usually some nonsense phrase like "ring a ding", etc. or "diddle dum", etc. constitutes the refrain—many times in the form of a chorus. However, meaningful refrains do occur. See "oh how I love thee" in Duncan, *No Hamilton Cnty*, 85 (Tennessee). Also, a "raggle-taggle gypsy" line often occurs. See Cox, *Trd Bld W Va*, C.

The Flanders series in *Ancient Blds* demonstrates most of the American variations. The S version may have been corrupted by *A Frog Went a-Courtin'*.

The ballad has been the subject of a number of burlesques. Owens, *Texas Fsgs*, 47 reprints the DeMarsan broadside of c. 1860. This text is from minstrel tradition, with a refrain beginning "Elopements now are all the go / They set the darkies crazy". See also the *Forget-me-not Songster* (DeWitt, N.Y., 1872), 223.

An analogous Danish ballad appears in Svend Grundtvig's *Danmarks gamle Folkeviser* (Copenhagen, 1853 - - -), #369.

201. BESSY BELL AND MARY GRAY

Texts: Barry, *Brit Blds Me,* 278 / Cox, *Fsgs South,* 134 / Cox, *W. Va. School Journal and Educator,* 428 / Davis, *Fsgs Va,* 28 / Davis, *Trd Bld Va,* 432 / *Mother Goose's Melodies* (James Miller, N.Y., 1869) / Scarborough, *Sgctchr So Mts,* 191.

Local Titles: Bessy (Betsey) Bell and Mary Gray.

Story Types: A: The first four lines of the Child ballad exist as a song by themselves.

Examples: Davis, *Trd Bld Va* (C, D).

B: The first four lines of the Child ballad, with a nursery stanza added, exist as a nonsense rime.

Examples: Barry (A); Davis, *Trd Bld Va* (A).

C: A two-stanza song is made up of the first stanza used by Types A and B in addition to a stanza on the green, not red or yellow, shoes the girls wore.

Examples: Cox, *Fsgs South*

D: The first stanza is that of Type A. The second stanza tells of the death coming from the town and killing the girls.

Examples: Scarborough.

Discussion: This ballad is based on the old Scottish story concerning two girls, Mary Gray, daughter of a laird of Lednock; and Bessy Bell, daughter of the laird of Kinvaid. When the latter girl was visiting the former in 1645, a plague broke out. The two women sought refuge in a bower. However, before long they were infected by a young man who was in love with one or both and who brought them food. They were buried near-by. *The London Times* of July 8, 1832 (and again of July 8, 1932) prints a report of the fencing in of the girls' grave by Lord Lynedoch in order to protect it from sightseers.

Davis, *Trd Bld Va,* 432 reports that there are two mountains in County Tyrone in Ireland that have the same names as the girls. These titles have also been given to twin peaks near Staunton, Va. For further details consult Child, IV, 75-6.

The American texts are fragmentary, but this condition seems to be the rule in the New World. Davis, *op. cit.,* 433 notes that "several people have told me they had known the first stanza of the ballad all their lives, but had no idea it was a ballad". Type A is of this sort. Compare it with Child's text, Stanzas 1 or 4. See also *Ramsay's Poems,* Edinburgh, 1721, 80 as quoted by Child, IV, 75. Type B is found as a nursery rime in Halliwell's *Nursery Rhymes of England,* 1874, 246 and is the most common American type. See *MWF,* 1958, 192. Type C seems to have been corrupted by *The Gypsie Laddie* (Child 200), while Type D constitutes an incomplete form of the Child text. See Stanzas 1 and 2 in Child.

204. JAMIE DOUGLAS

Barry, *Brit Blds Me,* 469f. presents evidence that this song will be found in Maine. He prints a text (*O Waly Waly*) which derives from a song that

Child, IV, 92 notes has shared stanzas with *Jamie Douglas* (Child A-M versions). *O Waly Waly* appeared in Ramsay's *Tea Table Miscellany*, II, under the title *Waly Waly Gin Love Be Bonny.*

208. LORD DERWENTWATER

Texts: JAF, 1934, 95 / Morris, *Fsgs Fla,* 308 / *SFQ,* 1944, 158.

Local Titles: The King's Love Letter.

Story Types: A: The Duke is summoned to England by a "love letter" from the King. He calls his eldest son and tells the lad that he is leaving for London. Before the city, he meets a man who fortells the Duke's death and asks for his will. The will is given; thereupon the Duke's nose begins to bleed as he stoops over to smell flowers. The song is incomplete, and it ends with the Duke's wish that his children be cared for.

Examples: Morris.

Discussion: The story of the incomplete Florida version can be reconstructed from the Child texts (especially Child D) where Derwentwater, who was actually an agitator for the Pretender, is summoned as a Scotsman to the court. His wife, with child, forseeing his death, tells him to make his will before he goes. Derwentwater complies. He then sets forth. En route, by some omen such as a bleeding nose, the stumbling of his horse, etc. he knows his days are numbered. At London, he is branded a traitor. An old man with an axe then steps up (undoubtedly this man is the original of the American questioner) and demands the Lord's life. Derwentwater is slain after a few generous dying requests.

For a discussion of the one American text of the ballad and the folk superstition in the nose-bleeding see *SFQ,* 1944, 158. A. C. Morris, the editor of this item, sees this discovery as an indication of the retention of English eighteenth century culture in the South.

209. GEORDIE

Texts: Barry, *Brit Blds Me,* 475 (trace) / Belden, *Mo Fsgs,* 76 / Brown, *NC Flklre,* II, 168 / Carlisle, *Fifty Sgs Blds NW Ark,* 33 / Chappell, *Fsgs Rnke Alb,* 37 / Cox, *Fsgs South,* 135 / Creighton, *Maritime Fsgs,* 27 / Creighton and Senior, *Trd Sgs N Sc,* 73 / Davis, *Fsgs Va,* 28 / Davis, *More Trd Blds Va,* 262 / Davis, *Trd Bld Va,* 435 / Flanders, *Ancient Blds,* III, 231 / Flanders, *Vt Fsgs Blds,* 241 / Gardner and Chickering, *Blds Sea Sgs Newfdld,* 40 / *Green Mountain Songster,* 33 / Hummel, *Oz Fsgs* / *JAF,* 1907, 319; 1919, 504; 1947, 245; 1957, 340 / Niles, *Sgs Hill Folk,* 12 / Pound, *Nebr Syllabus,* 11 / Randolph, *Oz Fsgs,* I, 161 / Randolph, *Oz Mt Flk,* 224 / Scarborough, *Sgctchr So Mts,* 213 / SharpC, *Eng Fsgs So Aplchns,* #28 / SharpK, *Eng Fsgs So Aplchns,* I, 240 / Shoemaker, *Mt Mnstly,* 162 / Shoemaker, *No Pa Mnstly,* 158 / *SFLQ,* V, 170 / *Va FLS Bull,* #s, 7, 9 / Wells, *Bld Tree,* 116 / Wetmore and Bartholomew, *Mt Sgs NC,* 13.

Local Titles: Charlie and Sally, Charley's Escape, Geordie, Georgia, George E. Wedlock, Georgie, Georgy-O, Go Saddle Up My Milk-White Steed, Johnny Wedlock, The Laird of Gigh, The Life of Georgia, London's Bridge, Lovely Georgia.

Story Types: A: A man crossing London Bridge sees a girl weeping for Georgie. Georgie, in prison for a crime calling for capital punishment, has

sent for his sweetheart or wife. She has hurried to him and knows that he can be rescued by a large ransom. She raises the money. However, Georgie in denying one capital offense admits another and is sentenced to death. He is hung. The girl often expresses the wish that she were armed so that she might fight for him.
Examples: Belden (A); Davis, *Trd Bld Va* (A); Randolph, *Oz Fsgs* (D).

B: The same general story is told in this type. However, in some texts, upon her arrival at the prison the lady is offered aid by an old man. At any rate, the king or judge says she has come too late and that Geordie is already condemned for horse or deer stealing. Geordie is hung in silk robes (or similar suitable style) because he is of royal blood and loved by a virtuous lady. The wish of the girl that she had weapons with which to fight for her lover is sometimes found in this type too.
Examples: Cox, Greenleaf and Mansfield.

C: The story is the same as that of Type A. However, it is told differently, and the ransom and the girl's pleas are successful so that Charlie and his Sally go free.
Examples: Flanders, *Ancient Blds* (B); Shoemaker, *Mt Mnstly.*

D: This type of story rises from the traditional British texts in which Geordie is freed by his wife (true love). Geordie is in trouble. He sends a man to tell his lady of his plight. She hurries to the King and produces enough money to free her man.
Examples: Randolph, *Oz Fsgs* (C); Scarborough.

Discussion: Because of the existence of the Scottish traditional song, *Geordie,* and two not dissimilar broadsides *Georgie Stoole* (early seventeenth century) and *The Life and Death of George of Oxford* (late seventeenth or early eighteenth century), this ballad presents a definite scholarly problem. (See Child, IV, 123—7, 140-2.) The chances are that the two broadsides represent literary reworkings and contemporary adaptations of the old Scottish song. (See Cox, *Fsgs South,* 135.) However, Ebsworth, *Roxbourghe Ballads,* VII, 67-73 thought the opposite to be the case.

Although the ransom motif is generally vague or lacking and the crime charged may be murder, as well as stealing the king's cattle, the Type A-C American texts derive from *George of Oxford* and the variant British broadsides. See Child, IV, 124 and 127, and *JAF,* 1907, 319. In the broadsides, the hero is hung in the end, although the girl's pleas are successful in the traditional texts as well as in the *Green Mountain Songster* version (Type C). Barry (see a letter quoted by Henry, *Fsgs So Hghlds,* 142) discusses this point in connection with the derivative songs such as the Henry *The Judge and the Jury, op. cit.,* 142.

The Type A-C American texts are difficult to classify. The Type A and Type B stories are certainly from the same broadside tradition, having many stanzas in common, and sometimes fusing into one narrative. (See Wells, *Bld Tree,* 118). However, as far as their plot outlines go, they do fall into two types, if only because of the material retained or forgotten in each group. Both these types contain stanzas that have not been traced to either the known broadsides or the traditional texts in Child. Type C, although it shares much material with Types A and B, seems to have an ancestor with a sentimentalized close.

Type D texts are localized variants of the traditional form of the song, even though they seem to have passed unrecognized as such. Randolph, *Oz Fsgs*, C parallels Child F rather closely through its first seven stanzas and summarizes the story of Child F in the last four stanzas. Of course, Child F is not a pure example of the traditional form of the song, its first and second stanzas having been corrupted by the *Oxford* broadside, but it does tell the traditional tale. Randolph's variant has an *Oxford* first stanza like Child F, but from there on shows no relation to any form but the traditional. However, certain localizations and repetitive features have clouded the identity to some degree. The Scarborough text (See Wetmore and Bartholomew, *Mt Sgs NC, 13* for a very similar text taken from the same informant) is abbreviated, but obviously related to the Randolph song. See *SFQ*, 1949, 161-168.

Chappell, *Fsgs Rnke Alb*, 37 prints a fragment called *Johnny Wedlock* (the Randolph text has the title *George E. Wedlock*). However, it is too brief to be clearly identified.

210. BONNIE JAMES CAMPBELL

Texts: Barry, *Brit Blds Me*, 279 / Beard, *Personal Fsg Coll Lunsford*, 94 / Combs, *Fsgs États-Unis*, 144 / Davis, *Fsgs Va*, 28 / Davis, *More Trd Blds Va*, 267 / Flanders, *Ancient Blds*, III, 237 / *JAF*, 1905, 294 / Worthington, *Nine Rare Trd Blds Va*, 105.

Local Titles: Bonnie George Campbell, Bonnie Johnnie Campbell, Willie Campbell.

Story Types: A: The story is lost in Britain as well as in America, so that we only know that Bonnie James Campbell rode out armed one day and that, although his saddled horse came home, he did not. His bride, mother, etc., went out to meet him, but he was never to return. The place was uncared for; his baby unborn.

Examples: Barry (A, B), Combs (A, B).

Discussion: The tale behind this ballad is unknown. Child, IV, 143 cites Motherwell's and Maidment's theories, and Barry, *Brit Blds Me*, 281 reconstructs the story as it stands in the known fragments.

The American texts are similar to those in Child and show a close relationships with the versions given in Smith's *Scotish Minstrel*, V, 42. See Barry, *op. cit.*, 297f.; Davis, *More Trd Blds Va*, 267-268; and Worthington, *Nine Rare Trd Blds Va*, 105-119 for discussion of the Anglo-American tradition of this song, as well as for a modification of some of Child's remarks.

213. SIR JAMES THE ROSE

Texts: American Speech, I, 481 / Barry, *Brit Blds Me*, 284 / Creighton, *Maritime Fsgs*, 23 / Creighton and Senior, *Trd Sgs N Sc*, 75 / Flanders, *Ancient Blds*, III, 239 / Flanders, *Blds Migrant NE*, 147 / MacKenzie, *Blds Sea Sgs N Sc*, 48.

Local Titles: Sir James the Rose, Sir James the Ross.

Story Types: A: The Ross Story: James the Ross learns at a meeting in the woods with his true love Matilda that she must marry the hated John Grames on her father's orders. Donald Grames overhears the conversation between the lovers and, after the girl departs, makes himself known to Ross. Ross kills the eavesdropper. Fearful of revenge by the Grames clan, Ross then sets out to get aid from his kinsman, stopping en route to awaken Matilda and tell her what he has done. She detains him and hides him, saying that a page will rouse his clansmen. The page, however, meets John Grames on the way, tells him what has taken place, and is bribed into revealing James' whereabouts. When the Grames come to Matilda's house, they find Ross sleeping in the wood much to the dismay of the girl. Ross is able to kill four (or fifteen) of his attackers before John Grames stabs him from behind. Matilda then kills herself, and the page follows suit.

Examples: *Am Speech,* I, 481; Barry; MacKenzie (A,B).

Discussion: The Child *Sir James the Rose* ballad is not in America. The American texts are highly sophisticated and based on *Sir James the Ross,* a song Child, IV, 156 thought to have been composed by Michael Bruce. Barry, *Brit Blds Me,* 290—1, citing Alexander Keith (editor) in Greig's *Last Leaves of Traditional Blds,* points out that both the Ross (not in Child's collection) and Rose (which Child printed) ballads are derived from eighteenth century broadsides and stall copies and that Michael Bruce is mistakenly considered the composer of the former. He also points out on Keith's authority that the Ross version has ousted the Rose in Scotland and that his American copy of Ross is identical with the 1768 and oldest known Scottish (*150 Scots Songs,* London, 1768) text of the story. His version being that old and well established in oral tradition, Barry therefore rates the Ross texts as a primary, rather than a secondary, form of the story in America. Also see MacKenzie, *Blds Sea Sgs N Sc,* 48. MacKenzie's A version is particularly sophisticated. The Pound, *American Speech,* Nebraska version does not differ materially from the northern texts.

214. THE BRAES OF YARROW

Texts: Barry, *Brit Blds Me,* 291 / Cazden, *Abelard Fsg Bk,* I, 40 / Cox, *Fsgs South,* 137 / Flanders, *Ancient Blds,* III, 255 / Flanders, *Blds Migrant NE,* 235 / *JAF,* 1955, 203 / *NYFQ,* 1952, 248 / Siegmeister, *Sgs Early Am,* 40 / *SFQ,* 1958, 195, 198.

Local Titles: The Dens of Yarrow, The Dewy (Dewy) Dens of Yarrow (Darrow), The Derry Dems of Arrow.

Story Types: A: Seven sons, two of them twins, battle for their true love in the dens of Yarrow. The girl dreams she has been gathering pretty heather blooms in Yarrow. Her mother reads her dreams to mean that her Jimmy has been slain. The girl then searches him up and down through Yarrow and finds him dead behind a bush. She washes his face, combs his hair, bathes the wound, and, wrapping her yellow hair about his waist, pulls him home. She tells her mother to make her death-bed, and, although her mother promises her a better love than the one slain, she dresses in

clean white clothes, goes to the river, and lies down to die on the banks.
Examples: Siegmeister, Cazden.

B: A Texas version recorded in Arkansas tells of a cowboy who is hired by his sweetheart's father. She sends him out one day, and as he rides the hills and valleys he is attacked by nine men. The girl's brother slays him from behind, after he has put up a fine fight. The slayers go to tell the girl, who has meanwhile dreamed a dream of sorrow about her love. Her father reads her dream and tells her her love is dead. She goes to the body, after removing her jewels, and cleanses it and buries it. When she returns her father offers her "a better lad", but she is heartsick.

Examples: *SFQ*, 1958, 198.

Discussion: The story in Child is that of a girl who dreams she has been pulling heather on the braes of Yarrow and wishes her true-love not to go to the highlands as she fears her cruel brother will betray him for stealing her from her family (other similar reasons are given in certain texts). Nevertheless, while drinking the night before, he has pledged himself to a fight on the braes at dawn and sets out in spite of her pleas. At Yarrow, he is attacked by nine of her family and, although killing four and wounding five, is knifed to death from behind. One of the brothers then goes to tell the sister of the deed. She hastens to the braes and, seeing her lover dead, faints and/or drinks his blood, kisses him, and combs his hair in her grief. She either ties her own three-quarter-length hair about her neck and chokes herself to death, takes her lover's body home and pregnant dies of a broken heart, or refuses the sympathy offered her by her father. In some versions, she curses the oxen and kye that have caused the original trouble between the two families. (See Child, IV, 164.)

Type A texts do not follow the Child texts (A-L) summarized above, but rather seem a variation of the Q-S (*The Dowie Dens of Yarrow*) series, a group of texts in which ten lovers fight over a girl and in which the father or sister is the dream-reader and clairvoyant of the lover's death. The American texts, from the Northeast and Southwest, and Child's Q-S series have almost identical titles, "dewy" usually replacing "dowie". The fight among the seven sons over the girl is a logical step from the confused ten lovers beginning in Child Q-S. The presence of the mother, instead of the father or sister, as reader of the dream and encourager of the bereft girl, is no great change, particularly when we note the insertion of the "make my bed" cliche in the Siegmeister text and remember the similarity of this situation to the ones in *Barbara Allen* (Child 84) and *Lady Alice* (Child 85) where the mother is present. And, finally, the girl does die in both Child Q and S, even though the dressing in white and the return to the river are not in Child.

The Type B version, however, is close to Child L, in spite of its westernization, and is an unusual American find for that reason. In addition, it includes two actions not in any of the Child 214 or 215 versions—the removal of the jewels and the burial of the body.

There are a number of American texts that cannot be traced to Child's *The Braes of Yarrow* with any finality. Cox, *Fsgs South,* 137 points out that his West Virginia text, which came to America from Scotland, is from the William Hamilton poem that Ramsay printed on p. 242 of the third or London edition of the *Tea-Table Miscellany,* 1733. (See also *Anderson's British Poets,* Edinburg, 1794, IX, 426.) This poem is noted by Child, IV, 163, footnote to have affected his J, K, and particularly L versions. Hamilton based it on the ballad story, and it consists of a conversation between three speakers. A man is requesting a bride to forget her past and rejoice in him, while a friend wonders why she is so sad and what story lies behind the situation. It is then revealed that the man has slain the girl's lover on the braes of Yarrow, and she cannot forgive him or forget. The poem ends indefinitely with the new lover still trying to persuade the girl of the futility of her mourning. The Cox text retains this story, although it is incomplete and the speakers are not marked as in the poem. Stanzas 1—6 (Cox 1—6) and 15—16 (Cox 7—8) are reproduced with almost no textual variation. Thus the lyricism and poetic style of the sophisticated work have been retained in oral tradition. See JAF, 1950, 328-335 for further remarks on this and other points in connection with Child 214 and 215, *Rare Willie Drowned in Yarrow.*

In *NYFQ,* 1952, 245-266, Norman Cazden discusses the "Yarrow" ballads, their historical content, and the social impact of their poetry. He suggests that Child 215, *Rare Willie Drowned in Yarrow,* is actually two ballads—one dealing with a drowning at Gamrie, one with a drowning at Yarrow. He further suggests that the versions of 215 with the Yarrow drowning belong to the tradition of 214, contrary to Child's classification, and that the drowning is an intrusion into the story. Willie of 215 was slain, and his body thrown in the water. He also argues that the "bed wide and narrow" cliché is inappropriate to *Barbara Allen* (84) with which it is usually associated, as unmarried Barbara would not request a narrow bed when hers had never been wide. He says the cliché fits not only the circumstances, but also the rime and prosody of Child 214.

Cazden continued his probings of Child 214 in *JAF,* 1955, 201-209, where he links it with *The Bold Soldier* (Laws M27, see Child 8 in this volume) to demonstrate that a ballad's "formal qualities are all dependent upon the truth of the ballad's social reference".

The New England texts, collected by Barry and Flanders, do nothing to help clear the confusion of the traditions of Child 214 and 215. Barry, *Brit Blds Me,* 291, reports a stanza from what he terms a lost version of Child 214 in a song sung by a Maine woman to the tune of *Barbara Allen.* The stanza, which begins "Last night I made my bed so wide, Tonight I'll make it narrow", is similar to Stanza 19 in Child L, but is also of a very conventional nature. Barry also prints a fragment that contains the word "Yarrow" and a stanza similar to one that Child, IV, 179, thought had intruded into *Rare Willie Drowned in Yarrow* (Child 215) from 214. See Child 215 in this study. And, finally, he found another Maine woman who had heard Child A of *The Braes of Yarrow* sung in Ireland in her youth. Flanders (see *Ancient Blds,* III, 257) prints an A text, which, while like Child's Q-S series, also shows certain similarities to the A-L series, especially in the questions and answers (see Child A, B, I) and the murder of the lover by an arrow shot from behind a tree (see Child D). Flanders B, moreover, includes a stanza, the third, which is not in Child's texts of 214, but is found in somewhat similar form in 215, D-H.

The answer to all this can only lie in the fact that Child 214 as sung in Child A-L; Child 214 as sung in Child Q-S, and Child 215 have become as mixed in oral tradition as they have in the anthologies of Anglo-American ballads.

Leach, *Bld Bk,* 570 prints a text of a Scandinavian analogue. The song always includes a great deal of ancient superstition, as Leach notes.

215. RARE WILLIE DROWNED IN YARROW or THE WATER o GAMRIE

Texts: Barry, *Brit Blds Me,* 292 (listed as Barry B of Child 214) / Eddy, *Blds Sgs Ohio,* 69.

Local Titles: Yarrow.

Story Types: A girl's betrothed lover has gone hunting and sent a letter back to her that he is too young to marry. She ominously dreams that she is pulling heather on the braes of Yarrow. She then goes searching for her lover and finds him drowned. She wraps her long yellow hair about his waist and pulls him out of Yarrow.

Examples: Eddy.

Discussion: This ballad has become confused with *The Braes of Yarrow* in Britain as well as in this country. (See JAF, 1950, 328f. and the discussion of Child 214 in this book.) The story of *Rare Willie* in Child is as follows: Willie, his mother's darling, fails (in most cases) to get parental blessing for his marriage. On the way to church, he is washed from his horse while crossing a river or some such body of water. The bride, hearing what has happened, sets out to find the missing groom. In texts A, B, and C, which do not give many preliminary details, she discovers the body in the cleft of a rock and by wrapping her three-quarter-length hair about Willie's waist draws him from the water (B, C).

The three "southern" versions of the story (A, B, C) are said by Child, IV, 178, to be the older tradition of this ballad. It is probable that these texts, which now only state that Willie is to marry the girl, originally contained a similar, if not identical, story background to the one given above from the "northern" texts. Child also points out that the wrapping of the hair about the lover's waist in his 215 B and C belongs to 214, as do the "dream", the "letter", and "the wide and narrow bed" stanzas of the six stanza 215 C. In short, four of the half dozen stanzas of this version of *Rare Willie* have come from *The Braes of Yarrow*. The situation becomes further confused when he notes (IV, 163) that the drowning of 214L probably belongs to 215.

The Eddy, *Blds Sgs Ohio*, 69 text is printed under the contradictory heading *Rare Willie Drowned in Yarrow*, Child 214. This text is, in reality close to Child 215C, which, as noted above, has been badly corrupted by 214 and undoubtedly brought with it across the ocean the large amount of borrowed material. As the Eddy notes and remarks (see pp. 69—70) seem to reveal some confusion on this point and as *Rare Willie* is rare indeed in this country, I have compiled a stanza by stanza analysis of the Ohio text.

The first stanza of the Ohio song is closely paralleled in all four lines by the opening stanzas of both Child 215 A and C. The second Ohio stanza is not to be found in Child 215, but it is of a conventional sort that turns up frequently in love song. These lines are probably a corruption, although the fact that they mention the hunt is of interest as almost all the Child 214 texts include this feature. The third Ohio stanza is quite like the second stanza of Child 215 C, which lends extra credance to the corruption theory for Ohio Stanza 2. The second stanza of 215 C is one of those that Child believed to have been borrowed from *The Braes of Yarrow*. The fourth Ohio stanza relates to Child 214 in that the girl goes up a hill to spy her lover and is closest to 214J, Stanza 14 of all the Child stanzas in the two ballads. The drowning, however, is like 215, and thus like 214L also, while the use of a rock as the repository of the body is in 215A and B. The final Ohio stanza compares closely to 215C, Stanza 5 and 215B, Stanza 2. This evidence would serve to indicate that the Ohio text is a version of Child 215 and perhaps a variant of 215C. See, however, Cazden's remarks in *NYFQ*, 1952, 245f.

Barry, *Brit Blds Me*, 292 prints a fragment containing the line "Between two hills of Yarrow", beginning with lines similar to Child 215A, Stanza 2, and mentioning Willie. See also Child 214H, Stanza 17. Child said that his 215A, Stanza 2 had entered *Rare Willie* from his 214, and, therefore, Barry has seen fit to put the fragment under the title *The Braes of Yarrow*.

217. THE BROOM OF COWDENKNOWES

Texts: Barry, *Brit Blds Me*, 293.

Local Titles: None given.

Story Types: A: A group of gentlemen ride past a milkmaid, and one of them stops to seduce her. He gives her three guineas when he is through and says if he is not back in half a year that she must look no more for him. She shows him the highway by Tay and he departs. Her father suspects her when she returns home, but she denies anyone has been with her.

Examples: Barry.

Discussion: The Maine fragment ends upon the denial by the girl that anyone has been with her. The Child A text, close to the Maine song, rounds out the story as known to one Maine Irishwoman in her youth. See Barry, *Brit Blds Me*, 295. A few months later, the girl is out with the sheep when another group of riders comes by. One, to her shame, asks her who got her with child. This man subsequently reveals himself to be the lover and turns out to be a very rich one at that.

There is a popular song, not traditional however, of similar name and story structure also known in Maine. See Child, IV, 192 and 208. Consult also *The Warbler* (Peter Edes, printer), Augusta, Me., 1805.

218. THE FALSE LOVER WON BACK

Texts: Belden, *Mo Fsgs,* 78 / *Golden Book,* IX, 50 / *JAF,* 1921, 395.

Local Titles: The True Lover.

Story Types: A: A girl watches her lover pass her door and asks him where he is going. He replies that he is on his way to woo a girl lovelier than she. She is philosophical about his fickleness, but warns him that she will turn to other men. Then she follows him, and at each town he buys her a present and tells her to go home. She persists, and finally he buys her a wedding gown.

Examples: Belden.

Discussion: This ballad is not easy to find in America. The Missouri text is like Child A. However, John Moore (*JAF,* 1921, 396) points out that the Missouri version suppresses three stanzas in which the girl persistently asks her lover if he will not be fond of her again and one stanza in which he says she can turn to other men if she wishes but he will be true to his new love. These four stanzas all appear in Child 218A.

219. THE GARDENER

Reed Smith, *SFQ,* 1937, #2, 9-11 lists this ballad among the survivals of Child texts in America. His reference is to the Child C ballad from a Dr. Thomas Davidson, a Scotsman who lived in a number of places in the States. The text, which is not really from American oral tradition, is fragmentary, though it preserves the "summery" offer of the gardener and the "wintery" response of the maid.

221. KATHERINE JAFFRAY

Texts: Katherine Jaffray: Brown, *NC Flklre,* II, 169.

Squire of Edinborough: Barry, *Brit Blds Me,* 400 / Child, IV, 218 (headnote) / Creighton, *Sgs Blds N Sc,* 22 / Creighton and Senior, *Trd Sgs N Sc,* 79 / Flanders, *Ancient Blds,* III, 261 / Flanders, *New Gn Mt Sgstr,* 141.

Local Titles: Katherine Jeffrys.

A Scotch Ditty, Katherine Joffray, The Squire of Edinboroughtown.

Story Types: A: Lord Willie courts Katherine and gains the consent of her parents to the marriage. Although promised, the girl falls in love with a second, dashing suitor, Lord Robert from across the border. She says that she will marry him if there is any way. Robert thus attends the wedding as a guest, saying simply that he came because he wished to see Kate on her wedding day. Katherine toasts Robert with a glass of wine, and at that sign the lover takes the girl by her white hand and grass green sleeve, and they flee, galloping over the border. "Her kin did them no harm".

Examples: Brown.

B: *The "Squire of Edinborough" type:* A girl, ready to marry a squire's lad, is forced to accept another gentleman. She writes her lover of her plight, and he sends his answer with a ring, telling her to wear green at her nuptials. She answers that she will marry him in spite of all. On the wedding day, the lover brings a large group of men and attends the ceremony. He mock-toasts the groom, and, in response to the latter's challenge to a fight, asks for a kiss from the bride, after which he promises to leave. The request granted, he slips his arm about the girl and whisks her away to Edinborough.

Examples: Barry (A) ; Creighton; Flanders, *Ancient Blds* (A).

Discussion: The Type A text, a rare find in this country, follows the Child A version closely for ten stanzas, although it displays some contact with print. The battle at Cowden Banks is omitted, however, and the lovers merely escape in the North Carolina version. Also, the Scottish-English rivalry is no longer a feature of the song, even if the border locale is still discernable.

The Squire of Edinboroughtown is a later remodelling of *Katherine Jaffray,* probably from print. See Child, IV, 217—8 and Barry, *Brit Blds Me,* 406. This song (Type B) has survived in both Scottish and Irish versions in Northeastern United States and Canada.

Flanders, *New Gn Mt Sgstr,* 144 suggests that *Katherine Jaffray* was recomposed in Scotland as *The Squire,* but the wearing of green by the bride (see Child, IV, 218) surely points to Irish tradition for those texts that include it. No Scots girl would dare clothe herself in that "ill-starred" color.

225. ROB ROY

Texts: Barry, *Brit Blds Me,* 296.

Local Titles: Rob Roy.

Story Types: A: Rob Roy attacks a border house to carry off as his wife a woman who detests him. He surrounds the place, enters, and takes the girl from her mother's embrace, although she refuses to go willingly.

Examples: Barry.

Discussion: The Canadian fragment consists of the first five stanzas of Child A and was not sung. The Child song continues the story through the forced marriage, the return to Scotland, Rob Roy's departure for France, and his promise to teach the girl to dance. The ballad is based on history (see Child, IV, 243—5). Robert Oig abducted Jean Key, a young, rich widow, and forced her to marry him in 1750. Four years later he was taken and executed.

226. LIZIE LINDSAY

Texts: Advertiser (Aurora, Mo.), 5-22-'41 / Barry, *Brit Blds Me,* 297 / Brewster, *Blds Sgs Ind,* 135 / Cox, *Trd Bld W Va,* 36 / Flanders, *Ancient Blds,* III, 269 / Randolph, *Oz Fsgs,* I, 164 / Bull Tenn FLS, XVI, #2, 26.

Local Titles: Leezie Lindsay, New Yealand.

Story Types: A: There are a few extremely abbreviated versions of the Child story in America. A man asks a girl to go to the highlands with him.

She refuses, for she knows neither him nor his home. However, the girl's maid wishes she were in a position to accept the man's offer. The girl then dresses up and leaves with her suitor. Upon their arrival at his home, she is shown the land into which she has married. The real story seems forgotten.

Examples: Brewster, Randolph.

B: A little lyric request of a lover, in which he asks a girl "to go to the highlands", exists as a song. She refuses.

Examples: Barry.

Discussion: A derivative of Lizie Lindsay is to be found in this country. But, because of the fragmentary nature of some of the texts, it is difficult to be certain just how much of the traditional song is and has been in America. Barry, *Brit Blds Me,* 298—9 discusses this point in some detail in connection with his Northern fragments. It seems certain that a few stanzas of the traditional ballad have come over in the derivative form of the song, and the incomplete Midwestern and Southern texts appear to be genuine.

In the Child B version we are told how a young nobleman goes to get a wife in Edinburgh under the disguise of being a shepherd. The girl selected is reluctant to leave home and go with a poor stranger, but is persuaded to do so by her maid. She goes and is homesick, but learns the next day on getting up to milk the kye that she has married a rich man.

The Blaeberry Courtship (see Laws, *Am Bldry Brit Bdsdes,* N 19), the song derived from *Lizie Lindsay,* exists in a number of American versions. See *JAF,* 1922, 345 from Illinois and MacKenzie, *Blds Sea Sgs N Sc,* 69 from Nova Scotia. This story tells of an educated and disguised highlander who convinces a lowland girl to go with him against her parents' advice and who makes her a great lady. The "milk cows" refrain allies it closely to Child 226.

The New Brunswick text, which may be influenced by both the tradition of the Child ballad and the derivative song, has lost the story and retains only a four-stanza request "to go to the highlands". The Arkansas version consists of a single stanza of request and a second stanza concerning the departure which is somewhat similar to Child C. Stanza 12. Nor can the Indiana fragment be allied directly to any Child version, although it resembles Child, IV, 524 in the first stanza and the name of the hero, Donald MacDonald. The West Virginia text is quite similar to this one.

232. RICHIE STORY

There is a song, which originally seems to have been a romantic re-writing of *Richie Story* (see Child, IV, 299), that had wide British circulation under the name *Huntingtower.* This song, which Laws classifies as O 23 (see *Am Bldry Brit Bdsdes,* 236 for remarks and bibliography) is known in Northeastern oral tradition. See Creighton and Senior, *Sgs Blds N Sc,* 217 and Flanders, *Ancient Blds,* III, 273 for texts and further commentary. *Richie Story,* Child 232, is not known to the New World in its traditional form.

233. ANDREW LAMMIE

Texts: MacKenzie, *Blds Sea Sgs N Sc,* 60.

Local Titles: None given.

Story Types: A: A fragmentary story of a girl whose father beats her, and whose mother and brother scorn and mistrust her. Her love died for her today; she will die for him tomorrow.

Examples: MacKenzie.

Discussion: This Nova Scotia fragment, which was received in two parts from two singers, is closest to the Child C text. The story, as told there, is of a rich miller's daughter who falls in love with a trumpeter in the service of Lord Fyvie. She wants to marry him, but finds the match scorned by her father. When the trumpeter has to go to Edinburgh for a time, the girl Annie, knowing she will die before he returns, plans a tryst with him at a bridge. (In Scotland, lovers who part at a bridge shall never meet again.) He says he will buy her a wedding gown while away, and they are to marry on his return. But she bids him farewell forever. The trumpeter goes to the top of the castle and blows a blast that is heard in the girl's home. Her parents beat her, and her brother breaks her back. Lord Fyvie passes and tries to convince the miller to change his mind, but to no avail. The father insists on a better match. The girl is put to bed where she dies of a broken heart. The father laments, and Andrew, on his return, dies of grief. However, in the New World fragment we have an example of a cliche ("make my bed") overriding the story to the extent that the lover is said to have died before his true love.

236. THE LAIRD O DRUM

Texts: Barry, *Brit Blds Me,* 300 / Creighton, *Maritime Fsgs,* 28 / Gardner and Chickering, *Blds Sgs So Mich,* 149.

Local Titles: The Laird (Knight) and the Shepherd's Daughter, The Laird o' Drum.

Story Types: A: A nobleman out hunting spies a shepherd's lass who immediately captivates him. In Barry's text, he offers to marry her and, in spite of her protests that he is joking, says he will go with her to herd sheep.

Examples: Barry, Gardner and Chickering.

B: The same opening as Type A, but the girl implies that both are already married as she refuses his offer. However, she says that if they were dead and in the same grave, she would gladly have their dust mingle.

Examples: Creighton.

Discussion: The event, the marriage of Alexander Irvine to a woman of mean birth against his family's wishes, on which this ballad is based is given in Child, IV, 322. The American fragments have garbled the story to some extent and make little recognizable reference to the family's objections. These objections are, however, discernible in the last stanza of Barry's text and in Stanzas 5 and 6 of Creighton's text, even though the Creighton stanzas appear to be spoken by the maid instead of Drum's brother, John. They create a new story in that the girl refuses a man because he is already married. Barry's ending with its lines "For it's herdin' sheep on yon hillside I'll gang wi' you my lovely Nancy" could also result in a change in story.

Barry, *Brit Blds Me*, 301 points out that the Child versions of this ballad fall into two groups: the older forms that stick close to history (A, C, D, E, etc.) and the more recent forms which do not mention the suitor by name and do not indicate a previous marriage (B). Child, IV, 122 suspects his B version to have been contaminated by a song in the Motherwell Mss. concerning an earl and a shepherd's daughter. Barry's fragment reflects the influence of this song, too, in the fact that the suitor's father is alive. (Barry, *op. cit.*, 301—3.)

Gardner and Chickering, *Blds Sgs So Mich*, 149 indicate that Robert Chambers (ed.) in *The Songs in Scotland Prior to Burns* (London, 1862), 440—1 names a song with identical words to the Michigan fragment which was composed by a well-born vagabond, Jean Glover. The text also resembles the Barry fragment. Stanza 3 of the Michigan text is almost identical to Stanza 3 of the Barry fragment.

239. LORD SALTOUN AND AUCHANACHIE

Child 239 has not been collected from the oral tradition of the New World. However, songs that tell much the same story were popular with broadside composers, and a number of stall songs have entered oral tradition and are to be found in America. See Belden, *Mo Fsgs*, 165-166; SharpK, *Eng Fsgs So Aplchns*, II, 385; and Laws, *Am Bldry Brit Bdsdes*, M 2 (*Johnny Doyle*) and P 31 (*The Nobleman's Wedding*) for remarks and bibliography.

240. THE RANTIN LADDIE

Texts: Barry, *Brit Blds Me*, 303 / Combs, *Fsgs États-Unis*, 145.
Local Titles: The Rantin' Laddie.

Story Types: A: A poor girl, with a dubious past, has a bastard child by a nobleman. Her family scorns her; so she sends one of her father's servants to tell her "laddie" of her plight. He responds gallantly and sends a retinue to fetch the girl, Maggie, home as his bride.

Examples: Combs.

B: A short song remains from the ballad. It implies a dubious past and that the child of the girl, is illegitimate.

Examples: Barry.

Discussion: The Combs, *Fsgs États-Unis*, version follows Child A and C in story, while the Canadian fragment represents a lyric remain which contains only the first stanza of the actual ballad. A "hush-a-by" refrain, unknown elsewhere to this song, rounds out the piece.

243. JAMES HARRIS (THE DAEMON LOVER)

Texts: Adventure, 7-30-'23, 191 / Barry, *Brit Blds Me*, 304 / Beard, *Personal Fsg Coll Lunsford*, 97 / Belden, *Mo Fsgs*, 79 / Brewster, *Blds Sgs Ind*, 136 / Brown, *NC Flklre*, II, 171 / BFSSNE, VI, 7; VII, 10 / *Bull U SC*, #162, #11 / Carlisle, *Fifty Sgs Blds NW Ark*, 36 / Cazden, *Abelard Fsg Bk*, I, 82 / Chappell, *Fsgs Rnke Alb*, 38 / Child, IV, 361 / Cox, *Fsgs South*, 139 / Cox, *Trd Bld W Va*, 38 / Cox, *W Va School Journal and Educator*, XLIV, 388 / Crabtree, *Overton Cnty*, 208 / Cutting, *Adirondack Cnty*, 69 / Davis, *Fsgs Va*, 28 / Davis, *More Trd Blds Va*, 270 / Davis, *Trd Bld Va*, 439 / Dean, *The Flying Cloud*, 55 / Duncan, *No Hamilton Cnty*, 91 / Eddy, *Blds Sgs Ohio*, 70 / Flanders, *Ancient Blds*, III, 287 / Flanders, *Blds Migrant NE*, 132 / Flanders, *Garl Gn Mt Sg*, 80 / Flanders, *New Gn Mt Sgstr*, 95 / *Focus*, IV, 162 / Gardner and Chickering, *Blds Sgs So Mich*, 54 / Garrison, *Searcy Cnty*, 27 / Gilbert, *Lost Chords*, 35 / *Grapurchat*, East Radford (Va.) State Teachers College, 8—25—'32 / Alberta P. Hannum, *Thursday, April*, 89 / *Harper's Mgz* (May, 1915), 911 / Henry, *Fsgs So Hghlds*, 116 / Henry, *Sgs Sng So Aplchns*, 59 / High, *Old Old Fsgs*, 16 / Hubbard, *Blds Sgs Utah*, 28 / Hudson, *Fsgs Miss*, 119 / Hudson, *Spec Miss Flklre*, #19 / Hummel, *Oz Fsgs* / *JAF*, 1905, 207; 1906, 295; 1907, 257; 1912, 274; 1913, 360; 1917, 325; 1922, 346; 1929, 274; 1932, 21; 1935, 295; 1936, 209; 1939, 46; 1944, 74; 1947, 231; 1951, 48; 1957, 340 / *The Ky Folk-Lore and Poetry Mgz*, II, #2, 7; II, #4, 17 / *Ky Folklore Record*, 1960, 127 / A. Lomax, *Fsgs No Am*, 182 / Luther, *Amcns Their Sgs*, 17 / MacIntosh, *So Ill Fsgs*, 33 / Mason, *Cannon Cnty*, 19 / McDowell, *Memory Mel*, 2 / *MLN*, XIX, 238 / *Mod Phil*, II, 575 / Morris, *Fsgs Fla*, 311 / Musick, *Flklre Kirksville*, 10 / Neal, *Brown Cnty*, 69 / N.Y. broadside: *The House Carpenter* (J. Andrews, N.Y., c. 1850) / Owens, *Studies Tex Fsg*, 34 / Owens, *Texas Fsgs*, 56 / *Ozark Life*, V, #8 / Perry, *Carter Cnty*, 160 / Pound, *Am Blds Sgs*, 43 / Pound, *Nebr Syllabus*, 10 / PTFS, X, 159 / Randolph, *Oz Fsgs*, I, 166 / Randolph, *Oz Mt Flk*, 201 / Sandburg, *Am Sgbag*, 66 / Scarborough, *Sgctchr So Mts*, 150 / SharpC, *Eng Fsgs So Aplchns*, #29 / SharpK, *Eng Fsgs So Aplchns*, I, 244 / Shearin and Combs, *Ky Syllabus*, 8 / SFQ, 1938, 75; 1944, 160 / Reed Smith, *SC Blds*, 151 / Smith and Rufty, *Am Anth Old Wrld Blds*, 44 / Stout, *Flklre Ia*, 11 / Thomas, *Devil's Ditties*, 172 / *Va FLS Bull*, #s 2—12 / *W Va Folklore*, II, #2 (1952), 12 / WF, 1959, 43 / Wilson, *Bckwds Am*, 96 / Wyman and Brockway, *20 Ky Mt Sgs*, 54.

Local Titles: The Banks of Claudy, The Carpenter's Wife, The Demon Lover, The Faithless Wife, The House Carpenter, The House Carpenter's Wife, James Harris, Little Closet Door, (Well Met, Well Met) My Own (Old) True Love, On the Banks of the Sweet Willie (Laurie, etc.), Said an Old True Love, The Salt, Salt Sea, The Salt Water Sea, The Sea Captain, The Ship Carpenter, Sweet Wilder, A Warning for Married Women, Young Turtle Dove.

Story Types: A: A sailor returns home and, though faithful himself even to the point of refusing a princess, finds his true love happily married to a carpenter. However, by promises and cajoling, he persuades the woman to leave her husband and children and sail off with him. She consents, but soon regrets leaving her baby and sometimes envisions torment that is in store for her. The ship sinks. Often, a stanza is added telling of her contrition or of the condition of her deserted babe and husband. But curses on deceiving men and warnings to erring women also conclude various texts.

Examples: Barry (A); Belden (C); Davis, *Trd Bld Va* (B); SharpK (A).

B: The story is similar to that of Type A. However, the demonaic quality of the lover is still evident to some degree through his ability to interpret the woman's vision, or through some similar hint.

Examples: Davis, *Trd Bld Va* (M, N); Scarborough (D, E); SharpK (B, L).

C: The usual story is told. However, after the lover identifies Heaven and Hell "where you and I must go", he sinks the ship purposely.

Examples: *PTFS*, X, 161 (B).

D: The story is similar to that of Type A. However, the girl leaps overboard and drowns, while the lover goes down with the ship or merely rues the fact that lovers must part.

Examples: Cox, *Fsgs South* (D); Eddy (A); Owens, *Texas Fsgs.*

E: The usual story is told. However, the boat does not sink, although the girl rues her decision to run away. This type is of course the result of fragmentation.

Examples: Chappell.

F: A type of story, independent of *The House Carpenter* tradition, has been found. In this type George Allis reminds the wife of her late promises that she would go with him in seven years and a day. She goes, in what prove to be golden ships with silken sails, but is "sorry sore" on seeing the banks of Claudy where seven ships sink to the bottom and are never more seen. Allis is clearly a ghost, but his demonaic qualities are not made fully apparent.

Examples: *BFSSNE*, VI, 7.

Discussion: The story of the Child (IV, 361) versions is that of Jane Reynolds and a sailor, James Harris, who exchange marriage vows. The young man is pressed into service and reported dead after three years. Jane marries a ship carpenter, and they live happily for four years and have children. One night when the carpenter is absent from home, a spirit raps on the window and says that he is James Harris come to claim his love after seven long years. She explains what has happened, but consents to go where he says he can support her well. In most versions, she repents on shipboard, but the boat goes down and she dies in one manner or another. Anyway, she is never heard of again, and her husband hangs himself.

In America, the lover and the wife (except for the "Fair Ellen" name that seems to have drifted into the song from *Lord Thomas and Fair Annet;* see Davis, *Trd Bld Va,* E, F, K, N, Q) have lost their names (Type A). The carpenter is usually a "house" carpenter and not a "ship" carpenter. (In Gilbert's text the ship carpenter steals the house carpenter's wife.) The action before the arrival of the spirit and the aftermath concerning the death of the carpenter are left out. And the demonaic nature of the lover has been rationalized. In connection with his final point, a number of versions (Type B) retain vestiges of the eerie lover in the form of the "hills of heaven" stanzas (Child E and F), although the cloven foot is not present. The *PTFS,*

X, 161, B version (Type C) follows Child E and F somewhat further in that the lover sinks the ship to get to Hell. Type D stories show a variation not in Child, as the grief of the girl reaches a suicidal peak. This change seems to me to be a sentimentalization. Type E is caused by omission and could result from the cutting short of any text. However, such abbreviation might well be important enough to cause a new version. Type F follows Child A in keeping the name of the lover and, with the text in Greig, *Last Leaves Traditional Bld*, 196, is one of the few versions surviving that is not a part of *The House Carpenter* tradition. The text was also recognized by an Irish woman in New York. The miraculous gilded ship(s) is in Child A, B, C, and F. Check *BFSSNE*, VII, 10 for an additional line.

Most American copies are close to the deMarsan (N. Y.) broadside (c. 1860), printed by Barry in *JAF*, 1905, 207. This text resembled Child B most closely. Belden, *Mo Fsgs*, 79 expresses the opinion that print has perpetuated this ballad orally, and on p. 80 he discusses the Missouri American texts in detail. Davis, *op. cit.*, 439 and Cazden, *Abelard Fsg Bk*, I, 122 are also sources of information.

James Harris has been subject to much corruption in its American travels. Davis, *op. cit.*, 440, 463f. discusses these changes and prints examples. His list of corrupting songs includes *The False Young Man, The True Lover's Farewell, The Rejected Lover, The Wagoner's Lad, Cold Winter's Night,* and *Careless Love*. See also the Duncan, *No Hamilton Cnty*, "Little Closet Door" text, p. 91 and Flanders, *Ancient Blds*, G.

It should be noted that in only a few American versions does the girl weep for her husband. (See Belden, *op. cit.*, C and Davis, *op. cit.*, I), and in Davis, *op. cit.*, O the girl refuses to go, but leaves anyway. Also note the change in the first stanza ("I could have married a railroader . . . but I married a house carpenter") in Cox, *Trd Blds W Va*, 12 (D). The *WF*, 1959, 43 version from Utah, via Idaho, is unusual in the fact the demon bribes the girl to go with him by offering her jewels and clothes, but she points out she needs no such inducements. She's not so poor.

There is no parallel European tradition of this ballad. However, the Danes have a similar song concerning a treacherous woman, and the English song did originate in Scotland—two facts that may or may not be related.

248. THE GREY COCK or SAW YOU MY FATHER?

Texts: Barry, *Brit Blds Me*, 310 / Creighton and Senior, *Trd Blds N Sc*, 83 / Isaiah Thomas Collection, Worcester, Mass., III, 50 / SharpC, *Eng Fsgs Aplchns*, #30 / SharpK, *Eng Fsgs So Aplchns*, I, 259.

Local Titles: Margaret and John.

Story Types: A: A girl awaits her lover. After some confused hindrances, he comes to the door when all are asleep. She lets him in, pledges to love him, and entreats the cock not to crow too early. The lover is obviously a ghost. From Child we know that the cock crows too early, and the tryst is ended too soon.

Examples: Barry.

B: A girl is thinking of her lover and weeping for her parents, when the lover comes. Finding all the doors shut, he rings. She gets up and lets him in. They go to bed, and, in spite of the girl's entreaties, the fowls crow two hours too early. She sends her love away by moonlight, asking him when he will return. He replies a ballad "never", and she berates herself for thinking him to be true. The ghostly mood is gone; the song is just another night assignation story.

Examples: SharpK.

C: A man, out riding one evening, hears a girl crying for her mother, father, and true love John. John appears unexpectedly and knocks at the bedroom door. The girl lets him in. They embrace, and he asks her where her down-bed, fine sheets, and maids-in-waiting are. She is clearly a ghost and replies the grave is her bed, the linen robes her sheets, and the night-larks and worms her servants. The cock is told not to crow, but does so an hour too soon.

Examples: Creighton and Senior (A, B).

Discussion: Barry, *Brit Blds Me,* 313 capably refutes the tendency to place this ballad in the *aube* tradition (see Child, headnote; C. R. Baskerville, *PMLA,* XXXVI, 565f.) and shows that the bird belongs to Celtic (from Oriental) folklore. He also prints an old song, *The Lover's Ghost,* on p. 312, *op. cit.,* from Joyce's *Old Irish Music,* 219 that is connected to *The Grey Cock,* if not to the extent that Barry claims. See also *JAF,* 1954, 285-290 where Albert Friedman discusses a late 17th Century English text of *The Grey Cock* as re-writeen by Henry Bold. This text, Friedman feels, supports the thesis that Child 248 is a revenant, rather than an *aube,* ballad. The text also indicates the presence of the ballad in England at least 100 years before Herd found it in Scotland. Brown, *NC Flklre,* (A) reveals an intrusion of Child 148 into Child 4, *Lady Isabel and the Elf-Knight.*

In the American versions, the ghostly nature of the lover is nearly gone. See SharpK, *Eng Fsgs So Aplchns,* I, 259 where this feature is so obscured that the cocks have become fowls. Also note, Brown, *NC Flklre,* II, 15 (Child 4, Text A) where an intrusion of the crowing motif appears in *Lady Isabel and the Elf-Knight.*

Type A is very close to the Child text, but Type B is noticeably different, though the basic story outline is the same. Type C, from Nova Scotia, may well be a re-working of Child 248. The opening stanzas are not unlike Child 255, *Willie's Fatal Visit,* and the girl, not her lover, is the ghost. See Creighton and Senior, *Trd Blds N Sc,* 83 for a discussion of such texts.

George P. Jackson, *Spiritual Fsgs Early Am,* 44 points out that Anne Gilchrist (*JFSS,* VIII, 65—91) has stated that this song and the religious song, *Saw Ye My Saviour?,* are closely related.

250. HENRY MARTYN

This ballad has been treated under *Sir Andrew Barton* (Child 167).

252. THE KITCHIE-BOY

Reed Smith (*SFQ,* 1937, #2, 9-11) included this ballad on his list of Child ballads that have survived in the New World. His reference is to the Child Ms. text which was taken from Dr. Thos. Davidson, a Scot who lived in several parts of the States. The song is not in New World oral tradition.

Attention should be directed, nevertheless, to W. R. Nelles' article in *JAF,* 1909, 42f. on Hind Horn in which he discusses *The Kitchie-Boy* as an off-shoot of the *Horn* tradition. See the chart on p. 59 in his article.

266. JOHN THOMSON AND THE TURK

Texts: Flanders, *Ancient Blds,* IV / Flanders, *Blds Migrant NE,* 91 / *Vt Historical Society, Proceedings,* N.S., VII, 73-98.

Local Titles: The Trooper and the Turk.

Story Types: A: John Thomson, away from home for three years fighting the Turks, is nostalgic, when he meets his true love who has followed him all the way from Scotland. Later, after they part, she mistakes her way and falls into the hands of Vallantree, the Turkish leader. John, writing home, learns no one has seen her there for over a year. Thus, he disguises himself as a palmer and goes to Vallantree's castle. His lady answers the door and informs him she no longer loves Thomson and is quite happy with the Turks. Thomson reveals himself, and she does consent to hide him from Vallantree. But when the Turk returns and says he would pay 10,000 guineas in gold for the Scotsman, she brings Thomson forth. The Turk asks Thomson what he would do were their situations reversed. Thomson says he would hang the Turk.

Examples: Flanders, *Ancient Blds.*

Discussion: This discovery of a text of Child 266 in Vermont is unique. However, like most of the unusual material taken from the informant, George Edwards, the version is quite like Child A. The Vermont text has a bit more detail than Child A (for example, it takes six stanzas to cover the three-stanza opening in Child), but it fails to finish the story. Missing are the stanzas where Thomson signals his men, who come, capture Vallantree, burn him in his castle, and hang the deceitful lady.

This is an old story, widely known in Western European and Slavic tradition.

267. THE HEIR OF LINNE

Texts: Davis, *Fsgs Va,* 31 / Davis, *Trd Bld Va,* 479 / *Va FLS Bull,* #6.

Local Titles: The Heir of Linne.

Story Types: A: The heir of Linne sells his land to John o' Scales and squanders money for nearly a year. Then he is forced to beg without much luck. He recalls a note that his father gave him for use in a time of dire need, and the message reveals three chests of money in a castle wall. He takes the gold and goes back to John as if he were poor. John's wife will not trust him with a single cent. One man offers to lend him money. John offers to resell the lands for one hundred marks less than the original sale price. Linne takes the bargain to the consternation of John and wife, makes the man who offered to lend him money a keeper of his forest, and promises never to put his estate in jeopardy again.

Examples: Davis, *Trd Bld Va.*

Discussion: The Virginia version is derived from the text published by Percy in his *Reliques* (1765), II, 309 and (1794), II, 128. Thus the American form of the ballad is close to Child A, though much compressed and corrupted by some of the additions made by Percy and taken by him from *The Drunkard's Legacy* (see Child, V, 12 for a summary of the plot). The additions are noted by Davis, *Trd Bld Va*, 479 to be the introduction of the "lonesome lodge", "the rope", and "one hundred marks" instead of "twenty pounds".

The song *The Saucy Sailor* or *Jack Tar* (Laws K 38) is sometimes seen as a derivative of Child 267. However, there is not much shared by the two, the former being a typical broadside story. See Laws, *Am Bldry Brit Bdsdes*, 160-161 for remarks and bibliography.

268. THE TWA KNIGHTS

The Pioneer Songster (pp. 11-22) prints and discusses two songs called *The Hog's Heart* and *The Knight in Green* respectively. Thompson and Cutting suggests these songs are related to Child 268, and they are listed under this number. However, both songs are long accounts which merely cover widespread folktale material that *The Twa Knights* also covers. For example, the motif of the wager on the wife's chastity is common to all three ballads. The two *Songster* ballads are not variants of Child 268, although they may be translations of German or other European ballads that tell similar stories. *The Twa Knights* has not, to date, been printed from American oral tradition.

272. THE SUFFOLK MIRACLE

Texts: Barry, *Brit Blds Me*, 314 / Brown, *NC Flklre*, II, 180 / BFSSNE, V, 7 / Cox, *Fsgs South*, 152 / Creighton and Senior, *Trd Sgs N Sc*, 88 / Davis, *Fsgs Va*, 31 / Davis, *Trd Bld Va*, 482 / Duncan, *No Hamilton Cnty*, 98 / Flanders, *Ancient Blds*, IV / Flanders, *Blds Migrant NE*, 145 / Flanders, *New Gn Mt Sgstr*, 86 / Morris, *Fsgs Fla*, 315 / Randolph, *Oz Fsgs*, I, 179 / SharpC, *Eng Fsgs So Aplchns*, #31 / SharpK, *Eng Fsgs So Aplchns*, I, 262 / SFQ, 1944, 162.

Local Titles: The Holland Handkerchief, Jimmy and Nancy, A Lady Near New York Town, Lucy Bound, Miss Betsy, The Richest Girl in Our Town, The Suffolk Miracle, There Was a Farmer.

Story Types: A: A lovely girl who has fallen in love with a young man is sent far away by her father. The young man dies. After awhile he appears at the place where the girl is living. He is mounted on her father's horse and carries her mother's gear, and he says that he has come to take her home. As they ride, he complains of a headache, and she ties a handkerchief about his head. At home, the young man goes to put up the horse while she knocks on the door. The father is amazed to see her, and his amazement is greater when he learns how she arrived. Later, they find the horse alone and in a sweat. It is then decided to open the grave, and, sure enough, the handkerchief is found about the head of the twelve-months corpse.

Examples: Davis, *Trd Bld Va* (A, B); SharpK (A).

Discussion: Child, V, 58f. points out that the English text is not truly a popular ballad, but he has included it because it represents, in enfeebled form, a great European story. He summarizes a Cornwall prose tale on the same subject, which he states to be "much nearer to the Continental tale".

The American versions follow the Child story, although they are more compact and leave out the death of the girl. As Morris (*SFQ*, 1944, 162) points out, on the whole they show an improvement in the literary style and feeble narrative of Child's text. They also include a number of variations in narrative detail. The Cox, *Fsgs South*, 153 West Virginia version has lost the handkerchief sequence entirely. In Flanders, *Ancient Blds*, C the handkerchief is already around the dead man's head when he arrives at the girl's door. And the Morris (*SFQ*, 1944, 162) version has the unique feature of the wound which speaks and requests the lady to unloose the bonds binding it. See also *Fsgs Fla*, 315.

SharpK, *Eng Fsgs So Aplchns*, A has a moral stanza at the beginning and end (see also Creighton and Senior, *Trd Sgs N Sc*, B), while the Randolph, *Oz Fsgs*, A text and the Brown, *NC Flklre*, texts are quite corrupt. Flanders, *Ancient Blds*, A borrows its ending from *Barbara Allen* (84). Brown, *op. cit.*, 180 prints an interesting discussion of the development of the heroine's name, Lucy Bound. It is seen as developing from the ghost's request to "loosen these bonds".

For a discussion of the superiority of northern American versions and the relation of southern American versions to the "sophisticated Child A" see Barry in *BFSSNE*, V, 10.

273. KING EDWARD THE FOURTH AND THE TANNER OF TAMWORTH

Reed Smith, *SC Blds*, 171—4 lists this song among the American survivals of Child ballads. However, as the song is not on Smith's subsequent *SFQ*, 1937, #2, 9-11 list, the first entry seems to be a mistake.

274. OUR GOODMAN

Texts: Barry, *Brit Blds Me*, 315 / Beard, *Personal Fsg Coll Lunsford*, 103 / Beck, *Down-East Blds Fsgs*, 34 / Belden, *Mo Fsgs*, 89 / Best, *Sg Fest*, 102 / Brand, *Bawdy Sgs Bckrm Blds*, 76 / Brewster, *Blds Sgs Ind*, 149 / Brown, *NC Flklre*, II, 181 / Browne, *Variant Versions Humorous Blds*, 60f., 214f. / *Bull Tenn FLS*, VIII, #3, 72; XXV, 37 / Caravan, #13, 43 / Carlisle, *Fifty Blds Sgs NW Ark*, 41 / Chappell, *Fsgs Rnke Alb*, 41 / Chase, *Am Ftales Sgs*, 118 / Cox, *Fsgs South*, 154 / Cox, *W Va School Journal and Educator*, XLV, 58, 92 / Creighton and Senior, *Trd Sgs N Sc*, 91 / Davis, *Fsgs Va*, 31 / Davis, *More Trd Blds Va*, 300 / Davis, *Trd Bld Va*, 485 / Duncan, *No Hamilton Cnty*, 103 / Eddy, *Blds Sgs Ohio*, 82 / Finger, *Frontier Blds*, 161 / Flanders, *Ancient Blds*, IV / Gray, *Songs*, 33 / Haun, *Cocke Cnty*, 113 / Henry, *Beech Mt Fsg*, 14 / Henry, *Fsgs So Hghlds*, 119 / Henry, *Sgs Sng So Aplchns*, 14 / Hubbard, *Blds Sgs Utah*, 34 / Hudson, *Fsgs Miss*, 122 /

Hudson, *Spec Miss Flklre*, #20 / Hummel, *Oz Fsgs* / *JAF*, 1905, 294; 1916, 166; 1917 199; 1953 44 / *Ky Folklore Record*, 1957, 94; 1960, 127 / Linscott, *Fsgs Old NE*, 261 / Lomax and Lomax, *Our Sgng Cntry*, 300 / Luther, *Amcns Their Sgs*, 18 / Lynn, *Sgs for Singin'*, 176 / MacKenzie, *Blds Sea Sgs N Sc*, 62 / McDowell, *Memory Mel*, 65 / Morris, *Fsgs Fla*, 317 / *Musical Quarterly*, II, 125 / Musick, *Flklre Kirksville*, 14 / *NYFQ*, 1956, 93 / *Oregon Folklore Bull*, I (1961), 3 / Owens, *Texas Fsgs*, 65 / Palmer, *Songs*, 165 / Parsons, *Ftales Andros Is*, 162 / Randolph, *Oz Fsgs*, I, 181 / Randolph, *Oz Mt Flk*, 225 / Scarborough, *Sgctchr So Mts*, 231 / Seeger, *Am Fav Blds*, 22 / SharpC, *Eng Fsgs So Aplchns*, #32 / SharpK, *Eng Fsgs So Aplchns*, I, 267 / Shay and Held, *More Pious Friends and Drunken Companions*, 104 / Silber, *Reprints People's Sgs*, 40 / *Sing Out*, XI, #1 (1961), 26 / Reed Smith, *SC Blds*, 159 / *SFQ*, 1938, 76; 1941, 169 / Stout, *Flklre Iowa*, 13 / *Va FLS Bull*, #s 2-5 / *The Weavers' Sg Bk*, 120 / *W Va Folklore*, I, #1 (1951), 4; V, #2 (1955), 27; IX, #2 (1959), 22 / *WF*, 1960, 83 / J.G. Whittier, *Yankee Gypsies* / Williams, *Blds Sgs*, 248.

Local Titles: The Adultress, Arrow Goodman, A Blackguard Song, Cario Girl, Down Came the Old Man, The Drunkard's Song, Four Nights, Hobble and Bobble, Home Came the Old Man, Home Comes the (Good) (Old) Man, I Called to My Loving Wife, In Came the Gay Old Man, Kind Wife, The Old Man (Came Tumbling Home), Our (The) Goodman, Parson Jones, Third Night of Married Life, Three Nights (of) Experience (Spree) / When I Came Home the Other Night.

Story Types: A: A man returning home finds another man's horse, hat, sword, etc. standing where his should be. His wife tells him that his eyes are deceiving him, that the objects that he sees are really cows, churns, milk dashers, etc. However, he is not to be duped.

Examples: Barry (A); Belden (A); Davis, *Trd Bld Va* (A).

B: The story and motif are identical to those in Type A, except for the fact that the woman is entertaining three lovers.

Examples: Davis, *Trd Bld Va* (B); *JAF*, 1905, 294.

C: The story and motif are identical to those in Type A. However, the action takes place on three or four consecutive nights.

Examples: Henry, *Sgs Sng So Aplchns;*
Lomax and Lomax; Scarborough (A, B).

Discussion: In America, the objects seen by the returning husband vary greatly, but the story itself is always approximately the same. Type A follows the outline of the Scottish Child A; Type B, that of English Child B; while Type C seems to be a more recent variation. Duncan, *No Hamilton Cnty*, 102 notes that the song is often recited as a dialogue. See also *JAF*, 1917, 199. The definitive study of this ballad is, of course, being prepared by Joseph Hickerson at Indiana. His work will include a broader bibliography than appears above, including numerous references to archived, but unprinted, texts and to foreign version and analogues. See also Browne, *Variant Versions Humorous Blds*, 60f., 214f.

The story, of course, readily lends itself to crudity and ribaldry. Cox, *Fsgs South,* points out that there are several such stanzas to be found in West Virginia and other states, while Randolph, *Oz Fsgs*, I, 183, headnote, reports encountering a man who said he no longer sings certain verses of this song since he has joined the church. See Hudson, *Fsgs Miss*, 122 and Duncan, *op.*

cit., 102 as well. There are also a number of manuscript collections that include bawdy versions of this song. See in particular J. Kenneth Larson's *Typical Specimens of Vulgar Folklore from the Collection of Gershon Legman* (Indiana University Folklore Archive), 6, 36-37 and Vance Randolph's *"Unprintable" Songs from the Ozarks* (Kinsey Institute for Sex Research, Indiana University), I, 22-28.

The SharpK, *Eng Fsgs So Aplchns,* A version reveals the shrewish nature of the wife at once. Davis, *Trd Bld Va,* 493 and Creighton and Senior, *Trd Sgs N Sc,* 91 print Jacobite adaptions from the British Navy in which the lover is a Tory cousin of the husband named MacIntosh. See also Smith's *Scotish Minstrel,* IV, 66.

The relationship of Child 274 to the Russian *ballada* is treated in *PTFS,* XXV, 90f. in a general essay by Robert C. Stephenson entitled *The Western Ballad and the Russian "Ballada".*

275. GET UP AND BAR THE DOOR

Texts: Barry, *Brit Blds Me,* 318 / Brown, *NC Flklre,* II, 183 / Brown, *Variant Versions Humorous Blds,* 91f., 280f. / Combs, *Fsgs États Unis,* 147 / Cox, *Fsgs South,* 516 / Creighton and Senior, *Trd Sgs N Sc,* 92 / Davidson's *Universal Melodist,* I, 275 / Davis, *Fsgs Va,* 32 / Davis, *Trd Bld Va,* 495 / Flanders, *Ancient Blds,* IV / Gardner and Chickering, *Blds Sgs So Mich,* 371 / Greenleaf and Mansfield, *Blds Sea Sgs Newfdld,* 41 / Jones, *Flklre Mich,* 5 / Morris, *Fsgs Fla,* 320 / Randolph, *Oz Fsgs,* I, 186 / *SFQ,* 1944, 170 / *Va FLS Bull,* #9.

Local Titles: Arise and Bar the Door-O, Get Up and Bar the Door, John and Joan Blount, Old John Jones.

Story Types: A: A housewife is boiling pudding when a cold wind blows the door open. The husband tells her to bar the door; however, she is busy and refuses. They agree that the first one who speaks must shut the door. Two travellers, attracted by the light from the open door, enter the house. Getting no reply to any of their questions or remarks, they eat and drink what they find. The husband and wife watch, saying nothing. One of the travellers proposes to take off the man's beard (and in some texts decides to use the hot pudding to soften it), while the other traveller plans to kiss the wife. The last proposal brings some words from the husband, and he has to bar the door.

Examples: Barry (A), Combs, Gardner and Chickering.

B: The story is essentially the same as that of Type A. However, the husband and wife get sleepy on home-brewed ale and go to bed forgetting to bar the door. The agreement is made, and the travellers come. They eat and drink downstairs and then go up and pull the wife out of bed and begin to kiss her on the floor. This freedom is too much for the husband.

Examples: Greenleaf and Mansfield.

Discussion: The Type A texts follow the Child A and B story closely. However, Type B seems to be of a different sort from anything in Child. It resembles Child C in that the couple go to bed, there are three travellers, and the wife is laid on the floor, but the narrative is fuller and the door is not blown open. as in Child.

The fragmentary B version in Randolph's *Oz Fsg* indicates that the men actually shave off the husband's beard.

Crude lyrics are easily and often inserted into this ballad. For other tales of the same sort see Aarne-Thompson, Mt. 1351 and Child, V, 96-98. For a burlesque of the ballad see Delehanty and Hengler's *Song and Dance Book* (1874), 169. See *Browne, Variant Versions Humorous Blds,* 91f., 280f. for further remarks.

277. THE WIFE WRAPT IN WETHER'S SKIN

Texts: Arnold, *Fsgs Fla,* 110 / Barry, *Brit Blds Me,* 322 / Beck, *Down-East Blds Fsgs,* 35 / Beck, *Flklre Me,* 112 / Belden, *Mo Fsgs,* 92 / Brewster, *Blds Sgs Ind,* 151 / Brown, *NC Flklre,* II, 185 / Browne, *Variant Versions Humorous Blds,* 102f., 295f. / Cazden, *Abelard Fsg Bk,* II, 36 / Chase, *Am Ftales Sgs,* 122 / Chase, *Sgs All Times,* 22 / Child, V, 304 / *Colorado Fsg Bull,* I, #2, 3, 4 / Cox, *Fsgs South,* 159 / Cox, *Trd Blds W Va,* 46 / Cox, *W Va School Journal and Educator,* XLV, 92 / Creighton and Senior, *Trd Sgs N Sc,* 94 / Davis, *Fsgs Va,* 32 / Davis, *More Trd Blds Va,* 305 / Davis, *Trd Bld Va,* 497 / Downes and Siegmeister, *Treasury Am Sg,* 226 / Flanders, *Ancient Blds,* IV / Flanders, *Blds Migrant NE,* 221 / Flanders, *Garl Gn Mt Sg,* 84 / Flanders, *Vt Fsgs Blds,* 222, 224 / *Focus,* V, 280 / Gordon, *Fsgs Am,* 89 / Haun, *Cocke Cnty,* 78 / Henry, *Fsgs So Hghlds,* 125 / Hubbard, *Blds Sgs Utah,* 38 / Hudson, *Fsgs Miss,* 123 / Hudson, *Ftunes Miss,* 12 / Hudson, *Spec Miss Flklre,* #21 / Ives, *BI Sg Bk,* 178 / *JAF,* 1894, 254; 1906, 298; 1917, 328; 1926, 109; 1935, 309; 1951, 51; 1957, 344 / Korson, *Pa Sgs Lgds,* 41 / A. Lomax, *Fsgs No Am,* 167 / McDowell, *Memory Mel,* 49 / Morris, *Fsgs Fla,* 322 / *N.Y. Times Mgz,* 1-8-'28 / Owens, *Texas Fsgs,* 66 / Pound, *Am Blds Sgs,* 16 / Randolph, *Oz Fsgs,* I, 187 / Ring, *NE Fsgs,* 8 / SharpC, *Eng Fsgs So Aplchns,* #33 / SharpK, *Eng Fsgs So Aplchns,* I, 271 / Shearin and Combs, *Ky Syllabus,* 8 / *SFQ,* 1949, 172 / Smith and Rufty, *Am Anth Old Wrld Blds,* 49 / *Va FLS Bull,* #s 4, 5, 7-10 / Wells, *Bld Tree,* 121 / *W Va Folklore,* IX, #2 (1959), 21 / *WF,* 1952, 178.

Local Titles: Bandoo, Dandoo, Dan-Doodle-Dan, Dan-you, Dindo-Dan, Gentle Fair Ginny, Gentle Virginia, Jennifer Gently, Jenny Flow (Fair) Gentle Rosemary(ie), John Dobber, Jock O'McKee, Kitty Lorn, Nickety Nackety, Old Man Come In from His Plow, The Old Man (Who Lived) in the West, The Old Sheepskin, Robin He's Gone to the Woods, The Scolding Wife, Sweet Robin, The Wee Cooper o' Fife, The Wife Wrapt in Wether's Skin.

Story Types: A: A man marries a girl who is too proud or too shrewish to work. When he returns from the fields at evening, she will not give him his supper. To reform her, he kills a sheep, cuts a rod, and beats her after wrapping her in the sheepskin, a device which frees him of responsibility. When she threatens to tell her family, he reminds her that he was only tanning the hide. She reforms completely.

Examples: Barry (A) ; Child (F) ; Davis, *Trd Bld Va* (A).

B: Certain West Virginia versions mention the old man's running away in the end. The Cox, *Fsgs South,* C version has four stanzas of nonsense inserted about the old man's running to his father and saying his wife has lice. All omit the bringing home of the bride.

Examples: Cox, *Fsgs South* (A, B, C).

C: The "wether's skin" has been forgotten in some texts, and a man merely beats his wife to reform her, sometimes without the sheepskin to help. Examples: Cox, *Fsgs South* (E), Owens (A, B).

Discussion: Barry, *Brit Blds Me,* 325 states that "Child F may be a possible intermediary between the earlier English texts and the later American". Whether this belief is true or not, the Child version does seem to me to tell the complete American story, and I have therefore used it as a model for Story Type A. As none of the British Child texts include the man's coming home from his plowing and asking for supper, some of the American texts omit this feature also. On the other hand, other American texts that I have grouped in Type A as well, omit the bringing home of the new bride who will not work and begin the story with the husband's return from the fields. Still other American texts can be found which include both opening scenes. See the examples listed under Type A. Types B and C are, of course, degenerations of this material, one through expansion, the other through loss. However, Davis, *More Trd Blds Va,* 307 suggests that as the texts with "dandoo" refrains do not really include a reform of the wife, they should make up a different story type from other Type A texts.

Like the story, the refrains of this ballad are varied and change place and character frequently. Belden, *Mo Fsgs,* 92, notes that two general divisions may be made with respect to these refrains: the "dandoo-clish ma clingo" types of the South and Midwest, and the "rosemary-thyme" types of the South and Northeast which probably have been borrowed from *The Elfin Knight* (Child 2). The "rosemary-thyme" lines may derive from the old plant burden, "juniper, gentian, and rosemary", which can be found rationalized to proper names in Child F and Barry, *op. cit.,* A and B and which has created a new title for the song. See Cox, *Fsgs South,* 162. McDowell, *Memory Mel,* 49 prints a text with the refrain "Jock O'McKee, Kitty alone tonight."

The ballad and its developments are discussed in some detail by William H. Jansen in *HFQ,* IV, #3, 41, and by Browne, *Variant Versions Humorous Blds,* 102f., 295f. Jansen divides the American tradition much in the fashion of Belden, and also notes that there is no reform of the wife in the *Dandoo* texts.

Child, V, 104 states that the ballad is, in all likelihood, derived from the traditional tale, *The Wife Lapped in Morrel's Skin,* which he summarizes. See Aarne-Thompson, Mt. 1370 for bibliography. It is possible the ballad blended with another tale in its travels. Lucy Broadwood, *JFSS,* II, 12-15, in a note on plant burdens states that plants were regarded as protection against demons and when a demon vanished the burden often remained. In that case, and providing the plant refrain has not been recently borrowed by the ballad, the wife may have originally had evil spirits, a feature which was later rationalized to her being too proud of kin or too shrewish by nature to work.

The Brewster, *Blds Sgs Ind,* A version has almost lost the story, and, instead of the husband's rationalization of his deed at the end, has the cliché, "if you want any more, you can sing it yourself." See also the fragment in Beck, *Flklre Me,* 112, which is a nonsense song about a 300 lb. wife who "washed pigs in the kitchen sink", as well as *JAF,* 1943, 103 text. Such songs may well not be versions of Child 277.

The Flanders, *Ancient Blds,* L text, about "Riddleson's daughter Dinah" is unusual and may show localization.

278. THE FARMER'S CURST WIFE

Texts: Barry, *Brit Blds Me,* 325 / Beck, *Sgs Mich Lmbrjks,* 107 / Beard, *Personal Fsg Coll Lunsford,* 108 / Belden, *Fsg Mo,* 94 / Brand, *Fsgs for Fun,* 105 / Brewster, *Blds Sgs Ind,* 155 / Brown, *NC Flklre,* II, 188 / Browne, *Variant Versions Humorous Blds,* 13f., 151f. / Bull Tenn FLS, VIII, #3, 73; XXIV, #2, 73 / Cazden, *Abelard Fsg Bk,* II, 74 / Chappell, *Fsgs Rnke Alb,* 42 / Chase, *Sgs All Times,* 55 / Cox, *Fsgs South,* 164 / Crabtree, *Overton Cnty,* 98 / Creighton, *Sgs Blds N Sc,* 18 / Creighton and Senior, *Trd Sgs N Sc,* 95 / Cutting, *Adirondack Cnty,* 71 / Davis, *Fsgs Va,* 33 / Davis, *More Trd Blds Va,* 316 / Davis, *Trd Bld Va,* 505 / Downes and Siegmeister, *Treasury Am Sg,* 228 / Duncan, *No Hamilton Cnty,* 108 / Flanders, *Ancient Blds,* IV / Flanders, *Blds Migrant NE,* 49 / Flanders, *Vt Fsgs Blds,* 226 / Folkways Monthly (May '62), 14 / Fowke and Johnston, *Fsgs Canada,* 172 / Gardner and Chickering, *Blds Sgs So Mich,* 373 / Garrison, *Searcy Cnty,* 13 / Haufrecht, *Folk Sing,* 25 / Haun, *Cocke Cnty,* 69 / Henry, *Fsgs So Hghlds,* 125 / Hubbard, *Blds Sgs Utah,* 40 / Hudson, *Fsgs Miss,* 124 / Hummel, *Oz Fsgs* / Ives, *BI Sg Bk,* 172 / JAF, 1906, 298; 1911, 348; 1914, 68; 1917; 329; 1935, 299 / Kolb, *Treasury Fsg,* 8 / Korson, *Pa Sgs Lgds,* 39 / Linscott, *Fsgs Old NE,* 188 / A. Lomax, *Fsgs No Am,* 187 / Lomax and Lomax, *Cowboy Sgs Frntr Blds,* 110 / Lomax and Lomax, *Our Sgng Cntry,* 152 / *Louisville Courier-Journal,* 1-14-'17 / MacKenzie, *Blds Sea Sgs N Sc,* 64 / Mason, *Cannon Cnty,* 75 / McDowell, *Memory Mel,* 51 / Morris, *Fsgs Fla,* 323 / Musick, *Flklre Kirksville,* 11a / Niles, *Anglo-Am Bld Stdy Bk,* 31 / Niles, *Blds Lv Sgs Tgc Lgds,* 2 / Owens, *Texas Fsgs,* 54 / PTFS, X, 164 / Randolph, *Oz Fsgs,* I, 189 / Randolph, *Oz Mt Flk,* 227 / Ritchie, *Sgng Family,* 143 / Seeger, *Am Fav Blds,* 58 / SharpC, *Eng Fsgs So Aplchns,* #34 / SharpK, *Eng Fsgs So Aplchns,* I, 275 / Silber, *Reprints People's Sgs,* 18 / Stekert, "The Farmer's Curst Wife"—a Mdfd Hist-Geog Stdy / Siegmeister, *Sgs Early Am,* 44 / Smith and Rufty, *Am Anth Old Wrld Blds,* 53 / SFQ, 1938, 77; 1940, 157 / Va FLS Bull, #s 4-6, 8-10 / Wells, *Bld Tree,* 122 / W Va Folklore, III, #2 (1953), 21; V, #2 (1955), 28.

Local Titles: Brave Old Anthony Marela, The Devil and the Farmer's Wife, The Devil Came to the Farmer's One Day, The Devil's Song, The Farmer's Curst Wife, The Farmer's Wife, Hi Lum Day, Jack, Jack's Wife, Kellyburnbraes, The Old Devil Come to My Plow, The Old Farmer, The Old Jokey Song, The Old Man Under the Hill, The Old Man Learned How (Went Out) to Plow, The Old Wife, The Old Woman and the Devil, The (Old) Scolding Wife, Ten Little Devils, The Two Little Devils.

Story Types: A: The Devil comes to take the farmer's shrewish wife, much to the farmer's delight. The woman is no more controllable in Hell than she was on earth. She kicks the imps about and is generally unmanageable. For the sake of peace and his own safety, the Devil is forced to take her back to the farmer. Upon her return, she sometimes asks for the food she was cooking in the pot when she left. Once and awhile she hits her husband, too. There is usually a comic philosophic last stanza.

Examples: Belden (A); Davis, *Trd Bld Va* (A); SharpK (A).

B: The story is like that of Type A. However, this feature is added: the farmer, having no oxen to plow his farm, hires the Devil, who abducts the wife as payment.   Examples: Barry (C).

C: The Devil takes so many things from the farmer in accordance with a pact between them that soon the poor man has only his hogs left to plow with. The Devil then abducts the wife, and the usual story ensues.
Examples: Gardner and Chickering (E).

D: The usual story is told. In the end, however, the farmer welcomes his wife back and congratulates her for killing the imps and ruling Hell.
Examples: Barry (D).

E: The usual story is told but, as in some of Type A texts, the woman asks for the food in the pot on her return, only to find that it has all been eaten up. She also brags to her husband of her accomplishments in Hades.   Examples: Cox.

F: The usual story is told. As in Types A and E the woman asks for the food in the pot on her return. She follows this query by beating her husband, who is sick in bed, on the head with a pipe.
Examples: Randolph, *Oz Fsgs* (B); SharpK (B).

G: Here, the wife is the farmer. She harnesses the cattle herself and goes to the gates of Hell.
Examples: Flanders, *Ancient Blds* (C).

Discussion: This ballad and a related song, *The Devil in Search of a Wife,* were London broadsides of the nineteenth century. Child prints only two versions of the traditional song, of which the A text is most like the majority of the American ballads. In this country, however, a mock aphoristic closing stanza on shrewish women is almost universally found, and the Child B ending, in which the returning wife asks for the food (mush, chicken, bread, etc.) she was cooking when abducted is not at all uncommon. See Types E and F.

Barry, *Brit Blds Me,* 332, pieces together his conception of the original story. The farmer has made a pact with the Devil for aid, as he has no oxen to plow his fields. Satan returns for the soul of one member of the family as payment. As in Child A, the farmer is relieved that his eldest son is not desired. This explanation would account for Type B stories and is lent support by the Maine, Tennessee, Texas, and Virginia versions that find the farmer yoking the swine to his plow. (In Siegmeister, *Sgs Early Am,* 44, from New York the farmer uses his wife as well as the swine.) See also the Gardner and Chickering, *Blds Sgs So Mich,* E text (Type C) which was recited as a story outline, the exact words of the song having been forgotten. However, definitive comments on the story matter of Child 278 can be found in Ellen Stekert's M.A. thesis at Indiana University, "*The Farmer's Curst Wife*", a *Modified Hisorical-Geographical Study.*

Beck, *Sgs Mich Lmbrjks,* 107 prints a text from the woodsmen that substitutes a lumberjack for the farmer, and the Randolph, *Oz Fsgs,* I, 89 version is long, with many details added. Nevertheless, the story matter of both these texts can be considered Type A. Except for the sentimentality of D, all the American texts have the same jocular mood. The refrains, in keeping with this mood, are whistles as in Child A, or nonsense of the "sing fol-roll dolli" and "clish-ma-clango" sort. See the Flanders, *Ancient Blds,* C-I series with the "right leg, left leg" refrains.

Flanders, *Ancient Blds,* U is a quite accurate copy of a poem which Robert Burns based on the ballad and called *Kellyburn Braes.*

Belden, *Mo Fsgs,* 95 suggests that the devils dancing on a wire, as they do in Missouri and Nova Scotia, may reflect mystery plays.

279. THE JOLLY BEGGAR

Texts: Barry, *Brit Blds Me,* 333, 475 (trace) / Cox, *Trd Blds W Va,* 50 / Creighton and Senior, *Trd Sgs N Sc,* 99 / Davis, *Fsgs Va,* 34, 35 / Davis, *More Trd Blds Va,* 328 / Goose Hangs High Songster (deWitt, Philadelphia, 1866) / Randolph, *Oz Fsgs,* I, 194 / John Templeton, "Jolly Beggar" (Oliver Ditson, Boston, n.d.).

Local Titles: The Beggar's Bride.

Story Types: A: A man gives lodging to a beggar who then runs off with his daughter. When the parents find the girl gone, they swear they will never take in another beggar. Seven years later the beggar returns, and, upon being told why no more beggars are lodged, he reveals that he is bringing the daughter back, not only full of fine stories, but a gay lady as well.   Examples: Barry.

Discussion: In *More Trd Blds Va,* 328-332, Davis discusses his fragment of Child 279 from Virginia in great detail. Davis feels this text and the slightly longer one collected by Randolph, *Oz Fsgs,* I, 194 in Missouri are the only texts of *The Jolly Beggar* that have survived in America without the aid of print. He bases his argument on the absence of Scottish dialect and of the "gang nae mair a roving" stanza from these two fragments. Both the Virginia and Missouri fragments seem to relate to Child B. Davis' point is subject to question. While there is no doubt about the influence of the song books on American forms of *The Jolly Beggar* (see Barry, *Brit Blds Me,* 475-476), Davis has had to base his arguments on extremely brief fragments. Until a lot more is known about the tradition from which these fragments came, it seems safe to say that Child 279 has no real oral tradition in America. Also see Worthington, *Nine Rare Trd Blds Va,* 152-165.

The Jolly Beggar (see also *The Beggar Laddie,* Child 280) was published in revised form as *The Gaberlunyie-Man* in the 1724 *Tea-Table Miscellany* of Allan Ramsay. This derivative form of Child 279 has been found in the New World. These texts, which have turned up in the South and the Northeast, are clearly related to songster versions. See Child, V, 115; Davis, *More Trd Blds Va,* 333-338; and Worthington, *Nine Rare Trd Blds Va,* 166-186 for detailed remarks on these matters.

The California (Cox, *Trd Bld W Va*) and the Missouri-Arkansas (Randolph, *Oz Fsgs*) fragments have two stanzas that correspond to the Maine (Barry, *Brit Blds Me*) text, and Barry, *JAF,* 1909, 79 notes a tune from Massachusetts. The Maine and Nova Scotia versions reflect the American tendency to omit lustier parts of a story. Compare also Child's *The Jolly Beggar* in this respect.

281. THE KEACH I THE CREEL

Texts: Barry, *Brit Blds Me,* 336 / Cazden, *Abelard Fsg Bk,* II, 10 / Flanders, *Ancient Blds,* IV.

Local Titles: The Little Scotch Girl.

Story Types: A: A young maid captivates a clerk. To win her from her parent's strict watch, the hopeful lover gets his brother to build him a ladder. He then enters the locked house in a basket let down the chimney and gets in bed with the girl. Investigation by the father and mother is thwarted by the girl's telling her father she is praying with a large book in her arms and by the mother's falling in the basket and being pulled up and down the flue by the clerk's brother.

Examples: Cazden.

Discussion: The Cazden text is a rare find, as it is complete and both the Barry and Flanders texts are brief fragments. However, it was learned from George Edwards, whose repertoire has a number of rare traditional ballads that are remarkably close to the Child versions. The Barry fragment tells only of the bump the mother gets in the basket, while the Flanders text gives the two stanzas that open the song and one in which the mother gets tossed about. Herbert Halpert also has a fairly complete text that has not been published, so there is no doubt that the song did survive in the New World. It is well enough known in Scotland, though the English tradition seems dead.

283. THE CRAFTY FARMER

Texts: Barry, *Brit Blds Me,* 477 (trace) / Cox, *Fsgs South,* 166.

Local Titles: None given.

Story Types: A: *The Crafty Farmer.* A farmer is going to pay his rent when a gentleman thief overtakes him. As they ride along, the farmer, through conversation, reveals the large amount of money that he is carrying on him. He even reveals the hiding-place of the money in his saddle-bags. The thief then pulls a pistol. However, the farmer throws an old saddle-bag over a hedge and, when the robber goes after this decoy, rides off upon the culprit's horse. The desperate thief offers to split fifty-fifty with the farmer, if the latter will only come back. This proposition is ignored, and the farmer goes to the landlord, pays his rent, and finds a lot more money in the robber's portmanteau. On his way home, the farmer finds his own horse tied to a tree. At home, his wife runs about the house in glee when she hears the news.

Examples: Cox.

Discussion: The Crafty Farmer itself is rare indeed in America. Cox, *Fsgs South,* prints a West Virginia text that is almost identical to Child A, although there are eight additional lines in the American text that do not affect the story and a rearrangement of stanzas in the final stages of the song. Barry, *Brit Blds Me,* 477 notes that the same text was recognized by a Maine sea-captain as a song his sailors used to sing.

During the last 250 years, many ballads telling how simple folk have outwitted thieves have circulated in print and oral tradition. Why Child chose *The Crafty Farmer* for inclusion in his anthology, and did not choose the others, is not at all clear. The songs that Laws, *Am Bldry Brit Bdsdes,* has labelled L 1, L 2, and L 3 all seem to have as good claims to the select circle as Child 283. L 1, *The Yorkshire Bite,* in which a boy spreads his money on the grass and rides off on the thief's horse when the latter dismounts to gather it, is the best known in America, appearing in many collections. A good bit rarer are L 2, *The Highwayman Outwitted,* in which a girl is stripped naked by the robber before she outwits him and rides away, and L 3, *The Undaunted Female,* in which a girl and a confederate rout a group of robbers. See Laws, *op. cit.,* 165-166 for remarks, plot outlines, and bibliography for all three.

The Yorkshire Bite has been included in many American anthologies as Child 283. A start on a bibliography would include: Barry, *Brit Blds Me,* 406 / Brown, *NC Flklre,* II, 188 / Combs, *Fsgs États-Unis,* 149 / Creighton, *Sgs Blds N Sc,* 29 / Flanders, *Ancient Blds,* IV / Flanders, *Cntry Sgs Vt,* 26 / Flanders, *New Gn Mt Sgstr,* 97 / Flanders, *Vt Fsgs Blds,* 234 / Gardner and Chickering, *Blds Sgs So Mich,* 382 / Greenleaf and Mansfield, *Blds Sea Sgs Newfdld,* 46 / Henry, *Fsgs So Hghlds,* 135 / Hubbard, *Blds Sgs Utah,* 263 / *JAF,* 1910, 451; 1917, 367; 1932, 30 / Sandburg, *Am Sgbag,* 118 / Thompson and Cutting, *Pioneer Songster,* 22.

Also check *JAF,* 1926, 214-217 where an American (Massachusetts via Ireland) text of *The Undaunted Female* (called *The Robber Maid*) appears with discussion and bibliography, and note Morse, *Fsgs Caribbean,* 138 where a text of *The Highwayman Outwitted* (called *The Highway Robber*) seems to end in the marriage of the girl and the robber. This text from the Virgin Islands may have mixed with *The Undaunted Female.* Greenleaf and Mansfield, *Blds Sea Sgs Newfdld,* 47 and Hubbard, *Blds Sgs Utah,* 265 also print texts of *The Highwayman Outwitted.*

285. THE GEORGE ALOE AND THE SWEEPSTAKE

Texts: JAF, 1905, 134 / Shay, *Deep Sea Chanties,* 58.

Local Titles: The George Aloe and the Sweepstake.

Story Types: A: Two merchant ships, the *Aloe* and the *Sweepstake,* are sailing by Barbary. The *Aloe* anchors, but the *Sweepstake* goes on and is attacked and boarded by a French man o'war. When those aboard the *Aloe* hear this, they sail out to meet the Frenchmen. They sight the enemy.

Examples: Shay.

B: A man o' war (originally she was a merchant ship) out cruising sights a frigate and, on hailing her, learns that she is a privateer (originally she was a French man o' war). A battle ensues, and the man o' war shoots the pirate's mast away. The robber calls for mercy, but none is shown.

Examples: *JAF,* 1905, 134.

Discussion: The American Types A and B, if placed together, give the complete story of the ballad. However, the Type B text has been changed to the extent that the merchantman and French man o'war have become a man o'war and a privateer respectively. As this version was collected from a United States Navy sailor and is of Civil War vintage, the change is understandable. See Child, V, 133 for his outline of the narrative and a discussion of a possible second part to the English ballad.

There are many American versions of a derivative of Child 285 that go under a variation of a *Coast of Barbary* title. These tell of a sea-fight between a privateer and a victorious man o'war (a feature that may account for the switch noted above in Type B) and trace back to a song based on the ballad and written for the British Navy by Charles Dibden (1745—1814). Little except the alternating refrain and the phrase "coast of Barbary" is retained of the Child song, however. Versions are easy enough to find in coastal regions. A start on a bibliography to *Coast of Barbary* texts would include: Barry, *Brit Blds Me,* 413 / Chappell, *Fsgs Rnke Alb,* 51 / Colcord, *Roll and Go,* 78 / Colcord, *Sgs Am Sailormen,* 153 / Flanders, *Ancient Blds,* IV / Flanders, *Vt Fsgs Blds,* 229 / *Forget-me-not Songster* (Turner and Fisher, Philadelphia and New York, c. 1840) / Harlow, *Chanteying Am Ships,* 161 / Hurgill, *Shanties 7 Seas,* 420 / Lomax and Lomax, *Our Sgng Cntry,* 212 / Morris, *Fsgs Fla,* 91 / Nesser, *Am Naval Sgs Blds,* 303 / Shay, *Am Sea Sgs Chanties,* 91 / Shay, *Deep Sea Chanties,* 98 / Shay, *My Pious Frnds Drkn Cmpns,* 140 / Smith and Rufty, *Am Anth Old Wrld Blds,* 56 / Thompson and Cutting, *Pioneer Songster,* 24.

286. THE SWEET TRINITY (THE GOLDEN VANITY)

Texts: Anderson, *Coll Blds Sgs,* 53 / Barry, *Brit Blds Me,* 339 / Beard, *Personal Fsg Coll Lunsford,* 111 / Belden, *Mo Fsgs,* 97 / *Berea Quarterly,* XVIII, 18 / Bowles, *Am Fsgs* / Brewster, *Blds Sgs Ind,* 158 / Brown, *NC Flklre,* II, 191 / *BFSSNE,* V, 10 / Cambiaire, *Ea Tenn Wstn Va Mt Blds,* 93 / Carlisle, *Fifty Sgs Blds NW Ark,* 45 / Carmer, *Am Sings,* 185 / Cazden, *Abelard Fsgs Bk,* I, 46 / Chappell, *Fsgs Rnke Alb,* 43 / Chase, *Am Ftales Sgs,* 120 / Chase, *Sgs All Times,* 14 / Colcord, *Roll and Go,* 79 / Colcord, *Sgs Am Sailormen,* 154 / Coleman and Bregman, *Sgs Am Flk,* 16 / Cox, *Fsgs South,* 169 / Cox, *Trd Blds W Va,* 52 / Cox, *W Va School Journal and Educator,* XLV, 58 / Creighton, *Sgs Blds N Sc,* 20 / Creighton and Senior, *Trd Sgs N Sc,* 101 / Davis, *Fsgs Va,* 35 / Davis, *More Trd Blds Va,* 339 / Davis, *Trd Bld Va,* 516 / Duncan, *No Hamilton Cnty,* 111 / Flanders, *Ancient Blds,* IV / Flanders, *Cntry Sgs Vt,* 40 / Flanders, *Vt Fsgs Blds,* 230 / *Focus,* IV, 158 / Fowke, *Canada's Story in Sg,* 38 / Gardner and Chickering, *Blds Sgs So Mich,* 214 / Grenleaf and Mansfield, *Blds Sea Sgs Newfdld,* 43 / Harlow, *Chanteying Am Ships,* 37 / *Harper's Mgz* (May, 1915), 912 / Henry, *Fsgs So Hghlds,* 127 / Hubbard, *Blds Sgs Utah,* 43 / Hudson, *Fsgs Miss,* 125 / Hudson, *Spec Miss Flklre,* #22 / Hummel, *Oz Fsgs* / Hurgill, *Shanties 7 Seas,* 62 / Ives, *BI Sg Bk,* 42 / Ives, *Sea Sgs,* 32 / *JAF,*

1905, 125; 1910, 429; 1917, 330; 1932, 25; 1935, 312, 386; 1939, 11; 1951, 52 / Leach, *Fsgs Labr Cst* / A. Lomax, *Fsgs No Am*, 191 / Lomax and Lomax, *Our Sgng Cntry*, 210 / MacIntosh, *So Ill Fsgs*, 21 / McDonald, *Selctd Fsgs Mo*, 17 / McGill, *Fsgs Ky Mts*, 97 / Ruth Moore, *Spoonhandle* (N.Y. '46) / Morris, *Fsgs Fla*, 326 / *Musical Quarterly*, III, 374 / Niles, *Anglo Am Bld Stdy Bk*, 28 / Niles, *Blds Lv Sgs Tgc Lgds*, 18 / *NC Folklore*, III #1 (1955), 8 / *Ozark Life*, VI, #1 / Perry, *Carter Cnty*, 197 / Pound, *Am Blds Sgs*, 24 / Raine, *Land Sddle Bags*, 121 / Randolph, *Oz Fsgs*, I, 195 / Randolph, *The Ozarks*, 177 / Richardson, *Am Mt Sgs*, 28 / Elizabeth M. Roberts, *The Green Meadow*, N.Y., 1930, 3—4 / Scarborough, *Sgctchr So Mts*, 184 / SharpC, *Eng Fsgs So Aplchns*, #35 / SharpK, *Eng Fsgs So Aplchns*, I, 282 / Shearin and Combs, *Ky Syllabus*, 9 / Shoemaker, *Mt Mnstly*, 132, 299 / Shoemaker, *No Pa Mnstly*, 126 / *Singer's Journal*, II, 686 / Smith and Rufty, *Am Anth Old Wrld Blds*, 59 / *SFQ*, 1938, 79; 1954, 180 / *Va FLS Bull*, #s 3, 4, 8-10 / Wells, *Bld Tree*, 53 / Wyman and Brockway, *Lnsme Tunes*, 72.

Local Titles: The Bold Trellitee, Cabin Boy, The Cruise in the Lowlands Low, The Fate of the Turkish Revelee (Revelrie), The French Galilee, The Gold China Tree, The Golden Vanity (Funnitee, Merrilee, Vallady, Willow Tree, etc.), The Green Willow Tree, The Little Cabin Boy, The Little Ship, The Lonesome Low, The Lonesome Sea, The Lowland Sea, The Lowlands, The Lowlands (Lonesome) Low, Merry (Mary) Golden Tree, The Pirate Ship, The Turkeyrogherlee and the Yellow Golden Tree, The Turkish Revoloo, The Turkey Shivaree, The Weepwillow Tree.

Story Types: A: A boat is sailing in the lowlands when attacked by a feared pirate. A cabin boy volunteers to sink the robbers. As a reward, he is to get money and the hand of the captain's daughter. He accomplishes his task by swimming to the other ship and cutting some gashes in her. The pirate goes down. When the boy has swum back to his ship, the captain refuses to keep his word. Out of respect for his mates or the girl, the boy reluctantly does not sink the captain's boat. He either dies of exhaustion in the water or in a hammock on deck after his mates hoist him aboard.

Examples: Barry (A); Davis, *Trd Blds Va* (A); SharpK (A).

B: The story is the same as that of Type A. However, the cabin boy is rescued by his shipmates. He scorns the gold and fee, but accepts the girl's hand in marriage.   Examples: *JAF*, 1905, 125

C: The story is identical to that of Type A. However, the ghost of the boy returns to haunt the captain or the Lowlands.

Examples: Belden (A), Coleman and Bregman.

D: The usual story is told. But, after the boy drowns, the crew throws the captain overboard and drowns him.

Examples: Shoemaker, *Mt. Mnstly*, p. 132.

E: The usual story is told. However, the boy swears that he will sink the captain, too.

Examples: Shoemaker, *Mt Mnstly*, p. 299.

F: The usual story is told. However, a storm arises after the lad dies. He speaks from Heaven and tells the captain he will sink the ship. The ship goes down, and the captain drowns, though the kinder mate survives.

Examples: Creighton and Senior (A).

G: This type is much like Type F, except the lad speaks from Heaven on a clear day. The mainmast then breaks, and the ship goes down. Examples: Fowke.

Discussion: The American versions of this song should not be confused with the more recent Lowlands Low group (*Young Edmund*), which traces back to the English *Edwin in the Lowlands Low*. See Laws, *Am Bldry Brit Bdsdes*, M 34, pp. 197-198 for bibliography.

The Sweet Trinity in the New World does not really follow any of the Child versions textually, although on the whole there is a closer relationship to Child B-C than to Child A. In America, Sir Walter Raleigh is almost never connected with the song (though see Flanders, *Ancient Blds,* FF), while the ships have variations of the names "Golden Vanity" and "Turkish Revelee".

The main variation in the New World story types comes in the conclusion. Type A is not unlike Child A and Child C, though there is no definite parallel. The gallant refusal of the cabin boy to follow his inclination to sink the ship is American. Type B seems to derive from Child B, while Types C-G reflect a desire to see justice done. F and G seem to be Canadian, while the texts in Colcord, *Roll and Go,* 79 and *JAF,* 1905, 125 show a tendency toward sentimentalization. Flanders, *Ancient Blds* prints a great number of texts, which reflect quite well the American variations. Her A[1], with stanzas on the phantom ship; R, with lines borrowed from *The Mermaid* (Child 289); and V, with its lone Ishmael-like survivor are particularly noteworthy. The Colcord, *Sgs Am Sailormen,* 154 text contains a great deal of sea lingo, while the Henry, *Fsgs So Hghlds,* 130, B version finds the *Golden Willow Tree* sunk by a lad from the *Turkish Revelee.* Note also the BFSSNE, V, 11 text where the boy "upsets the tea-kettle and drowns all the mice". The Brown, *NC Flklre,* II, 662 text is mixed with a ballad on the sinking of the *Titanic.* Roger Abrahams has collected a children's game rime that seems to use a part of this ballad.

Barry, *Brit Blds Me,* 347 points out that the similarity between the Southern and New England versions of this ballad indicates that the height of the song's popularity in England was at the time of the big American emigration.

For a parody of the song, see Sandburg, *Am Sgbag,* 343. For other college versions, note *The American College Songster* (Ann Arbor, Mich., 1876), 101; Waite's *Carmina Collegensia* (Boston, cop. 1868), 171; and White's *Student Life in Song* (Boston, cop. 1879), 58.

287. CAPTAIN WARD AND THE RAINBOW

Texts: Barry, *Brit Blds Me,* 347 / Broadsides: Coverly, Boston Public Library; Harvard University Library 25242.5.5, 25276.4381 / Chappell, *Fsgs Rnke Alb,* 45 / Flanders, *Ancient Blds,* IV / Flanders, *Blds Migrant NE,* 204 / Flanders, *Vt Fsgs Blds,* 242 / *Forecastle Songster* (Nafis and Cornish, N.Y., 1849) / *Forget-me-not Songster* (Locke, Boston, c. 1842) / *Forget-me-not Songster* (Nafis and Cornish, N.Y.), 41 / *Forget-me-not Songster* (Turner and Fisher, Philadelphia), 200 / Gardner and Chickering, *Blds Sgs So Mich,* 216 / *Green Mountain Songster,* 56 / *JAF,*

1905, 137; 1912, 177 / *Pearl Songster* (Huestis, N.Y., 1846), / Shoemaker, *Mt. Mnstly*, 300 / Thompson, *Bdy Bts Brtchs*, 33 / Thompson and Cutting, *Pioneer Songster*, 25.

Local Titles: Captain Ward (and the Rainbow), Captain Ward the Pirate.

Story Types: A: The English king has a ship, the *Rainbow*, built and sent out to sea. She encounters the Scot, Captain Ward, who, upon being recognized as a pirate who had robbed the English and ordered to surrender, fights her and routs her with the taunt that the king can rule the land, but Ward rules the sea.

Examples: Barry (B), Gardner and Chickering, Shoemaker.

B: The Scotsman Ward writes the English King and requests that he be taken into the Royal Navy with his ship for £ 10,000 of gold. The King (or Queen) refuses him as being untrustworthy. Ward sets off again, undismayed, and robs, among others, an English merchantman. When the news reaches the King, he has the *Rainbow* built. This boat attacks Ward, captures him and takes him back to England. Ward speaks right up to the King and says that he hates France and Spain and has robbed but three English ships. Nevertheless, he is hung.

Examples: Barry (C).

C: The story is similar to that of Type B. However, after losing the fight, the *Rainbow* returns to the King and tells him Ward will never be taken, and the monarch bewails the three great men he has recently lost. They would have captured Ward had they been alive.

Examples: Barry (D), Flanders (B).

Discussion: Child, V, 163 dates the events of this ballad as having occurred between 1604 and 1609 and cites John Ward of Kent as the hero. The deaths of Essex, Clifford, and Mountjoy in 1601, 1605 and 1606 respectively tend to back up these statements. They are the three heroes who would have taken Ward had they been alive. Barry, *Brit Blds Me*, 358—63, in a difficult, but informative discussion, investigates the British and American versions of the story in detail.

From his arguments, it seems very possible that the Type B ballads give the end of the story as it occurred in actuality and that, although Ward escaped once, he was later captured by other men in James' service and hung. The Type A and C texts do not reveal these subsequent events and only tell of the escape—Type A, the most common of the three in America, being a shorter version of the Type C (Child) story. If this reasoning is true, then the name the *Rainbow* has been confused and appears both on James' defeated ship (A, C) and on his victorious ship (B). However, it is equally possible that a tragic ending and a happy ending exist on the same ballad because of contact with *Sir Andrew Barton* (see my discussion under Child 167, as well as Barry, *op cit.*, 253f.), or some other reason.

The savage opening stanza of the Chappell, *Fsgs Rnke Alb*, 45 text is worth note. In it, the King calls Ward a "wanton, lying, stinking thief".

289. THE MERMAID

Texts: Barry, *Brit Blds Me,* 363 / Beard, *Personal Fsg Coll Lunsford,* 116 /
Belden, *Mo Fsgs,* 101 / Botkin, *Am Play-Party Sg,* 56 / Botkin, *Treasury NE
Flklre,* 872 / Brown, *NC Flklre,* II, 195 / Chappell, *Fsgs Rnke Alb,* 47 / Cox,
Fsgs South, 192 / Creighton, *Maritime Fsgs,* 26 / Creighton and Senior, *Trd Sgs
N Sc,* 106 / Davis, *Fsgs Va,* 35 / Davis, *More Trd Blds Va,* 344 / Davis, *Trd
Bld Va,* 521 / DeMarsan Broadside List 14, #56 / Deming Broadside (Boston,
c. 1838) / Flanders, *Ancient Blds,* IV / *Focus,* II, 447; IV, 97 / *Forget-me-not
Songster* (Locke, Boston, c. 1842) / *Forget-me-not Songster* (Nafis and Cornish,
N.Y.), 79 / *Forget-me-not Songster* (Sadlier, N.Y., 46 / *Forecastle Songster* (Nafis
and Cornish, N.Y., 1849), 112 / Harlow, *Chanteying Am Ships,* 147 / Haun, *Cocke
Cnty,* 112 / *Heart Songs,* 360 / Henry, *Fsgs So Hghlds,* 133 / Hudson, *Fsgs Miss,*
127 / Hudson, *Spec Miss Flklre,* #23 / Hurgill, *Shanties 7 Seas,* 560 / *JAF,* 1905,
136; 1912, 176; 1913, 175; 1947, 237; 1957, 341 / Lomax and Lomax, *Our Sgng
Cntry,* 151 / Luce's *Naval Songs,* 1902, 118 / MacKenzie, *Blds Sea Sgs N Sc,* 65 /
McGill, *Fsgs Ky Mts,* 46 / Morris, *Fsgs Fla,* 328 / Musick, *Flklre Kirksville,* 12 /
NYFQ, IV, 179 / *Pearl Songster* (Huestis, N.Y., 1846), 155 / Pound, *Am Blds Sgs,*
26 / Pound, *Nebr Syllabus,* 10 / *PTFS,* X, 162 / Randolph, *Oz Fsgs,* I, 202 /
Scarborough, *Sgctchr So Mts,* 189 / SharpK, *Eng Fsgs So Aplchns,* I, 291 /
Shoemaker, *No Pa Mnstly* (1919), 157 / *Singer's Journal,* I, 301 / *SFQ,* 1954,
182 / Spaeth / *Read 'em and Weep,* 81 / Stout, *Flklre Iowa,* 14 / Thompson,
Bdy Bts Brtchs, 216 / Thompson and Cutting, *Pioneer Songster,* 29 / *Uncle Sam's
Naval and Patriotic Songster* (Cozzens, N.Y.), 40 / *Va FLS* Bull, #s, 2-5, 8-10
/ Alfred Williams, *Street Blds and Sgs* (pre-1895).

Local Titles: As I Sailed Out One Friday Night, Doom Ship, The (Our)
Gallant Ship, Maid o' Home, The Mermaid, Oh the Lamp Burns Dimly Down
Below, The Raging Sea, The Royal George, The Saillers, The Shipwrecked Sailors,
The Sinking Ship, The Stormy Winds, The Stormy Winds How They Blow (Do
Blow), The Three Sailor Boys, The Wreck.

Story Types: A: A ship sets sail on a Friday, a day of ill-omen. It sights
a mermaid at sea, a fact which bodes ill-weather. The men on board all
resign themselves that the ship will go down. It does.

Examples: Barry (A); Belden; Davis, *Trd Bld Va* (A).

B: The story is the same as that of Type A. However, the captain
"plumbs" the sea fore and aft and realizes the boat will sink and that all
the men on board will be in Heaven or Hell "this night". The other crew
members do not appear.

Examples: Lomax and Lomax.

C: This text is localized to the Sandy Hook, N.Y. area. It follows
Child A, but omits mention of the mermaid completely.

Examples: Creighton, *Maritime Fsgs.*

Discussion: The Type A texts of this song are the most common and
follow the Child B-D series rather closely. However, Child A does have
a tradition in the New World as can be seen from my Type C (check also
JAF, 1913, 175, Stanza 1 and Davis, *More Trd Blds Va,* AA). Of the
Type A texts, Brown, *NC Flklre,* B is the most interesting. This version
from Cape Cod, Mass. names the ship *Maid o' Home,* has an unusual
refrain, and closes with a stanza about the church at Plymouth where
"many a woeful wife" mourns. The text is an excellent specimen of story

localization. Also of interest is the *JAF*, 1957, 342 text from West Virginia in which a girl is among the crew. She weeps for her sweetheart in New York Town. The Type B version has no parallel in Child.

The ballad has been included in many published works both in Britain (see Cox, *Fsgs South*, 172) and in America. Cox, *op. cit.*, and MacKenzie, *Blds Sea Sgs N Sc*, 65 give lists of college songbook texts. Some references of this sort are *The American College Songster* (Ann Arbor, 1876), 56; Noble's *Songs of Harvard* (cop. 1913), 82; W. H. Hill's *Student's Songs*, 27; and Waite's *Student Life in Song* (Boston, cop. 1879), 47. It has been parodied frequently. See Scarborough, *Sgctchr So Mts*, 190; *The Slam-Bang Songster* (cop. 1870), 8; and *The We Won't Go Home Until Morning Songster* (cop. 1869), 8. For its use as a children's game see Gomme, *Traditional Games*, II, 143, 422; For its use as a play-party game see Botkin, *Am Play-Party Sg*, 56. For other published texts, which have had a large influence on the form of this song, see the broadside and songster references included in the bibliography above.

American texts usually have a "stormy winds" chrous which will vary in position and use in the different versions and variants.

293. JOHN OF HAZELGREEN

Texts: Barry, *Brit Blds Me*, 369 / *BFSSNE*, III, 9 / Davis, *Fsgs Va*, 36 / Davis, *More Trd Blds Va*, 350 / Davis, *Trd Bld Va*, 529 / Flanders, *Ancient Blds*, IV / Flanders, *Blds Migrant NE*, 237 / *MLN*, XLVI, 304 / Morris, *Fsgs Fla*, 330 / Scarborough, *Sgctchr So Mts*, 225 / SharpK, *Eng Fsgs So Aplchns*, I, 294 / Smith and Rufty, *Am Anth Old Wrld Blds*, 62 / *SFQ*, 1949, 173 / *Va FLS Bull*, #s 3-7, 10.

Local Titles: John (Jack, Jock) o' Hazelgreen, John of (over) Hazelgreen, Willie of Hazel Green, Young Johnny of Hazelgreen.

Story Types: A: A walker discovers a girl crying, and he offers her his eldest son in marriage. However, she refuses, saying that she loves John of Hazelgreen, whom she describes glowingly. She then rides to town and is met by John, who kisses her and promises fidelity.

Examples: Davis, *Trd Bld Va* (A); SharpK.

B: The story is parallel to that of Type A, except that instead of going to town the girl rides home with the walker after she has refused the offer of his son's hand. At the house she is met by her Willie, who conveniently turns out to be the son.   Examples: *BFSSNE*, III, 9.

Discussion: The full story of the ballad as given by Child, V, 160 is as follows:

> A gentleman overhears a damsel making moan for Sir John of Hazelgreen. After some complaint on his part, and some slight information on hers, he tells her that Hazelgreen is married; then there is nothing for her to do, she says, but to hold her peace and die for him. The gentleman proposes that she shall let Hazelgreen go, marry his eldest son, and be made a gay lady; she is too mean a maid for that, and, anyway, had rather die for the object of her affection. Still she allows the gentleman to take her up behind him on his horse and to buy clothes for her at Biggar, though all the time dropping tears for Hazelgreen.

After shopping they mount again, and at last they come to the gentleman's place, when the son runs out to welcome his father. The son is young Hazelgreen, who takes the maid in his arms and kisses off the still-falling tears. The father declares that the two shall be married the next day, and the young man shall have the family lands.

The Type B version cited here, although obviously a fragment of the same story, does not follow any Child version. The Type A stories are not close to Child's version either and frequently in America appear as little more than a maid's lament and a lover's reunion.

The Davis, *Trd Bld Va*, 536, J version has been the subject of some scholarship because of the influence that Scott's *Jock of Hazeldean* has had upon it. For a discussion of the role played by Scott in the composition of the English text in the light of this Virginia version, see Maurice Kelley's article, *MLN*, XLVI, 304. Check also Davis, *op. cit.*, 529 and Morris, *Fsgs Fla*, 482. See *BFSSNE*, III, 9 where a New Brunswick song that corrupts Scott's poem with lines from the traditional ballad is printed. Scott's poem and its history are fully treated here. There is no clear story to be seen in this fragmentary Canadian version, however.

295. THE BROWN GIRL

Note: Reed Smith (*SFQ*, I, #2, 9-11) lists *The Brown Girl* in its traditional form among the survivals of Child ballads in America. I have not, however, been able to locate a published text or the text to which he made reference. The texts that sometimes go under the title, *A Rich Irish Lady* (Laws P 9), may be considered derivatives of Child 295.

"A Rich Irish Lady" Texts: Barry, *Brit Blds Me*, 418 / Beard, *Personal Fsg Coll Lunsford*, 120 / Belden, *Mo Fsgs*, 111 / Brewster, *Blds Sgs Ind*, 164 / Brown, *NC Flklre*, II, 299 / Cambiaire, *Ea Tenn Wstn Va Mt Blds*, 119 / Cox, *Fsgs South*, 366 / Davis, *Fsgs Va*, 36 / Davis, *Trd Bld Va*, 537 / Flanders, *Ancient Blds*, IV / Flanders, *Vt Fsgs Blds*, 244 / Gardner and Chickering, *Blds Sgs So Mich*, 150 / *Green Mountain Songster*, 23 / Haun, *Cocke Cnty*, 83 / Henry, *Fsgs So Hghlds*, 134 / Hubbard, *Blds Sgs Utah*, 46 / Hudson, *Fsgs Miss*, 128 / Hudson, *Ftunes Miss*, 8 / Hudson, *Spec Miss Flklre*, #25 / *JAF*, 1914, 73; 1916, 178; 1919, 502; 1926, 110; 1932, 53; 1939, 12; 1947, 214; 1950, 259; 1957, 342 / Lomax and Lomax, *Our Sgng Cntry*, 160 / McDowell, *Memory Mel*, 19 / Morris, *Fsgs Fla*, 330 / Owens, *Studies Tex Fsgs*, 18 / Owens, *Texas Fsgs*, 37 / Powell, *5 Va Fsgs*, 9 / Randolph, *Oz Fsgs*, I, 205 / Scarborough, *Sgctchr So Mts*, 97 / SharpC, *Eng Fsgs So Aplchns*, #36 / SharpK, *Eng Fsgs So Aplchns*, I, 295 / Smith and Rufty, *Am Anth Old Wrld Blds*, 67 / *SFQ*, 1954, 178 / *Va FLS Bull*, #s 5, 7-9, 11.

Local Titles: The Bold Sailor, A Brave Irish Lady, The Brown Girl, The Fair Damsel (Rich Lady) from London, Fair (Pretty) Sally, A Irish (Young) Lady, Love Billie, A New Ballad, Pretty Sally of London, The Rich (Irish) Lady, Rose of Ardeen, The Royal Fair Damsel, The Sailor from Dover, Sallie, Sally, (Pretty) Sally and Billy, Sally and Her True Love Billy, Sally Sailsworth, Sweet Sally, There Was a Young Lady.

Story Types: A: A young girl, once attached to a man, tells him she cannot love him as she has fallen for another. He becomes proud. Later, when she falls deathly ill, she sends for the scorned one and requests that he restore her faith and love. He arrives and mocks her situation, reminds her how she scorned him, and says he will dance with glee on her grave. Often, she gives him a ring to wear while dancing on her grave, a gift which he scorns.

Examples: Brewster; Davis, *Trd Bld Va* (A); SharpK (A).

B: See *The Death of Queen Jane* (Child 170): Type D.

Examples: Davis, *Trd Bld Va*, p. 420; SharpK, p. 303.

C: The story is like that of Type A, except that the man repents his cruelty and says he will soon die and wed the girl in death.

Examples: SharpK (G).

D: The same story is told as was told in Type A, but the ending is happy. The lover repents and tells the girl to "cheer up". He then marries her.

Examples: Barry (A, E), Gardner and Chickering, Flanders.

E: The story is the same as that of Type A, but it is the man who gets ill and the girl (like Barbara Allen) who goes to see him, scorns him a second time, and is given the rings to wear when she dances on his grave.

Examples: *JAF*, 1939, 12.

F: The story is very like that of Type A. However, the man spurns the girl at the start by telling her that he will marry her only if forced. She then puts the best face possible on things. She later becomes ill, sends for the man that "she has denied". He scorns her and says he will dance on her grave.

Examples: *JAF*, 1950, 259.

G: A degeneration exists in which a sea-captain, Pretty Polly, and Miss Betsy are involved in a confusion in which the "are you the doctor" stanzas are the only intelligible part.

Examples: *JAF*, 1932, 53.

H: A happy lyric tells of a man who loves a girl. He offers her pearls and gold, but is rejected. As he is getting his hat to leave, she tells him to stay.

Examples: *JAF*, 1947, 214.

Discussion: American forms of this ballad, unless Reed Smith's reference is correct, can all be traced back to the songs referred to in Laws, *Am Bldry Brit Bdsdes,* as P 9. See pp. 252-253 for discussion and bibliographical references to broadside texts. Such ballads, usually appearing under a *Rich Irish Lady* or *Sally and Billy* title are no doubt closely related to Child 295 and do form the American tradition of that song. In the New World, the girl is no longer brown, and the sexes are reversed so that the lover scorns the dying girl. See Belden, *Mo Fsgs,* 111 and Laws, *op. cit.,* 253 for detailed discussions of the Anglo-American characteristics of the song. Laws sees two closely related broadside forms that have spread through the New World. In one the man asks the girl if her pains are in her head or in her side; in the other the "Are you the doctor?" stanzas are a feature.

There has been a certain amount of doubt and hesitation among the collector-editors in deciding whether or not to include the American *Brown Girl* as part of the Child 295 tradition or not. Barry and Gardner and Chickering publish their finds as secondary versions of the traditional song, while Randolph, Brewster, Sharp-Karpeles, and Davis include theirs as American variants. See Hudson, *Fsgs Miss,* 128; the Kirklands, *SFQ,* 1939, 79; and Powell, *5 Va Fsgs,* 7—8 for discussions of the problem.

The story of The Brown Girl, as given by Child, V, 166, is as follows:

> A young man who has been attached to a girl sends her word by letter that he cannot fancy her because she is so brown (he has left her for another). She sends a disdainful reply. He writes again that he is dangerously ill (he is lovesick), and begs her to come to him quickly and give him back his faith. She takes her time in going, and when she comes to the sick man's bedside, cannot stand for laughing. She has, however, brought a white wand with her, which she strokes on his breast, in sign that she gives him back the faith which he had given her. But as to forgiving and forgetting, that she will never do; she will dance upon his grave.

The American story types are, of course, quite dissimilar to this narrative. Type A is the normal American tale. The Type B variation is due to the corruption of Child 170, *The Death of Queen Jane* (See Type D under 170). Types C and D reflect different degrees of sentimentality and, particularly in the latter case, weaken the story considerably. Type E is interesting in that the sexes reverse back to the British form, although the girl remains the scorner at the start. Part of this story was narrated, and the change may be due in some degree to faulty memory. Type F echoes the British *Brown Girl* also in that the man spurns the girl before she becomes haughty. However, this text is clearly the derivative song, and the variation is probably connected to the fact that some of the verses were unknown to the singer. Type G is one of the most garbled texts of a ballad ever collected in America and is completely confused. H is an unusual song, and although it has certain affinities with the American *Brown Girl,* may well be some other piece. It was taken from a 19th Century songbook.

The SharpK, *Eng Fsgs So Aplchns,* F text should be noted in that it reveals the "doctor" stanzas taken so literally that the lover has become a physician. See also Powell, *5 Va Fsgs.*

299. THE TROOPER AND THE MAID

Texts: Barry, *Brit Blds Me,* 371 / Brewster, *Blds Sgs Ind,* 166 / Brown, *NC Flklre,* II, 198 / BFSSNE, VIII, 11 / Davis, *Fsgs Va,* 36 / Davis, *More Trd Blds Va,* 356 / Davis, *Trd Bld Va,* 544 / Focus, V, 280 / Randolph, *Oz Fsgs,* I, 213 / Randolph, *Oz Mt Flk,* 209 / SharpC, *Eng Fsgs So Aplchns,* #37 / SharpK, *Eng Fsgs So Aplchns,* I, 305 / *Va FLS Bull,* #s 4, 7-8.

Local Titles: The Bugle Boy, A Soldier Rode from the East, The Trooper, The Trooper and the Maid.

Story Types: A: A trooper comes to his mistress' house to spend the night with her. After feeding the horse and feasting, they go to bed and are awakened by a trumpet in the morning. The trooper has to leave; the girl fearing she has been ruined follows him. He begs her to turn back. She asks him repeatedly when they are to meet and marry. He replies with a typical ballad "never, never" motif, such as that used in *Edward, The Two Brothers,* etc.

Examples: Davis, *Trd Bld Va* (A, B); SharpK (A, C).

B: The story is much like that of Type A. However, the trooper says he will return to the girl, though marriage is not mentioned.

Examples: Barry.

C: The story is similar to that of Type A, but the trooper says he will marry the girl in the future.

Examples: Randolph, *Oz Fsgs,* I.

D: A version, badly corrupted by *Young Hunting,* in which the lady stabs the trooper as he bends from his horse after telling her he will never marry her, exists in Indiana. In this text, the girl also persuades the man to spend the night with her after he has told her he is on his way to see his real love.   Examples: Brewster.

Discussion: The American Type A stories follow Child's summary as given in V, 172. Type B, however, as does the Greig, *Last Leaves Trd Bld,* B, version (see his Note 107 on p. 278), begins to show a modification of the realistic ending. Here the mention of the marriage is left out, but an intention to return is expressed. The Barry, *Brit Blds Me,* B text, it should be noted, is similar to Greig A (p. 246) except for this one final stanza where the idea of the return is given: "But, bonnie lassie, I'll lie near ee yet". This final stanza may be a variation from the second stanza (which is repeated in Greig A) with influence from the Greig B ending. Type C carries the tendency to its ultimate conclusion in an ending where the trooper replies that he'll marry the girl "when peace is made an' the soldiers are at home" instead of the usual "when cockle shells grow silver bells", etc. Whether this ending has been affected by the *Pretty Peggy* of Gibb Ms., #13, p. 53 or *The Dragoon and Peggy* of Maidment's *Scotish Ballads and Songs* (1859), 98 which Child, V, 172 notes end happily is hard to say. Type D demonstrates the manner in which a new song can grow from two old ones. Brewster, *Blds Sgs Ind,* 166 points out that his text contains a half-stanza from the Manx *Va shiaulteyr voish y twoiae* (*JFSS,* VII, 216). Brown, *NC Flklre,* II, 198 prints a version that concludes with a paraphrase of the "bell-bottom trousers" refrain.

THE TRADITIONAL BALLAD AS AN ART FORM

The Traditional Ballad as an Art Form[1]

Anglo-American ballad poems are the texts of ballads, printed without music and judged by the literary standards of Anglo-American culture. These texts, comprising the greatest single art form that oral tradition has produced, are seldom discussed as art by the amateurs and anthropologically-trained researchers who work with them. As a result, most teachers and many scholars think of Anglo-American ballad poetry as something a bit unusual in the realm of human endeavor, something a breed apart from "conscious" arts like drama, concert music, poetry in print. Today, it is frequently assumed that such ballad poetry "just happens" or that the folk, working in communion, have mystically borne what we recognize as great literature. Yet we know better. We know things don't "just happen"; and we know the old "communal theory of ballad composition" to be almost completely wrong. It seems long past high time that the whole subject of the Anglo-American ballad text as art were brought up for review.

MacEdward Leach has characterized all ballads as follows:

> A ballad is story. Of the four elements common to all narrative—action, character, setting, and theme—the ballad emphasizes the first. Setting is casual; theme is often implied; characters are usually types and even when more individual are undeveloped, but action carries the interest. The action is usually highly dramatic, often startling and all the more impressive because it is unrelieved. The ballad practices rigid economy in relating the action; incidents antecedent to the climax are often omitted, as are explanatory and motivating details. The action is usually of a plot sort and the plot often reduced to the moment of climax; that is, of the unstable situation and the resolution which constitutes plot, the ballad often concentrates on the resolution leaving the listener to supply details and antecedent material.
>
> Almost without exception ballads were sung; often they were accompanied by instrumental music. The tunes are traditional and probably as old as the words, but of the two—story and melody—story is basic.[2]

Leach's definition would be disputed by few folklorists. Add to his points the idea that ballads are individually composed, and are most often fed down to the folk from a somewhat more highly educated stratum of society, and one has a good picture of the ballad as modern scholarship sees it. Ballads, thus, are widely considered to be plotted narratives, rising from relatively trained minds, taken over and fostered by the folk until they become the verses and masterpieces that our collectors uncover.

The word "plotted" is of particular significance. It shall be a main purpose of this essay to suggest that plotting is vestigial, rather than vital, in the make-up of Anglo-American ballads. Unified action is a sign of the trained artist from the time of Homer through the Renaissance to the twentieth century.[3] Such organization of narrative tends to distinguish a man with training in the traditions of Western European literature from the ignorant or primitive. Plotting is honored by the tradition in which the Anglo-American ballad is born, but there is little evidence to support a contention that the folk, in whose oral heritage the ballad lives, care very much at all for unified action. Their myths and their tales lack unified action, except as a vestige. Generally, the folk tend to discard plotting in favor of something one might call "impact" or "emotional core."

Leach, as other writers on the ballad, stresses action as the most essential ingredient. I feel, however, that Anglo-American ballads stress impact over action and retain, in the long run, only enough of the original action or plot unity to hold this core of emotion in some sort of focus. In our ballad, details are kept and discarded to fit the core, and little real attention is paid to plot consistency or structure. Plot is present, but in the background. The emotional core, a part of the musical as well as the textual meaning of the song, is emphasized and cherished.

To understand the process by which an Anglo-American ballad becomes a poem, one must go into the problem of "emotional core" in some detail. It is essential that we understand what our folk consider a ballad to be and how it should be sung. Two things are certain: to our folk a ballad is song, not poetry; for us ballads become poems because certain variants (often by sheer chance) measure up to Western European aesthetic standards.

A ballad survives among our folk because it embodies a basic human reaction to a dramatic situation. This reaction is reinterpreted by each person who renders the ballad. As an emotional core it dominates the artistic act, and melody, setting, character, and plot are used only as means by which to get it across. This core is more important to the singer and the listeners than the details of the action themselves. For while a singer is often scrupulous not to change the version of a song as he sings it, he shows little interest in the consistency or meaning of the details he is not changing. Ballads resemble gossip. They are transmitted like gossip, and their variation comes about in much the way gossip variation occurs.

The thesis presented above accounts for a number of the unique qualities of folk art and, through these qualities, designates the pattern of development that our ballads take over a stretch of time.

1. That many singers actually miss the point of the ballad action may well be because they focus attention on the emotional core of the song rather than on the plot detail. For example, thirteen years ago I published a paper dealing with an Arkansas version of "The Drowsy Sleeper."[4] My informant considered "The Drowsy Sleeper" to be an incest tale, but the woman who had taught the song to him had considered it a suicide-love story. Although the factual detail was the same (actually all the words were the same) in both texts, my informant had changed the emotional core that these details went to make up.

2. Such focus on the emotional core of a song may also account for the fact that the folk tolerate contradictions and preposterous images in their songs. So lines like "he mounted a roan, she a milk-white steed, whilst

himself upon a dapple gray" and "up spoke a pretty little parrot exceeding on a willow tree"[5] survive even from generation to generation.

3. Finally, if we accept the thesis of the "emotional core," the difficulties encountered by all scholars who attempt to define the Anglo-American ballad are accounted for. Every text of every ballad is in a different stage of development and derives from a different artistic environment. The details of the action are never precisely conceived. As a result, there is nothing exact enough about a ballad to define.

As an Anglo-American ballad survives in oral tradition, the details become conventionalized so that songs of the same general type (love songs, ghost songs, etc.) tend to grow more and more alike, to use more and more of the same clichés. As Moore said, "In a way the ballad resembles the proverb: there is nothing left in it which is not acceptable to all who preserve it by repetition. The simple ballads, which have served a general public are non-technical in diction, whereas the modern songs of special classes . . . are highly technical. The same levelling process destroys whatever individual character the original poem may have."[6] And (p. 400), "After a painstaking study of the subject, I have yet to find a clear case where a ballad can be shown to have improved as a result of oral transmission, except in the way of becoming more lyrical." Moore's words, along with other things, have led me to believe that the life of an Anglo-American ballad can be charted somewhat like this:

Stage 1. A poem, created by an individual, enters or is retained in oral tradition. This poem has three major parts: an emotional core, details of action, frills of a poetic style that are too "sophisticated" for the folk. At this stage the poem is frequently not for singing and may well be closer to literature than to musical expression. The Frazer broadside of "Sally and Billy" or "The Rich Lady from London" (the song so often cited erroneously as Child 295) offers a relatively modern example:

> 'Tis of a young sailor, from Dover he came,
> He courted pretty Sally, pretty Sally was her name,
> But she was so lofty, and her portion was so high,
> That she on a sailor would scarce cast an eye.
>
> .   .   .   .
>
> "So adieu to my daddy, my mammy, and friends,
> And adieu to the young sailor for he will make no amends.
> Likewise this young sailor he will not pity me,
> Ten thousand times now my folly I see."[7]

So, of course, do any number of other newspaper, almanac, and broadside texts.

Stage 2. This is the "ballad" stage. The frills of sub-literary style have been worn away by oral tradition; some of the action details have been lost. Any so-called "traditional" ballad can serve as an illustration of Stage 2, although in the cases of both "Sally and Billy" and "Geordie" the American texts are close enough to print so that the transition from Stage 1 to Stage 2 is not complete. In fact, a majority of American songs lie in the area between the first two stages and were in the process of evolving toward traditional balladry when hindered by print and the urbanization of the folk. Some songs are born at this mid-point, to be sure. Individuals like Booth Campbell or Sir Walter Scott, who are used to singing or working within the conventions of folk tradition, may compose songs that never pass through Stage 1, that are traditional in language and detail at their birth.[8]

Stage 3. In this final stage the ballad develops in one of two ways. Either unessential details drop off until lyric emerges, or essential details drop off until only a meaningless jumble, centered about a dramatic core, is left. The so-called "degenerate" ballad (and that is a poor term) is either a lyric or a nonsense song. The Scarborough text of "Geordie" beginning,

> Come bridle me up my milk-white steed
> The brownie ain't so able, O.
> While I ride down to Charlottetown.
> To plead for the life of my Georgie, O.[9]

shows the start of a development toward something like the lyrical "Rantin' Laddie" that was quoted in toto in the discussion on variation.[10] In much the same way the nonsensical Wisconsin "Sally and Billy" that begins with the meaningless lines,

> There was a ship captain
> That sailed on the sea.
> He called on Miss Betsy;
> Pretty Polly did say
> You go to that sea captain
> And grant me love or ruined I'll be.[11]

has its counterparts in "Bessy Bell" nursery rhymes and that amazing Texas version of Child 84, "Boberick Allen."[12] Both lyric and nonsense stages develop, of course, from forgetting. Yet it is significant to note that it is the detail, not the emotional core, that is forgotten. The emotional core may be varied or modified, but it is the essential ingredient of any one song as long as that song exists.[13]

Ballads in Stage 3 and ballads in the process of moving from Stage 2 to Stage 3 are the only Anglo-American ballads that can meet the requirements of Western European poetry.[14] While it is certainly true that collectors are always finding Anglo-American ballads with complete or nearly complete plot unity, the variants that subordinate plot detail and focus on the emotional impact are the variants that are accepted as art. To become great poetry, our ballads must lose so much of their original style, atmosphere, and detail that they must become lyrics as well.

Which of our ballads will meet the requirements of Western European poetry as they move toward lyric is governed by chance. A balance attained in oral tradition between stress on plot unification and stress on emotional impact gives some texts a magnificent half-lyric, half-narrative effect. Individuals, coming in series, often generations apart, change lines, phrases, and situations to fit their personal fancies and to render what they consider to be the song's emotional core before giving the ballad back to oral tradition. Some of these individuals are untrained geniuses, a few may be trained geniuses like Burns or Scott, most are without artistic talent. The geniuses give us the texts, or parts of texts, that measured by Western European standards are art. Their efforts are communal in the sense that there are usually many "authors" working on the tradition of any one song or version of a song. But it must be remembered that often these geniuses live decades apart, handle the song separately, and store it in an ineffectual oral tradition in between. Oral tradition is an aimless thing. It will stumble into art—but not with any sort of consistency.

The widely anthologized Child A version of "Mary Hamilton" is an example of an Anglo-American ballad poem that has gained artistic acceptance. The plot of the song is quite simple. Mary, Queen of Scots, has four maids-in-waiting, each selected for her virginal name and her beauty. One of the maids, Mary Hamilton as she is called in the ballad, not only flaunts the conventions of society by having an affair with the Queen's husband, but is unfortunate enough to bear a child as fruit of this indiscretion. She attempts to destroy the baby, is caught, tried, and hanged for murder. Characterization and real setting are almost nonexistent, but the emotional core of the ballad is given great emphasis. This core, the tragedy of beauty and youth led astray, the lack of sympathy within the law, the girl's resigned indifference to her lot, are driven home with full force.

1. Word's gane to the kitchen,
   And word's gane to the ha,
   That Marie Hamilton gangs wi bairn
   To the hichest Stewart of a'.

2. He's courted her in the kitchen,
   He's courted her in the ha',
   He's courted her in the laigh cellar,
   And that was warst of a'.

3. She's tyed it in her apron
   And she's thrown it in the sea;
   Says, Sink ye, swim ye, bonny wee babe!
   You'l neer get mair o me.

4. Down then cam the auld queen,
   Goud tassels tying her hair:
   "O Marie, where's the bonny wee babe
   That I heard greet sae sair?"

5. "There was never a babe intill my room,
   As little designs to be;
   It was but a touch o my sair side,
   Come oer my fair bodie."

6. "O Marie, put on your robes o black,
   Or else your robes o brown,
   For ye maun gang wi me the night,
   To see fair Edinbro town."

7. "I winna put on my robes o black,
   Nor yet my robes o brown;
   But I'll put on my robes o white,
   To shine through Edinbro town."

8. When she gaed up the Cannogate,
   She laughd loud laughters three;
   But whan she cam down the Cannogate
   The tear blinded her ee.

9. When she gaed up the Parliament stair,
   The heel cam aff her shee;
   And lang or she cam down again
   She was condemned to dee.

10. When she cam down the Cannogate,
   The Cannogate sae free,
   Many a ladie lookd oer her window,
   Weeping for this ladie.

11. "Ye need nae weep for me," she says,
   "Ye need nae weep for me;
   For had I not slain mine own sweet babe,
   This death I wadna dee.

12. "Bring me a bottle of wine," she says,
   "The best that eer ye hae,
   That I may drink to my weil-wishers,
   And they may drink to me.

13. "Here's a health to the jolly sailors,
   That sail upon the main;
   Let them never let on to my father and mother
   But what I'm coming hame.

14. "There's a health to the jolly sailors,
   That sail upon the sea;
   Let them never let on to my father and mother
   That I cam here to dee.

15. "Oh little did my mother think,
   The day she cradled me,
   What lands I was to travel through,
   What death I was to dee.

16. "Oh little did my father think,
   The day he held up me,
   What lands I was to travel through
   What death I was to dee.

17. "Last night I washd the queen's feet,
   And gently laid her down;
   And a' the thanks I've gotten the nicht
   To be hangd in Edinbro town!

18. "Last nicht there was four Maries,
   The nicht there'l be but three;
   There was Marie Seton, and Marie Beton,
   And Marie Carmichael, and me."

Only the first five of the eighteen stanzas that make up Child A are devoted to the rumors of Mary Hamilton's pregnancy, the courtship by Darnley, the murder of the child, and the Queen's discovery that she has been deceived. This juicy copy could not be dispatched more decorously had Mary of Scotland written the lines herself. The next five stanzas are devoted to the trial and conviction of Mary Hamilton, although again no effort is made to capitalize upon dramatic potentialities. Mary Hamilton, somewhat ironically, decides to dress in white, laughs and cries conventionally before and after the trial, and has her misfortune symbolized by losing the heel to her shoe. If the folk as a whole really cared about plot it is doubtful that the narrative possibilities of these events would be so ignored.

Stanzas 11-18, almost half the text, show what really interested the folk who preserved the Child A variant. Stanzas 11-18 deal with material that reflects the girl's feelings as she stands on the gallows waiting to die. The first ten stanzas have remained in the song only because they bring into focus the last eight. The folk recognize that the emotional situation brought on by the seduction and subsequent murder is the artistically vital part of the ballad.

That these stanzas are primarily cliché stanzas is not of importance. They are admirably suited to the emotional situation at hand. Mary tells the sentimentalists that congregate at every hanging not to weep for her, her death is her own doing. She calls for wine in a burst of braggadocio. Her toast mentions her parents, and her mood changes. Mary becomes sentimental herself, and the ballad draws to its end in four heart-rending stanzas. This is the essence of the story: the beauty and youth of a girl snuffed out by law.

It is true that one can turn the page in Child and read the B text to discover that Mary Hamilton would not work "for wantonness and play" and that Darnley came to the gallows to ask Mary Hamilton to "dine with him." But these details, as the ones in Scott's composite version,[16] do nothing to increase the impact of the emotional core. Nor does it matter that Mary Hamilton was really a girl in the Russian court of Peter the Great and that, besides Seaton and Beaton, Livingston and Fleming were the names of Mary of Scotland's other Maries. A girl is a girl, the law is the law, in any age, in any place.

As an Anglo-American ballad survives in oral tradition more and more of the plot material can be expected to vanish, until only a lyric expressing the emotional core is left. Barry's collection from Maine (see n. 10) includes, page 258, the following variant of "Mary Hamilton":

> Yestre'en the queen had four Maries,
> This nicht she'll hae but three;
> There was Mary Beaton, an' Mary Seaton,
> An' Mary Carmichael an' me.

Last nicht I dressed Queen Mary
An' pit on her braw silken goon,
An' a' thanks I've gat this nicht
Is tae be hanged in Edinboro toon.

O little did my mither ken,
The day she cradled me,
The land I was tae travel in,
The death I was tae dee.

They've tied a hanky roon me een,
An' they'll no let me see tae dee:
An' they've pit on a robe o' black
Tae hang on the gallows tree.

Yestre'en the queen had four Maries,
This nicht she'll hae but three:
There was Mary Beaton, an' Mary Seaton,
An' Mary Carmichael an' me.

Here is a lyric poem with but the merest suggestion of plot. Only the facts that the girl was one of the Queen's favored maidens and is now about to die remain clear. Yet the emotional core, girlhood and its beauty snuffed out by law, is as clear as it was in Child A.

It is certain that the Maine lyric did not evolve from Child A (or some similar text) merely through the miracles of forgetting and fusing alone. A member of the folk, or some learned poet, framed Mary's lament with the "Beaton and Seaton" stanza. Perhaps this poet, or another, purposefully discarded some of the plot detail as well. These points are relatively unimportant. The basic thing is that "Mary Hamilton" as it is found today is almost always a lyric and that the tendency to preserve the core and not the plot of the song is typical.

The tendency is also typical of the American song "Charles Guiteau"—an example of mediocre poetry. Here the murderer of James A. Garfield waits for his death with the "little did my mither ken" cliché on his lips. The lines are just as adequate for a nineteenth century assassin as they are for a medieval flirt, and the folk have sloughed nearly all the plot detail included in the original sub-literary text; but "Charles Guiteau," unlike "Mary Hamilton," never passed through the hands of a genius or series of geniuses who could lift it above sentimental verse.

In the hands of A. E. Housman, the "Mary Hamilton" situation was touched by a great poet. "The Culprit," the poem that opens with the lines "The night my father got me / His mind was not on me,"[17] tells of the musings of a man about to be hung. It is in reality a re-statement of the emotions Mary Hamilton expressed in stanzas 11-18 in the Child A text. Why the youth is on the gallows, how he got there, are too clinical for Houseman's poetic purpose. Like the folk singer who shaped "Mary Hamilton" and even "Charles Guiteau," Housman did not clutter his lyric with action detail.

Beyond the observations made on the Child A "Mary Hamilton" lie similar observations that can be made on the Scott "Twa Corbies," the Percy "Sir Patrick Spens," the Percy "Edward," the Mackie-Macmath "Lord Randal," and the other most widely anthologized of our ballads.[18] All of them are basically lyrics. In each case there is a full plot, now lost forever, that the folk have seen fit to discard. A realization of the importance of the "emotional core" to the folk is essential to a sensitive evaluation of Anglo-American ballad poems. The teacher, the critic, the poet, even the researcher, must know that in certain ballad variants there is to be found a fine blend of plot residue and universal emotion that produces priceless offspring from mediocre stock. An Anglo-American ballad may look like narrative. At its birth it may be narrative. But its whole life proceeds as a denial of its origin.

FOOTNOTES

[1] This chapter was first printed in *JAF*, 1957, 208-214 and later included in Mac-Edward Leach and Tristram P. Coffin, *The Critics and the Ballad* (Carbondale, Ill., 1961), 245-256. The word "ballad" should be read throughout to mean "Anglo-American ballad", although the remarks are pertinent to the ballads of Western Europe in general.

[2] *The Standard Dictionary of Folklore, Mythology, and Legend,* ed. Maria Leach (New York, 1949-1950), I, 106.

[3] Even the revolt against plotting that has taken place in much 20th century literature shows a definite consciousness of plotting.

[4] "The Problem of Ballad Story Variation and Eugene Haun's 'Drowsy Sleeper,' " *Southern Folklore Quarterly*, 1950, 87-96.

[5] See, respectively, Arthur K. Davis, *Traditional Ballads of Virginia* 188, and J. Harrington Cox, *Folk Songs of the South*, 18.

[6] *Modern Language Review*, XI (1916), 404-405.

[7] Broadside in the Yale University Library. See the Claude L. Frazer Collection, 2:5.

[8] Narrative accretion may occur during Stage 2 also. But the addition of narrative detail in Stage 2, even when two whole ballads fuse, offers only a temporary setback to the steady movement toward Stage 3—lyric or nonsense.

[9] Dorothy Scarborough, *A Songcatcher in the Southern Mountains,* 213.

[10] See p.   in this book.

[11] *JAF*, 1932, 54.

[12] *Publications of the Texas Folklore Society,* VII, 111, or X, 149.

[13] It should be noted that a composition can move back up these stages at any time that an individual inserts morals, sentiment, and other poetic frills. Parodists, broadside-writers, and the like, frequently made such changes, particularly in the 18th century. The Civil War parodies of "Lord Lovel" as printed in many Southern collections, and the moral version of "The Three Ravens" printed in *JAF*, 1907, 154, serve as examples. It is also true that a song may be composed at any one of the three stages, even at the lyric or nonsense stage (see many of the minstrel tunes).

[14] American ballads, which, as stated above, are usually in the process of moving from Stage 1 to Stage 2, are generally thought of as inferior to Child ballads when measured by Western European poetic standards.

[15] See Child's *The English and Scottish Popular Ballads,* III, 384.

[16] Sir Walter Scott, *Minstrelsy of the Scottish Border* (Edinburgh, 1833), II, 294 (Child I).

[17] A. E. Housman, *Collected Poems* (New York, 1940), p. 114.

[18] See Child for the texts of "The Twa Corbies," "Sir Patrick Spens," "Edward," and "Lord Randal" mentioned.

GENERAL BIBLIOGRAPHY OF
TITLES ABBREVIATED IN THE STUDY OF
STORY VARIATION

GENERAL BIBLIOGRAPHY OF
TITLES ABBREVIATED IN THE STUDY OF
STORY VARIATION

Aarne, Antti and Thompson, Stith. *The Types of the Folktale,* Helsinki, 1961.
Adams, E. C. L. *Nigger to Nigger,* N.Y., 1928.
Adler, Kurt. *Songs of Many Wars, N.Y.,* 1943.
Allen, Jules V. *Cowboy Lore,* San Antonio, Texas, 1933.
Ames, Russell. *The Story of American Folk Song,* N.Y., 1960.
Anderson, Geneva. *A Collection of Ballads and Songs from East Tennessee,* Master's Thesis, University of North Carolina, 1932.
Anderson, Robert. *Works of the British Poets,* 14 vols., Edinburgh, 1795.
Arnold, Byron. *Folksongs of Alabama,* University, Alabama, 1950.

Barbeau, Marius. *Folk Songs of French Canada,* New Haven, 1925.
Barbour, Frances M. *Six Ballads of the Ozark Mountains,* Radcliffe College, 1929.
Baring-Gould, S. and Sheppard, H. Fleetwood. (Sharp, C.: musical ed.). *Songs of the West,* London, 1905.
Barnes, Ruth. *I Hear America Singing,* Philadelphia, 1937.
Barry, Phillips. *Ancient British Ballads,* a privately printed list.
Barry, Phillips (with Eckstorm, Fannie H. and Smyth, Mary W.). *British Ballads from Maine,* New Haven, 1929.
Barry, Phillips. *Maine Woods Songster,* Cambridge, Mass., 1939.
Beard, Anne. *The Personal Folksong Collection of Bascom Lamar Lunsford,* Master's Thesis, Miami University, Oxford, Ohio, 1959.
Beck, Earl C. *Lore of the Lumberjack,* Ann Arbor, 1948.
Beck, Earl C. *Songs of the Michigan Lumberjacks,* Ann Arbor, 1941.
Beck, Horace P. *Down-East Ballads and Songs,* Ph.D. thesis, University of Pennsylvania, 1952.
Beck, Horace P. *Folklore of Maine,* Philadelphia and N.Y., 1957.
Beckwith, Martha. *Folklore in America,* Poughkeepsie, N.Y., 1931.
Belden, H. M. *A Partial List of Song Ballads and Other Poetry Known in Missouri* (Second Edition), 1910.
Belden, H. M. *Missouri Folk Songs* (University of Missouri Studies, Vol. XV), 1940.
Best, Dick and Beth. *Song Fest,* N.Y., 1948, 1955.
Blades, W. C. *Negro Poems, Melodies, etc.,* Boston, 1921.
Boatright, Mody C. *Backwoods to Border,* Dallas, 1943.
Boni, Margaret B. *Fireside Book of Favorite American Songs,* N.Y., 1952.
Boni, Margaret B. *Fireside Book of Folk Songs,* N.Y., 1947.
Botkin, Benjamin. *American Play Party Song,* Lincoln, 1937.
Botkin, Benjamin. *Treasury of American Folklore,* N.Y., 1944.
Botkin, Benjamin. *Treasury of New England Folklore,* N.Y., 1947.
Botkin, Benjamin. *Treasury of Southern Folklore,* N.Y., 1949.
Botsford, Florence. *Songs of the Americas,* N.Y., n. d.
Bowles, Paul F. *American Folk Songs,* N.Y., 1940.
Brand, Oscar. *Folksongs for Fun,* N.Y., 1961.
Brewster, Paul G. *Ballads and Songs of Indiana,* Bloomington, Ind., 1940.
Brown, F. C. *Folk Ballads from North Carolina,* Vol. II, Durham, 1952.
Browne, Earl W. *Variant Versions of Scottish and English Humorous Popular Ballads in America,* Master's Thesis, University of Southern California, 1951.
Burns, Robert. *Complete Poems* (Cambridge Edition), Cambridge, Mass., 1897.

Cambiaire, Celeste P. *East Tennessee and Western Virginia Mountain Ballads,* London, 1935.
Carlisle, Irene. *Fifty Songs and Ballads from Northwest Arkansas,* Master's Thesis, University of Arkansas, 1958.

Carmer, Carl L. *America Sings*, N.Y., 1942.
Cazden, Norman. *Abelard Folk Song Book*, N.Y., 1958.
Chambers, Robert. *The Songs in Scotland Prior to Burns*, Edinburgh, 1890.
Chappell, Louis W. *Folk Songs of the Roanoke and Albemarle*, Morgantown, W. Va., 1939.
Chapple, J. M. (ed.) *Heart Songs*, Boston, 1909.
Chase, Richard. *American Folk Tales and Songs*, N.Y., 1956.
Chase, Richard. *Old Songs and Singing Games*, Chapel Hill, N.C., 1938.
Chase, Richard. *Traditional Ballads, Songs, and Games*, Chapel Hill, N.C., 1935.
Chase, Richard; Ritchie, Edna; McLain, Raymond K.; Marvel, Marie. *Songs of All Time*, Berea, Ky., 1946.
Child, Francis J. "Ballad Poetry" in *Johnson's Universal Cyclopaedia*, Vol. I., 1893.
Child, Francis J. *English and Scottish Popular Ballads* (edited by Kittredge, G. L. and Sargent, H. C.), Cambridge Edition, Cambridge, Mass., 1904.
Child, Francis J. *The English and Scottish Popular Ballads*, 5 Vols., Boston, 1882—98.
Coffin, Robert P. T. *Lost Paradise*, N.Y., 1934.
Colcord, Joanna. *Roll and Go*, Indianapolis, 1924.
Colcord, Joanna. *Songs of American Sailormen*, N.Y., 1938.
Coleman, Satis and Bregman, Adolph. *Songs of American Folk*, N.Y., 1942.
Combs, Josiah. *Folk Songs du Midi États-Unis*, Paris, 1926.
Combs, Josiah. *Folk Songs of the Kentucky Highlands*, N.Y., 1939.
Cox, John H. *Folk Songs of the South*, Cambridge, Mass., 1925.
Cox, John H. *Traditional Ballads Mainly from West Virginia*, N.Y., 1939.
Crabtree, Lillian G. *Songs and Ballads Sung in Overton County*, Master's Thesis, George Peabody College, Nashville, 1936.
Creighton, Helen. *Maritime Folksongs*, Toronto, 1962.
Creighton, Helen. *Songs and Ballads from Nova Scotia*, Toronto, 1933.
Creighton, Helen and Senior, Doreen H. *Traditional Songs from Nova Scotia*, Toronto, 1950.
Cunningham, Allan. *The Songs of Scotland*, 4 Vols., London, 1825.
Cutting, Edith. *Lore of an Adirondack County* (Cornell Studies in American History, Literature, and Folklore, I), Ithaca, N.Y.

Davis, Arthur K. *Folk Songs of Virginia: A Descriptive Index and Classification*, Durham, N.C., 1949.
Davis, Arthur K. *More Traditional Ballads of Virginia*, Chapel Hill, N.C., 1960.
Davis, Arthur K. *Traditional Ballads of Virginia*, Cambridge, Mass., 1929.
Dean, M. C. *The Flying Cloud, etc.*, Quickpoint, Virginia, Minn., 1922.
Deutsch, Leonhard. *Treasury of the World's Finest Folk Songs*, N.Y., 1942.
Doerflinger, William M. *Shantymen and Shantyboys*, N.Y., 1951.
Dolph, Edward A. *Sound Off*, N.Y., 1942.
Downes, Olin and Siegmeister, Elie. *Treasury of American Song*, N.Y., 1940.
Duncan, Ruby. *Ballads and Folk Songs in North Hamilton County*, Master's Thesis, University of Tennessee, 1939.

Eckstorm, Fannie H. and Smyth, Mary W. *Minstrelsy of Maine*, Boston, 1927.
Eddy, Mary O. *Ballads and Songs from Ohio*, N.Y., 1939.
Emerich, Duncan. *Casey Jones and Other Ballads of the Mining West*, Denver, 1942.

Farwell, Arthur. *Folk Songs of the West and South*, Newton Center, Mass., 1905.
Fauset, Arthur H. *Folklore from Nova Scotia*, MAFS, XXIV, N.Y., 1931.
Flanders, Helen H.; Coffin, Tristram P.; Nettl, Bruno K. *Ancient Ballads Traditionally Sung in New England*, 4 Volumes, Philadelphia, 1960 f.
Flanders, Helen H. and Olney, Marguerite. *Ballads Migrant in New England*, N.Y., 1953.
Flanders, Helen H., etc. *Country Songs of Vermont*, N.Y., 1937.

Flanders, Helen H. *Garland of Green Mountain Song*, Boston, 1934.
Flanders, Helen H.; Ballard, Elizabeth F.; Brown, George; and Barry, Phillips. *New Green Mountain Songster*, New Haven, 1939.
Flanders, Helen H. and Brown, George. *Vermont Folk Songs and Ballads*, Brattleboro, Vt., 1931.
Finger, Charles J. *Frontier Ballads*, N.Y., 1927.
Ford, Ira. *Traditional Music of America*, N.Y., 1940.
Ford, Worthington C. *Broadsides, Ballads, etc. in Massachusetts, 1639—1800*, (Massachusetts Historical Society Collection, Vol. LXXV), Boston, 1922.
Fowke, Edith; Mills, Alan; Blume, Helmut. *Canada's Story in Song*, Toronto, 1960.
Fowke, Edith and Johnston, Richard. *Folk Songs of Canada*, Waterloo, Ontario, 1954.
Fuson, Harvey H. *Ballads of the Kentucky Highlands*, London, 1931.

Gardner, Emelyn E. *Folklore from the Schoharie Hills*, Ann Arbor, 1937.
Gardner, Emelyn E. and Chickering, Geraldine J. *Ballads and Songs of Southern Michigan*, Ann Arbor, 1939.
Garrison, Theodore. *Forty-five Searcy County Songs*, Master's Thesis, University of Arkansas, 1939.
Gilbert, Douglas. *Lost Chords*, Garden City, 1942.
Gordon, Robert W. *Folk Songs of America*, National Service Bureau Publication, 1938.
Gray, Otto. *Songs*, Stillwater, Oklahoma, 1930.
Gray, Roland P. *Songs and Ballads of the Maine Lumberjacks*, Cambridge, Mass., 1924.
Green, Charles P. *Ballads of the Black Hills*, Hot Springs, Va., 1930.
Green Mountain Songster (in possession of Harold Rugg, a librarian at the Dartmouth College Library), Sandgate, Vt., 1823.
Greenleaf, Elisabeth B. and Mansfield, Grace Y. *Ballads and Sea Songs of Newfoundland*, Cambridge, Mass., 1924.
Greig, Gavin. *Last Leaves of Traditional Ballads* (ed. A. Keith), Aberdeen, 1925.
Gummere, Francis J. *Ballads* (in *CHEL*, Chapter 17), Cambridge, Mass., 1908.
Gummere, Francis J. *Old English Ballads*, N.Y., 1894.
Gummere, Francis J. *The Popular Ballad*, N.Y., 1902.

Halliwell, James O. *Nursery Rhymes of England*, London, 1874.
Halliwell, James O. *Popular Rhymes and Nursery Tales*, London, 1849.
Hannum, Alberta P. *Thursday April*, N.Y., 1931.
Harlow, Frederick P. *Chanteying Aboard American Ships*, Barre, Massachusetts, 1962.
Hart, Walter M. *Ballad and Epic*, Boston, 1907.
Hart, Walter M. *English Popular Ballad*, N.Y., 1916.
Haufrecht, Herbert (ed.) *Folk Sing*, N.Y., 1959.
Haufrecht, Herbert (ed.) *The Wayfarin' Stranger*, N.Y., 1945.
Haun, Mildred. *Cocke County Ballads and Songs*, Master's Thesis, Vanderbilt University, 1937.
Hendren, Joseph W. A Study of Ballad Rhythm, Princeton, N. J., 1936.
Henry, Mellinger. *A Bibliography of American Folk Songs*, London, 1937.
Henry, Mellinger. *Folk Songs from the Southern Highlands*, N.Y., 1938.
Henry, Mellinger. *Songs Sung in the Southern Appalachians*, London, 1934.
Henry, Mellinger and Matteson, Maurice. *Twenty-nine Beech Mountain Folk Songs and Ballads*, N.Y., 1936.
High, Fred. *Old, Old Folksongs*, Berryville, Arkansas (n.d.)
Hubbard, Lester A. *Ballads and Songs of Utah*, Salt Lake City, 1961.
Hudson, Arthur P. *Folk Songs of Mississippi and their Background*, Chapel Hill, N.C., 1936.
Hudson, Arthur P.; Herzog, George; Halpert, Herbert. *Folk Tunes from Mississippi*, N.Y., 1937.
Hudson, Arthur P. *Specimens of Mississippi Folklore*, 1928.

Hughes, Langston and Bontemps, Arna W. *The Book of Negro Folklore,* N.Y., 1958.
Hummel, Lynn E. *Ozark Folk Songs,* Master's Thesis, University of Missouri, 1936.
Hurgill, Stan. *Shanties from the Seven Seas,* N.Y. and London, 1961.

Ives, Burl. *Burl Ives Song Book,* N.Y., 1953.
Ives, Burl. *Sea Songs,* N.Y., 1956.

Jackson, George P. *Down-East Spirituals,* N.Y., 1939.
Jackson, George P. *Spiritual Folk Songs of Early America,* N.Y., 1937.
Jackson, George P. *White and Negro Spirituals,* N.Y., 1943.
Jackson, George P. *White Spirituals in the Southern Uplands,* Chapel Hill, N.C., 1934.
Jeckyll, Walter. *Jamaican Song and Story,* London, 1907.
Johnson, Guy B. *John Henry,* Chapel Hill, N.C., 1929.
Johnson, Guy B. and Odum, Howard W. *Negro Workaday Songs,* Chapel Hill, N.C., 1926.
Johnson, Guy B. and Odum, Howard W. *The Negro and His Songs,* Chapel Hill, N.C., 1925.
Johnson, Margaret and Travis. *Early American Songs,* N.Y., 1943.
Jones, Bertrand L. *Folklore in Michigan* (reprinted from the *Kalamazoo Normal Record,* May 1914, Western State Normal School, Kalamazoo, Mich.)
Jordan, Philip D. *Singing Yankees,* Minneapolis, 1946.

Karpeles, Maud. *Folk Songs from Newfoundland,* Oxford, 1934.
Kennedy, Charles O. *A Treasury of American Ballads, Gay, Naughty, and Classic,* N.Y., 1954.
Kennedy, Charles O. and Jordan, David. *American Ballads, Naughty, Ribald, and Classic,* N.Y., 1952.
Kennedy, Tolbert H. *Cultural Effects of Isolation on a Homogeneous Rural Area,* Doctoral Dissertation, George Peabody College, Nashville, 1942.
(*Kentucky Counties Songs*). Songs Collected by Workers of the Federal Music Project (WPA) in Boyd, Floyd, and Rowan Counties, Ky. Mss. New York Public Library, 1938.
Kincaid, Bradley. *Favorite Mountain Ballads and Old Time Songs,* Chicago, 1928.
Kolb, John and Kolb, Sylvia. *A Treasury of Folk Song,* N.Y., 1948.
Korson, George P. *Pennsylvania Songs and Legends,* Philadelphia, 1949.

Lane, Rose. *Cindy,* N.Y., 1928.
Lane, Rose. *Hill Billy,* N.Y., 1926.
Larkin, Margaret. *Singing Cowboy,* N.Y., 1931.
Leach, MacEdward. *The Ballad Book,* N.Y., 1955.
Lengyel, Cornel. *A San Francisco Songster* (History of Music in San Francisco Series, II), 1939.
Linscott, Eloise H. *Folk Songs of Old New England,* N.Y., 1939.
Loesser, Arthur. *Humor in American Song,* N.Y., 1942.
Logan, W. H. *A Pedlar's Pack of Ballads and Songs,* Edinburgh, 1869.
Lomax, Alan. *The Folk Songs of North America in the English Language,* N.Y., 1960.
Lomax, Alan and Colwell, S. A. *American Folk Song and Folklore* (A Regional Bibliography), N.Y., 1942.
Lomax, John and Lomax, Alan. *American Ballads and Folk Songs,* N.Y., 1941.
Lomax, John. *Adventures of a Ballad Hunter,* N.Y., 1947.
Lomax, John. *Cowboy Songs,* N.Y., 1910.
Lomax, John and Lomax, Alan. *Cowboy Songs and Other Frontier Ballads,* N.Y., 1938.
Lomax, John. *Folk Song U.S.A.,* N.Y., 1947.
Lomax, John and Lomax, Alan. *Negro Folk Songs by Leadbelly,* N.Y., 1936.

Lomax, John and Lomax, Alan. *Our Singing Country,* N.Y., 1941.
Lomax, John. *Songs of the Cattle Trail and Cow Camp,* N.Y., 1919.
Lunsford, Bascom and Stringfield, Lamar. *Thirty and One Folk Songs from the Southern Mountains,* N.Y., 1929.
Luther, Frank. *Americans and Their Songs,* N.Y., 1942.
Lynn, Frank. *Songs for Singin',* San Francisco, 1961.

MacCaskey, J. P. *Franklin Square Song Collection,* N.Y., 1887.
MacIntosh, David S. *Some Representative Southern Illinois Folk Songs,* Iowa City, 1935.
MacKenzie, W. Roy. *Ballads and Sea-Songs from Nova Scotia,* Cambridge, Mass., 1928.
MacKenzie, W. Roy *Quest of the Ballad,* Princeton, N.J., 1919.
Mason, Robert. *Folk Songs and Folk Tales of Cannon County,* Master's Thesis, George Peabody College, Nashville, 1939.
Mattfeld, Julius. *Folk Music of the Western Hemisphere,* New York Public Library, 1925.
McCarthy, Helen. *Return of the Dead,* Master's Thesis, Brown University, 1937.
McDonald, Grant. *A Study of Selected Folk Songs of Missouri,* Master's Thesis, University of Iowa, 1939.
McDowell, Lucien L. and Flora L. *Memory Melodies,* Smithville, Tenn., 1947.
McGill, Josephine. *Folk Songs of the Kentucky Mountains,* N.Y., 1917.
Moore, Ruth. *Spoonhandle,* N.Y., 1946.
Morris, Alton C. *Folk Songs of Florida,* Gainesville, Fla., 1950.
Musick, Ruth. *Folklore In and Near Kirksville, Missouri,* in manuscript.

Neal, Mabel. *Brown County Songs and Ballads,* Master's Thesis, University of Indiana, 1926.
Neely, Charles and Spargo, J. W. *Tales and Songs of Southern Illinois,* Menosha, Wisc., 1938.
Neeser, Robert W. *American Naval Songs and Ballads,* New Haven, 1938.
Newell, William W. *Games and Songs of American Children,* N.Y., 1883.
Niles, John J. *Anglo-American Ballad Study Book,* N.Y., 1945.
Niles, John J. *The Ballad Book,* Boston, 1961.
Niles, John J. *Ballads, Carols, and Tragic Legends,* N.Y., 1938.
Niles, John J. *Ballads, Love Songs, and Tragic Legends,* N.Y., 1937.
Niles, John J. *More Songs of the Hill Folk,* N.Y., 1936.
Niles, John J. *Seven Kentucky Mountain Tunes,* N.Y., 1928.
Niles, John J. *Songs of the Hill Folk,* N.Y., 1934.
Northcote, Sydney. *The Ballad in Music,* N.Y., 1941.
Notes from the Pine Mountain Settlement School, Harlan County, Ky., 1935.

Owen, Mary, *Voodoo Tales,* N.Y., 1893.
Owens, William A. *Southwest Sings,* Austin, 1941.
Owens, William A. *Studies in Texas Folk Song,* Doctoral Dissertations, University of Iowa, 1941.
Owens, William A. *Texas Folk Songs,* Austin and Dallas, 1950.

Palmer, Edgar A. *G.I. Songs,* N.Y., 1944.
Parsons, Elsie C. *Folklore of the Antilles,* MAFS, XXVI, N.Y., 1933.
Parsons, Elsie C. *Folklore of the Cape Verde Islands,* MAFS, XV (2 vols.), N.Y., 1923.
Parsons, Elsie C. *Folklore of the Sea Islands,* MAFS, N.Y., 1923.
Parsons, Elsie C. *Folk Tales of the Andros Islands,* MAFS, XIII, N.Y., 1918.
Perry, Henry W. *A Sampling of the Folklore of Carter County,* Master's Thesis, George Peabody College, Nashville, 1938.

Pound, Louise. *American Ballads and Songs*, N.Y., 1922.
Pound, Louise. *Folk Song of Nebraska and the Central West. A Syllabus.*
Pound, Louise. *Poetic Origins and the Ballad*, N.Y., 1921.
Powell, John. *Five Virginia Folk Songs*, N.Y., n. d.

Raine, James W. *Land of the Saddle Bags*, Texarkana, 1924.
Ramsay, Allen. *Tea-Table Miscellany*, London, 1733.
Randolph, Vance. *Ozark Folk Songs*, Vol. I, Columbia, Mo., 1946.
Randolph, Vance. *Ozark Mountain Folk*, N.Y., 1932.
Randolph, Vance. *The Ozarks*, N.Y., 1931.
Rayburn, O. E. *Ozark Country*, N.Y., 1941.
Rickaby, Franz. *Ballads and Songs of the Shanty-Boy*, Cambridge, Mass., 1926.
Richardson, Ethel P. *American Mountain Songs*, N.Y., 1927 .
Richmond, W. Edson. *Place Names in the English and Scottish Popular Ballads and Their American Variants*, Doctoral Dissertation, Ohio State University, 1947.
Ring, Lyle R. *New England Folk Songs*, Boston, 1934.
Ritchie, Jean. *Singing Family of the Cumberlands*, N.Y., 1955.
Roberts, Elizabeth M. *The Great Meadow*, N.Y., 1930.
Robison, Carson. *The Top Album of Carson J. Robison*, N.Y., 1936.

Sackett, S. J. and Koch, William E. *Kansas Folklore*, Lincoln, 1961.
Sandburg, Carl. *The American Songbag*, N.Y., 1927.
Seeger, Pete. *American Favorite Ballads*, N.Y., 1961.
Scarborough, Dorothy. *On the Trail of Negro Folk Songs*, Cambridge, Mass., 1925
Scarborough, Dorothy. *Songcatcher in the Southern Mountains*, N.Y., 1937.
Scott, Thomas J. *Sing of America*, N.Y., 1947.
Sharp, Cecil. *100 English Folk Songs*, N.Y., 1916.
Sharp, Cecil and Campbell, Olive. *English Folk Songs from the Southern Appalachians*, N.Y., 1917.
Sharp, Cecil and Karpeles, Maud. *English Folk Songs from the Southern Appalachians*, 2 vols., Oxford, 1932.
Shay, Frank. *American Sea Songs and Chanties*, N.Y., 1948.
Shay, Frank. *Deep Sea Chanties*, London, 1925.
Shay, Frank. *Drawn from the Wood*, N.Y., 1929.
Shay, Frank. *Iron Men and Wooden Ships*, N.Y., 1925.
Shay, Frank. *More Pious Friends and Drunken Companions*, N.Y., 1928.
Shay, Frank. *My Pious Friends and Drunken Companions*, N.Y., 1927.
Shearin, Hubert and Combs, Josiah. *A Syllabus of Kentucky Folk Songs* (Transylvania Studies in English, Lexington, Ky.), 1911.
Sheppard, Muriel. *Cabins in the Laurel*, Chapel Hill, N.C., 1935.
Sherwin, Sterling. *Singin in the Saddle*, Boston, 1944.
Shoemaker, Henry W. *North Pennsylvania Minstrelsy*, Altoona, Pa., 1923. (Mention is also made of the 1919 edition in connection with *The Mermaid.*)
Shoemaker, Henry W. *Mountain Minstrelsy* (a third edition of *North Pennsylvania Minstrelsy*), Philadelphia, Pa., 1931.
Sidgwick, Frank. *The Ballad*, London, 1914.
Siegmeister, Elie. *Songs of Early America*, N.Y., 1944.
Siegmeister, Elie. *Work and Sing*, N.Y., 1943.
Silber, Irwin. *Reprints from the People's Song Bulletin (1946-1949)*, N.Y., 1961.
Spaeth, Sigmund. *Read 'em and Weep*, N.Y., 1935.
Spaeth, Sigmund. *Weep Some More My Lady*, N.Y., 1927.
Smith, R. A. *The Scotish Minstrel*, 6 vols., Edinburgh, 1820-4.
Smith, Reed. *South Carolina Ballads*, Cambridge, Mass., 1928.
Smith, Reed and Rufty, H. *An American Anthology of Old World Ballads*, N.Y., 1937.
Stout, Earl J. *Folklore from Iowa*, MAFS, XXIX, N.Y., 1936.

Stringfield, Lamar. *America and her Music* (University of North Carolina Extension Bulletin, X, #7), March, 1931.
Sturgis, Edith B. and Hughes, Robert. *Songs from the Hills of Vermont,* N.Y., 1919.
Sulzer, Elmer G. *Twenty-Five Kentucky Folk Ballads,* Lexington, Ky., 1936.

Thomas, Jean. *Ballad Makin' in the Mountains of Kentucky,* N.Y., 1939.
Thomas, Jean. *Blue Ridge Country,* N.Y., 1942.
Thomas, Jean. *Devil's Ditties,* Chicago, 1931.
Thomas, Jean. *Singin' Fiddler,* N.Y., 1938.
Thomas, Jean. *The Singin' Gatherin',* N.Y., 1939.
Thompson, Harold W. *Body, Boots, and Britches,* N.Y., 1940.
Thompson, Harold W. and Cutting, Edith. *A Pioneer Songster: Texts from the Stevens-Douglass Manuscript of Western New York (1841-1856),* Ithaca, N.Y., 1958.
Thompson, Stith. *Motif Index to Folklore,* Bloomington, Ind., 1955-58.

The Vagabonds: Old Cabin Songs of the Fiddle and Bow, n. p., n. d.
Vincent, Elmore. *Lumberjack Songs,* n. p., 1932.

The Weavers. *The Weavers' Song Book,* N.Y., 1960.
Wells, Evelyn. *The Ballad Tree,* N.Y., 1950.
Wetmore, Susannah and Bartholomew, Marshall. *Mountain Songs of North Carolina,* N.Y., n. d.
Wheeler, Mary. *Kentucky Mountain Folk Songs,* Boston, 1937.
White, Newman I. *American Negro Folk Songs,* Cambridge, Mass., 1928.
Whittier, John G. *Yankee Gypsies* in *Prose Works,* Boston, 1889.
Williams, Alfred. *Folk Songs of the Upper Thames,* London, 1923.
Williams, Alfred M. *Studies in Folk Song and Popular Poetry,* N.Y., 1894.
Williams, Cratis D. *Ballads and Songs,* Master's Thesis, University of Kentucky, 1937.
Wilson, H. R. *Songs of the Hills and Plains,* Chicago, 1943.
Wilson, Charles M. *Backwoods America,* Chapel Hill, N.C., 1934.
Wimberly, Lowry C. *Death and Burial Lore in the English and Scottish Popular Ballads,* Lincoln, 1927.
Wimberly, Lowry C. *Folklore in the English and Scottish Ballads,* Chicago, 1928.
Wyman, Loraine and Brockway, Howard. *Lonesome Tunes, Folk Songs from the Kentucky Mountains,* N.Y., 1916.
Wyman, Lorraine and Brockway, Howard. *Twenty Kentucky Mountain Songs,* Boston, 1920.

Zielonko, Jane. *Some American Variants of Child Ballads,* Master's Thesis, Columbia University, 1945.

PERIODICALS AND SPECIAL VOLUMES

(For references to specific articles consulted see the individual bibliographies and discussions under the various ballads.)

Adventure, New York.
Advertiser, Aurora, Mo.
American Speech, Baltimore.
Altoona Tribune, Altoona, Pa.
Arizona Quarterly, Tucson.
Arkansas Historical Quarterly, Fayetteville, Ark.
Art World, New York.

Ballad Society Publications, London.
Ballads Surviving in the United States, a Ballad Circular, Department of Public Instruction of Virginia, 1916.

Bangor Daily News, Bangor, Me.
Berea Quarterly, Berea, Ky.
Blackwood's Magazine, Edinburgh.
Boletin Latino-Americano de Musica, Montevideo.
Bookworm, London.
Boston Evening Transcript, Boston.
Boston Sunday Globe, Boston.
Bulletin of the Folk Song Society of the Northeast, Cambridge, Mass. (*BFSSNE*).
Bulletin of the Tennessee Folklore Society, Marysville and Athens, Tenn.
Bulletin of the University of South Carolina, Columbia, S.C.

California Arts and Architecture, San Francisco.
California Folklore Quarterly (now *Western Folklore Quarterly*), Berkeley, Calif. (*CFQ*).
Caravan, New York.
Caravan, Washington, D.C.
Charlotte Observer, Charlotte, N.C.
Colorado Folksong Bulletin, Boulder, Colo.

Dalhousie Review, Halifax, N. Sc.
Detroit News, Detroit.
Direction, Darien, Conn.

German Quarterly, Lancaster, Pa.
Greensboro Daily News, Greensboro, N.C.

English Journal, Chicago.
English Studies in Honor of James S. Wilson, University of Virginia Studies, IV (1951), 99-110.
Étude, Philadelphia.
Explicator, Fredericksburg, Va.

Farm Life, Spencer, Ind.
Federal Writers Project: Louisiana: *Gumbo Ya-Ya,* Cambridge, Mass., 1945.
Focus, Farmville, Va.
Folk-Lore, London.
Folklore Fellows Communication, Helsinki (FFC).
Folk-Lore Journal, London.
Folk Say, Norman, Okla.
Folk Sing, New York.
Folkways Monthly, State College, Pa.

Golden Book, New York.
Grapurchat, East Radford State Teacher's College, Va.

Harper's Magazine, New York.
Hoosier Folklore Quarterly, Bloomington, Ind. (HFQ).

Illinois State Historical Society Journal, Springfield, Ill.

Journal of American Folklore, Boston, Lancaster, Pa., New York, and Richmond, Va. (*JAF*).
Journal of the Folk Song Society, London. (*JFSS*).
Journal of the Irish Folk Song Society, Dublin.

Kentucky Folklore Record, Bowling Green, Ky.
Keystone Folklore Quarterly, Lewisburg and Lycoming, Pa.

Midwest Folklore, Bloomington, Ind. (*MWF*).
Midwest Quarterly (Nebraska University), New York.
Missouri Historical Society Bulletin, St. Louis.
Modern Language Notes, Baltimore. (*MLN*).
Modern Language Quarterly, Seattle. (*MLQ*).
Modern Language Review, Cambridge, Eng. (*MLR*).
Modern Philology, Chicago.
Musical America, New York.
Music Educator's Journal, Madison, Wisc. and Ann Arbor, Mich.
Musical Quarterly, New York.
Music Teacher's National Association Papers.

Narragansett Times, Wakefield, R.I.
Nation, New York.
Nebraska Academy of Sciences Publications, Lincoln.
Nebraska Folklore Pamphlets, Lincoln.
New Jersey Journal of Education, New Egypt, N.J., and Newark, N.J.
New Republic, New York.
New York Folklore Quarterly, Ithaca, N.Y., (*NYFQ*).
New York Sunday Times, Magazine Section, New York.
New York Tribune, New York.
North American Review, Boston and New York.
North Carolina Booklet, Raleigh, N.C.
North Carolina Folklore, Chapel Hill, N.C.
Northeast Folklore, Orono, Me.

Oregon Folklore Bulletin, Eugene, Ore.
Outlook, New York.
Ozark Life, Kingston, Ark.

Publications of the Modern Language Association, New York. (*PMLA*).
Publications of the Texas Folklore Society, Dallas, Texas. (PTFS).

Sewanee Review, Sewanee, Tenn.
Sing Out, New York.
Singer's Journal (Henry deMarsan), New York.
Southern Folklore Quarterly, Gainesville, Fla. (*SFQ*).
Speculum, Cambridge, Mass.
Springfield Sunday Union and Republican, Springfield, Mass.
Survey, New York.

Texas Folklore Society Bulletin, Austin, Texas.
Travel, New York.

University of Kansas Publications, Humanistic Studies, Lawrence, Kans.
University of Virginia Magazine, Charlottesville, Va.

Vermont Historical Society, Proceedings, New Series, Montpelier, Vt.
Virginia Folklore Society Bulletin, Charlottesville, Va.

West Virginia Folklore, Fairmont, W. Va.
West Virginia School Journal and Educator, Morgantown, W. Va.
West Virginia University Studies, III (*Philological Papers,* II), Morgantown, W. Va.
Western Folklore, Berkeley, Calif. (*WF*).
William and Mary Literary Magazine, Williamsburg, Va.

INDEX TO BALLADS DISCUSSED

Andrew Lammie 135
Archie o Cawfield 117

Babylon 40
The Baffled Knight 99
The Bailiff's Daughter of Islington 97
Bessy Bell and Mary Gray 123
The Bold Pedlar and Robin Hood 104
Bonnie Annie 46
Bonny Barbara Allen 82
Bonny Bee Hom 89
The Bonny Earl of Murray 116
The Bonnie House of Airlie 118
Bonnie James Campbell 126
The Boy and the Mantle 49
The Braes of Yarrow 127
The Broom of Cowdenknowes 131
The Broomfield Hill 51
The Brown Girl 159

Captain Car (Edom o Gordon) 116
Captain Ward and the Rainbow 155
Captain Wedderburn's Courtship 53
The Cherry-Tree Carol 60
Child Maurice 81
Child Waters 64
Clerk Colvill 51
The Crafty Farmer 151
The Cruel Brother 36
The Cruel Mother 44

The Death of Queen Jane 113
Dick o the Cow 117
Dives and Lazarus 61

Earl Brand 29
Edward 39
The Elfin Knight 23
Erlinton 30

Fair Annie 63
Fair Margaret and Sweet William 70
The False Knight upon the Road 24
The False Lover Won Back 132
The Famous Flower of Serving-Men 98
The Farmer's Curst Wife 148

The Gardener 132
The Gay Goshawk 94
Geordie 124
The George Aloe and the Sweepstake 152
Get Up and Bar the Door 145
Glasgerion 65
The Grey Cock (Saw You My Father?) 139
Gude Wallace 110
The Gypsie Laddie 119

The Heir of Linne 141
Henry Martyn 140

Hind Horn 41
The Hunting of the Cheviot (Chevy Chase) 110

James Harris (The Daemon Lover) 137
Jamie Douglas 123
Jellon Grame 89
Jock o the Side 117
John of Hazelgreen 158
John Thomson and the Turk 141
Johnie Armstrong 113
Johnie Cock 100
Johnie Scot 95
The Jolly Beggar 150

Katherine Jaffray 132
King Edward the Fourth and a Tanner of Tamworth 143
King Henry the Fifth's Conquest of France 111
King James and Brown 116
King John and the Bishop 52
King Orfeo 44
The Kitchie-Boy 141
The Knight and the Shepherd's Daughter 99
The Keach i the Creel 151

Lady Alice 86
Lady Isabel and the Elf-Knight 25
Lady Maisry 64
The Laily Worm and the Machrel of the Sea 49
The Laird o Drum 135
Lamkin 89
The Lass of Roch Royal 73
Little Musgrave and Lady Barnard 79
Lizie Lindsay 133
Lizie Wan 57
Lord Derwentwater 124
Lord Ingram and Chief Wyet 65
Lord Lovel 72
Lord Randal 36
Lord Saltoun and Auchanachie 136
Lord Thomas and Fair Annet 68

The Maid Freed from the Gallows 91
The Marriage of Sir Gawain 49
Mary Hamilton 114
The Mermaid 157
Musselburgh Field 114

Northumberland Betrayed by Douglas 115

Our Goodman 143

Prince Robert 87
Proud Lady Margaret 55

Queen Eleanor's Confession 109
The Queen of Elfan's Nourice 51

The Rantin Laddie 136
Rare Willie Drowned in Yarrow (The Water o Gamrie) 130

Richie Story 134
Riddles Wisely Expounded 22
Rob Roy 133
Robin Hood and Allen a Dale 105
Robin Hood and the Beggar 104
Robin Hood and the Bishop 107
Robin Hood and Guy of Gisborne 101
Robin Hood and Little John 102
Robin Hood and the Prince of Aragon 103
Robin Hood and the Shepherd 105
Robin Hood and the Tanner 103
Robin Hood Rescuing Three Squires 106
Robin Hood Rescuing Will Stutly 106
Robin Hood's Birth, Breeding, Valor, and Marriage 107
Robin Hood's Death 102
Robin Hood's Progress to Nottingham 105
The Rose of England 111

Saint Stephen and Herod 45
Sir Andrew Barton 112
Sir Hugh (The Jew's Daughter) 107
Sir James the Rose 126
Sir Lionel 42
Sir Patrick Spens 62
The Suffolk Miracle 142
The Sweet Trinity (The Golden Vanity) 153
Sweet William's Ghost 75

Tam Lin 50
Thomas Rymer 49
The Three Ravens (The Twa Corbies) 46
The Trooper and the Maid 161
The Twa Brothers 55
The Twa Knights 142
The Twa Sisters 32
The Twa Magicians 52

The Unquiet Grave 77

The Wee Wee Man 50
The Whummil Bore 48
The Wife of Usher's Well 77
The Wife Wrapt in Wether's Skin 146
Willie and Earl Richard's Daughter 97
Willie Macintosh 117
Willie o Douglas Dale 96
Willie o Winsbury 96
Willie's Lyke-Wake 46
Willie's Lady 28

Young Beichan 58
Young Benjie 88
Young Hunting 66
Young Johnstone 88

A Supplement to
The British Traditional Ballad in North America

Preface

The word *supplement* in the title of this modest addition to Tristram Potter Coffin's *The British Traditional Ballad in North America* is to be taken in its literal sense: that parent work has been, to a major extent, both my formal and epistemological guide throughout the research and writing stages of this enterprise. (Other approaches to identifying similarities and differences among ballad narratives may be found in George List, "Toward an Indexing of Ballad Texts," *Journal of American Folklore*, 81 [1968], 44–61; Eleanor R. Long, "Thematic Classification and 'Lady Isabel,'" *Journal of American Folklore*, 85 [1972], 32–41; D. K. Wilgus, "A Type-Index of Anglo-American Traditional Narrative Songs," *Journal of the Folklore Institute*, 7 [1970], 161–177.) Moreover, this addition is intended to cover as completely as possible only material published since the last revision of its parent in 1963; I have not made any special attempt to discover source works omitted from the main guide, though if something important came to hand I have included it—Helen Creighton's *Folklore of Lunenburg County, Nova Scotia*, for instance, published in 1950, or Carrie B. Grover's *A Heritage of Songs*, another pre-1963 publication. The references to the fourth volume of *The Frank C. Brown Collection of North Carolina Folklore* also belong to this category.

In addition, I have not sought to discover and correct any existing errors of printer or editor in the main work, whether errors of commission or omission of the sort that inevitably appear in a publication of any scope. About the sole exception to this policy is my inclusion of the reference to Arthur Fauset's version of Child 221, its omission from the parent work having been pointed out to me by Edith Fowke, and because it is an unusual version of that story-song—in cante-fable form. In short, this Supplement is just that, dealing with works published since the last edition of *The British Traditional Ballad in North America* in 1963 and up to the spring of 1975; it is not a revision of that book.

I have also followed previously set limits and not dealt with phonograph recordings. This is an area so in need of systematic data gathering, sorting, transcription, and codification that it deserves nothing but the best treatment. Rather than attempt an incomplete and haphazard sortie into that field, I have simply declared it outside my boundaries, so that when someone does take that particular plunge the results will be a deservedly seminal work, not a *pro forma* one. This lacuna is mitigated somewhat in that many more transcriptions of ballad texts from phonograph records are available now in printed works than was the case up to the early sixties. The efforts of Bertrand Bronson and Duncan Emrich are especially notable in this respect; we are fortunate that they have allowed us access to at least some of this large body of data, even though through such a secondary and more traditional mode of presentation as the printed page.

The same constraints and the same rationale that have kept primary recordings out of this guide apply to unpublished manuscripts, master's theses, doctoral dissertations, and the like. Of course, such compilations which contain texts of traditional ballads recorded firsthand by fieldworkers are not nearly so numerous as they were in the thirties and forties —already surveyed in the original work. But, again, the inevitable incompleteness that would result from such a survey has restrained me. If such a task cannot be done completely, it seems ultimately detrimental to attempt it at all. That should be a separate undertaking unto itself.

The reader of the following pages will immediately notice one important departure from the format of *The British Traditional Ballad in North America*: each text is given its own story type designation. This should be an additional aid to any who use this work as a reference tool for detailed comparative study of individual ballads. Such a format did raise the editorial problem of how to categorize the frequent one- or two- (or even more) stanza fragments that appear in source books. Rather than exclude them from the references, a new category, not found in the main work, has been instituted—Fragments & Title Lists. Needless to say, in some cases it was a moot point as to whether a particular piece could be considered a fragment or a complete (if truncated) statement in song unto itself, but indecision on this point rose infrequently. Any decision eventually made was based on an unanalyzable combination of subjective reasoning, knowledge of other versions of the same ballad, and the internal logic of the individual item.

As is the case in the main work, I have avoided referencing reprints of already published texts, since that would have swollen the size of this addition unnecessarily. I have made certain exceptions to this policy, however: First, when both printings of the same text are made by the same editor in two different works and are taken from field recordings (the several collections of Edith Fowke are the most prominent examples of this), I have referenced both source works. Second, I have included references to texts which are taken from early, hard to obtain printed sources (for instance, an issue of *Outlook* for September 9, 1899). Third, when different editors print transcriptions of the same field tape (the works of Maud Karpeles and Bronson exemplify this kind of overlap) or of the same phonograph recording (as do Bronson and Emrich), I have indicated both references. Reprintings of texts from such standard works as those of Phillips Barry or John Harrington Cox or Arthur Kyle Davis or a host of others have not been indicated, however.

This Supplement was prepared with the intent that it be used in conjunction with *The British Traditional Ballad in North America*; no section of it should be studied by itself, but always alongside the corresponding section in its parent. References are often made here to specific portions of the main text, but even when these are not given, my underlying assumption in the discussions is that the reader will cross-check the matching parts of the major work, thus the frequent use of such relational terms as "also," "new," "more recent," and the like.

The British Traditional Ballad in North America is referenced in this Supplement as *BTBNA*. Whenever individual ballads are referred to by a numeral in the discussions, that numeral denotes the same ballad type as it does in Francis James Child's *The English and Scottish Popular Ballads*, in *BTBNA*, and in other parts of this Supplement. Any ballad referred to by the "Laws ———" designation is a version of the ballad indexed under the same letter and numeral combination in one of G. Malcolm Laws's two syllabi, *American Balladry from British Broadsides* and *Native American Balladry*. (The complete bibliographical information on these and any other works mentioned in this Supplement will be found in the Bibliography. The exceptions are those more ancient works of such figures as William Motherwell, Thomas Percy, or Walter Scott, any references to which are not to their original works as such but to excerpts from them that appear in Child's volumes.)

I wish to thank Richard Bauman, Edith Fowke, Hugh Shields, and D. K. Wilgus for their help in bringing certain source material to my attention; Roger D. Abrahams and Archie Green for their most useful critical comments on the first draft of the introductory "Note on Variation in the British Traditional Ballad in North America"; Sally M. Yerkovich for duplicating several texts and journal articles that I could not get hold of myself; and Frances Terry for typing the manuscript. Kenneth S. Goldstein conceived of this project and first requested that I undertake it; he also made his personal library available for the research, without which this work would have been unacceptably incomplete. Tristram Potter Coffin not only agreed, perhaps incautiously, to my supplementing his original book, but also pointed out several naïvetes and omissions in the first draft of the Guide.

A NOTE ON VARIATION IN THE BRITISH
TRADITIONAL BALLAD IN NORTH AMERICA

A Note on Variation in the British
Traditional Ballad in North America

The purpose of this introductory note is to draw attention to work done in the area of variation in narrative folksong since 1963 when *The British Traditional Ballad in North America* was last revised and prefaced with Coffin's wide-ranging essay on the subject, "A Description of Variation in the Traditional Ballad of America" (pp. 1–19). In the course of this review, I shall also point to a few aspects of ballad variation that recently published texts reveal. In keeping with the supplemental nature of this whole work, my discussion will follow the organization that underlies the *BTBNA* introductory essay: categories of print, general trends in folk art, and personality as they affect both verbal and narrative elements in ballad texts are major headings, with the stipulation that these three are not mutually exclusive categories or forces of change. With this in mind, we can most usefully categorize the essential differences between these factors as follows: print is exogenous to the system that is the native oral tradition of song learning and performing; general trends in folk art are indigenous to that system in its normal evolutionary development; and personal factors, of course, reside primarily in the sensibilities of the individual performer.

As far as print is concerned, we can add little to Coffin's statements on the general principles that appear to underlie its common effects on oral tradition. One phenomenon, however, which is exhibited far more in recent recoveries of Child ballads in North America than in the past may be mentioned: published works—designed primarily for academic, learned, or urban audiences—have undoubtedly influenced many song repertoires of rural and oral cultures. Greater literacy and the more extended dissemination of information by means of print, radio, phonograph recordings, and public performances to large audiences are both part of this influence, to which may be added the very increase in awareness and knowledge of and interest in "folklore" as a concept itself and its relationship to traditional song.

This kind of influence is certainly not a phenomenon entirely of the twentieth century or the New World. Scott's *Minstrelsy*, for instance, appears to have taken on the function of a chapbook to Scottish singers in the last century, as Alexander Keith says in his notes to Greig's *Last Leaves* (p. 92), and on this continent resemblances of several traditional singers' texts to *Minstrelsy* versions are marked (see the discussions to 76 and 214 in this Supplement). It is not necessary, of course, to posit a home edition of the *Minstrelsy* as the only possible source for such versions; the collections of Scott and other nineteenth-century British ballad gleaners whose texts have influenced our modern traditions have often been reproduced in anthologies of verse and disseminated through primary and secondary school teachings in both Britain and America. Such a milieu has certainly been the immediate source of many texts sung (and sometimes recited) by Scottish immigrants to this country; this is epitomized in texts recorded from many of those Oklahoma residents who supplied ballads for Moore and Moore's *Ballads and Folk Songs of the Southwest* (see, for example, the discussion to 106 in this Supplement).

In North America, among singers whose association with this country dates back farther than their own generation, it is not too surprising to learn that professional hillbilly singers drew upon published folksong collections as sources for repertoire (see *JEMF Quarterly*, VIII, 3 [1972], 147–148); we must grant, moreover, that the same applies to some of those very active, talented, and occasionally semiprofessional singers who have supplied many of our more recent versions of traditional ballads (see the discussions to 65, 76, 215, and 228 in this Supplement). However, we may observe the same thing occurring among amateur rural singers as well, the dominant reason possibly being that the very emphasis on collecting and teaching folklore, on "reviving" it, or on making a culture aware of its traditional heritage—particularly prevalent in Appalachian Kentucky and West Virginia—has resulted in the introduction of ballad versions into traditional repertoires that have their immediate sources in such popular anthologies as Sargent and Kittredge's edition of Child (see the discussions to 13 and 295 in this Supplement). The major results of this development on North American ballad tradition have been the recent appearance in folk repertoires of versions of British ballads which had evidently been long absent from communal circulation; the lengthening of normal American textual forms to more closely approximate the often greater complexities of their pre-twentieth-century Old World counterparts; and the appearance of certain more archaic elements within songs (on this last, see especially the Gainer, *Folk Songs from the West Virginia Hills*, version of Child 13 [pp. 18–19] and the *Kentucky Folklore Record*, 18 [1972], 41–43 version of Child 243).

The second factor used by Coffin—general trends in folk art—refers to patterns that are characteristic of community ideas and practices rather than personal, idiosyncratic ones. This notion seems to be a rationale, for instance, behind Abrahams' concept of "tropisms," which are either attractions toward certain songs, motifs, values, and themes or, conversely, adverse reactions against such elements. Both of these responses, approach and avoidance, can lead to significant patterns of not only repertoire selection but change in received materials as well. The point is that such reactions are largely learned, accepted by individuals from surrounding cultural preferences, rather than created or imposed by those individuals themselves, hence the biological term rather than some other that implies predominantly personal cognitions, interpretations, choices, and volitions (see Roger D. Abrahams, "Patterns of Structure and Role Relationships in the Child Ballads in the United States," *Journal of American Folklore*, 79 [1966], 448).

That one such general trend in the course of the British ballad in tradition is toward compression of ballad texts is so well established that it needs no repetition here. Attempts to talk about such tendencies in terms of "deteriorating process" (or even its opposite) are of fairly limited use in understanding the fundamentals at work in ballad variation (see Douglas J. McMillan, "A Survey of Theories Concerning the Oral Transmission of the Traditional Ballad," *Southern Folklore Quarterly*, 28 [1964], 299–309). Those whose purposes are more analytical than evaluative find it useful to talk in relatively neutral terms about such a process as compression; Coffin's concept of the emotional core (see "The Traditional Ballad as an Art Form," *BTBNA*, pp. 164–172) and Judith W. Turner's of the symbol (see her "A Morphology of the 'True Love' Ballad," *Journal of American Folklore*, 85 [1972], 21–31) are of this class (see also Abrahams, "Patterns of Structure," pp. 456–458). The notion that underlies both of these concepts is that there is a single (usually) dominant proposition or sentiment anchoring the aesthetic relationship between community and song, a core element that gives the song meaning and relative universality. Narrative and technical detail are secondary; thus, while this core provides stability and continuity on one hand, as a very object of focus it is in a sense responsible for variation, since textual details which relate to it only tangentially tend to be forgotten, discarded, or adapted in some way.

Such changes may often seem, to the observer, haphazard and illogical, in that we sometimes find within a single version inconsistencies in matters that involve action, characterization, or specification. One of the more common manifestations of this is perhaps in names, both of people and of places. In a Tennessee version of "Sir Hugh" (155), for instance, the young protagonist is named at different points in the story as both "Hugh" and "Dew," the latter also the name of his murderess, obviously a derivation from "Jew" (see Burton and Manning, *The East Tennessee State University Collection of Folklore: Folksongs*, pp. 1–2). In an Oklahoma version of "Young Beichan" (53) the hero is incarcerated in Turkey, is rescued by the Turk's daughter, sails homeward, and is later followed by his rescuer; but the hero's home turns out to be also Turkey, and matters are further complicated when Susan recounts their earlier experiences—she had set him free, she says, from "Ireland's chains" (see Moore and Moore, *Ballads and Folk Songs of the Southwest*, pp. 41–43). The principle of "universalization" (see Abrahams and Foss, *Anglo-American Folksong Style*, pp. 29–31) alone cannot account for such inconsistencies; we must also posit that they are the effect—literally, a byproduct—of emphasis directed toward the affective or symbolic core of the ballad, which lies elsewhere.

Such minor textual variations signal the unimportance of those nonessential aspects of the song's message, but they do not usually affect

either the nature or the length of the story. Most such intratextual variations are what Tom Burns, in the article "A Model for Textual Variation
in Folksong," *Folklore Forum*, 3 (1970), 49–56, and others designate as
"substitution": a given element in a song text is replaced by another
element taken from a source outside the song itself. Focus on the emotional core, however, more often leads to the kind of compression Burns
calls "subtraction," which is simply the shortening of a text by deletion.
This is a well-known trend in Anglo-American folk balladry and is a
major emphasis of Coffin's discussion of the emotional core; it results in
such lyrical statements, complete unto themselves even though detached
from a longer narrative ballad, as are exhibited by the impossible-tasks
stanzas of "The Elfin Knight" (see the more lyrical texts of Child 2 referenced under Story Type B in *BTBNA*), the shoe-your-foot query and
answer of Child 76 (see Story Type B), and the last-goodnight lament of
the condemned girl in Child 173 (see Story Type B).

Some cases of subtraction, however, present difficulties for the analyst
in that it is sometimes not clear whether a text can be considered a fragment or a complete statement from the singer's point of view. Highly
shortened texts of ballads which have, in their normal forms, relatively
complex narratives are not uncommon (Child 10, for instance). Often,
versions of such lengthy pieces simply drop an episode or two and still tell
a complete story, even though a simpler one. The criterion for the analyst—and I assume that it would be the same for the singer—need be but
a simple one: when we see a text in which a problem arises but is not
resolved, it is a reasonable hypothesis that the singer considered his song
incomplete. Thus, we can safely call a version of Child 73 that ends with
Fair Annet arriving at Lord Thomas' wedding (see *North Carolina Folklore Journal*, 22 [1974], 151–152) a "fragment." It is not so simple, however, to characterize a text of "Young Hunting" (68) which lacks the
episodes of the bird witness, the attempted bribe and its refusal, and the
punishment of the murderess (see Joyner, *Folk Song in South Carolina*,
pp. 43–44). Yet, despite the uniqueness of this truncation, the text does
end with the girl's remorse for her action, and this seems enough of a
resolution, especially since it does have analogues of some sort in other
ballads—though hardly exact ones (e.g., certain story types of 13, 20, 49,
51, 74, 295). We are also aided by extratextual factors: the version is
from a commercial phonograph recording, an unlikely place for a conscious "fragment" (though yet further extratextual or extrapersonal factors may be applicable here; see *Journal of American Folklore*, 61 [1948],
216).

Burns also recognizes that "rearrangement," the shifting of an element
from one part of a song to another position in the same song, is another
logical possibility in textual change. The type of compression which
combines rearrangement and subtraction has effected some of the more
interesting variations in the British traditional ballad in North America.
A form of this sort of variation is that which often occurs in ballads that

have more than two active dramatis personae: the tendency is to drop one of the actors and assign some of his deeds to one of the major figures retained. When this type of compression appears in the fairy-lover ballad of Child 85 (see Boette, *Singa Hipsy Doodle*, pp. 20–21; Gainer, *Folk Songs from the West Virginia Hills*, pp. 59–60; the discussion to 85 in *BTBNA*, p. 87), we can suspect rationalization of the supernatural also to be at work; the same process can be observed, however, in ballads where there is no need to rationalize. In some versions of "The Gypsy Laddie" (200), for instance, the husband has disappeared, and speeches normally his, delivered toward the end of the song, have been shifted to the beginning and assigned to the abductor. The ballad becomes a simple tale of successful courtship and departure, somewhat in the manner of "The Green Bushes" (Laws P2). In this case, a new story type is developed (see Story Type K under 200 in this Supplement).

Such subtraction and rearrangement are not always so drastic in that they effect a major change in the narrative; in the text of "Geordie" (209) found in Grover, *A Heritage of Songs*, pp. 82–83, the old man on the bridge and the court official have been fused into a single figure, but the story is not affected. Similarly, in several texts of "John of Hazelgreen" (293) the father and son figures have been merged into one (see Bronson, *The Traditional Tunes of the Child Ballads*, IV, 395–396 [#12]; see also the discussion to 293 in this Supplement). In many compressions of this sort we can suggest that more common thematic models which flourish in the general Anglo-American ballad repertoire are being superimposed on the individual song. Thus, the narrative theme of seduction in such popular pieces as "Seventeen Come Sunday" (Laws O17) may be exercising influence on "The Gypsy Laddie" to cause the dropping of the husband figure in favor of concentration on the lover-wife relationship, while the influence of the "returned unrecognized lover" theme of such ballads as "Pretty Fair Miss" (Laws N42) and a host of others on "John of Hazelgreen" may cause the elimination of the father figure. The same sort of phenomenon has been noted in the tradition of the native American ballad of "Pearl Bryan" (Laws F1, F2, F3, dF51, and others) by Anne B. Cohen, *Poor Pearl, Poor Girl!* (p. 73).

Another logical form of structural change, as Burns points out, is "addition." While this does not appear to be as common a trend in the tradition of Anglo-American folk balladry as subtraction (or as substitution—the combining of the two processes of adding and dropping), it is not uncommon in its more minor manifestations of superimposed sentimental or moralistic stanzas which do not materially affect a basic story. When additions are of such a radical kind as to bring about major story changes, the text is usually unique to a single singer (e.g., see Story Type U and its discussion under Child 10 in this Supplement), and its influence can be more validly attributed to personal factors. The norm among North American singers seems to be minor textual changes rather than major narrative ones, as we can infer from the published results of one of the few studies that report singers' own testimonies on conscious variation (though, alas, no texts are given; see John Quincy Wolfe, "Folksingers and the Re-Creation of Folksong," *Western Folklore*, 26 [1967], 101–111). Almeda Riddle's conservative nature and respect for tradition, for instance, forbade her incorporating an ending onto her version of "The Sweet Trinity" (286) that she learned from another singer, even though the variant ending (in which the captain was punished for his deeds) fit her moral sense more closely than did her own version (see Abrahams, *A Singer and Her Songs*, pp. 146, 156–157).

One interesting kind of addition which has not been closely attended to until fairly recently can be alluded to here as an example of a cultural trend, or oikotypification, even though it occurs not in North America itself but in Ireland; but the fact that such expanded texts have been disseminated to America and turn up in tradition in this country warrants its mention. This addition is the interpolation of supernatural elements into previously nonsupernatural ballads, which seems to have been the case with the Story Type A and C versions of "The Grey Cock" (248). These two are revenant stories, whereas the earlier version appears to have been the Type B story, which is more simply one of a night visit between two purely mortal lovers (see the discussion to 248 in this Supplement for references to scholarship on this subject). A similar Irish addition has been made to "The Sweet Trinity" (286), which has the ghost of the drowned cabin boy appearing to wreak vengeance on the ship after his death has been caused by the captain's perfidy (Story Types F and G). That all the Irish supernatural versions of these two ballads have been collected from Canadian tradition may be significant and may also suggest Irish provenience for certain unusual Canadian versions of Child 2, "The Elfin Knight" (see Story Type D in this Supplement), and Child 46, "Captain Wedderburn's Courtship" (see Story Types B and C in this Supplement). In these latter cases, however, the stories and sometimes the texts of the ballads are so closely related to others in which supernatural elements are an intimate and ancient feature (e.g., Child 1, 3, and 278) that they may be a case of more simple textual and narrative association rather than conscious, intentional supernaturalizing. A unique version of "Barbara Allen" (84) which has a minor supernatural interpolation may also be of this class; it was sung by a Kentucky man with Irish forebears on his mother's side (see Roberts, *Sang Branch Settlers*, pp. 95–96).

Finally, we may point to several examples in which addition follows substitution to the extent of varying the received story substantively. Simple substitution most frequently involves the changing of a word or phrase only and may be a result of such passive operations as mishearing or misunderstanding or of the more intentional activities of modernizing, localizing, universalizing, conventionalizing, and the like. We have some interesting examples, however, in which such substitution, for whatever reasons, goes hand-in-hand with the adding of additional textual or narrative material in order to develop implications that logically stem from the substitution. Such a process may have lain behind the North American Story Type D tradition of Child 243. In most of the older British versions the woman goes down with the ship which, sometimes, her demonaic lover sinks (cf. Story Types B and C). In the most common American form, Story Type A (close to the DeMarsan broadside text), the sinking takes place on stage and is not directly attributed to the lover's actions: the ship usually "springs a leak" after hitting a rock, which leads to the drowning. In the Type D story, however, the woman brings about her own death by jumping overboard, usually couched in a line such as "overboard she sprang a leap." The substitution by printer or singer of a single phoneme has thus appeared to transform "leak" to "leap" and to have led to the adding of "overboard" or its equivalent in order to satisfy the logic of the new meaning. The fortuitous synonymy of "springing" in both contexts and the feminine gender of "she" being applicable to both ship and woman have aided this significant change in the narrative with, in this case, quite minor textual changes.

In cases where such synonyms do not already haply exist, a major addition around a restructured word or phrase is necessary. Several North American versions of "Young Hunting" (68) include, for instance, statements by the murderess who has just stabbed her lover or by the dying man himself that doctors may be sought or sent for to heal the wound for which the girl has just been responsible. This episode, unparalleled in Old World texts, may encompass as many as two stanzas in its North American manifestations. In some older British texts, however, duckers (or divers) are sent for to search the water for Young Hunting's body. It seems likely that either this word or this custom must have been unintelligible or foreign to North American copyists or singers, and thus "duckers" changed to the similar but more familiar "doctors." Subsequently, surrounding stanzas were constructed in order to give the episode more substance. It may also have conceivably led to the eventual dropping of the somewhat contradictory later episodes of disposing of the body and conversing with the parrot and, thus, the unique Story Type H discussed earlier.

Personal factors constitute Coffin's third category of forces which account for textual change in traditional ballads. While some of the most significant work in Anglo-American folksong scholarship over the last decade has treated the individual folk artist, most of it has dealt with song makers rather than singers of traditional songs. Enough accounts of the tradition bearers have appeared in folklore studies at large, however, to permit Eleanor R. Long to suggest a useful typology of folksingers' personalities as they affect manifested texts. The four main types she proposes are (1) perseverator, (2) confabulator, (3) rationalizer, and (4) integrator ("Ballad Singers, Ballad Makers, and Ballad Etiology," *Western Folklore*, 32 [1973], 225–236).

Singers who are predominantly perseverators are, in their most extreme forms, faithful to received texts. They repeat what they have heard and remember, whether intelligible to themselves or not, and consequently are partially responsible for the extreme stability of certain invariant textual forms of the same ballad over wide areas, as well as for the many obvious fragments, sometimes for intratextual inconsistencies, often for certain meaningless words and phrases. In short, the perseverator subordinates self to external forces of print or to the texts *qua* texts which he learns from his culture. His "positive tropism" is not toward the emotional core, but to the textual materials as fixed and inviolable. In his hands a tradition is, inevitably, a dying one.

Long calls the second personality type the confabulator, whose chief characteristic is a high degree of sensitivity to immediate context of performance, of audience response, of momentary personal mood. While inclined toward the antinomian and the individualistic, he tends to lack commitment to the perpetuation of any single manifestation of the same ballad text from one performance to another; thus, he does not contribute greatly to the tradition of a ballad, because a high degree of stability is necessary for such longevity and wider circulation. The confabulator probably manipulates the more easily varied aspects of performance, such as singing style and minor phrasing, with more frequency than he does basic narrative. Since documented studies of individual singers seldom present the kind of detail needed to exemplify such a singer, it is difficult to reference specific performers as unequivocal illustrations. One can suggest that Marybird MacAllister might be of this sort; as Abrahams describes her, she appears to have a somewhat existentialist world view and little sustained memory of past events, varying her mood greatly to the immediate moment. However, published data on several of her performances of the same ballad are lacking, and we have no empirical support for this conjecture (see Abrahams, "Creativity, Individuality, and the Traditional Singer," *Studies in the Literary Imagination*, 3 [1970], 5–34). The confabulator's ability to work quantitatively substantial changes upon texts is probably limited most often to cases of addition that are cumulative—by adding diverse kin to an existing sequence of relatives, say, as in Phillips Barry's example of Child 95 ("The Part of the Folk Singer in the Making of Folk Balladry," in Leach and Coffin, *The Critics and the Ballad*, p. 64), or in adding further riddles and tasks to an already existing set (compare the two versions of Child 3 contributed by the same singer a year apart in Bronson, *The Traditional Tunes of the Child Ballads*, IV, 442 [#10.1], and Manny and Wilson, *Songs of Miramichi*, pp. 199–200.)

Long's third personality type is the rationalizer, and it is probably this sort of tradition bearer who is most responsible for the adaptive capability, along with the very important relative stability, of individual ballads over large areas and extended periods of time. As Long characterizes him, the rationalizer is governed neither by blind allegiance to received texts as texts nor by the exigencies of the moment, but by a reasonably enduring set of values, a *stance*, to which form, meaning, and function of song must conform. It is ultimately a rationalizer who at some point brings about the kind of attitudinal changes of the conscious sort that ballads are commonly subject to in a North American environment—moralization, sentimentalization, the discarding of the supernatural, and others that we ascribe to responses generated by the stimuli that are general trends in folk art. Texts that have passed through the re-creative hands of such singers or printers often enter the song repertoire of the culture because they are determined chiefly by cultural relevance.

A great many of the kinds of changes that bring about narrative variation directed toward the support of a thesis may be reasonably ascribed to such a personality (see Story Types G of Child 4 and D of 81 and the discussions to them in this Supplement). In a modified sense, Almeda Riddle, on whom we have more detailed information than most other North American traditional singers (see, especially, Abrahams, *A Singer and Her Songs* and "Creativity, Individuality, and the Traditional Singer"), displays certain characteristics of the rationalizer in her approach to traditional ballads. Mrs. Riddle's conception of the nature of tradition, of her role as a bearer of that tradition, and of her value system as it relates to the messages in her ballads, as well as to the values of her society, presents a picture of a strong personality cognizant of the ethical and aesthetic dimensions of public behavior and art. She refrains from performing trivia or impropriety, and she will not sing illogical texts or fragmented waifs and strays. She will go to great lengths to learn songs which fit this world view, but which at the same time come from the tradition of her own culture as she sees it.

In keeping with the rationalizer's sense of wholeness, permanence, and intelligibility, Mrs. Riddle does not manifest the radical kinds of variation which bring about uniquely different story types in traditional ballads. She understands and respects the notion of what her tradition connotes, though she is not enslaved by it as a perseverator might be enslaved by the notion of the text. Her rationalizing tends to be manifested chiefly in an editorial role: she selects and rejects, with occasional collation and modification; she is not a transformer or creator. The effects of this approach may be seen in its most extreme form, perhaps, in Mrs. Riddle's version of "Glasgow Peggie" (228), which she apparently learned from print. She has dropped the stanzas which deal fairly explicitly with lovemaking, since that does not fit her ethos as a suitable topic for public expression. But the deletions do not in any way harm the force or sense of the ballad (see the discussion to 228 in this Supplement); if that had been the case, she doubtless would simply never have incorporated "Glasgow Peggie" into her repertoire.

While the rationalizer may be the force behind the continuity and stability of ballads in tradition, Long's fourth personality type, the integrator, may be responsible for most of their truly major variations and sometimes for their popularity, since he is the one who injects distinct freshness into tradition and revitalizes it at key points. In his extreme manifestation the integrator is a maker of songs. Less extremely, he may fashion secondary ballads from older models, telling the same story but with topical language, referents, and dramatis personae (e.g., Laws P9 from Child 295, Child 250 from 167). Or, he may make functional revisions of the sort exemplified by Story Type E of Child 93 in this Supplement (cf. also Bertrand H. Bronson, "Fractures in Tradition among the 'Child' Ballads," in *The Ballad as Song*, pp. 266–270). At the very least, he may reword the phrasing of ballads into a more imaginative, aesthetically pleasing mold without necessarily effecting any narrative changes (see, for instance, the unusual renditions of Captain Nye discussed under 112 and 278 in this Supplement). He is of most interest to us when his revisions encompass story as well as text, however, for without his handiwork there would indeed be not as much occasion for this very guide to story variation as there is.

Certainly, many of the integrator's articulations never enter community tradition for any sustained period (cf. MacEdward Leach, *The Ballad Book*, p. 31). Moreover, his creative impulse may sometimes cause difficulties for the ballad annotator when the product departs so much from the model that it becomes a question as to whether the former can be legitimately called a "version" of the latter. Such is the case with a Kentucky song, "Down in the Green Wood's Valley," obviously modeled on "The Cruel Mother" (20); but the story is so much indebted to some local event, a theme from popular fiction, or perhaps a personal fantasy, that it seems more fitting to call it a distinct song unto itself, standing in the same sort of nebulous thematic relationship to Child 20 that "Nancy of Yarmouth" (Laws M38), say, stands to Child 252, "The Kitchie-Boy" (see the discussion to 20 in this Supplement).

In sum, changes made by integrators best synthesize influences from the two causal forces of individual artist and group (the locus of general trends in folk art); the rationalizer is more open to influence from his culture; and the confabulator is dominated primarily by his own unique perceptions and tastes. These three ideal personality types, in the mingling of their diverse degrees and kinds, are essential parts of the process of variation in oral tradition.

The works of Long and others sketched in this survey indicate that there is a fair amount of theoretical and empirical studies on traditional ballads available to those who wish to plot both general and particular processes of stability and change in song traditions. Any complete explanations of such processes must take account of both quantitative and qualitative aspects of text change and the several variables that effect them, such as the personality of bearers of tradition, the motives which underlie purposive adaptations, the community ethos to which individual singers respond, and the external factors, such as print, which influence singers' approaches to their oral traditions.

To be sure, it is not possible to claim that our knowledge is virtually complete. On the theoretical side, for instance, we lack models of how the subtleties of situational factors in performance may affect traditional texts (Kenneth S. Goldstein, "On the Application of the Concepts of Active and Inactive Traditions to the Study of Repertory," *Journal of American Folklore*, 84 [1971], 62–67, has several suggestions relevant to this). We are also unsure of how the nature of oral re-creation as a process may be applicable to some of our twentieth-century regional ballad traditions (cf. David Buchan's analysis of pre-1750 Scottish Northeast ballad tradition in *The Ballad and the Folk*). On the empirical side, we especially lack studies of individual singers and their treatment of ballad texts over an extended period of time, detailed information of the sort that Henry Glassie was able to gather from New York State song maker Dorrance Weir (" 'Take That Night Train to Selma': An Excursion to the Outskirts of Scholarship," in Henry Glassie et al., *Folksongs and Their Makers*, pp. 1–68).

In the meantime, the old and honored tradition of serious text collection and publication which has, since Percy in England and Lomax in America, been the bedrock of ballad studies continues to expand our available resources of folksong data. Bibliographical and descriptive guides like *The British Traditional Ballad in North America* are one kind of tool that should contribute to further explanatory studies of variation in traditional ballads as they continue to be the subject of scholarly research.

A BIBLIOGRAPHICAL GUIDE TO
STORY VARIATION IN THE BRITISH
TRADITIONAL BALLAD IN NORTH AMERICA

A Bibliographical Guide to Story Variation in the British Traditional Ballad in North America

1. RIDDLES WISELY EXPOUNDED

Local Titles: Child Riddles, The Devil's Questions.

Texts: *Story Type* A: Abrahams & Foss, *Anglo-Am Fsg Style*, 86–87 / Boette, *Singa Hipsy Doodle*, 36 / Brown, *NC Flklre*, IV, 331–333 / Emrich, *Am Flk Ptry*, 248 / Gainer, *Flk Sgs West Va Hills*, 3.

C: Moore & Moore, *Blds & Flk Sgs SW*, 6.

Fragments & Title Lists: Rosenberg, *Fsgs Va*, 107.

Discussion: This ballad shares the theme of a riddling exchange—and often even the same riddles—with 46, "Captain Wedderburn's Courtship." Several scholars have remarked on additional textual affiliations between the two (see *BTBNA*, p. 23), most noticeable perhaps in certain Labrador and Newfoundland variants (see the discussion to 46 in this Supplement). Yet another key to these connections, covertly underlying the manifest riddling content, may be that both 1 and 46 (and the similar "The Elfin Knight" [2] and "Proud Lady Margaret" [47] as well) contain figurative references to sex (see also the discussion to 3 in this Supplement). This thesis is supported by J. Barre Toelken in " 'Riddles Wisely Expounded,' " *WF*, 25 (1966), 1–16.
See also the discussions to 2 and 46 below.

2. THE ELFIN KNIGHT

Local Titles: Blow Ye Winds, Cambree Shirt, Every Rose Grows Merry in Time, Rosemary and Thyme, Rose Mary and Tide.

Texts: *Story Type* A: Bronson, IV, 440 (#34.1) / *Ky Flklre Record*, 1973, 117–118 / Moore & Moore, *Blds & Flk Sgs SW*, 7–8 (A) / Parler, *Ark Ballet Bk*, 49–50 / Peacock, *Sgs Newfdld Outpts*, I, 7–8 (B) / Scott, *Lvng Dcmts Am Hstry*, I, 57–58.

B: Bronson, IV, 440–441 (#38.1) / Carey, *Md Flk Lgds & Flk Sgs*, 93 / Gainer, *Flk Sgs West Va Hills*, 4–5 / *NE Flklre*, 1965, 88–89.

C: Moore & Moore, *Blds & Flk Sgs SW*, 8–9 (B).

D: The usual sets of impossible tasks are imposed between an old woman and the devil. There is no romance involved. Peacock, *Sgs Newfdld Outpts*, I, 6 (A).

Fragments & Title Lists: Abrahams, *Sngr & Her Sgs*, 180 (Story Type A) / Brown, *NC Flklre*, IV, 3–4 / Combs, *Fsgs So US*, 199 (Story Type A) / Moore & Moore, *Blds & Flk Sgs SW*, 9–10 (C, D) / Rosenberg, *Fsgs Va*, 31.

Discussion: The new Story Type D shares with Type C the lack of any expressly stated amorous relationship between the two dramatis personae, if one regards as not too significant the fact that she is in bed when the devil pays his visit. It is the appearance of this latter figure in the New-foundland text that gains for it recognition as a distinct story type. He may have been borrowed from other ballads in that select group which deals with the imposition of riddles and tasks: "Riddles Wisely Ex-pounded" (1), "The False Knight upon the Road" (3), or even certain unusual Newfoundland texts of "Captain Wedderburn's Courtship" (see the discussion of Story Types B and C to 46 in this Supplement). Less likely is that he is a direct, modern-day transformation of the elfin knight himself. Whatever his thematic provenience might be, his textual source is a little clearer: it is either "The Farmer's Curst Wife" (278), the first two stanzas of which parallel the first two in this version, with the sub-stitution of the woman for the farmer, or the traditional British nursery rhyme which is an almost exact verbal replica of the first stanza of the Peacock text (see Baring-Gould & Baring-Gould, *The Annotated Mother Goose*, p. 28). See the discussion to 2 in *BTBNA*, p. 24, for reference to other connections between Child 2 and the genre of nursery song.

There may be support for Toelken's thesis on the covert sexual refer-ents of the tasks in Child 2 (see the discussion to 1 in this Supplement) in the Peacock B text (Story Type A): the girl instructs the suitor to "knock it all out with a shoe-maker's awl," which implement appears quite ex-plicitly in a later British folksong, "The Long Peggin' Awl," as a sexual metaphor. See A. L. Lloyd, *Folk Song in England*, pp. 212–213; the same symbol also appears in a British version of Child 2—see Bronson, I, 22–23 (#31).

The Combs text, from West Virginia, may not have been a traditional recovery. Bernth Lindfors, "A Fraudulent 'Elfin Knight' from West Vir-ginia," *WF*, 27 (1968), 107–111, shows that the text was probably copied by "a student 'collector' " from *JAF*, 1894, 228, or from Child, V, 284, where it was reprinted in the additions. For a discussion on the possible lack of authenticity of some of the Combs collection, see the foreword by D. K. Wilgus to Combs, *Fsgs So US*, pp. xvii–xxi, and the discussions to 11 and 13 in this Supplement.

3. THE FALSE KNIGHT UPON THE ROAD

Local Titles: The Devil and the School Child, The False Knight to the Row, The Nightman.

Texts: *Story Type* A: Bronson, IV, 442 (#10.1) / Emrich, *Am Flk Ptry*, 250 / Manny & Wilson, *Sgs Miramichi*, 199–200 / Moore & Moore, *Blds & Flk Sgs SW*, 11–12 / Parler, *Ark Ballet Bk*, 44 / Roberts, *Sang Branch Settlers*, 89–90.

Fragments & Title Lists: Rosenberg, *Fsgs Va*, 34.

Discussion: The textual influence of "Riddles Wisely Expounded" (1) on this ballad, previously seen to a significant extent only in Creighton's *Sgs Blds N Sc*, pp. 1–2, text (which caused Barry to call it "an extraordinary version" in *BFSSNE*, XI, 8), is even more pronounced in the recent New Brunswick version from Manny & Wilson, *Sgs Miramichi*. This text, collected in 1963, is a much fuller one than that in Creighton and again emphasizes the close relationships among Child 1, 2, 3, and 46 (see discussion to 1 in this Supplement). It should be noted that a year earlier the same informant provided the Bronson, IV, 442, text, which is quite different in that it is closer to the more usual Child 3 versions and does not include the riddling sequence more normally associated with 1 and 46.

The Moore & Moore text in *Blds & Flk Sgs SW* is from a native of Scotland who emigrated to the U.S. as a child. It is an "emigrant" text (see discussion to 199 in this Supplement) that is entirely Scots in content and diction. It was recited by the informant and is quite similar to Child's A and C versions. Many of the texts in Moore & Moore are of this class and might not be usefully called traditional American versions (see discussions to 40 and 219 in *BTBNA*, pp. 51, 132).

A French ballad from Nova Scotia in Barbeau, *Jongleur Songs of Old Quebec*, pp. 9–10, bears some striking resemblances to Child 3.

4. LADY ISABEL AND THE ELF-KNIGHT

Local Titles: The Dapherd Grey, The False-Hearted Knight and the Pretty Carol Lynn, False Hearted William, False William, The Gates (Doors) of Ivory, The King's (Seventh) Daughter, The Lord from the West, May Collins, My Pretty Cold Rain (Golden), The Seventh King's Daughters, A Young Man Came Over.

Texts: *Story Type* A: Bush, *Flk Sgs Cntrl West Va*, II, 90–93 / Fowke, *Trd Sngrs & Sgs Ont*, 102–104 / Gainer, *Flk Sgs West Va Hills*, 6–7 / Grover, *Hrtge Sgs*, 25–26 / *JAF*, 1964, 156–157; 1968, 45 / Karpeles, *Flk Sgs Newfdld* (1971), 23–24 / Manny & Wilson, *Sgs Miramichi*, 202–203 / Moore & Moore, *Blds & Flk Sgs SW*, 13–15 (B) / Peacock, *Sgs Newfdld Outpts*, I, 206–207 / Ritchie, *Flk Sgs So Aplchns*, 8–9.

G: The usual story is told, but there is no parrot and no father. On her safe return home she gets on her knees and thanks God for her narrow escape. *WF*, 1968, 94–95.

Fragments & Title Lists: Bronson, IV, 443 (#101.1) / Brown, *NC Flklre*, IV, 4–8 / Combs, *Fsgs So US*, 199 (Story Type A) / *JAF*, 1968, 51–53 / Moore & Moore, *Blds & Flk Sgs SW*, 12–13 (A) / *MWF*, 1963, 135 / Rosenberg, *Fsgs Va*, 67.

Discussion: The single example of the new Type G story is West Indian, from oral tradition in Nevis, and was credited by informants to a local song maker, Charles Walters, who died in 1959. The ending which warrants its designation as a separate story type is unusual in the Anglo-American tradition of this ballad and, in not mentioning the parrot/family episode, is closer to the Continental forms and the Canadian Story Type F. The final episode of the prayer may be indebted to the tradition of Child 4 represented by the unique Peter Buchan text that is Child B. Since its other stanzas, however, are textually the common British "outlandish knight" form (Child E), it is not necessary to posit such a connection: creating a pious ending of this sort would be quite in keeping with general Christian beliefs and with Walters' song-making abilities. Another of its unusual features is that it is told throughout in the first person by the maid.

In the Moore & Moore, *Blds & Flk Sgs SW*, Type A text, that portion of the final dialogue usually exchanged between the parrot and the father or mother is ascribed to parrot and maid. In Peacock's *Sgs Newfdld Outpts* (Type A) text her spirited nature is emphasized even more than usual: she does not attempt to bribe the bird, presumably since its cage is already richly furnished, but instead threatens to wring its neck "like a common crow" should it tattle on her.

As far as the international distribution of "Lady Isabel and the Elf-Knight" is concerned, two studies which bear on some of Nygard's conclusions in *The Ballad of Heer Halewijn* should be noted: Lajos Vargyas, *Researches into the Mediaeval History of Folk Ballad*, pp. 129–157, brings important evidence to bear from Hungarian tradition which questions Nygard's hypotheses on paths of diffusion and on the archaism of supernatural elements, and David D. Buchan, "Lady Isabel and the Whipping Boy," *SFQ*, 34 (1970), 62–70, refutes the validity of Nygard's "Animadversions" on the verity of the Peter Buchan texts. (If Buchan is correct, then the charming title by which Child 4 had long been known may again come into general favor.) Also pertinent to the question of Continental tradition is Edith Rogers, "A New Genealogy for 'Rico Franco,'" *JAF*, 82 (1969), 367–375.

Eleanor R. Long, "Thematic Classification and 'Lady Isabel,'" *JAF*, 85 (1972), 32–41, shows important thematic parallels between Child 4 and other Anglo-American narrative songs not usually considered in conjunction by folksong scholars.

7. EARL BRAND

Local Titles: Lord William and Lord Douglas, The Seven Sons, Sweet William and Fair Ellen.

Texts: *Story Type* A: Abrahams & Foss, *Anglo-Am Fsg Style*, 7–8 / Emrich, *Am Flk Ptry*, 253–255 / Jameson, *Sweet Rivers Sg*, 50–51 / Moore & Moore, *Blds & Flk Sgs SW*, 16–17 (A).

D: Boette, *Singa Hipsy Doodle*, 17–18 / Gainer, *Flk Sgs West Va Hills*, 8–9 / Warner, *Flk Sgs & Blds Estn Sbrd*, 8–9.

Fragments & Title Lists: Brown, *NC Flklre*, IV, 8–13 / *JEMF Quarterly*, IX, 2 (1973), 58 / Moore & Moore, *Blds & Flk Sgs SW*, 18 (B) / Rosenberg, *Fsgs Va*, 30.

Discussion: The Warner *Flk Sgs & Blds Estn Sbrd* (Story Type D) version has the Type A ending, but also contains the harsh words that Willie imparts to his love after the battle, the distinctive feature of the Type D story. The repetition of the motif of hanging the bugle about the neck (see Child's B text), which Coffin points to as unusual in North American versions (*BTBNA*, p. 30), appears in Emrich's *Am Flk Ptry* (Type A) text from North Carolina.

8. ERLINTON

Note: There is still no published North American ballad that is demonstrably a direct relative of Child 8. As in *BTBNA*, the following references are all to "The Bold Soldier" (Laws M27).

Local Titles: The Jolly Soldier, Lady Flower, Little Soldier Boy, The Rich Lady from London.

Texts: *Story Type* A: Burton & Manning, *E Tenn State U Coll Flklre: Fsgs*, 47–48 / Emrich, *Am Flk Ptry*, 90–91 / Grover, *Hrtge Sgs*, 92–93 / Moore & Moore, *Blds & Flk Sgs SW*, 177–178 / *NYFQ*, 1966, 117–119; 1967, 21–22.

Fragments & Title Lists: Brown, *NC Flklre*, IV, 158–160 / Fowke, *Trd Sngrs & Sgs Ont*, 58 / *MWF*, 1963, 147.

10. THE TWA SISTERS

Local Titles: Balance Unto Me, The Bonny Busk of London, Bow and Balance, Bow Down, Bow Your Bend to Me, The Lord of the North Country, Old Man from the North Countree, The Sister's Murder, There Was an Old Lady, The Twin Sisters, Wind and Rain.

Texts: Story Type A: Abrahams & Foss, *Anglo-Am Fsg Style*, 20–23 / Boette, *Singa Hipsy Doodle*, 32–33 / Burton & Manning, *E Tenn State U Coll Flklre: Fsgs*, 29–30 / Carey, *Md Flk Lgds & Flk Sgs*, 94–95 / Jameson, *Sweet Rivers Sg*, 41 / *Ky Flklre Record*, 1965, 18–20 / Leach & Coffin, *Critics & Bld*, 65 / Moore & Moore, *Blds & Flk Sgs SW*, 19–20 (A) / Ritchie, *Flk Sgs So Aplchns*, 63 / Scott, *Lvng Dcmts Am Hstry*, I, 61–63 / *Sing Out!*, XIII, 2 (1963), 4 / Sweeney, *Fct Fctn & Flklre So Ind*, 51–53.

C: Boette, *Singa Hipsy Doodle*, 163–165 / Gainer, *Flk Sgs West Va Hills*, 10–12.

H: Emrich, *Am Flk Ptry*, 255–256.

L: *Colorado Fsg Bull*, 1964, 32–33.

M: *Ky Flklre Record*, 1969, 67.

R: The story follows the common Type A outline to the point where the miller's attention is drawn to the girl's body in the water. He observes that it is neither fish nor swan, but Sweet William's love. Sweet William then takes his own life "because he could not have the one he loved for his wife." Burton & Manning, *E Tenn State U Coll Flkre: Fsgs II*, 82–83.

S: The courtship, jealousy, and attempted murder occur in the customary sequence, but the girl is rescued by the miller who declares his love for her. She replies that she loves him as well. He boasts of his wealth which he says will be hers if she marries him, and she gives the somewhat startling (despite its commonplace nature) reply: "Your riches great may be / But all I do crave is your fair body." They ride to his castle where they are married the same day. The ballad ends with a description of her wedding finery. Peacock, *Sgs Newfdld Outpts*, I, 179–180.

T: Two sisters are walking by the river and one pushes the other in. The drowning girl floats down to the miller's pond, where the miller pulls her out with hook and line. He makes fiddle strings of her hair and fiddle screws of her bones. The only tune the fiddle would play was "the dreadful wind and rain." Abrahams & Foss, *Anglo-Am Fsg Style*, 23–24 / *SFQ*, 1964, 120–121.

U: Two lovers go fishing. The man proposes marriage, then knocks the girl down, beats her viciously, and throws her body into the water. She floats down to the miller's dam and the rest of the story is as Type T. *Sing Out!*, XVIII, 1 (1968), 19.

Fragments & Title Lists: Bronson, IV, 447 (#23.1) / Brown, *NC Flklre*, IV, 13–18 / Combs, *Fsgs So US*, 199 / *JEMF Quarterly*, IX, 2 (1973), 58 / *Ky Flklre Record*, 1965, 65 / Moore & Moore, *Blds & Flk Sgs SW*, 21 (B) / Rosenberg, *Fsgs Va*, 128.

Discussion: This ballad continues to be popular among North American singers and to show great variation in its story types (cf. *BTBNA*, p. 34)—perhaps due in part to the relative complexity of its fullest form. Even texts within the same story type display significant variations: in the Sweeney, *Fct Fctn & Flklre So Ind*, text, for instance, no one is punished, either for the murder or for the theft; in Carey, *Md Flk Lgds & Flk Sgs*, p. 94, there is no theft and the elder sister only is hanged, while in the second text, p. 95, there is the unusual feature of the story being told in the first person by the suitor. Yet all three tell essentially the Type A story.

The new Story Type S text, from Newfoundland, is textually similar to the only other published version of 10 from that province, found in Greenleaf & Mansfield, *Blds Sea Sgs Newfdld*, a text which Coffin was understandably moved to characterize as "amazing" and which represents the sole example of Story Type G (*BTBNA*, p. 33). The Type S text, however, from Peacock's *Sgs Newfdld Outpts*, is far more internally logical and coherent by analytical standards than the Greenleaf & Mansfield one in that there is no ghost and the coverings of silver and gold are made integral parts of the bride's wedding outfit. While these elements in the Greenleaf & Mansfield version more closely approximate their place in the Old World versions of Child B–F, O, and Q, they appear far more functional in the role assigned to them in the Peacock copy.

The texts that provide the examples of the new Story Types T and U are closely related to the previously unique Type N text from *BFSSNE*, XII, 10, with the important exception that Types T and U include the murder, while N does not. All four texts which exemplify these three story types resemble the parody (or, in Child's words, I, 121, "buffoonery") versions of Child A and L in their details of the girl-fiddle anatomy, but the North American versions do not have the comical tone of their British counterparts. Barry considered his Type N text to be "perhaps the most primitive that has survived in English tradition" (*BFSSNE*, XII, 10). Part of the uniqueness of these four texts resides in their common refrain, "the wind and the rain," which is found in the Fools' songs in both *King Lear* and *Twelfth Night* but which appeared in no other known versions of Child 10 from either Old or New World tradition until Hugh Shields published a fragment of the ballad from the manuscripts of the nineteenth-century Irish poet William Allingham, which includes a similar refrain. Allingham had collected the fragment from "a nurse in the family of a relative." See Hugh Shields, "William Allingham and Folk Song," *Hermathena*, 117 (1974), 23–36 (the quotation above is from p. 28). George Foss, "More on a Unique and Anomalous Version of 'The Two Sisters,' " *SFQ*, 28 (1964), 119–133, subjects the three texts that exemplify Types N and T to a comparative textual and musicological analysis. They were all learned within a small area of the North Carolina and Virginia border.

The fourth of this group of texts, the Story Type U example from *Sing*

Out!, 1968, evidently not known to Foss when he wrote his article, is from the singing of Kilby Snow, also from Virginia. Its distinctiveness lies in the introduction of the common Anglo-American "murdered girl" narrative theme (see Anne B. Cohen, *Poor Pearl, Poor Girl!*) into the ballad. This version is at the present unique to this singer; the song "has been in his family for generations," but there have been "four new verses added by Kilby Snow" (*Sing Out!*, XVIII, 1 [1968], 19).

Kenneth Peacock has published a text in Russian, with English translation, of a ballad collected in a Saskatchewan Doukhobor community which is manifestly a version of the British Child 10. Versions have been collected from tradition in the USSR itself, and Peacock speculates in his notes how the ballad may have traveled eastward from Great Britain. See his *Songs of the Doukhobors*, pp. 152–154.

11. THE CRUEL BROTHER

Local Titles: The Bride's Murder, The Three Maids.

Texts: Story Type A: Combs, *Fsgs So US*, 199–200 / Gainer, *Flk Sgs West Va Hills*, 13–15.

Fragments & Title Lists: Brown, *NC Flklre*, IV, 18–19 / Rosenberg, *Fsgs Va*, 21.

Discussion: The newly published text from the Combs collection was reported by a student fieldworker, Carey Woofter, to be " 'doctored' by one Daniel De Weese." D. K. Wilgus, editor of the Combs edition, adds that this doctoring may have been responsible for the unsual refrain, "All along the chip-yards so clean" (Combs, *Fsgs So US*, p. 199). For references to other speculations on the nature of some of Combs's student collections, see the discussions to 2 and 13 in this Supplement.

12. LORD RANDAL

Local Titles: Jimmy Random My Son, Johnny Ellis My Son, Lord Ransome, My Ramboling Son, Randall (Randy) My Son, Seigneur Randal, Sweet Harry, Willie Randalls.

Texts: Story Type A: Gainer, *Flk Sgs West Va Hills*, 16–17 / Joyner, *Flk Sg SC*, 23–24 / Leach & Coffin, *Critics & Bld*, 62–63 / *McNeese Review*, 1964, 18–19 / Moore & Moore, *Blds & Flk Sgs SW*, 22–23 (A) / Raim & Dunson, *Grass Roots Harmony*, 56–57 / Ritchie, *Flk Sgs So Aplchns*, 56–57.

Fragments & Title Lists: Abrahams, *Sngr & Her Sgs*, 180 (Story Type A) / Brown, *NC Flklre*, IV, 19–22 / Combs, *Fsgs So US*, 200 (Story Type

A) / *JEMF Quarterly*, IX, 2 (1973), 58 / Moore & Moore, *Blds & Flk Sgs SW*, 23 (B) / *MWF*, 1963, 135 / Rosenberg, *Fsgs Va*, 74.

Discussion: The Raim & Dunson, *Grass Roots Harmony*, Type A text is the normative American version in all respects but lacks the testament stanzas and the revelation of the murderer.

The version in *McNeese Review* is in French, from Louisiana (the "Seigneur Randal" in the local titles). It has been in the informant's family tradition for a hundred years and was originally taught to his grandmother by the nuns of a local Catholic convent she attended as a child in the 1860's. Theodore Toulon Beck, who published the text, recognizes that it is an almost word-for-word equivalent of Child D from Scott's *Minstrelsy* and suggests the possibility that it stems directly from a seventeenth-century French version which also traveled independently to Scotland and formed the basis for the Scott text. Given the sophisticated context of the convent culture, the international popularity of Scott's works, the close textual similarity of the two versions, and the English name "Randal," however, it seems more likely that the origin of this version was a direct translation of a *Minstrelsy* text (by the convent sisters?) and can safely be said to be a *British* traditional ballad in North America.

E. Flatto analyzes "Lord Randal" from a literary-aesthetic perspective in *SFQ*, 34 (1970), 331–336, as does Graham S. Kash in *Tenn FLS Bull*, 36 (1970), 6–10.

13. EDWARD

Local Titles: Blood of the Red Rooster, Edward Edward, Edward My Son, The Father's Murder, The Hazel Nut Tree, How Come That Blood on Your Coat Sleeve?, My Own Darling Boy, My Son Come Tell It to Me, Son Davie Son Davie.

Texts: Story Type A: Burton & Manning, *E Tenn State U Coll Flkre: Fsgs*, 40–41 / Emrich, *Am Flk Ptry*, 258–259 / Grover, *Hrtge Sgs*, 199–200 / Moore & Moore, *Blds & Flk Sgs SW*, 24–25 / Parler, *Ark Ballet Bk*, 28–29 / Ritchie, *Flk Sgs So Aplchns*, 12–13.

C: Brown, *NC Flklre, IV*, 24–25 / *WF*, 1966, 77–79.

D: In the usual question-and-answer exchange with his mother, the son reveals he has killed his father. He implicates his mother in the crime. Gainer, *Flk Sgs West Va Hills*, 18–19.

Fragments & Title Lists: Abrahams, *Sngr & Her Sgs*, 180 (Story Type A) / Bronson, IV, 452 (#16.1) / Brown, *NC Flklre*, IV, 23 / *Colorado Fsg Bull*, 1964, 1 / Combs, *Fsgs So US*, 201 (Story Type C) / Rosenberg, *Fsgs Va*, 31.

Discussion: The Percy text of this ballad (Child B), in which Edward slays his father rather than his brother (or brother-in-law), has been much anthologized in collections of British poetry and expressively rendered on concert platforms. Its unique feature of the father-victim, however, has never appeared in published versions of "Edward" that have been collected from oral tradition since the *Reliques* in either Britain or America. The sole exception to this is the recently published text in Gainer, *Flk Sgs West Va Hills*, which constitutes the new Type D story. It is possible that this version owes its unusual feature to the ubiquitous Percy text entering tradition.

Relevant to this point is an article by James Twitchell, "The Incest Theme and the Authenticity of the Percy Version of 'Edward,' " *WF*, 34 (1975), 32–35 (published before the Gainer text), which adds to the fair body of scholarship that has already subjected the unusual Percy version to inquiry (see *BTBNA*, p. 40, for references and synopses). While agreeing with others before him that the Percy version has had no real currency in oral tradition as far as the recorded evidence shows, Twitchell suggests that in its Oedipal implications it may be thematically the oldest version of "Edward" and legitimately folklore rather than a clerical (Percy) or aristocratic (Dalrymple) re-creation—a conclusion contrary, in certain respects, to Taylor's thesis (see *BTBNA*, p. 40). His suggestion is that taboos against mother-son incest relationships would have been strong enough to force the sublimation of this concern and prevent its being so openly expressed in song, with the result of its subsequent transformation into intersibling incest and rivalry. Gainer's own quite original interpretation of the events that lie behind the story of the ballad should be consulted (p. 18).

Gainer's West Virginia text shares a further, rarely seen element with the Percy text: it couples patricide with the condemnation of the mother for her role in that action—"For such you taught to me, oh!" Implication of the mother in the crime has previously turned up in only five versions: Child A (Motherwell) and B (Percy); Brown, *NC Flklre*, IV, 24–25; Davis, *More Trd Blds Va*, pp. 62–64 (AA); and *WF*, 1966, 77–79 (which may have been largely authored by the collector—see below). Of this group, however, except for the Percy and Gainer texts, all implications of the mother's role in the crime are coupled with the killing of the brother, not the father, and are Type C stories.

The *WF*, 1966, Type C text is from Combs's unpublished collection and is given in an article by D. K. Wilgus, "The Oldest (?) Text of 'Edward,' " pp. 77–92. Wilgus suggests that it was not collected from oral tradition as claimed but fabricated by a contributor from earlier printed sources (cf. discussions to 2 and 11 in this Supplement).

In the Ritchie, *Flk Sgs So Aplchns*, Type A text Edward has murdered his brother-in-law, as he has in several other North American versions. There is no tendency in this or any other text for the ballad to become associated with "family opposition to lovers" or "lowly suitor" themes, however, which often include such slayings (e.g., Child 214, Laws M32). This may be partly because the latent incest theme is too strong or, more simply, because the narrative element is so minimal in the ballad's tradition.

14. BABYLON

Local Titles: The Bonny Banks of Airdrie-O, Fair Flowers in the Valley, Heckry-Hi Si-Bernio.

Texts: *Story Type* A: Gainer, *Flk Sgs West Va Hills*, 20–21 / Karpeles, *Flk Sgs Newfdld* (1971), 27–28 (A) / *NYFQ*, 1966, 119–120 / Peacock, *Sgs Newfdld Outpts*, III, 809–810 (A).

B: *NYFQ*, 1966, 120–121.

Fragments & Title Lists: Karpeles, *Flk Sgs Newfdld* (1971), 28–29 (B–D) / Peacock, *Sgs Newfdld Outpts*, III, 810 (B).

Discussion: No specific source is credited for the *NYFQ*, 1966, Type A text, presented as being "sung three generations ago in my mother's family" (p. 119), but it is Motherwell's (Child A) down to practically every dialect peculiarity and archaism.

17. HIND HORN

Local Titles: I Gave My Love a Gay Gold Ring, In Scotland Town (Where I Was Born).

Texts: *Story Type* A: Bronson, IV, 454–455 (#4.1) / Emrich, *Am Flk Ptry*, 260–262 / Fowke, *Trd Sngrs & Sgs Ont*, 80–82 / Gainer, *Flk Sgs West Va Hills*, 22–23 / Karpeles, *Flk Sgs Newfdld* (1971), 30–31 (A) / Manny & Wilson, *Sgs Miramichi*, 206–208 / Moore & Moore, *Blds & Flk Sgs SW*, 26–27 / *MWF*, 1963, 136–137 / *NE Flklre*, 1963, 20–22.

Fragments & Title Lists: Karpeles, *Flk Sgs Newfdld* (1971), 31 (B).

Discussion: This ballad, previously confined to tradition in New England, the Maritimes, and Newfoundland, has now been reported from Oklahoma (Moore & Moore, *Blds & Flk Sgs SW*) and West Virginia (Emrich, *Am Flk Ptry*, and Gainer, *Flk Sgs West Va Hills*, independent recoveries from the same informant), as well as from Ontario, but the story continues to show little variation.

J. Kieran Kealy, "The Americanization of Horn," *SFQ*, 37 (1973), 355–384, presents the results of a detailed comparative study of North American texts, British texts in Child, and the three Romance versions of the Horn legend.

Edith Fowke, "American Cowboy and Western Pioneer Songs in Canada," *WF*, 21 (1962), 247–256, gives the text of a song (pp. 249–250) collected in Ontario about a cowboy and his sweetheart which, while it has no observable textual relationship to "Hind Horn," has many of the elements of that ballad which are not found in the numerous broadside derivatives on the similar "returned unrecognized lover" and "broken token" themes.

18. SIR LIONEL

Local Titles: Bangham, Bangum Rid by the Riverside, Bangum Rode the Riverside, The Jobal Hunter, Old Badman (Bangdum, Bangem, Banghum).

Texts: Story Type A: Abrahams & Foss, *Anglo-Am Fsg Style*, 60 / *Colorado Fsg Bull*, 1964, 2, 16 / Gainer, *Flk Sgs West Va Hills*, 24–25 / Parler, *Ark Ballet Bk*, 45 / Ritchie, *Flk Sgs So Aplchns*, 91 / *Tenn FLS Bull*, 1971, 9–10.

D: A hunter meets a girl in the woods who tells him of a wild boar that has slain the lord and his men. She leads him to the boar's den, where he kills the creature after a lengthy battle. He goes on his way and meets a "witch-wife" who curses him for slaying her "pig" and demands three things: his hawk, hound, and lady. He refuses, kills her, and continues on his journey. Burton & Manning, *E Tenn State U Coll Flklre: Fsgs II*, 44 / Emrich, *Am Flk Ptry*, 262–263 / Moore & Moore, *Blds & Flk Sgs SW*, 30–32 (B).

Fragments & Title Lists: Bronson, IV, 455 (#9.2) / Moore & Moore, *Blds & Flk Sgs SW*, 29 (A) / Rosenberg, *Fsgs Va*, 117.

Discussion: The three examples of the new Story Type D are by no means all of a piece. The story description given above is of the fullest version, from Emrich, *Am Flk Ptry*, but variations in the other examples should be noted: in Burton & Manning, *E Tenn State U Coll Flklre: Fsgs II*, there is no girl and the hunter kills the witch *before* he meets and slays the boar, while in Moore & Moore, *Blds & Flk Sgs SW*, the girl is also absent and it is only implied that he kills the old woman. The three texts are all unusual in the North American tradition of the ballad, however, in that the witch figure makes an appearance, and in this they are closest to the Child C and D texts. In addition, the Emrich and the Burton & Manning versions are clearly related to these Child texts by not featuring the usual nonsense refrain, having instead the more intelligible "blow thy horn" internal burden which is found in the older British tradition. The Emrich text has many other interesting verbal parallels with Child C.

20. THE CRUEL MOTHER

Local Titles: The Babes in the Greenwood, Down by the Greenwood Sidee (Tree), Greenwood Sides, There Are Fine Flowers in the Valley, There Was a Girl Her Name Was Young, Two Little Babes.

Texts: Story Type A: Combs, *Fsgs So US*, 201 / Creighton, *Flklre Lunenburg Cnty*, 79–80 / Gainer, *Flk Sgs West Va Hills*, 26–27 / Karpeles, *Flk Sgs Newfdld* (1971), 34–36 (C, D) / Manny & Wilson, *Sgs Miramichi*, 209–210 / Moore & Moore, *Blds & Flk Sgs SW*, 32–34 (A, B) / Parler, *Ark Ballet Bk*, 14 / Peacock, *Sgs Newfdld Outpts*, III, 804–805 (A).

B: Karpeles, *Flk Sgs Newfdld* (1971), 32–34 (A, B), 37–38 (G) / Leach & Glassie, *Guide for Collectors of Oral Traditions*, 27–28.

C: The Story is as Type A except for the introduction: she marries a fisherman's son and has two daughters whom she then proceeds to murder with no apparent motive. *Ky Flklre Record*, 1965, 21–22 / Sweeny, *Fct Fctn & Flklre So Ind*, 54–56.

Fragments & Title Lists: Karpeles, *Flk Sgs Newfdld* (1971), 36–37 (E, F) / Peacock, *Sgs Newfdld Outpts*, III, 805 (B) / Rosenberg, *Fsgs Va*, 22.

Discussion: Some minor variations among Story Type A examples should be noted: the most persistent portion of "The Cruel Mother" in tradition is the dialogue between the mother and her dead children, and the Moore & Moore, *Blds & Flk Sgs SW*, version emphasizes this by having the woman unaccountably bind and bury her children *after* they return and accuse her. This might indicate a functional shift in the story: she is trying to prevent them from haunting her. The Manny & Wilson, *Sgs Miramichi*, Type A text is unusual in that the dialogue between mother and children is not present; the murder of the baby (one only) comprises almost the entire song, with a single homiletic stanza at the end declaring that she will go to hell for her crime. In the Peacock, *Sgs Newfdld Outpts*, Type A version there is the unique inference that she is paid to murder her children, though whether by her father or by her lover is not stated.

The texts which exemplify the new Story Type C (both from the same informant) have no counterpart that I can find. This story type renders the motive for the crime even more obscure than do those frequent versions in which the illegitimacy of the births is not mentioned.

Attention should be drawn to a ballad in Jameson, *Sweet Rivers Sg*, called "Down in the Green Wood's Valley" (p. 55). It tells of a widow with two small children who falls in love with a young man, but he does not return her affection. Suspecting that her children are an impediment to her chances of gaining the young man's love and an offer of marriage, she kills them. He still will not court her, however, and she eventually wanders "through the wild" with a lost soul, no lover, and no children. While the maker of this interesting piece obviously had a version of "The Cruel Mother" in mind (the similarities in the air, the refrain, the title, and the phrasing are manifest), the story is too close to being an original composition to be properly called a version of Child 20.

23. JUDAS

Cheney, *Mormon Sgs Rocky Mts*, contains a song called "Thirty Pieces of Silver" (pp. 169–170) which treats some of the same subject matter as Child 23 but is in no way a clear derivative of the ancient piece.

Julie Reich Mackey, in her doctoral dissertation, "Medieval Metrical Saints' Lives and the Origin of the Ballad," devotes some space to a discussion of the unique Trinity MS text of "Judas" (pp. 190–203). She thinks that it was not a popular or traditional ballad but a section of a longer, didactic legend composed and delivered to a congregation by some mendicant friar.

26. THE THREE RAVENS (THE TWA CORBIES)

Texts: Story Type A: Abrahams & Foss, *Anglo-Am Fsg Style*, 176 / Creighton, *Fsgs So NB*, 5 / Killion & Waller, *Treasury Ga Flklre*, 256 / Moore & Moore, *Blds & Flk Sgs SW*, 34–35 / Parler, *Ark Ballet Bk*, 52.

B: Gainer, *Flk Sgs West Va Hills*, 28 / *SFQ*, 1965, 181–182.

Fragments & Title Lists: Combs, *Fsgs So US*, 201 (Story Type A) / Rosenberg, *Fsgs Va*, 126.

Discussion: Both examples of Story Type B referenced above have certain elements of Type A, especially in the brevity of their narratives. Their common thematic link with the Type B story, however, is that the crows' prospective meal is a dead man rather than an animal. The Gainer, *Flk Sgs West Va Hills*, text is also serious in tone, a further Type B feature. The *SFQ*, 1965, version, on the hand, is extremely merry.

Vernon V. Chapman III, " 'The Three Ravens' Explicated," *MWF*, 13 (1963), 177–186, subjects the British text of this ballad to interpretation and suggests that the song's origin was in Gaelic Ireland. He relies heavily on Celtic mythology in decoding various symbols in the text. Such studies should be read in conjunction with the strictures of John Greenway, "The Flight of the Grey Goose: Literary Symbolism in the Traditional Ballad," *SFQ*, 18 (1954), 165–174, and Eleanor Long, *"The Maid" and "The Hangman,"* pp. 96–107.

27. THE WHUMMIL BORE

There is a bawdy item in both British and North American tradition which, whether directly related to Child 27 or not, tells substantially the same story. Traditional North American texts of this song, "The Keyhole in the Door," may be found in Cheney, *Mormon Sgs Rocky Mts*, 17–18; Huntington, *Sgs Whalemen Sang*, 315–317; Jackson, *Flklre & Society*, 47–48.

31. THE MARRIAGE OF SIR GAWAIN

There are still no published texts of Child 31 from North American tradition. Add to the bibliography for its thematic relative, "The Half-Hitch" (Laws N23), Cheney, *Mormon Sgs Rocky Mts*, 19–22.

43. THE BROOMFIELD HILL

Texts: *Story Type* A: Combs, *Fsgs So US*, 113–114.

Discussion: Add to the references for texts to "The Maid on the Shore" (Laws K27), a narrative analogue of Child 43, Creighton, *Fsgs So NB*, 110–111; Emrich, *Am Flk Ptry*, 527–528; Grover, *Hrtge Sgs*, 154–155; Huntington, *Sgs Whalemen Sang*, 136–137; Karpeles, *Flk Sgs Newfdld* (1971), 117–121; Peacock, *Sgs Newfdld Outpts*, I, 296–297.

45. KING JOHN AND THE BISHOP

Texts: *Story Type* A: Emrich, *Am Flk Ptry*, 267–268.

46. CAPTAIN WEDDERBURN'S COURTSHIP

Local Titles: An Old Man's Courtship, The Riddle Song.

Texts: *Story Type* A: Moore & Moore, *Blds & Flk Sgs SW*, 37–38 (B).

B: The story is as Type A, save that he is unable to perform the final task (summon a priest unborn) and so departs with his desires unfulfilled. Karpeles, *Flk Sgs Newfdld* (1971), 40–41 (B).

C: The roles are reversed: he asks the questions; she answers all correctly; she does not lie with him. Karpeles, *Flk Sgs Newfdld* (1971), 39–40 (A).

D: An old man asks a girl what she desires for supper, and she gives the enigmatic reply in riddle form (a chicken without a bone, etc.). He replies that there are no such things, whereupon she answers her own riddles. He then tries to outwit her by posing riddles of his own, but she answers them successfully and will not lie with him. He is angry at being outsmarted and will have nothing more to do with her. Moore & Moore, *Blds & Flk Sgs SW*, 36 (A).

Fragments & Title Lists: Brown, *NC Flklre*, IV, 25–27 / Rosenberg, *Fsgs Va*, 15.

Discussion: The three new Story Types B, C, and D all feature the failure of the attempted seduction, and this may be due in part to a certain amount of moralization, though none have specific moral tags attached to them. What is more likely is that they show the effects of association with the Child 1 idea of a battle, not only of wit and sex, but also between womankind and the devil. In the Karpeles, *Flk Sgs Newfdld* (1971), Type B text the linking of Captain Wedderburn (here a bold sea captain) with the devil is clearly intimated in his inability to "call the priest unborn," whether it be the Biblical Melchizedek or the more topical figures of Child A and B. In the Type C example, also from Karpeles (1971), this association is less clear but can be inferred from her answer to one of his first riddles—"the devil he passes the female's heart." Thus, he is identified by his inability to pass hers.

The Story Type D example, from Moore & Moore, *Blds & Flk Sgs SW*, intersperses verse and prose in cante-fable format but was recited *in toto* by the informant. Most of the narrative is in the prose portions, the verses being the various riddles and impossible tasks. However, the story and the repeated "lie against the wall" line identify it clearly as a version of 46. There is no intimation that he is to be considered the devil in this text.

These three new Story Types B, C, and D most closely resemble the most unusual published version of "Captain Wedderburn's Courtship" in Leach, *Flk Blds & Sgs Lwr Labr Cst*, pp. 26–27, the informant's title for which was, significantly, "The Devil and the Blessed Virgin Mary." Consult Leach's suggestions on the possible history of his text-type on pp. 27–28. See also the discussion to 1 in this Supplement.

Further references to "I Gave My Love a Cherry" lyric songs are Burton & Manning, *E Tenn State U Coll Flklre: Fsgs*, 88; Gainer, *Flk Sgs West Va Hills*, 29; Jameson, *Sweet Rivers Sg*, 46–47; Scott, *Bld of Am*, 9–10.

48. YOUNG ANDREW

Rosenberg's *Fsgs Va* title checklist of WPA holdings at the University of Virginia lists two versions of Child 48 under the title "Young Andrew"

(p. 143). The only relationship this song bears to Child 48, however, is its title. The song itself is a homiletic piece about a young man being killed by a fall from his horse; for a text, see Brown, *NC Flklre*, II, 659–660. (As a functional genre, this may have been a narrative obituary poem; see Tristram Potter Coffin, "On a Peak in Massachusetts: The Literary and Aesthetic Approach," in Boatright, Hudson, and Maxwell, *A Good Tale and a Bonnie Tune*, pp. 201–209, and Mark Tristram Coffin's Ph.D. dissertation, "American Narrative Obituary Verse and Native American Balladry.") No other versions of Child 48 have as yet been reported in print from oral tradition in North America.

49. THE TWA BROTHERS

Local Titles: John G. Billups, Our Young Son John, Willie and Johnny, Yonder School.

Texts: Story Type A: Brunvand, *Guide for Collectors of Folklore*, 73–74 / Moore & Moore, *Blds & Flk Sgs SW*, 38–39 (A) / *Rocky Mt Coll*, 18.

B: Gainer, *Flk Sgs West Va Hills*, 30–31 / *Ky Flklre Record*, 1965, 22–23 / Sweeney, *Fct Fctn & Flklre So Ind*, 57–58.

C: Emrich, *Am Flk Ptry*, 270–271 / Moore & Moore, *Blds & Flk Sgs SW*, 39–41 (B) / Parler, *Ark Ballet Bk*, 53–54 / Peacock, *Sgs Newfdld Outpts*, III, 827–828 (A).

Fragments & Title Lists: Combs, *Fsgs So US*, 201 (Story Type C) / Peacock, *Sgs Newfdld Outpts*, III, 829 (B) / Rosenberg, *Fsgs Va*, 128.

Discussion: Like many other reported versions of this ballad from North American tradition, most of the above texts do not tell the fullest story by including the postburial scene between the two lovers. The principal distinguishing feature between the story types is whether the conflict is a result of a love relationship (Type A); is purposeful, but for some such reason as refusal to play at ball (Type C); or is accidental (Type B).

The *Rocky Mt Coll* (Type A) text is prefaced with the rather startling note, "Collected from Cecil Sharp who was collecting songs in the Southern Appalachians in 1901 for Child," which may be its author, Bruce ("Utah") Phillips, in a winsome mood. The text bears no closer resemblance to any of Sharp's published copies than would normally be expected.

The Utah informant who supplied the Brunvand, *Guide for Collectors of Folklore*, Type A text provides an interesting gloss on the "Brother comb my sister's hair" line: it "doesn't mean he's combing his sister's hair; it's a game they used to play" (p. 72).

52. THE KING'S DOCHTER LADY JEAN

Local Titles: Queen Jane.

Texts: *Story Type* A: Queen Jane leaves off sewing at home to go gather nuts in the woods. A forester appears and censures her for doing so without his permission. After he has laid her down and had his will of her, she reviles him, promising that he will suffer for his action, as she is the king's daughter. He reveals that he is her brother who, long away, has not seen her since childhood. He laments the meeting and the wrong he has done; she wishes that her baby were born and she were dead. Bronson, IV, 464–465 (#1.1) / Emrich, *Am Flk Ptry*, 273–274 / *Sing Out!*, XVIII, 5 (1968–1969), 5.

Discussion: All the above references are to the only version of Child 52 found so far in North American tradition, from the singing of Sara Cleveland of Brant Lake, N.Y. Its discovery adds to the select corpus of ballads in contemporary tradition which deal overtly with the subject of intersibling incest.

Mrs. Cleveland's version is textually closest to Child A but does not have the episode of Jane's confrontation with her family on her return from the woods which all four versions in Child do. Nor does she kill herself (Child A), or be killed by her brother (Child B), but rather wishes her baby's birth and her own death in a commonplace stanza.

For the significance of gathering nuts in the forest and other related actions, see Scott Elliott, "Pulling the Heather Green," *JAF*, 48 (1935), 353–361, and Eleanor Long, *"The Maid" and "The Hangman,"* pp. 96–104.

53. YOUNG BEICHAN

Local Titles: Lord Akeman (Baker), The Man in Anglon Bound, Susan Price, Young Beham.

Texts: *Story Type* A: Abrahams & Foss, *Anglo-Am Fsg Style*, 101–103 / Emrich, *Am Flk Ptry*, 275–277 / *Folkways Monthly*, I, 2 (1963), 16–18 / Gainer, *Flk Sgs West Va Hills*, 32–33 / Jameson, *Sweet Rivers Sg*, 42–43 / Joyner, *Flk Sg SC*, 28–30 / Karpeles, *Flk Sgs Newfdld* (1971), 42–46 (A, B) / Moore & Moore, *Blds & Flk Sgs SW*, 41–43 / Peacock, *Sgs Newfdld Outpts*, I, 210–212 (A) / Ritchie, *Flk Sgs So Aplchns*, 28–29 / Roberts, *Sang Branch Settlers*, 90–91.

B: Burton & Manning, *E Tenn State U Coll Flklre: Fsgs*, 81–82 / Burton & Manning, *E Tenn State U Coll Flklre: Fsgs II*, 47–48.

Fragments & Title Lists: Abrahams, *Sngr & Her Sgs*, 180–181 (Story Type A) / Bronson, IV, 465 (#14.1), 467 (#96.2) / Brown, *NC Flklre*,

IV, 27–28 / Combs, *Fsgs So US*, 201 (Story Type A) / Fowke, *Trd Sngrs & Sgs Ont*, 58 / *JEMF Quarterly*, IX, 2 (1973), 58 / Karpeles, *Flk Sgs Newfdld* (1971), 46 (C) / Peacock, *Sgs Newfdld Outpts*, I, 212 (B) / Rosenberg, *Fsgs Va*, 143–144.

Discussion: This ballad continues to enjoy wide popularity in North American tradition and to exhibit relatively strong stability in its story. Variations are most noticeable in minor details like geography, not surprising in view of the two distinct locales in which the action takes place —not a common feature of the traditional ballad. The Moore & Moore, *Blds & Flk Sgs SW*, Story Type A text exemplifies the confusion this may lead to: the initial episode takes place in Turkey, but Lord Bateman's home to which the fair Susan travels is also "on the Turkish shore," and the lady moreover requests the porter to remind his master of the one who set him free from "Ireland's chains."

The Burton & Manning, *E Tenn State U Coll Flklre: Fsgs II*, text has the Type B story but shows strong influence from the normal Type A form in its conclusion.

Recent references to the related broadside ballad of "The Turkish Lady" (Laws O26) are Huntington, *Sgs Whalemen Sang*, 191–193; Karpeles, *Flk Sgs Newfdld* (1971), 138–139.

54. THE CHERRY-TREE CAROL

Local Titles: Carol of the Cherry Tree, Joseph Was an Old Man.

Texts: *Story Type* A: Boette, *Singa Hipsy Doodle*, 154 / Lomax, *Penguin Bk Am Flk Sgs*, 77 / Scott, *Lvng Dcmts Am Hstry*, I, 64–65.

B: Combs, *Fsgs So US*, 202–203 (C) / Emrich, *Am Flk Ptry*, 402–403 (B) / Gainer, *Flk Sgs West Va Hills*, 34–35 / Jameson, *Sweet Rivers Sg*, 60 / Moore & Moore, *Blds & Flk Sgs SW*, 44–47 (A, B) / Ritchie, *Flk Sgs So Aplchns*, 42 / Roberts, *Sang Branch Settlers*, 91–92.

Fragments & Title Lists: Bronson, IV, 467 (#16.1) / Combs, *Fsgs So US*, 201 (Story Type A) / Rosenberg, *Fsgs Va*, 16.

Discussion: Some minor variations, involving for the most part just which character performs the usual actions, are common among the various examples of this ballad. In Boette, *Singa Hipsy Doodle*, and Gainer, *Flk Sgs West Va Hills* (both Type A stories), for instance, the tree bows down on its own accord, and in the Moore & Moore, *Blds & Flk Sgs SW*, (B) text (a Type B story) it is Mary who takes the infant to knee and poses the usual questions. In Scott, *Lvng Dcmts Am Hstry* (Type A), the Christ child does not appear; it is the tree that speaks to Mary.

Check Wilgus' notes in Combs, *Fsgs So US*, p. 202, for an indication that the singer did not consider this an entirely proper song and for a possible reason as to why this was so.

56. DIVES AND LAZARUS

Note: At the time of publication of the most recent edition of *BTBNA* in 1963 only a secondary version of Child 56 had appeared in the published record of the British traditional ballad in North America. Texts of this secondary ballad were given primary status in *BTBNA*, with the caveat that they were not directly related to the Child texts (p. 62). Since 1963, however, two versions of a "Dives and Lazarus" ballad from North American tradition have been published which are palpably direct textual relatives of Child 56. As a result, I have thought it best to separate the two textual traditions here, even though the same story is told in both. The "Dives and Lazarus" ballad referred to in *BTBNA*, therefore, is here called *Secondary Version*, and the recent recoveries which more closely approximate the Child 56 texts are cited below under *Primary Version* (cf. Child 295 in this Supplement).

Secondary Version: *Local Titles*: Lazarus and the Rich Man.

Texts: *Story Type* A: Burton & Manning, *E Tenn State U Coll Flklre: Fsgs*, 53–54 / Emrich, *Am Flk Ptry*, 277–278.

Fragments & Title Lists: Bronson, IV, 468 (#11.1) / Brown, *NC Flklre*, IV, 132 / Rosenberg, *Fsgs Va*, 26.

Primary Version: *Local Titles*: Diverus (Dives) and Lazarus.

Texts: *Story Type* A: As in Story Type A of Secondary Version in *BTBNA*, pp. 61–62. Bush, *Flk Sgs Cntrl West Va*, I, 41–44 / Gainer, *Flk Sgs West Va Hills*, 35–36.

Discussion: The Primary Version, though not uncommon in recent English folksong tradition, had not been reported from America until 1969, when it appeared in Bush, *Flk Sgs Cntrl West Va*. That text is very close to Child A, with minor verbal differences and without stanza 15 of the Child text. It tells the full story, including Dives's repentance, though it does not have Dives's request that his brethren be warned against his mistakes as in the Virginia text of the Secondary Version described under Story Type A in *BTBNA*. The other example of the Primary Version, however, in Gainer's *Flk Sgs West Va Hills* concludes with the summonses to the respective resting places of heaven and hell and does not contain the request for water. These same differences exist among the several texts of the Secondary Version tradition.

The Bush text has the motif that none of the Secondary Version texts exhibit: the strange inability of the dogs to harm the beggar Lazarus.

The Gainer text, however, follows the Secondary Version in that pity rather than some supernatural agency restrains the dogs' behavior toward that unwelcome visitor. Perhaps not too much significance should be attached to such a distinction, however, since only a minor sound—or typographical—change could make the difference between these two meanings (i.e., the change from "could not" to "would not," or vice versa). It is possible, of course, that the Gainer text has been crossed thematically with the Secondary Version tradition, though this is not evident so far as its verbal structure is concerned.

58. SIR PATRICK SPENS

Local Titles: Sir Patrick Song (Spence).

Texts: *Story Type* A: Creighton, *Fsgs So NB*, 6–8.

Fragments & Title Lists: Brown, *NC Flklre*, IV, 29 / Rosenberg, *Fsgs Va*, 117.

Discussion: The single new recovery from New Brunswick differs little from other North American texts of "Sir Patrick Spens." It was collected, however, from a lady who was born and raised in Aberdeenshire where she had been taught the ballad as a recitation in school; she herself had never heard it sung. See the discussion to 3 in this Supplement.

The paper by Norman L. McNeil analyzing the various theories concerning the historical background of the ballad and mentioned in *BTBNA*, p. 63, has since been published as "Origins of 'Sir Patrick Spens'" in Hudson, *Hunters and Healers*, pp. 65–72. See also William H. Matchett, "The Integrity of 'Sir Patrick Spence,'" *Mod Phil*, 68 (1970–1971), 25–31, for an analysis of the Child texts and a suggestion that philological evidence extracted from the Percy version (Child A) reveals the ballad to have originally contained sociopolitical protest. The Percy version is also subjected to analysis in R. L. H. Albright, "The Fate of Sir Patrick Spens: The Ballad as a Strategy for Living," *Keystone Folklore Quarterly*, 17 (1972), 19–26; the author sees the ballad—for the Scots folk—as a way of expressing and dealing with life, built around a certain conception of the role of fate in human affairs.

62. FAIR ANNIE

Texts: *Story Type* A: Combs, *Fsgs So US*, 114–118.

65. LADY MAISRY

Texts: *Story Type* B: *Rocky Mt Coll*, 8.

Discussion: The above text, credited to "the singing of Joe Hansen, 'The Stranger from the Sea,'" is virtually identical with that in Scarborough, *Sgctchr So Mts*, referenced under Story Type B in *BTBNA*.

68. YOUNG HUNTING

Local Titles: Henry Lee, (Lord) Barney, Lowe Bonnie, Parrot of Two Lovers, Young Heneree.

Texts: Story Type A: Abrahams & Foss, *Anglo-Am Fsg Style*, 97–99 / Bush, *Flk Sgs Cntrl West Va*, I, 75– 76 / Dunson & Raim, *Anth Am Flk Music*, 22–23 / Gainer, *Flk Sgs West Va Hills*, 37–38 / Jackson, *Flklre & Society*, 113–115 / *Ky Flklre Record*, 1972, 13–14 / Moore & Moore, *Blds & Flk Sgs SW*, 47–50 (A) / *Mt Life & Work*, XL, 3 (1964), 55–56 / *Sing Out!*, XIX, 1 (1969), 8–9.

H: The Type A story is told up to the stabbing. She then implores him not to die, saying she has sent for doctors in the town in hope of finding one who can heal him. He asks, in a manner reminiscent of Fair Annet in 73, how can he live now he is wounded and feels his heart's blood dripping down to his feet? Joyner, *Flk Sg SC*, 43–44 / *Sing Out!*, XVI, 4 (1966), 19.

Fragments & Title Lists: Brown, *NC Flklre*, IV, 29–30 / Combs, *Fsgs So US*, 203 (Story Type A) / *JEMF Quarterly*, IX, 2 (1973), 58 / *Ky Flklre Record*, 1965, 65 / Moore & Moore, *Blds & Flk Sgs SW*, 50–51 (B, C) / Rosenberg, *Fsgs Va*, 144.

Discussion: The talking bird, such a prominent retention in North American versions of both 68 and 4, is not present in the Bush, *Flk Sgs Cntrl West Va*, Type A text, which ends with the disposal of the body in the well.

The new Story Type H also lacks the bird but has an unusual conclusion which requires its recognition as a separate story: the girl immediately regrets her action and attempts to save her lover by sending for a doctor who can cure him. This episode appears in several North American texts of "Young Hunting" but is invariably followed by such actions as attempting to hide the body and conceal the affair by bribing the bird; concluding with the murderer's remorse, however, is unique to this story type. Of further interest is that this may be a transitional story type between the common A form and the not-nearly-so-common D: in the latter, the remorse is carried through to the point where the girl commits suicide (see the story description in *BTBNA*, pp. 66–67).

The episode of sending for doctors to heal the dying lover appears only in North American texts; it is entirely absent from the Scots tradition that supplied all the texts in Child. It is distinctly possible, therefore, that it is derived from the "send for the king's duckers" episode that does appear in Child A, H, J, and K. Thus may the searching of the waters for the body—the duckers' function—have been transformed in this country. In a couple of texts this transformation is carried even further from its origin by a certain refinement in language, exemplified by the Moore & Moore, *Blds & Flk Sgs SW*, Type A version: after fatally wounding her false lover, the maid instructs him to ride on in hope that he may "find some physicians" to cure his wound.

69. CLERK SAUNDERS

D. K. Wilgus, in "A New 'Child' from North Carolina," *JAF*, 83 (1970), 353–354, points out that a song in Brown, *NC Flklre*, III, 558–559, bears an unmistakable resemblance to the three related "family opposition to lovers" ballads of Child 69, 70, and 71. The song, "Raise a Ruckus Tonight," is similar to yet different from each of these three ballads and impossible to firmly classify as being a version of any one of them. The story, told in five stanzas, is as follows: a man makes a boat of his coat and shirt and sails to see his love. Before he can touch her, her four brothers burst into the room, seize the man, and throw him into the sea, his heart pierced by a dagger. She follows her lover to death.

70. WILLIE AND LADY MAISRY

See 69 above.

71. THE BENT SAE BROWN

See 69 above.

73. LORD THOMAS AND FAIR ANNET

Local Titles: Lord Thomas and Fair (Sweet) Ellender (Ellinor), Parrot of Two Lovers (*sic*; cf. local titles under 68, above).

Texts: Story Type A: Abrahams & Foss, *Anglo-Am Fsg Style*, 46–47 / Bronson, IV, 469 (#32.1) / Burton & Manning, *E Tenn State U Coll Flklre: Fsgs*, 25–27 / Bush, *Flk Sgs Cntrl West Va*, II, 96–101 (A, B) / Carey, *Md Flk Lgds & Flk Sgs*, 95–96 / Cohen & Seeger, *New Lost City Ramblers Sg Bk*, 73 / *Colorado Fsg Bull*, 1964, 31 / Emrich, *Am Flk Ptry*, 281–285 (A, B) / *Folkways Monthly*, I, 2 (1963), 11–13 / Gainer, *Flk Sgs West Va Hills*, 39–41 / *Green Mt Whittlin's*, XVII (n.d.), 2–4 / *JAF*, 1968,

56–57 / Joyner, *Flk Sg SC*, 35–37 / Moore & Moore, *Blds & Flk Sgs SW*, 51–53 / *NC Flklre*, 1974, 151–152 / Peacock, *Sgs Newfdld Outpts*, II, 617–619 (A) / Raim & Dunson, *Grass Roots Harmony*, 64–65 / Ritchie, *Flk Sgs So Aplchns*, 66–67 / *Sing Out!*, XIV, 4 (1964), 32–33 / *Studies Literary Imagination*, 1970, 28–29.

Fragments & Title Lists: Abrahams, *Sngr & Her Sgs*, 181 (Story Type B) / Brown, *NC Flklre*, IV, 30–40 / *Colorado Fsg Bull*, 1964, 1 / *JEMF Quarterly*, IX, 2 (1973), 58 / Peacock, *Sgs Newfdld Outpts*, II, 619 (B) / Rosenberg, *Fsgs Va*, 74–75.

Discussion: Child 73 continues to be extremely popular as well as extremely stable in American tradition. This stability is evident in the above list: all the published texts considered are of the same Story Type A.

Some minor deviations in individual texts should be noted: the *NC Flklre*, 1974, text ends with Ellender being admitted into the hall by Thomas; both of the Bush, *Flk Sgs Cntrl West Va*, texts are incomplete but are firmly enough in the Type A tradition as they stand; and it is assumed that the Raim & Dunson, *Grass Roots Harmony*, copy has suffered from some human error in the mechanics of the printing process, for it is inverted from its usual form: the block of stanzas which encompass the last section of the ballad, from Ellender's arrival at the wedding to the deaths, comes first, followed by what is normally the first half of the song.

74. FAIR MARGARET AND SWEET WILLIAM

Local Titles: The Fair Margaret, Fair Marjorie's Ghost, Lady Margaret and Lord William, Lilly (Lily) Margaret, Sweet William and Lili Margaret.

Texts: Story Type A: Karpeles, *Flk Sgs Newfdld* (1971), 47–48 (A) / Moore & Moore, *Blds & Flk Sgs SW*, 54–55 (A) / Ritchie, *Flk Sgs So Aplchns*, 18–19.

B: Abrahams, *Sngr & Her Sgs*, 139–141 / Gainer, *Flk Sgs West Va Hills*, 42–44 / Parler, *Ark Ballet Bk*, 39–40.

E: Emrich, *Am Flk Ptry*, 285–286 / *Sing Out!*, XV, 5 (1965), 33.

H: From her bower window, Fair Marjorie sees Willie and his bride enter the church. She throws down her comb and leaps to her death. That night, her ghost appears at the couple's bed and asks Willie how he likes his blanket, his sheet, his bride. He replies that he likes them well enough but prefers Marjorie to the lot. She takes her comb from her hair, strikes him on the breast, and tells him to come with her to his "final rest." He kisses the ghost three times and falls dead at its feet. Peacock, *Sgs Newfdld Outpts*, II, 383–384.

Fragments & Title Lists: Brown, *NC Flklre*, IV, 40–42 / Combs, *Fsgs So US*, 203–204 (Story Types A and E) / Karpeles, *Flk Sgs Newfdld* (1971), 49 (B, C) / Moore & Moore, *Blds & Flk Sgs SW*, 56 (B) / Rosenberg, *Fsgs Va*, 33.

Discussion: The new Story Type H condenses the more common, longer narrative of this ballad very neatly by eliminating Willie's visit to Marjorie's home and his run-in with her brothers. His kissing of the corpse and subsequent death have here been incorporated into the wedding-night scene. Besides this contraction, it is also clear that this version has been influenced by 77, "Sweet William's Ghost," in some versions of which the ghost lover has his troth returned in a similar manner—see Child C and E in which a hand is stroked or smoothed across the lover's breast and Child D in which the returned object is a key (see also 295). In 74 the dead/living roles are a reversal of 77 and the motive for the smiting on the breast is not the same, but there is an obvious textual and thematic connection. This motif also gives additional meaning to Marjorie's earlier action of throwing off her comb before she casts herself from her window, a common feature in this ballad's tradition; if the comb were Willie's troth, then throwing it off would seem to be a fitting response to her lover's deceit.

The examples of Story Type E referenced above are ambiguous, for she appears at the couple's bedside dressed in white, which may indicate a winding sheet and thus her ghostly condition; the preceding stanzas, however, seem to imply that she has not yet died and therefore still very much alive when she makes her nocturnal visit.

75. LORD LOVEL

Local Titles: Lord Lovel and Lady Nança Bell, Lord Lovel and Nancy Bell, Lord Lovell.

Texts: *Story Type A*: Boette, *Singa Hipsy Doodle*, 11–13 / Bronson, IV, 471 (#18.1) / Carey, *Md Flk Lgds & Flk Sgs*, 97 / Gainer, *Flk Sgs West Va Hills*, 45–46 / Joyner, *Flk Sg SC*, 41–42 / Moore & Moore, *Blds & Flk Sgs SW*, 57–58 / *NC Flklre*, 1963, 27; 1973, 143–144 / Ritchie, *Flk Sgs So Aplchns*, 22–23 / *Tenn FLS Bull*, 1971, 11–12 / Warner, *Flk Sgs & Blds Estn Sbrd*, 48–49.

Fragments & Title Lists: Brown, *NC Flklre*, IV, 43–47 / Combs, *Fsgs So US*, 204 (Story Type A) / Rosenberg, *Fsgs Va*, 74.

Discussion: In its North American tradition, "Lord Lovel" shows little variation in story or phrasing from version to version. Minor differences may result from the dropping of a stanza or two: the Joyner, *Flk Sg SC*, text, for instance, does not have the episode of opening the coffin and kissing the corpse but moves directly from the hero receiving the news of his love's death to his own demise and a rose-briar motif.

Add to the references of parodies and burlesques in *BTBNA*, p. 73, a War of Independence broadside from the DeMarsan press titled "Lord Lovel no. 2," in which the English Lord Lovel is defeated by "Sir Farragut" (reproduced in *Folkways Monthly*, no. 3 [1964], 45).

Arthur Kyle Davis, Jr., " 'Far Fannil Town': A Ballad of Mystery Examined," *SFQ*, 36 (1972), 1–13, discusses a unique ballad from oral tradition in Virginia which is patently of the Child ballad genre but which cannot be identified as a version of any known song. It bears certain resemblances to portions of Child 65, 76, and 208 but is closest to 75 (cf. Story Type B).

76. THE LASS OF ROCH ROYAL

Local Titles: A-Roving on a (One) Winter's Night, Fair Annie of the Lockroyan, The Foreign Lands, He's Gone Away to Stay a Little While, I Go Away, I Truly Understand, I Will Bid You a Sad Billet-doux, Last Saturday Night, Lord Gregory, A Lover's Lament, The Mournful Dove, Oh Who Will Shoe Your Bonney Feet, Pretty Little Dear, Storms on the Sea, Sweet Annie of Rock Royal, Sweet Wine, Ten Thousand Miles, Who Will Shoe My Little Feet?, Who Will Shoe Your Feet, Winter's Night, Wish I'd Never Been Born.

Texts: Story Type A: Combs, *Fsgs So US*, 118–121 / Gainer, *Flks Sgs West Va Hills*, 47–50.

B: Boette, *Singa Hipsy Doodle*, 67 / Burton & Manning, *E Tenn State U Coll Flklre: Fsgs*, 108 / Bush, *Flk Sgs Cntrl West Va*, II, 102–103 / Emrich, *Am Flk Ptry*, 96–97, 97–98 / Gainer, *Flk Sgs West Va Hills*, 131–132 / Jameson, *Sweet Rivers Sg*, 62 / Justus, *Complete Peddler's Pack*, 24–25 / *Ky Flklre Record*, 1973, 15–16 / Moore & Moore, *Blds & Flk Sgs SW*, 59–60 (A) / *Sing Out!*, XVIII, 6 (1969), 21 / Watson, *Sgs Doc Watson*, 51–52.

D: *SFQ*, 1965, 182–183.

E: The Type A story is told, but without the dialogue between Annie and Gregory about their former exchange of love tokens. The distinguishing feature of this type, however, is that it includes the episode during her voyage in which she meets a band of robbers on the high seas. They question her as to her identity and eventually direct her to her lover's dwelling. Ritchie, *Flk Sgs So Aplchns*, 84–85.

F: The story begins with Gregory telling his mother of his dream: his love was at the gate seeking entrance. The mother replies that it did indeed happen just "an hour and a half ago." He reviles her, mounts a horse, and rides till he comes to Lochland Lane, where he finds his love dead. There is a note in her bosom reminding him of their exchange of love tokens, of her fidelity, and his falseness, and prophesying that he will die on the following day. They are buried close by and there is a rose-briar motif. Fowke, *Trd Sngrs & Sgs Ont*, 106–107 / *MWF*, 1963, 138–139.

Fragments & Title Lists: Brown, *NC Flklre*, IV, 47–48 / Moore & Moore, *Blds & Flk Sgs SW*, 60–61 (B) / Rosenberg, *Fsgs Va*, 67–68.

Discussion: The recently published versions of 76 which exemplify the two new Story Types E and F are significantly different from the more common North American tradition of Type A. The Type A texts are closest to the Child D tradition, while the two new Type F texts (both from the same informant) approximate Child A most closely (cf. discussion in BTBNA, p. 75). Three aspects of this Type F which contribute to its uniqueness on this continent should be noted: it does not contain the usual introductory episode of Annie's journey to Gregory's home and her conversation with his mother; it features the motif of the heroine communicating with her lover in a note, not found in any other version of the ballad from either the Old or New World, through reminiscent of the common "Butcher Boy" (Laws P24), "Riley's Farewell" (Laws M8), and "Sailor's Tragedy" (Laws P34A); it does not have the ubiquitous "shoe-your-foot" stanzas. See Fowke's comments in *Trd Sngrs & Sgs Ont*, pp. 185–186.

The text which exemplifies the other new story, Type E, is also unique in American tradition in its inclusion of the episode in which Annie meets the robbers while on her journey. In this it is closest to Child B and F, and to a lesser extent Child A, but textually it is so much like the Scott version printed in Child IV, 471–474, that it might be considered directly descended from that particular text of the "Lass of Lochroyan" tradition.

All "shoe-your-foot" lyric texts are referenced above under Story Type B, but the Bush, *Flk Sgs Cntrl West Va*, and Jameson, *Sweet Rivers Sg*, texts deserve special mention: they each contain two narrative stanzas which, while ballad-commonplace ones, may show closer connections with the fuller 76 story than do the myriad other "shoe-your-foot" songs (cf. Story Type D).

77. SWEET WILLIAM'S GHOST

Texts: *Story Type* A: Karpeles, *Flk Sgs Newfdld* (1971), 50–51 (A).

B: Karpeles, *Flk Sgs Newfdld* (1971), 52–54 (B) / Peacock, *Sgs Newfdld Outpts*, II, 390–392 (A).

Fragments & Title Lists: Brown, *NC Flklre*, IV, 48 / Karpeles, *Flk Sgs*

Newfdld (1971), 54–57 (C–I) / Peacock, *Sgs Newfdld Outpts*, II, 393–395 (B–F).

Discussion: Note that the Peacock, *Sgs Newfdld Outpts*, Type B text is an editorial composite of four local versions. The nature of the collation is indicated to a certain extent (II, 392). For remarks on the crossing of this with other ballads of similar import, see discussions to 74 and 248 in this Supplement. See also Hugh Shields, "The Dead Lover's Return in Modern English Ballad Tradition," *Jahrbuch für Volksliedforschung*, 17 (1972), 105–106, which extends to an even greater extent the range of this ballad's influence on others in British and American tradition.

78. THE UNQUIET GRAVE

Local Titles: Cold Falling Drops of Dew.

Texts: *Story Type* A: Karpeles, *Flk Sgs Newfdld* (1971), 58–59 / Peacock, *Sgs Newfdld Outpts*, II, 412–413 (B).

B: Peacock, *Sgs Newfdld Outpts*, II, 410–411 (A) / Ritchie, *Flk Sgs So Aplchns*, 64.

Discussion: There is little substantive variation among texts of this ballad, which is in keeping with its general simplicity and internal cohesiveness. Two of the versions cited above, however, have elements which, while not unparalleled elsewhere, are not common. The first of these is the Karpeles, *Flk Sgs Newfdld* (1971), Type A text which ends with a reference to the lovers sailing away on board a ship, found in only two other versions—Child D (from Buchan's MSS), in which the mourner only is to set sail, and a Baring-Gould MS text (see Bronson, II, 235–236 [#3]), in which it is the mourned who will do the sailing. The second unusual feature is in the Peacock, *Sgs Newfdld Outpts*, Type B text (an editorial composite of two closely related variants) where the dead girl sets her mourning lover some impossible tasks similar to Child 2 and 46 —also paralleled in British texts of 78 (see Bronson, II, 235–238 [#3, #10, #12, #14], 244–245 [#41]; Child H). These enigmatic elements may be due to the metaphorical nature of much of this ballad, apropos of which see George Griffith, " 'The Unquiet Grave,' " *SFQ*, 31 (1967), 314–319.

79. THE WIFE OF USHER'S WELL

Local Titles: A Knight and a Lady Bride, The Lady from the North Country, The Lady's Dream, Little Lady Gay, Mary Hebrew, The Miracle of Usher's Well.

Texts: *Story Type* A: Abrahams, *Singr & Her Sgs*, 114–116 / Emrich,

Am Flk Ptry, 291–292 / Fowke & Johnston, *More Flk Sgs Can*, 24–25 / Gainer, *Flk Sgs West Va Hills*, 51–52 / Moore & Moore, *Blds & Flk Sgs SW*, 61–62 (A) / *NC Flklre*, 1969, 57–58 / Parler, *Ark Ballet Bk*, 38 / Ritchie, *Flk Sgs So Aplchns*, 75 / *Sing Out!*, XVIII, 4 (1968), 21.

Fragments & Title Lists: Bronson, IV, 474 (#7.1) / Brown, *NC Flklre*, IV, 48–52 / Combs, *Fsgs So US*, 204 (Story Type A) / *JEMF Quarterly*, IX, 2 (1973), 58 / Moore & Moore, *Blds & Flk Sgs SW*, 62–63 (B) / Rosenberg, *Fsgs Va*, 137.

Discussion: The Ritchie, *Flk Sgs So Aplchns*, version deserves special mention because it is not the usual North American Child D form but rather is a close textual relative of Child A. The only other North American version of Child 79 in this textual tradition is the Flanders, *Ancient Blds*, II, A copy (see *BTBNA*, p. 79); that New England version, however, clearly has as its immediate source some publication or other of the Child text (from Scott's *Minstrelsy*). These two are the only North American texts which specify Martinmas as the time of the sons' return, but the Ritchie version has less obvious analogues with Child A than does the Flanders, especially in its lack of the esoteric motif of birch hats gleaned from the woods at the gates of Paradise.

Ben Gray Lumpkin analyzes unusual features of the *NC Flklre*, 1969, version on pp. 56–60. Also noteworthy is the singer's exegesis on her understanding of the song in Abrahams, *Sngr & Her Sgs*, p. 116: she rejects the interpretation that the sons return as ghosts; they return in their mother's dreams.

Of some interest is Daniel McDonald, "The Baleful Wife of Usher's Well," *Ball State Teachers College Forum*, V, 2 (1964), 39–42, which subjects Child A to interpretation and concludes that the mother's character is a dominant cause in the tragic events (cf. Story Type B).

81. LITTLE MUSGRAVE AND LADY BARNARD

Local Titles: (Little) Mathey (Mathie, Matthy, Matty) Gove (Grones, Gross, Groves, Moscrow), Little Mathigrew, Little Musgrove and Lady Barnard, Lord Thomas (Vanners).

Texts: Story Type A: Gainer, *Flk Sgs West Va Hills*, 53–56 / Manny & Wilson, *Sgs Miramichi*, 204–205 / Moore & Moore, *Blds & Flk Sgs SW*, 64–68 (B) / Ritchie, *Flk Sgs So Aplchns*, 36–38 / *Sing Out!*, XIX, 5 (1970), 22–24.

B: Creighton, *Flklre Lunenburg Cnty*, 79 / Karpeles, *Flk Sgs Newfdld* (1971), 63–66 (B) / Peacock, *Sgs Newfdld Outpts*, II, 613–616 (A).

C: Roberts, *Sang Branch Settlers*, 92–94 / Watson, *Sgs Doc Watson*, 43–45.

D: The story is that of Type B except for the beginning: it is Lord Dannel who attends church one holiday where the news of his wife's infidelity is then delivered to him by his post boy. Karpeles, *Flk Sgs Newfdld* (1971), 60–62 (A).

Fragments & Title Lists: Brown, *NC Flklre*, IV, 53–57 / Combs, *Fsgs So US*, 204 (Story Type C) / *Ky Flklre Record*, 1965, 65 / Moore & Moore, *Blds & Flk Sgs SW*, 63–64 (A) / *MWF*, 1963, 135 / Peacock, *Sgs Newfdld Outpts*, II, 616 (B) / Rosenberg, *Fsgs Va*, 71 / *SFQ*, 1967, 328.

Discussion: Randolph's remarks on the "dirty" label some of his southern singers attached to this ballad (see *BTBNA*, p. 81; for additional evidence, see Roger D. Abrahams, "Creativity, Individuality, and the Traditional Singer," *Studies Literary Imagination*, 3 [1970], 9) are echoed by Manny & Wilson, *Sgs Miramichi*, p. 205, of New Brunswick singers. It is conceivable that this might be, in part, responsible for its considerable popularity on this continent; yet it is curious that such a dramatic and sensational piece should be so widespread in North American folk tradition while evidently being long forgotten in Great Britain (with the exception of Jeannie Robertson's version; see Bronson, IV, 474–476 [#29.1]). It may be that it is the very combination of the sensational transgression and the equally sensational punishment which holds such strong attraction for our singers, though in the Roberts, *Sang Branch Settlers*, Type C version this punishment is mitigated somewhat in that the husband does not murder his wife. In the *Sing Out!*, 1970, Type A text, on the other hand, he does render a uniquely modern revenge by placing "a special against her head" and discharging "a special ball."

The reticence of New Brunswick singers to perform the ballad for Manny may have resulted in some folk expurgation: in her *Sgs Miramichi* Type A text the details of the lovers' sport are somewhat slighted, though the additional absence of any mention of the foot page may indicate simply a more condensed version.

Interesting variations in both of Karpeles' *Flk Sgs Newfdld* (1971) texts may also be indebted to a certain extent to folk sensibility. In her Story Type B version the initial meeting and adulterous arrangement take place in "the play-house," where Matthy Groves has gone to hear some "funny words." While the nature of such a scene is analogous to that of a ball, or even playing at the ball—both of which are common in the early British and, on this continent, northern traditions—it has no exact counterpart in other texts; it is certainly more fitting to the licentious nature of the liaison than a church. Similarly, in Karpeles' A text, which exemplifies the new Story Type D, it is not the lovers but Lord Dannel who goes to church, which milieu is more suitable to the character who represents whatever moral center there is in the drama than it is to the adulterers.

84. BONNY BARBARA ALLEN

Local Titles: Barbary (Barbra, Barbro, Barb'ry) Allan (Allen), Barbery (Barbre, Barbro, Barbue) Ellen, Barbry Alone (Ella), John Graham (Sir John Greheme) and Barbara Allen. (See also the article by Ed Cray cited in the discussion below.)

Texts: Story Type A: Abrahams, *Sngr & Her Sgs*, 87–89 / Brown, *NC Flklre*, IV, 62–63, 68–69 / Burton & Manning, *E Tenn State U Coll Flklre: Fsgs*, 74–76 / Bush, *Flk Sgs Cntrl West Va*, I, 72–74 / Emrich, *Flklre Am Land*, 572–574 / *Flklre Forum*, 1974, 13–14 / Gainer, *Flk Sgs West Va Hills*, 57–58 / Jameson, *Sweet Rivers Sg*, 48–50 / *Mt Life & Work*, XL, 4 (1964), 20–22 / Peacock, *Sgs Newfdld Outpts*, III, 654–655 (B) / Ritchie, *Flk Sgs So Aplchns*, 79.

B: Boette, *Singa Hipsy Doodle*, 3 / Brown, *NC Flklre*, IV, 65–67 / Burton & Manning, *E Tenn State U Coll Flklre: Fsgs*, 7–8, 57–58 / Burton & Manning, *E Tenn State U Coll Flklre: Fsgs II*, 28–29 / Carey, *Md Flk Lgds & Flk Sgs*, 98 / *Colorado Fsg Bull*, 1964, 47 / Fowke, *Trd Sngrs & Sgs Ont*, 60–61 / Fowke & Johnston, *More Flk Sgs Can*, 20–21 / Joyner, *Flk Sg SC*, 45–46 / Killion & Waller, *Treasury Ga Flklre*, 255 / Moore & Moore, *Blds & Flk Sgs SW*, 68–70 / *NYFQ*, 1964, 48–50.

F: Peacock, *Sgs Newfdld Outpts*, III, 652–653 (A), 658–659 (D).

K: Somewhat in the spirit of Type J, this version begins with a tavern scene in which the lover dances "to" all the ladies until Barbery Ellen is slighted. This slighting results in his getting ill, at which point she visits his sickbed (unsummoned) and the story proceeds in the usual fashion, with the Type C feature that he acknowledges his guilt. Sweeney, *Fct Fctn & Flklre So Ind*, 59–61.

L: The usual Type A story is told, but there is no confrontation between the lovers or deathbed scene because she does not obey his summons to visit. She tells the servant that she knows his master is ill and dying; then as she goes through the fields she hears the accusing notes of the death bell and the birds' song. The rest of the story is the normal Type A. Burton & Manning, *E Tenn State U Coll Flklre: Fsgs*, 41–42.

M: The Type B story is told with the Type G feature that she blames her mother for causing the tragedy, and the mother joins the lovers in death. Its unique feature, however, is that when she encounters the corpse it is as active as any ballad revenant: she asks that it lie down so she may look upon it, and the corpse replies that it cannot lie down to save her and will not let her gaze at it. Roberts, *Sang Branch Settlers*, 95–96.

Fragments & Title Lists: Brown, *NC Flklre*, IV, 57–62, 64–65, 67, 69 / Burton & Manning, *E Tenn State U Coll Flklre: Fsgs*, 39, 51–52, 85 /

Combs, *Fsgs So US*, 204 / Fowke, *Trd Sngrs & Sgs Ont*, 100 / *JEMF Quarterly*, IX, 2 (1973), 58–59 / *Ky Flklre Record*, 1965, 65 / *MWF*, 1963, 136 / *NYFQ*, 1967, 121–122 / Peacock, *Sgs Newfdld Outpts*, III, 656–657 (C), 660 (E, F) / Rosenberg, *Fsgs Va*, 9–10 / *WF*, 1968, 93–94.

Discussion: The new Story Type L is unusual in that it does not contain the deathbed exchange between the two lovers, an affecting episode which one would expect to be attractive to traditional singers. Her realization of guilt, her repentance, and the twin deaths appear to constitute the emotional core of this version.

The Type M text, from the Kentucky mountains, is unique in this ballad's tradition (and in the traditions of the somewhat similar 75 and 85 as well) in having the corpse speak. This would seem to be a logical enough action since here, as in many other versions, she addresses the corpse directly rather than conveying her remarks to the pallbearers. Still, while walking and talking corpses are of course no strangers to traditional ballads, this kind of supernatural interpolation is contrary to what we commonly think to be normal to the course of more modern tradition (though, on this point, see Vargyas' analysis of the European tradition of Child 4, cited in the discussion to that ballad, as well as the discussion to 248 in this Supplement).

The distinguishing episode of the Type G story—the accusation against the parents of having had a hand in the abortive love affair—appears in only a few versions in North American tradition and not at all in British. It is probably a later addition, due to association with "parental opposition to lovers" themes perhaps, or, more functionally, it may be an attempt to mitigate Barbara's responsibility for the unfortunate course of events, somewhat in the manner of John Snead's version discussed by Leach in *The Ballad Book*, p. 31. On the other hand, it may conceivably be a trace of an even earlier story type than those known to us from Child's sources, as may the talking corpse of Type M. In the Killion & Waller, *Treasury Ga Flklre*, Type B text the mother follows the lovers to death as in Type G, though here she has not been accused of any wrongdoing. The characters are reversed in the Peacock, *Sgs Newfdld Outpts*, (A) Type F text to the extent that it is the parents who are the moral voices and cry shame on their daughter's head.

The two studies cited in *BTBNA*, p. 85, as in-process have since been published: Charles Seeger, "Versions and Variants of the Tunes of 'Barbara Allen,'" *Selected Reports*, I, 1 (1966), 120–163, is a musicological study, and Ed Cray, "'Barbara Allen': Cheap Print and Reprint," in Wilgus, *Flklre International*, pp. 41–50, is primarily a bibliography of broadsides, songsters, and periodicals, both British and American, which contained texts of the ballad.

Peacock, *Sgs Newfdld Outpts*, III, presents a text on pp. 649–651 which is an editorial composite for singing purposes; it has not been included in the references above, although a similar collation in Bush, *Flk Sgs Cntrl West Va*, I (Story Type A), has been cited. The Emrich, *Flklre Am Land*, Type A text as published also has two stanzas from another source interpolated by the editor, which I have not taken into account. With the editorial additions the text is Story Type B rather than A.

The *NYFQ*, 1964, Type B text is reprinted from an 1850 issue of *The Spirit of the Times* and is, as the contributor notes, substantially Percy's (Child Ab) and no doubt not from American oral tradition. Fowke's *Trd Sngrs & Sgs Ont*, Type B text (the same as in Fowke & Johnston, *More Flk Sgs Can*) is close enough to child Aa to cause the editor to remark that "someone in the oral chain must have seen a printed text" (p. 173).

85. LADY ALICE

Local Titles: George Giles, Lady Alice, One Cold December Day, Young Collins Green.

Texts: Story Type A: Boette, *Singa Hipsy Doodle*, 20–21 / Gainer, *Flk Sgs West Va Hills*, 59–60 / Karpeles, *Flk Sgs Newfdld* (1971), 67–68.

B: Burton & Manning, *E Tenn State U Coll Flklre: Fsgs II*, 17–18, 73–74 / Cohen & Seeger, *New Lost City Ramblers Sg Bk*, 48 / Emrich, *Am Flk Ptry*, 296–297 (A) / Jackson, *Flklre & Society*, 116–117 / Joyner, *Flk Sg SC*, 40 / Killion & Waller, *Treasury Ga Flklre*, 256–257 / Moore & Moore, *Blds & Flk Sgs SW*, 71–72 / *Sing Out!*, XVI, 2 (1966), 7.

C: Peacock, *Sgs Newfdld Outpts*, III, 738–739.

Fragments & Title Lists: Brown, *NC Flklre*, IV, 69–74 / Combs, *Fsgs So US*, 204 (Story Types A and C) / *JEMF Quarterly*, IX, 2 (1973), 59–60 / Rosenberg, *Fsgs Va*, 66.

Discussion: The Boette, *Singa Hipsy Doodle*, and Gainer, *Flk Sgs West Va Hills*, texts (both Story Type A examples and both from West Virginia) present the "washer at the ford" and the girl Ellen as the same figure, a fusion not uncommon in the North American tradition of this ballad that has been ascribed to rationalization of the supernatural (*BTBNA*, p. 87).

The text in Jackson, *Flklre & Society* (Type B), transcribed from the singing of Dick Justice and given in an article by Judith McCulloh, "Some Child Ballads on Hillbilly Records," pp. 107–129, has only three stanzas that are clearly related to the usual Child 85 ballad; the rest is normally associated with the lyric portions of the native American ballad "The Dying Hobo" (Laws H3). This amalgamation is paralleled—though to a lesser extent—in another hillbilly recording of Child 85 by Kelly Harrell (see Bronson, II, 402 [#30]).

87. PRINCE ROBERT

Texts: *Story Type* A: Combs, *Fsgs So US*, 121–123 / Gainer, *Flk Sgs West Va Hills*, 61–62.

Discussion: The Gainer version is only the second reporting of a full text of "Prince Robert" in North American tradition. It is from the singing of a Mrs. Nan Wilson of Nicholas County, West Virginia. The only previously reported version, in Combs, was from the singing of F. C. Gainer (p. 204), who was doubtless Francis C. Gainer, the grandfather of the collector of the Nan Wilson version (see Gainer, p. xiii). The two versions are textually so similar it would seem likely that one of the informants learned it from the other. Cf. discussion to 240 in this Supplement.

92. BONNY BEE HOM

Add to the references for texts of the related "Lowlands of Holland" ballad: Burton & Manning, *E Tenn State U Coll Flklre: Fsgs*, 101–102; Bush, *Flk Sgs Cntrl West Va*, II, 88–89; Emrich, *Am Flk Ptry*, 147–148; Emrich, *Flklre Am Land*, 570–571; Grover, *Hrtge Sgs*, 50. (The last three texts are from the same informant.)

93. LAMKIN

Local Titles: Beaulampkins, Bolakins, Bold Lamkin.

Texts: *Story Type* A: Emrich, *Am Flk Ptry*, 301–302 / Karpeles, *Flk Sgs Newfdld* (1971), 69–71 (A) / Moore & Moore, *Blds & Flk Sgs SW*, 72–74 / Peacock, *Sgs Newfdld Outpts*, III, 806–807 / *Sing Out!*, XVI, 1 (1966), 23.

E: Bolakin builds a castle for a lord and is not paid for his work. He comes to the castle gate where the lord's child is at play and abducts the boy. The child's dead body is later found by the road, but Bolakin is never seen again, and "he's alive to this day, they say." Gainer, *Flk Sgs West Va Hills*, 63.

Fragments & Title Lists: Brown, *NC Flklre*, IV, 74–76 / Combs, *Fsgs So US*, 204 (Story Type A) / Karpeles, *Flk Sgs Newfdld* (1971), 71–72 (B–D).

Discussion: The example of the new Story Type E is only three stanzas long but tells a complete story. We know that "Lamkin" has been used as a nursery rhyme in Great Britain (see p. 7 of the Gilchrist article cited in *BTBNA*, p. 91, and Child, II, 321), and it is possible that this version served a similar function, judging by its brevity and the implications of the last line, quoted in the description above.

The Karpeles, *Flk Sgs Newfdld* (1971), Type A text has the unusual feature that the lady offers Lamkin not her daughter but the nurse(!), which may be a change motivated by the distaste for the idea of a mother offering her daughter to the clutches of such a villain in order to save her own life.

95. THE MAID FREED FROM THE GALLOWS

Local Titles: The Hangman, Hangman Hangman (Hold Your Holts), Hangman (Hangman) Slack the (Your) Rope, Hangman Oh Hangman, Hangman on the Gallows Tree, (The) Hangman Song (Tree), The Highwayman, Hold up Your Hand, Joshua, My Golden Ball, The Raspel Pole, Ropesman, Rop'ry. (See also the monograph by Long, cited below.)

Texts: Story Type A: Boette, *Singa Hipsy Doodle*, 15–16 / Burton & Manning, *E Tenn State U Coll Flklre: Fsgs*, 85–87 / Gainer, *Flk Sgs West Va Hills*, 64–65 / Moore & Moore, *Blds & Flk Sgs SW*, 75–76 (A) / Sweeney, *Fct Fctn & Flklre So Ind*, 143–144.

B: Bronson, IV, 480–481 (#39.1) / McIntosh, *Flk Sgs & Sgng Games Ill Ozarks*, 39–41.

C: Abrahams, *Sngr & Her Sgs*, 110–111 / Abrahams & Foss, *Anglo-Am Fsg Style*, 41–42 / Ritchie, *Flk Sgs So Aplchns*, 33 / Roberts, *Sang Branch Settlers*, 96–97.

D: Coffin reported in *BTBNA* a colleague's recollection of a version of Child 95 in which the accused was hanged as the only example of this story type. Kenneth S. Goldstein, "The Ballad Scholar and the Long-Playing Record," in Jackson, *Flklre & Society*, pp. 38–39, draws attention to such a version recorded on Folkways FH 5723 by a traditional singer, Harry Jackson. Eleanor Long, *"The Maid" and "The Hangman,"* also reports having discovered several examples of this story type (p. 12), and in Brown, *NC Flklre*, IV, 78, the editor states in the notes to tune N that, in the text, "neither sweetheart nor father brings gold." The full text is not given.

G: *SFQ*, 1965, 179–181.

Fragments & Title Lists: Brown, *NC Flklre*, IV, 76–81 / Combs, *Fsgs So US*, 205 (Story Type A) / *JEMF Quarterly*, IX, 2 (1973), 60 / *Ky Flklre Record*, 1965, 65 / Moore & Moore, *Blds & Flk Sgs SW*, 76 (B) / Rosenberg, *Fsgs Va*, 78.

Discussion: Studies which bear on Child 95 in varying degrees may be cited: Dan Ben-Amos, "The Situation Structure of the Non-Humorous

English Ballad," *MWF*, 13 (1963), 163–176, subjects a normal form to sociological interpretation; Tristram Potter Coffin, "The Golden Ball and the Hangman's Tree," in Jackson, *Flkre & Society*, pp. 23–28, suggests a forgotten significance to the "golden ball" object and its influence on certain variations the ballad often exhibits in tradition; and Ingeborg Urcia, "The Gallows and the Golden Ball," *JAF*, 79 (1966), 463–468, presents a more story-oriented analysis while also searching for obscured motives that lay behind earlier forms. None of these three bear to any great extent on the matter of the North American textual tradition of the ballad.

These studies, as well as any others which touch on Child 95 to any extent, must be evaluated in the light of Eleanor Long's exhaustive analysis of primarily British and American traditions of this ballad in *"The Maid" and "The Hangman."* Among her findings are that (1) while the male sex of the victim is both the earlier form and the most common in tradition, whether male or female depends on regional preferences and in any event is frequently not of much relevance to the singers; (2) the narratives in cante-fables forms were later additions to an already existing traditional ballad of the basic 95 model of plea to an executioner and appeal for ransom; (3) any symbolic relationship between golden balls and sexuality was not a feature of Western European traditional literature, belief, or custom; golden ball elements were later additions to the ballad and probably came from printed, mass-culture forms; (4) the ballad was probably first introduced into English tradition in the last half of the seventeenth century by gypsies. There is much more; see also her bibliography of scholarly studies, of published and unpublished texts, and her discography.

See McIntosh, *Flk Sgs & Sgng Games Ill Ozarks*, p. 32, for an informant's recounting of the "Golden Ball" legend often associated with this ballad but here with the male in the role of transgressor (cf. Story Type C).

99. JOHNIE SCOT

Local Titles: Young Johnny Scott.

Texts: Story Type A: *SFQ*, 1965, 183–184.

C: The basic Type A story, minus several extraneous features, is told up to the point when Johnny defeats the king's champion. King Edward then calls for any knight to rescue his daughter; Johnny counters by calling for a priest to wed them. He will take his bride back to Ireland with him, despite the king's wishes. Moore & Moore, *Blds & Flk Sgs SW*, 78–80.

Discussion: For the most part, this ballad varies little in both its Old and New World traditions, and the new Type C story is no great exception to this. The text which tells this story, from Moore & Moore, *Blds & Flk Sgs SW*, has far more of the popular style than does the Barry, *Brit Blds Me*, (A) version (the prototype of the fuller A story type); it also lacks several elements that are tangential to the main narrative, but at no detriment to the ballad as a whole. It is this Oklahoma version's very similarity to the Scots textual tradition that is at the root of its unique characteristic and its status as a distinct story type, in fact: in most Scots versions the king calls for a clerk to set the "tocher fee"—i.e., the dowry of his daughter in the marriage to which he has finally assented. In the Moore & Moore text, however, this no doubt unintelligible phrase has been Anglicized to "daughter free," and the clerk has been transformed to a knight to preserve the logic of this new plea.

100. WILLIE O WINSBURY

Texts: Story Type A: Combs, *Fsgs So US*, 123–124 / Karpeles, *Flk Sgs Newfdld* (1971), 73–76 (A, B) / Peacock, *Sgs Newfdld Outpts*, II, 534–535 (A).

Fragments & Title Lists: Karpeles, *Flk Sgs Newfdld* (1971), 77 (C, D) / Peacock, *Sgs Newfdld Outpts*, II, 536 (B).

102. WILLIE AND EARL RICHARD'S DAUGHTER

Local Titles: The Birth of Robin Hood.

Fragments & Title Lists: Rosenberg, *Fsgs Va*, 140.

105. THE BAILIFF'S DAUGHTER OF ISLINGTON

Local Titles: The Bailey Daughter (Dear) of Hazelentown.

Texts: Story Type A: Burton & Manning, *E Tenn State U Coll Flklre: Fsgs*, 100–101 / Gainer, *Flk Sgs West Va Hills*, 66–67 / Karpeles, *Flk Sgs Newfdld* (1971), 78–79 / Moore & Moore, *Blds & Flk Sgs SW*, 80–81 / *Phil Papers*, 1966, 70–72.

Discussion: The *Phil Papers*, 1966, text is given in an article by Patrick W. Gainer, "The Bailiff's Daughter of Islington," pp. 70–75. The version, from a long family tradition, is in the author's opinion a very old one and quite removed from the influence of print. His analysis should be consulted.

The Karpeles, *Flk Sgs Newfdld* (1971), text is a shortened version that lacks the initial episodes of unrequited love and the departure of the youth. When the lovers do eventually meet, there is a recognition motif, not usually found in this ballad (though see Flanders, *Cntry Sgs Vt*, pp. 6–7); in this particular case he recognizes her by "the private mark she had on her hand." (For a similar motif see Laws K18, "Scarboro Sand.")

The Moore & Moore, *Blds & Flk Sgs SW*, text is from an informant who was born in England, but it does not differ substantially from other North American versions. See the discussion to 199 in this Supplement.

106. THE FAMOUS FLOWER OF SERVING-MEN

Local Titles: The Lady Turned Serving Man, Lament of a Border Widow.

Texts: Story Type B: A man builds his love a bower. It is discovered by a stranger who fetches the king, and the bower is broken and the lover killed. The bereaved girl buries her lover's body, laments both their fates, and vows never to love again. Moore & Moore, *Blds & Flk Sgs SW*, 83–84.

Fragments & Title Lists: Rosenberg, *Fsgs Va*, 34.

Discussion: The Oklahoma text which provides the new Story Type B was given by a Scottish emigrant. It is almost exactly the version from Scott's *Minstrelsy* given in Child's headnote, II, 429–430.

110. THE KNIGHT AND THE SHEPHERD'S DAUGHTER

Local Titles: The Shepherd's Daughter, Sir William.

Texts: Story Type A: Huntington, *Sgs Whalemen Sang*, 185–186.

B: Peacock, *Sgs Newfdld Outpts*, I, 230–232.

112. THE BAFFLED KNIGHT

Local Titles: The Foolish Shepherd, A Man and a Maid, On the Banks of Salee.

Texts: Story Type B: Creighton, *Flklre Lunenburg Cnty*, 80–81 / *JAF*, 1972, 178–179 / Peacock, *Sgs Newfdld Outpts*, I, 272–275 (A, B).

C: This story combines the introductory episode of Type A, in which the couple meet while out riding, with the fuller story of Type B that comprises the trickery of the maid and the foiling of the attempted seduction, as in the older British texts (e.g., Child A, B). Emrich, *Am Flk Ptry*, 175–176 / Moore & Moore, *Blds & Flk Sgs SW*, 84–86.

Fragments & Title Lists: Bronson, IV, 489 (#6.1) / Karpeles, *Flk Sgs Newfdld* (1971), 80.

Discussion: The new Type C story is simply the fuller form of the highly compressed Story Type A; it is distinguished from Type B chiefly by its initial episode in that the couple meet while on a walk or ride, and not while the maid is swimming naked and defenseless in a stream. The Moore & Moore, *Blds & Flk Sgs SW*, text of the Type C story begins with the couple riding off seeking a suitable place for love-making, but the singer provides a prose explanation of the prefatory situation. This shortened text may stem from folk expurgation, for the informant good-humoredly refers to it as a "dirty little song." The story description of Type C is that of the more complete version in Emrich, *Am Flk Ptry*, from the singing of a Captain Nye of Ohio. It is quite individualistic in its phrasing, though obviously a version of Child 112 (the editor does not include it in his section of Child ballads). It may either be descended from a broadside unknown to us or be a creative reworking by an imaginative singer; the latter seems likely (see the discussion to 278 in this Supplement).

The Peacock, *Sgs Newfdld Outpts*, A text (Story Type B) has the "blow ye winds" chorus which in American tradition is more usually found with the Type A versions. The *JAF*, 1972, Type B copy is of interest because it is a relatively early text, found in a MS compiled during the Revolutionary War, probably by an American privateersman while a prisoner in England.

Other songs from British broadside tradition that exhibit a similar kind of trickery are, besides "Katie Morey" (Laws N24), "Lovely Joan" (see Williams & Lloyd, *Penguin Book of English Folk Songs*, p. 64; not found in America) and "The Maid and the Horse" (see Peacock, *Sgs Newfdld Outpts*, I, 214–215).

114. JOHNIE COCK

Local Titles: James o' Broodies.

Texts: Story Type A: Moore & Moore, *Blds & Flk Sgs SW*, 86–89.

Discussion: The new text, from Oklahoma, differs from the only other American example of Type A (from Davis, *Trd Blds Va*) in several minor respects, the most notable being that the bird-messenger sequence is absent: the poacher dies in the woods after having sent the wounded forester home with the news. This version most closely resembles Child F and the several more recent Scottish recoveries dating from Greig to the present (see the texts in Bronson, III, 3–11). This is to be expected, since the Oklahoma informant was born in the Northeast of Scotland herself and came to the Southwest in 1925 via Canada. However, Keith remarked in his notes to the Greig versions in *Last Leaves* that they all bore such a striking resemblance to the version published in Scott's *Minstrelsy* (a Scott collation) there was little doubt the *Minstrelsy* itself formed the basis for all the Greig texts (p. 92), and the same may be true for this American version. Two central incidents common in the Northeast Scots version have been dropped, however: the extended dialogue between the old man and the foresters as well as the bird-messenger. Despite its Scottish origin, the Oklahoma text has been Americanized to a fair extent and can be characterized as a "first generation" text (see discussion to 199 in this Supplement).

125. ROBIN HOOD AND LITTLE JOHN

Texts: *Story Type* A: *SFQ*, 1972, 21–23.

Discussion: The recent recording of Child 125 is from the sister of the informant who sang the *SFQ*, 1938, version and does not differ significantly from that earlier rendition.

132. THE BOLD PEDLAR AND ROBIN HOOD

Local Titles: Robin Hood, Robin Hood and the Pedlar.

Texts: *Story Type* A: Bronson, III, 43 (#8) / Emrich, *Am Flk Ptry*, 311–313 / Grover, *Hrtge Sgs*, 78–79.

Discussion: The three texts cited above are all from the same informant and follow the texts in Child and *The American Songster* quite closely, with the exception that, as in the Flanders, *Ancient Blds*, III, (B) text, the peddler does battle with only one of the pair of outlaws, though here he fights Robin rather than Little John.

140. ROBIN HOOD RESCUING THREE SQUIRES

Local Titles: The Widow's Three Sons.

Fragments & Title Lists: Brown, *NC Flklre*, IV, 81–82 / Rosenberg, *Fsgs Va*, 107.

155. SIR HUGH or THE JEW'S DAUGHTER

Local Titles: The Duke's Daughter, Fatal Flower Garden, It Mist It Rained, It Rained All Day, It Rained All Day It Rained All Night or

The Minstrel Boy, It Rained It Mist, Jewish Lady, (Little) Sir Hugh, Little Son Hugh, Sonny Hugh, Twas on a Cold and Winter's Day.

Texts: *Story Type* A: Bronson, III, 81 (#12), 86–94 (#27, #29, #31, #33, #35–#37, #40, #41), 102–103 (#64) / Gainer, *Flk Sgs West Va Hills*, 68–69 / *Ind Flklre*, II, 2 (1969), 101–116 (8 texts) / Killion & Waller, *Treasury Ga Flklre*, 258–259 / Moore & Moore, *Blds & Flk Sgs SW*, 89–91 / Parler, *Ark Ballet Bk*, 35–36.

B: Bronson, III, 78–79 (#9), 80 (#10b) / Burton & Manning, *E Tenn State U Coll Flklre: Fsgs*, 1–2 / *NC Flklre*, 1969, 59–60 / *Tenn FLS Bull*, 1965, 45–47.

Fragments & Title Lists: Bronson, III, 83 (#18, #19), 89 (#32), 94 (#42) / Brown, *NC Flklre*, IV, 82–83 / Combs, *Fsgs So US*, 205 (Story Type A) / *JEMF Quarterly*, IX, 2 (1973), 60.

Discussion: Confusion of names is also evident in many of the above texts (cf. *BTBNA*, p. 109), epitomized in the most extreme form in the Burton & Manning, *E Tenn State U Coll Flklre: Fsgs*, Type B copy (the same as in *Tenn FLS Bull*, 1965): the phonetically alike "Jew," "Hugh," and "Dew" have been confused to the extent that the action takes place in the garden of the Dew family and it is "Miss Dew" who murders the boy, himself identified as both "Dew" and "Hugh" at different points in the song. Burton, who presents this text in an article, " 'Sir Hugh' in Sullivan County," *Tenn FLS Bull*, 31 (1965), 42–47, compares it with several traditional versions from North Carolina and suggests that his Tennessee text stems from an "older stock," basing his conclusions on its resemblance to the "less corrupted" Child F (the North Carolina versions more closely resembling Child N).

Ben Gray Lumpkin's notes to the *NC Flklre*, 1969, Type B text raise the possibility of cross-influence between his version and "The Bitter Withy" (cf. Wells, *The Ballad Tree*, p. 185). In the Bronson, III, 102–103 (#64), Type A version the boy is killed in much the same fashion as is the brown girl in 73 and Little Musgrave in 81.

Faith Hippensteel, " 'Sir Hugh': The Hoosier Contribution to the Ballad," *Ind Flklre*, II, 2 (1969), 75–140, discusses oral and written traditions of stories dealing with ritual murder and subjects texts of 155 from both Old and New Worlds to comparative analysis.

162. THE HUNTING OF THE CHEVIOT

Texts: *Story Type* B: Earl Percy goes poaching in Chevy Chase, and when the news of this raid is brought to Earl Douglas the Scots lord vows to prevent it. The two armies meet, the English and Scots earls exchange words, and battle is commenced. It lasts all day, and the English lose almost all their men. Though outnumbered three to one, the Scots are victorious. Moore & Moore, *Blds & Flk Sgs SW*, 91–93.

Discussion: The Moore & Moore version, which was recited by the informant, is textually a much condensed Child B but lacks the Percy-Douglas combat and the catalogue of heroes and their deeds. It does have a final stanza which is not paralleled elsewhere and which makes it a distinct story type, however: the Scots are declared to have been the clear victors. This would favor the argument put forward by David C. Fowler, " 'The Hunting of the Cheviot' and 'The Battle of Otterburn,' " *WF*, 25 (1966), 165–171 (also in his *A Literary History of the Popular Ballad*, pp. 108–114), that 162 was actually pro-Scots and probably the source of 161, "The Battle of Otterburn," which he sees as pro-English. These views are opposed to what Child and most other ballad scholars have considered to be the case. Fowler bases his argument on internal linguistic and metrical evidence, but Bronson, in *WF*, 1969, 280–286, questions Fowler's slighting of the process of oral transmission and thus his conclusions as well.

167. SIR ANDREW BARTON (including 250, HENRY MARTYN)

Local Titles: Andrew Bardan (Bardee, Bataan, Batann), Henry Martin, The Three Brothers.

Texts: Story Type A: Bronson, III, 133–134 (#1).

B: Bronson, III, 135 (#3), 137–138 (#6, #8) / Emrich, *Am Flk Ptry*, 315–317 (A) / Moore & Moore, *Blds & Flk Sgs SW*, 115–117.

C: Bronson, IV, 28 (#5), 38–39 (#35) / Karpeles, *Flk Sgs Newfdld* (1971), 104–106 (B, C).

D: Textually, this is the "Henry Martyn" Type C ballad, but with a significant difference in the story: Henry is killed and his ship sunk by the very first ship he meets and engages. Gainer, *Flk Sgs West Va Hills*, 82–83.

Fragments & Title Lists: Bronson, III, 135–137 (#4, #5a, #7) / Karpeles, *Flk Sgs Newfdld* (1971), 103 (A) / Rosenberg, *Fsgs Va*, 47.

Discussion: The new Type D example, in having the pirate defeated in his first major engagement on stage, resembles 167, "Sir Andrew Barton," though in that respect only; textually, it is the "Henry Martyn" (250) ballad. The Child Aa text of 250 also contains this feature, but it is quite unusual in the whole known tradition of the ballad. Child, in fact, remarked on this incident that it was "not quite in keeping with the rest of the story" (IV, 393) which follows most other versions: despite Henry's death, the merchant ship is sunk and the bad news carried to England.

In the West Virginia version that exemplifies Type D, however, there is no apparent contradiction, since the ballad ends quite logically with Henry dead and his enemy evidently victorious and still afloat.

There is a possibility that this American version is descended from that unusual strain of Child Aa, but it seems more likely that it is an independent remolding, perhaps under the influence of the more common 167 tradition (Story Type A). In Type D, the merchant ship may have become fused with the Lord Admiral's man-of-war, which is normally sent to capture the pirate after he has defeated the merchantman. This fusion is suggested not only by the course of the narrative but also by the description of the vessel—it is "a great and mighty ship." Also at work, of course, may be the unwillingness to let the pirate win any of his battles, or perhaps the influence of other ballads on similar topics in which pirates get the worst of it all along (e.g., Laws K29, K33).

170. THE DEATH OF QUEEN JANE

Local Titles: Queen Sally.

Texts: *Story Type* C: Bronson, III, 147 (#7) / Emrich, *Am Flk Ptry*, 319.

D: Jameson, *Sweet Rivers Sg*, 61.

Discussion: Both examples of the Type C story cited above are trancriptions of the same Library of Congress recording of Bascom Lamar Lunsford, who was also the informant for the Scarborough, *Sgctchr So Mts*, text that exemplifies Story Type C in *BTBNA*.

For some remarks on the relationship between oral and broadside traditions of the Queen Jane episode in balladry, see Holger Nygard, "Ballads and the Middle Ages," *Tennessee Studies in Literature*, 5 (1960), 85–96.

173. MARY HAMILTON

Local Titles: Four Marys.

Texts: *Story Type* A: Abrahams, *Sngr & Her Sgs*, 134–135 / Combs, *Fsgs So US*, 124–126 / Emrich, *Am Flk Ptry*, 319–320 / Emrich, *Flklre Am Land*, 592–594 / Gainer, *Flk Sgs West Va Hills*, 70–71.

B: Creighton, *Fsgs So NB*, 10 / Jameson, *Sweet Rivers Sg*, 54–55 / Moore & Moore, *Blds & Flk Sgs SW*, 94.

Fragments & Title Lists: MWF, 1963, 136 / Rosenberg, *Fsgs Va*, 79.

Discussion: Although the Abrahams, *Sngr & Her Sgs*, text tells the usual Type A story, it contains the unique feature that the baby "was stillborn." As the editor notes (pp. 178–179), this turns up in no other known text of "Mary Hamilton." The informant's remarks on her version, pp. 134–137, are worth studying in detail.

The Jameson, *Sweet Rivers Sg*, Type B lyric version also has an unusual stanza in which the condemned woman wishes she might be buried in the churchyard of her childhood. This whole text is an unusually compressed one and clearly in the tradition of Child BB, the only other version with the aforementioned stanza (which Child called "clearly modern"; but cf. Child 201). See Child, V, 299.

The Emrich, *Am Flk Ptry* and *Flklre Am Land* (both Type A texts), and the Rosenberg, *Fsgs Va*, copies are all from the singing of Texas Gladden; see the note by Scouten in *JAF* cited in *BTBNA*, p. 115. The Moore & Moore, *Blds & Flk Sgs SW*, Type B example is from the singing of an informant born in Edinburgh and is an "emigrant" text (see the discussion to 199 in this Supplement).

Carlos Drake, " 'Mary Hamilton' in Tradition," *SFQ*, 33 (1969), 39–47, presents a synthesis of the scholarship on 173 and surveys its history in tradition and literature, attempting to refine Coffin's concept of the "emotional core" in the process (see the reference in *BTBNA*, p. 115).

181. THE BONNY EARL OF MURRAY

Local Titles: The (Bonny) Earl of Moray.

Texts: Story Type A: Bronson, III, 161 (#6).

Fragments & Title Lists: Brown, *NC Flklre*, IV, 83.

Discussion: The new text in Bronson follows Child's A text closely. It was learned by the singer from "an old Scotchman in Buffalo" and has the diction of an "emigrant" text (see the discussion to 199 in this Supplement).

183. WILLIE MACINTOSH

Local Titles: Willie MacIntosh.

Texts: Story Type A: Moore & Moore, *Blds & Flk Sgs SW*, 95.

Discussion: The Moore & Moore version, recited by the informant (as was the only other text of 183 recovered in America; see *BTBNA*, p. 117), is, in the words of the editors, "almost word for word like Child A Version." The informant was born in Scotland and emigrated to America in 1867. See the discussion to 199 in this Supplement.

188. ARCHIE O CAWFIELD

Fragments & Title Lists: Rosenberg, *Fsgs Va*, 3.

199. THE BONNIE HOUSE O AIRLIE

Local Titles: Bonnie House of Airlie, Lady Ogalbie.

Texts: Story Type A: Moore & Moore, *Blds & Flk Sgs SW*, 96–97.

C: Bronson, III, 192 (#2) / Walker & Welker, *Reality & Myth*, 136.

Discussion: The Moore & Moore, *Blds & Flk Sgs SW*, Type A text follows the first half of the Child A–C versions quite closely but has a most unusual line in which Argyle "has stabbed her dear little babe." The only other version in which the baby is killed is from recent Scots tradition, published in Bronson, III, 196–197 (#14), where it is mentioned that the lady and all her children die in the ruins of the castle. The mother herself does not perish in the Moore & Moore text; it was collected from a lady who was born in Scotland and came to Oklahoma in 1925 from Canada (see below).

The Type C references to Bronson and Walker & Welker are to the same text, collected by Cecil Sharp from a lady in New York. It contains the unusual feature shared by Type C texts, not included in the description of this story type in *BTBNA*: Lady Ogilvie dies after witnessing the destruction of her home. This can be found in only three Old World texts: Child D, in which Argyle himself kills her by throwing her over the castle wall; the Bronson, III, 196–197 (#14), text cited above, in which she perishes along with her children in the ruins; and a Scottish version from the singing of Ewan MacColl (see Bronson, III, 193–194 [#7]). This last is closest to the American variant in that she lies down on the hill to die after witnessing the plunder.

The New York text is given in an article by Herschel Gower, "The Scottish Palimpsest in Traditional Ballads Collected in North America," Walker & Welker, pp. 117–144, in which he makes some useful distinctions between "emigrant" texts, which are copies that have "come recently to America on the lips of an emigrant and which still . . . [retain] Scottish diction and . . . native idiom" (p. 133); "first generation" texts, which display formal characteristics that are partly Old World and partly New, usually traceable to British-born sources; and texts that have been acclimatized to their new environment. He considers this New York version to be in the second category. For related concerns, see Tristram Potter Coffin, "American Balladry: The Term and the Canon," *Keystone Folklore*, 19 (1974), 3–10. See also the discussion to 3 in this Supplement.

The poem credited to an Illinois high school student discussed in *BTBNA*, p. 119, contains traditional elements beyond simply the stanzas incorporated from 199: Katharine M. Briggs has communicated to Coffin an excerpt from *Thatched with Gold: The Memoirs of Mabell Countess of Airlie* (1962) that mentions the legend of Airlie's drummer (pp. 47, 92), though it is not quite the same story as that presented in the student's poem.

200. THE GYPSY LADDIE

Local Titles: Amos Furr, Black Jack Davy Came a-Riding O'er the Plain, Black Jack Davy or Raggle-Taggle Gypsy, Black Jack Gypsy, David, The Davy, The Egyptian Davy O, Egyptian Laddie, Gipson Daisy, Gipsy Draly, Gyps of David, Gypsum Davy, The Gypsy Boy, Gypsy Laddie-O, The Gypsy Lady, I'm Seventeen Come Sunday, The Radical Gypsy David, Seven Gypsies (on Yon Hill), There's Some Gypsies in This Land, William Davey, The Wraggle Taggle Gypsies O.

Texts: Story Type A: Abrahams, *Sngr & Her Sgs*, 26–28 / Abrahams & Foss, *Anglo-Am Fsg Style*, 181–184 (#9–5, #9–6, #9–7) / Bronson, III, 204–205 (#8), 209–213 (#19, #22, #24, #27, #29), 230–231 (#81–#83), 239–240 (#105), 244–245 (#116) / Combs, *Fsgs So US*, 206–207 (B) / Creighton, *Fsgs So NB*, 12 / Emrich, *Am Flk Ptry*, 323–324 / Fowke, *Trd Sngrs & Sgs Ont*, 18–19 / Fowke & Johnston, *More Flk Sgs Can*, 22–23 / Gainer, *Flk Sgs West Va Hills*, 72–73 / Grover, *Hrtge Sgs*, 116–117 / Karpeles, *Flk Sgs Newfdld* (1971), 81 (A) / Lomax, *Penguin Bk Am Flk Sgs*, 112 / Moore & Moore, *Blds & Flk Sgs SW*, 97–100 / Parler, *Ark Ballet Bk*, 5–6 / Peacock, *Sgs Newfdld Outpts*, I, 196–197 (B) / Scott, *Settlers Estn Shore*, 188–189 / *SFQ*, 1965, 184–186 / Shellans, *Flk Sgs Blue Ridge Mts*, 36–37 / *Tenn FLS Bull*, 1964, 2–3 / Warner, *Flk Sgs & Blds Estn Sbrd*, 6–7.

B: Bronson, III, 213–214 (#30).

C: Bronson, III, 216–217 (#38) / Ritchie, *Flk Sgs So Aplchns*, 86.

E: Bronson, III, 208–209 (#16, #18).

H: Bronson, III, 204 (#7), 217 (#39), 245–246 (#117, #120) / Burton & Manning, *E Tenn State U Coll Flklre: Fsgs*, 97–98 / Dunson & Raim, *Anth Am Flk Music*, 108–109 / Jackson, *Flklre & Society*, 110–111.

I: Bronson, III, 236 (#96).

K: The usual story is told with the major exception that the husband does not appear. Black Jack Davy convinces the lady to leave her home and her lover to go with him. She consents, and they ride off together. She contrasts her present life with her past one. Bronson, III, 237–238 (#101, #102) / Parler, *Ark Ballet Bk*, 7.

L: The story is as Type A with the addition of a new figure: while in pursuit of the runaway lovers, the husband meets and is given directions on their whereabouts by an old man or "old farmer." Bronson, III, 221 (#52) / Karpeles, *Flk Sgs Newfdld* (1971), 82–84 (B, E) / Peacock, *Sgs Newfdld Outpts*, I, 194–195 (A).

M: The full Type A story is told with the addition of the old man episode of Type L and an ending similar to Type J: the gypsies are hanged for their offense. Fowke, *Penguin Bk Can Flk Sgs*, 176–177 / *MWF*, 1963, 139–140.

N: This is the normal Type A story with an unusual ending: after his wife has refused his pleas to return, the husband commits suicide by leaping into a nearby body of water ("In madness he was ravin' "). Bronson, III, 242 (#111).

Fragments & Title Lists: Bronson, III, 211 (#23, #25), 213–214 (#28, #31), 216 (#37), 225 (#63, #64), 230 (#80), 233 (#89), 234–235 (#92), 243 (#113), 250 (#127) / Brown, *NC Flklre*, IV, 84–91 / Combs, *Fsgs So US*, 205 (Story Type A) / Fowke, *Trd Sngrs & Sgs Ont*, 84, 101 / *JEMF Quarterly*, IX, 2 (1973), 60 / Karpeles, *Flk Sgs Newfdld* (1971), 83 (C, D) / Rosenberg, *Fsgs Va*, 45–46 / *SFQ*, 1967, 322 / *Tenn FLS Bull*, 1964, 1.

Discussion: The new Story Type K has been created by eliminating the husband as an actor in the drama and transferring words and deeds normally attributed to him to the abductor; thus it is Black Jack David rather than the husband who asks the lady whether she will forsake her possessions to go with him, and it is the fleeing lovers who ride all day and all night till they come to a "dark salt lake" rather than the husband in the course of his pursuit. The whole has been very well compressed into a less complex but quite coherent narrative.

The Type L texts are unusual in North American tradition and are all from Newfoundland: the husband is given directions by a man who has seen the couple on their journey. This feature appears in only one other North American text—also Canadian, from Ontario (Story Type M)—but can be found in Scots tradition (Child's E text and also IV, 74), in Irish tradition (see *JIFSS*, 1 [1904], 42), and (partially) in an English broadside (Child G). The Newfoundland versions do not display close textual relationships with any of these British ones, however, and the Peacock, *Sgs Newfdld Outpts*, (A) text has a further element that has no direct parallel anywhere: after the wife has refused his plea to return, the husband rips off her fine clothes and wishes her "to the devil with the gypsy-o."

The Type M example, which also features the old man, is textually closer to British versions than are the Newfoundland copies of Type L, the closest resemblance being to Child G. It has two further unusual elements: the gypsies are executed, common in British tradition but rare in this country (see Story Type J), and the wife is named as "Lord

Castle's" lady. Several British texts incorporate this pseudo-historical basis of the events described in 200, but the only other North American version which preserves this name is the Flanders, *Ancient Blds*, (E) copy.

The Combs, *Fsgs So US*, (B) text (Story Type A) is also nominally localized but to West Virginia, somewhat in the vein of another West Virginia version in Cox, *Fsgs South*, p. 133 (D). There may, however, be more than a hint of the student collector's personal hand in the Combs copy as elsewhere (see the discussion to 2 in this Supplement).

The distinctive characteristic of the new Type N story is the husband's suicide, unique to the single text that exemplifies this story type. Sung by Frank Proffitt of North Carolina, it also displays unusual phrasing throughout the ballad and may be a tribute to the more creative abilities of the exceptional folksinger. The abductor is presented as a more dashing and romantic figure than is usual, and the husband's final degradation does not seem out of place.

The tendency to moralize the conclusion of the narrative, noted in *BTBNA*, p. 122, as prominent in Story Types B and C, is often hinted in Type A versions. These may be transitional texts and more liable to story variation (for examples, see Abrahams & Foss, *Anglo-Am Fsg Style*, 183–184 [#9–7], where the lady soon dissipates the wealth she brought with her in her short career as the gypsy's mistress, and Bronson, III, 209–213 [#19, #22, #27]).

The Lomax, *Penguin Bk Am Flk Sgs*, Type A text is given both as being collected "from the singing of Woody Guthrie" (p. 7) and as "a composite of Texas and Oklahoma texts" (p. 112). The note to the *Tenn FLS Bull*, 1964, fragment suggests that the role of nineteenth-century outlaws as disseminators of traditional ballads in America might be profitably investigated: it was learned by the singer from his grandfather Robert Ford, Jesse James's executioner. Almeda Riddle's connection with the James family might also be noted (see Abrahams, *Sngr & Her Sgs*, p. 10); and one of the Oklahoma informants of Moore & Moore was a nephew of Cole Younger (*Blds & Flk Sgs SW*, p. 39).

201. BESSY BELL AND MARY GRAY

Texts: *Story Type* D: Essentially the same text and story as in Child: the two girls live in a house outside the city walls and expect to escape the plague but don't. They die and are buried close to their house, not among their own kin in the churchyard. Gainer, *Flk Sgs West Va Hills*, 74 / Moore & Moore, *Blds & Flk Sgs SW*, 100–101.

Fragments & Title Lists: Rosenberg, *Fsgs Va*, 6.

Discussion: The two recent texts from West Virginia and Oklahoma are the only ones so far recovered from North American tradition that tell the full story—or as full a tale as is in any of the Old World versions.

The Moore & Moore text is virtually the same as Child's and was probably learned from print. It is an "emigrant" text (see the discussion to 199 in this Supplement); the informant was born in Scotland and came to the U.S. in 1867. See also the informant's explanation of the subject matter of the ballad (p. 100).

204. JAMIE DOUGLAS

Additional references to "Waly, Waly" texts, which resemble certain lyric passages in the narrative ballad Child 204, are Burton & Manning, *E Tenn State U Coll Flklre: Fsgs*, 89; Emrich, *Am Flk Ptry*, 112; Scott, *Lvng Dcmts Am Hstry*, I, 59–60; Scott, *Settlers Estn Shore*, 196–197.

208. LORD DERWENTWATER

Texts: Story Type A: Bronson, III, 266 (#4a) / Emrich, *Am Flk Ptry*, 325–326.

Discussion: The two new references above to 208 are to a version recorded from the same informant who supplied the only other known versions of this ballad in American tradition (see the three references in *BTBNA*, p. 124). The Emrich text is an editorial collation of two separate performances by the singer.

209. GEORDIE

Local Titles: As I Walked Over London's Bridge, Georgie and Sally, Georgie Wedlock.

Texts: Story Type A: Bronson, III, 277 (#20), 283–284 (#40, #42) / Parler, *Ark Ballet Bk*, 21 / Watson, *Sgs Doc Watson*, 54–55.

B: Bronson, III, 275–276 (#13, #15), 287 (#47), 289 (#54) / Brown, *NC Flklre*, IV, 91–93 (footnote 1, #38 [I]) / Bush, *Flk Sgs Cntrl West Va*, II, 94–95 / Emrich, *Am Flk Ptry*, 326–327 / Gainer, *Flk Sgs West Va Hills*, 75–76 / Grover, *Hrtge Sgs*, 82–83 / Moore & Moore, *Blds & Flk Sgs SW*, 101–102.

D: Emrich, *Am Flk Ptry*, 327–328.

Fragments & Title Lists: Bronson, III, 276–277 (#14, #19) / Brown, *NC Flklre*, IV, 93–95.

Discussion: A common characteristic of oral tradition to compress action and reduce the number of persons in the drama is evident in the Grover, *Hrtge Sgs*, Type B version, where the figures of the old man on the bridge and the official of the court have become one: it is the king himself who meets her on the bridge and tells her she is too late to save her lover. A new figure, however, is added in the Bronson, 284 (#42), Type A text, for there her father appears to plead Georgie's case with the court.

The Watson, *Sgs Doc Watson*, Type A version is credited to "Cecil Sharpe's edition," with some alteration.

210. BONNIE JAMES CAMPBELL

Local Titles: (Bonnie) James Campbell, War Song.

Texts: Story Type A: Bronson, III, 291 (#2, #4) / Combs, *Fsgs So US*, 126–127 / Emrich, *Am Flk Ptry*, 329 / Moore & Moore, *Blds & Flk Sgs SW*, 103–104.

Fragments & Title Lists: Abrahams, *Sngr & Her Sgs*, 60.

Discussion: As is true of all previous North American recoveries of this short ballad, the more recently published texts do not differ substantially from one another or from the Scots versions. The Moore & Moore, *Blds & Flk Sgs SW*, text is an "emigrant" text (see the discussion to 199 in this Supplement), very close to Child A, and was collected from an informant born in Scotland.

213. SIR JAMES THE ROSE

Texts: Story Type A: Bronson, III, 305–308 (#17, #18) / Creighton, *Fsgs So NB*, 23–27 (B) / Karpeles, *Flk Sgs Newfdld* (1971), 85–93 (A, B) / Peacock, *Sgs Newfdld Outpts*, III, 715–719.

Fragments & Title Lists: Bronson, III, 309 (#24) / Creighton, *Fsgs So NB*, 22 (A) / Karpeles, *Flk Sgs Newfdld* (1971), 94 (C).

Discussion: The above texts are all from tradition in either Newfoundland or New Brunswick and are versions of the "Ross" ballad (see *BTBNA*, p. 127). The only substantial difference among them is that in some texts (e.g., Karpeles, *Flk Sgs Newfdld* [1971], B text; Peacock, *Sgs Newfdld Outpts*) the girl's suicide is absent. The Peacock text is a collation, to a small extent, of two separate versions.

214. THE BRAES OF YARROW

Local Titles: The Banks of Yorrow, The Braes o' (of) Yarrow, The Derry Downs of Arrow, The Dewy Dells of Yarrow.

Texts: *Story Type* A: Parler, *Ark Ballet Bk*, 12–13.

B: Bronson, III, 323 (#30) / Fowke, *Penguin Bk Can Flk Sgs*, 178–179 / Karpeles, *Flk Sgs Newfdld* (1971), 95–96 / *MWF*, 1963, 141–142 (A).

C: While drinking wine together in a tavern, a man and his brothers-in-law agree to do battle, despite their mutual kinship. The affair takes place the following day, and the hero, after slaying several of his opponents, is himself slain from behind by one of the brothers. He sends his murderer with the news of his death to his wife, the brother delivering the message by interpreting his sister's premonitory dream that her lord has been killed. She goes to her dead husband and grieves until her heart breaks. She asks her father to make her deathbed, and although he orders her to put aside her grief, offering her a better husband, she refuses, for there could be no better. Fowke, *Trd Sngrs & Sgs Ont*, 62–63 / *MWF*, 1963, 143–144 (B).

D: A wife who has had a premonitory dream that her husband will be slain begs him not to leave home. He replies that he must go nevertheless to meet her brothers. The brothers ambush and kill him as planned, leaving their sister to mourn the death of her husband. Gainer, *Flk Sgs West Va Hills*, 77 / Moore & Moore, *Blds & Flk Sgs SW*, 104–105 (A).

Fragments & Title Lists: Bronson, III, 323 (#32) / Moore & Moore, *Blds & Flk Sgs SW*, 105–106 (B).

Discussion: Coffin remarked in his headnote to Child 214 in Flanders, *Ancient Blds*, III, 256, that variants of this and other ballads "have become as mixed in oral tradition as they have in the minds of American scholars" (cf. *BTBNA*, p. 130), and the recently published texts do not aid the confused scholar any. The whole "Braes of Yarrow" tradition would benefit greatly from a systematic comparative study; an episode which might appear in an example of one story type—carrying the body with the hair, for instance—may be shared with a text of another story type, yet be absent from a version of the same type. Or the girl's death may appear in Type A and in one Type B text, yet be absent from another example of the Type B story. The criteria used for distinguishing the new story types above, therefore, should be made explicit.

The distinguishing features of the new Type C story are, first of all, that the husband is of noble blood, as are his wife and brothers-in-law. (In Type B he is their social inferior. There is no hint in any of the North American texts of the element unique to Child's C text—that the husband regards himself as superior to his wife's family. Child thought this "perhaps too much of a refinement for ballads, and may be a perversion" [IV, 161].) Second, the battle in Type C is arranged in an opening scene in which the husband and brothers-in-law drink wine in a tavern. No other North American texts have this, but it is common in the Child texts—B, C, D, E, F, H, I, M(?), Q, S. This Canadian text, in fact, is closer to the Child A–L series than any other North American text; Fowke, *Trd Sngrs & Sgs Ont*, places it closest to Child F and I, while suggesting that the version of the Child E text printed in Scott's *Minstrelsy* may also have had some influence, since a localization to "Tennies' Bank" (not traditional, but made by Scott himself) turns up in the Ontario version. See her notes on pp. 173–174, as well as her comparative notes on the Type B example in *MWF*, 1963, 144.

The new Type D, the description of which is culled from the Gainer, *Flk Sgs West Va Hills*, text, has shortened the story considerably. The distinguishing feature here is that the wife has a premonitory dream about her husband's death before he goes to fight, and she uses this to try and restrain him from keeping his fatal appointment. This text is also in the Child A–L tradition; the murderers are the wife's brothers, not rival suitors, and there is no hint of social inferiority.

The other example of Type D, from Moore & Moore, *Blds & Flk Sgs SW*, is yet another sophisticated rewrite of the "Braes of Yarrow" ballad, and its narrative resemblance to the traditional version in Gainer's West Virginia collection is surely coincidence. I am unable to identify the original poem; it is not any of those referred to by Child in his headnote to 214 (see also *BTBNA*, p. 129). The Moores evidently collected two versions of this unusual ballad in Oklahoma, but give only one text in full. Both informants were born in Scotland and emigrated to North America in the first quarter of this century (see the discussion to 199 in this Supplement).

215. RARE WILLIE DROWNED IN YARROW or THE WATER O GAMRIE

Local Titles: Rare Willie Drowned in Yarrow, Willie Drowned in Ero.

Texts: Story Type A: Abrahams, *Sngr & Her Sgs*, 124–125 / Fowke, *Penguin Bk Can Flk Sgs*, 180–181.

Discussion: Both of the above texts are the fullest and most intelligible of the very few relatives of Child 215 found in North American tradition. Both are closest to Child's C text, the Abrahams, *Sngr & Her Sgs*, version especially so; the Child C text itself was reprinted in 1955 in Leach's *The Ballad Book* (see *Sngr & Her Sgs*, pp. 60, 152, and the discussion to 228 below).

217. THE BROOM OF COWDENKNOWES

Local Titles: The Bonny Broom.

Texts: Story Type B: The Type A Story is continued so that the maid's seducer returns and takes her away with him. Moore & Moore, *Blds & Flk Sgs SW*, 106–109.

Discussion: The new text from Oklahoma tells the fuller story that the Child versions do, but in such a condensed and confusing manner that one has to be familiar with the Child texts in order to discern just what happens in the American version. While it is much shorter than the Old World copies, the stanzas it does contain closely resemble the corresponding ones in Child A. The informant was born in Scotland before emigrating to the U.S., and the text displays many Scots dialect words and phrases. See the discussion to 199 in this Supplement.

218. THE FALSE LOVER WON BACK

Local Titles: Young John and His Sweetheart.

Fragments & Title Lists: Rosenberg, *Fsgs Va*, 34.

221. KATHARINE JAFFRAY

Local Titles: The Green Wedding, Hembrick Town, Kath'rine Jaffrey, The Lord in Edinburgh, The Scotchman Who Loved an Irish Girl.

Texts: *Story Type* B: Fauset, *Flklre NS*, 124–125 / Karpeles, *Flk Sgs Newfdld* (1971), 97–99 / Peacock, *Sgs Newfdld Outpts*, I, 200–201.

C: For the most part, this tells the story of "The Squire of Edinburgh" Type B, but in a condensed version. The rival suitor comes alone to the wedding, steals the bride away, incurs the groom's wrath, and engages in a bloody battle with the betrayed husband. Moore & Moore, *Blds & Flk Sgs SW*, 109–110.

Fragments & Title Lists: Fowke, *Trd Sgrs & Sgs Ont*, 100 / *MWF*, 1963, 136.

Discussion: All the above references are to versions of "The Squire of Edinboroughtown," a later remodeling of the traditional ballad recognized by Child but so close in its narrative to the earlier ballad that Bronson, III, does not separate the two. Only one text that is demonstrably a version of the traditional ballad has been found in American oral tradition (Story Type A); the others are all primarily the later reworking (Story Types B and C).

These statements must be qualified slightly in the face of the Oklahoma text in Moore & Moore, *Blds & Flk Sgs SW*, which provides a new story Type C. It is only seven stanzas long and compresses the action considerably, but it is very much in the popular style (except perhaps for part of stanza 6: "That churlish dog of an Englishman / Has whisked my bride away") and shows evidence of having long been in domestic oral tradition. While textually and musically it is primarily the later "Squire of Edinboroughtown" ballad, its uniqueness lies in its obvious crossing with the earlier traditional ballad of "Katharine Jaffray," evident in three features shared by no other texts of the later ballad: first, the name Katherine Jaffray appears in the text; second, it retains the aspect of Scottish-English rivalry, though reversed in that it is the Englishman who successfully steals the bride; and, third, it not only features the battle between the abductor and the groom but also tells of it in a final stanza that is paralleled in fully half of the Child texts of 221: the blood runs down "Camden" banks and the trumpets cry "foul play."

The Nova Scotia version in Fauset, *Flklre NS* (Type B), overlooked in the references to versions of 221 in *BTBNA*, is in cante-fable form.

226. LIZIE LINDSAY

Local Titles: Leetsey Linsey, Lizie Lindsay.

Texts: *Story Type* A: Moore & Moore, *Blds & Flk Sgs SW*, 110–111.

Fragments & Title Lists: Rosenberg, *Fsgs Va*, 72 / *SFQ*, 1967, 322.

Discussion: The version in Moore & Moore is the lyrical derivative of Child 226, containing only the short dialogue between the girl and the lord and her departure with him. This Oklahoma text is almost a word-for-word analogue of that in a popular nineteenth-century Scottish songbook, *The Songs of Scotland*, ed. J. Pittman and others, p. 152 (similar to Bronson, III, 366–367 [#4]). The informant was born in Scotland and later emigrated to the U.S. See the discussion to 199 in this Supplement.

228. GLASGOW PEGGIE

Local Titles: Peggy of Glasgow.

Texts: *Story Type* A: A highland trooper meets the lovely Peggy when his regiment comes to Glasgow and persuades her to go off with him against the wishes of her parents. In the course of their journey Peggy begins to lament the grief she will have caused her mother by leaving; her lover then reveals that he is the Earl of the Isle of "Sky" and comforts her by telling of the property and position that will now be hers. Abrahams, *Sngr & Her Sgs*, 181–182.

Discussion: This is the first reporting of Child 228 from North American oral tradition, though the informant had no tune for the ballad and did not sing it. The editor points out that the text is very close to the

Child A version (reprinted in Leach's *The Ballad Book*, pp. 588–589; see the discussion to 215 above) with certain differences of conventional phrasing, which suggests that "this text is authentically in oral tradition" (p. 182). This version, interestingly, also omits the two stanzas, 6 and 8, of the Child text which deal with the couple's love-making. See the comments of both informant and editor on p. 182.

240. THE RANTIN LADDIE

Texts: *Story Type* A: Combs, *Fsgs So US*, 127–128 / Gainer, *Flk Sgs West Va Hills*, 78–79.

Discussion: Other than a lyric fragment from Maine (Story Type B), the Combs version from West Virginia has previously been the only full text of 240 reported from North American tradition (Story Type A). The new example in Gainer is also from West Virginia, and, while the informant was not the same one who supplied the Combs text, the two versions are almost identical, which suggests a small network of local singers who learned songs from each other. See the discussion to 87 in this Supplement.

243. JAMES HARRIS (THE DAEMON LOVER)

Local Titles: Fair Janie, House Carpenter's Song, The King's Daughter, My Little Carpenter, Nice Young Man, The Old House Carpenter, Sweet William, Well Met, We're Met We're Met, the Young Ship's Carpenter.

Texts: *Story Type* A: Boette, *Singa Hipsy Doodle*, 9–10 / Bronson, III, 437–438 (#15), 442–447 (#27, #28, #31, #33, #38), 449–450 (#45, #47, #49), 453–457 (#56, #59, #63), 460–461 (#70), 467–468 (#85), 473–480 (#98, #100, #103, #105, #108), 495–496 (#144, #145) / Burton & Manning, *E Tenn State U Coll Flklre: Fsgs*, 4–5, 65–66 / Burton & Manning, *E Tenn State U Coll Flklre: Fsgs II*, 3–5, 76–78, 105–107 / Bush, *Flk Sgs Cntrl West Va*, I, 77–79 / Carey, *Md Flk Lgds & Flk Sgs*, 103–104 / *Colorado Fsg Bull*, 1964, 3, 17, 34 / Creighton, *Fsgs So NB*, 14–15 / Dunson & Raim, *Anth Am Flk Music*, 24–25 / Emrich, *Am Flk Ptry*, 331–334 (A, B) / Gainer, *Flk Sgs West Va Hills*, 80–81 / Lloyd & Rivera, *Flk Sgs Americas*, 50–51 / Moore & Moore, *Blds & Flk Sgs SW*, 112–113 / Parler, *Ark Ballet Bk*, 26–27 / *Rocky Mt Coll*, 5–6 / Shellans, *Flk Sgs Blue Ridge Mts*, 30–31 / *Studies Literary Imagination*, 1970, 14–15.

B: Abrahams, *Sngr & Her Sgs*, 8–9 / Abrahams & Foss, *Anglo-Am Fsg Style*, 25–27 / Bronson, III, 440 (#20), 448–449 (#44), 454–455 (#57), 461 (#71), 464 (#78), 466–467 (#84), 480 (#109b), 490 (#132) / Ritchie, *Flk Sgs So Aplchns*, 90–91 / *Studies Literary Imagination*, 1970, 15–16.

C: *Ky Flklre Record*, 1972, 41–43.

D: Fowke, *Penguin Bk Can Flk Sgs*, 186–187 / *NC Flklre*, 1973, 142–143 / Peacock, *Sgs Newfdld Outpts*, III, 740–741.

E: Bronson, III, 436–437 (#13), 442 (#26), 488–489 (#129) / Brown, *NC Flklre*, IV, 99–100 (E).

G: A departing youth tells his love that he is going away but will return. They exchange mutual vows of fidelity during his absence. On his return he finds that though he has been faithful—refusing the Queen's daughter, power, and wealth—she has married another man. The rest of the story is as Type A. Bronson, III, 438–439 (#18) / Coffin & Cohen, *Flklre Wkng Flk Am*, 77.

Fragments & Title Lists: Bronson, III, 433–434 (#1, #3, #4), 436 (#11, #12), 438–440 (#16, #17, #19, #22), 443 (#30), 445–448 (#34, #35, #37, #39–#41, #43), 456 (#60, #61), 459 (#68), 461–462 (#72, #75), 468 (#87), 480–481 (#110–#112), 487 (#126), 490 (#133) / Brown, *NC Flklre*, IV, 95–99, 100–101 / Combs, *Fsgs So US*, 207 (Story Type A) / Fowke, *Trd Sngrs & Sgs Ont*, 100 / *JEMF Quarterly*, IX, 2 (1973), 60 / *Ky Flklre Record*, 1965, 65 / *MWF*, 1963, 136 / Rosenberg, *Fsgs Va*, 58–59.

Discussion: The description of the new Story Type G above follows the Bronson, III, (#18) text which was sung by a Wisconsin man. Its noteworthiness lies in the first three stanzas which precede the "well met, well met" lines that begin most full versions of 243 in North American tradition: they tell of the earlier relationship between the abductor and the wife and thus resemble to a significant extent the narrative of Child's unique A text which tells the story of James Harris and Jane Reynolds. Aside from the other example of Type G, from Coffin & Cohen's *Flklre Wkng Flk Am*, the only previously known version that even hints at a connection with this feature of Child A is the fragmented *BFSSNE* text (Story Type A) in which the lover is called George Allis, a name that Barry says is a "traditional distortion" of Harris (VI, 8).

While the Wisconsin example may be distantly related to this oldest known version of Child 243 that is the A broadside copy, textual evidence would indicate that this introductory episode is instead a later addition to the usual form made in fairly recent American tradition. Two things suggest this: first, the major portion of the ballad, from the "well met, well met" stanza to the end, is very close textually to the common American form (if in somewhat more elegant phrasing than is usual), which is substantially that of the DeMarsan broadside (see *BTBNA*, p. 139); and, second, the three antecedent stanzas are obviously indebted to the ubiquitous "Ten Thousand Miles"–"True Lover's Farewell" lyric complex rather than to the James Harris broadside. This is not the only instance in which these lyric stanzas have become attached to this ballad (see the

references in *BTBNA*, p. 139), though their position here as an introductory episode is unparalleled elsewhere.

Whatever their ultimate source, they are well integrated into the ballad,
with the result that there is here a far stronger motivation for the abductor's actions than is usually the case. And they have further interest for
comparative study of folksong as well since they provide the wife not only
with a name (she is named only in Child A, in some of Davis' Virginia
texts [see *BTBNA*, p. 138], and in the other example of Type G from
Coffin & Cohen), but with a name—Mary Anne—that turns up in tradition only in a unique version of the "True Lover's Farewell" lyric collected by Barbeau in Quebec (see Fowke & Johnston, *Flk Sgs Can*, pp.
142–143; for an English broadside text, see Henderson, *Victorian Street
Ballads*, p. 61), though that is about all they share textually with that
highly unusual Anglo-Canadian version.

The other example of the new Type G story, from Coffin & Cohen,
Flklre Wkng Flk Am, is no less an anomaly than the Wisconsin text. Its
seven stanzas concentrate mostly on the initial episode, the subsequent
return, flight, and death being synopsized in the final two verses, more
allusion than narrative. It names the girl as Janie (cf. Jane Reynolds) and
is localized to a logging milieu—"near Richmond, logging town" in the
"Northwest"; she also marries a logger. This text is clearly a direct relative of the unique Child A broadside tradition, and in its language, phrasing, and meter it seems to be more recitation than song. Consult the
editors' notes, p. 427, for information on collector, informant, and related
matters.

The tendency for many versions of 243 to utilize stanzas and motifs
from related songs and ballads such as "true love" lyrics, Child 73, and
Child 289, has been noted by many analysts, particularly Davis, *More Trd
Blds Va*, p. 273 (the stanza on her rich clothing, indebted textually to 73,
may be a thematic trace of the related stanza 8 of Child's E text without
the magical significance); a previously unseen correspondence with Child
4 is displayed in the new Burton & Manning, *E Tenn State U Coll Flklre:
Fsgs*, pp. 65–66, Type A version, in which the runaway lovers journey to
the sea in a stanza usually reserved for that other notable ballad of
maiden-robbing (cf. also discussion to 248 below).

A role switch of not-too-great significance should be noted in two texts:
in *Colorado Fsg Bull*, 1964, 3, 17 (both Type A), it is *she* who delivers the
"well met, well met" greeting and who could have married a "rich young
man," and *he* who replies that she is to blame for not doing so. The rest
of the ballad continues as usual, however, with he taking the active role
in all that follows, so I have not considered this a significant enough difference to warrant a new story type. The second example is more minor:
in the Bronson, III, #20, Type B text it is *he* who asks the identity of the
banks they spy, and *she* who replies that they are the banks of hell. Had
these two role reversals taken place in the same text, a new and unusual
story type would indeed have been recognized.

The demonaic nature of the lover is usually exhibited in American versions only through his connection with hell (Types B and C), but the *Ky Flklre Record*, 1972, Type C text is unique in this country in also mentioning his cloven foot, as in Child E, F, and G. The Peacock, *Sgs Newfdld Outpts*, III, Type D has several relatively rare features: the husband is a ship's carpenter rather than the far more common (in this country) house carpenter; when the news of his wife's abduction and death reaches him the husband swears and tears his hair, in the manner of Child B (stanza 12); and there is an interesting localization in the place names, for the action takes place in England, the lady's home, while the lover is from Newfoundland, and it is to there he attempts to take her, where they "will pass for man and wife." This could be a touch of either local satire or personal fantasy; it could also be a borrowing from the more recent "Oh No, Not I," in which a Newfoundland sailor also tempts an English girl into an illicit relationship with unfortunate—though not quite so disastrous—results (see Peacock, *Sgs Newfdld Outpts*, I, 304–305).

It is suggested in the discussion to 243 in *BTBNA*, p. 139, that the Type D story, in which the girl jumps overboard to her death, may result from sentimentalization. Also at work, however, may have been some confusion by singers (or printers) between the similar words "leap" and "leak." The Types A and B stories, in which the ship springs a leak and sinks, are undoubtedly older than the Type D, in which the girl leaps overboard. It is possible that the substitution of "leap" for "leak," and not sentimentalization necessarily, has led to the change in the surrounding circumstances. Support for this suggestion comes from texts in Brewster's *Blds Sgs Ind*: in his C text the "ship sprung a leak under deck" (Story Type A), while in his A text "over the deck she sprang a leap" (Story Type D). The similar sounds of the two words, the same feminine gender of both girl and ship, and the synonymity of "springing" in both contexts may all combine to bring about the change. (See also the *NC Flklre*, 1973, Type D text.) Brewster's D text carries this sort of change even further, for there "over the deck in the lake she sprung."

The Emrich, *Am Flk Ptry*, pp. 332–334, B text (Type A), as printed, is an editorial amalgamation of a Type A text and two final stanzas from another version, which makes it a Type B story. I have not taken the interpolated stanzas into consideration and have categorized it as Type A.

The two texts from *Studies Literary Imagination*, 1970 (Types A and B), are given in an article by Roger D. Abrahams, "Creativity, Individuality, and the Traditional Singer," pp. 5–34, in which he uses these two versions as sung by two different singers to illustrate their respective world views and aesthetics.

A song from Kentucky, "Mines of Coal Creek," in Roberts, *Sang Branch Settlers*, pp. 119–120, should be consulted, for it contains three stanzas of 243 within what seems to be a local white blues lyric or banjo song.

The British tradition of this ballad is the subject of an article by John Burrison, " 'James Harris' in Britain since Child," *JAF*, 80 (1967), 271–

284, while Alisoun Gardner-Medwin looks at the American tradition in "The Ancestry of 'The House-Carpenter': A Study of the Family History of the American Forms of Child 243," *JAF*, 84 (1971), 414–427.

248. THE GREY COCK or SAW YOU MY FATHER?

Local Titles: The Gray Cock, The Little Fishes, The Lover's Ghost, Pretty Crowin' Chicken, Saw You My True Love John.

Texts: *Story Type* A: Bronson, IV, 17–18 (#3, #5) / Karpeles, *Flk Sgs Newfdld* (1971), 100–102 (A, B).

B: Bronson, IV, 19 (#7) / Burton & Manning, *E Tenn State U Coll Flklre: Fsgs II*, 78–79 / Moore & Moore, *Blds & Flk Sgs SW*, 114–115.

Fragments & Title Lists: Bronson, IV, 18 (#4).

Discussion: The basic differences among the three story types of 248 in North American tradition may be briefly summarized: in Type A, the visiting lover is clearly a ghost; in Type B, he is mortal, and the ballad is simply one of a lovers' assignation; in Type C, the story is parallel to Type A but the roles are reversed—the girl is the ghost, the visiting man mortal. The Barry, *Brit Blds Me*, text cited in *BTBNA* as an example of Type A is more properly a Type B story, for there is little in the text to denote the lover's ghostly status, unless one infers it from the slender evidence of the cock's crow in the text and one's knowledge of general Oriental and Occidental folklore. On the other hand, the recently published examples of Type A cited above are explicit about the ghostly nature of the visitor: not only are his hands "colder than clay" but also, as in Type C texts (where the ghostly state of the girl is explicit and of which these Type A versions are close textual relatives), there is reference to the winding sheet and the worms.

Since much scholarship has been devoted to Child 248 and similar ballads (see references in *BTBNA*, p. 140) in attempts to discern genetic relationships, I will try here to clarify what I see to be the similarities and, more importantly, the differences among the various ballads which bear on the matter of "The Grey Cock" complex. There are six distinct ballads in British and American tradition which have been most emphasized by scholars as bearing on this song cluster, and these are (1) Child 248 itself, "The Grey Cock"; (2) Child 255, "Willie's Fatal Visit"; (3) Child 77, "Sweet William's Ghost"; (4) an Irish ballad which goes by more than one title that I will identify here as "Willy O!" (for texts see Bronson, IV, 20 [#9]; Morton, *Come Day, Go Day, God Send Sunday*, pp. 5, 155–156; *Traditional Topics*, I, 2 [February 1968], 5; Leader Records, LEA 4055), not collected from any but Irish-born singers to my knowledge; (5) "Here's a Health unto All True Lovers" (and many other titles; for texts see Creighton, *Maritime Flk Sgs*, p. 63; Fowke, *Trd Sngrs & Sgs*

Ont, p. 105; MacColl, *Folk Songs and Ballads of Scotland*, p. 47; *MWF*, 1963, 145; Purslow, *The Wanton Seed*, p. 86; Seeger & MacColl, *The Singing Island*, p. 24; Prestige/International Records, INT 25016); and (6) "O Once I Loved a Lass" (for texts see Brocklebank & Kindersley, *A Dorset Book of Folk Songs*, p. 7; *JAF*, 1954, 286–287; Purslow, *Marrow Bones*, p. 52; Reeves, *The Everlasting Circle*, pp. 136–138).

Individually considered, (2), Child 55, shares with (1), Child 248, its opening two, perhaps three stanzas, but while it does feature a ghost, that figure is never one of the two lovers. The ballad is extremely rare in tradition and, the purely introductory stanzas aside, has not influenced either the textual or the narrative tradition of 248 to any discernible extent. It is, in part, a night-visit ballad; it is never a revenant one. (3), Child 77, also shares with 248 and 255 an introductory stanza in question form which usually goes something like "Is that my father, Is that my brother? Is that my true lover William?" which, while not exactly the same as the similar questions in 248 and 255, are close enough to suggest a possible direct relationship. But, other than the rampant ballad cliche of "twirling at the ring" and the cock-crowing motif in the Child A text, that is all the three ballads share textually.

Thematically, 77 shares with the Story Types A and C versions of 248 the feature that one of the lovers is a revenant and that he or she therefore cannot stay long in the living world, but very little else. The characteristic features of 77, such as the return of the troth, the night journey, the description of the resting place, and the wish of the living lover to go with the dead, are nowhere paralleled in 248. (4), "Willy O!," is thematically similar to 248 and 77 in that it is a revenant ballad, but that is all. There are no textual similarities. It is more than likely of Irish broadside origin and probably dates from the first half of the nineteenth century. My suspicion is that it may be a remake by an Irish broadside versifier of a very popular Scots song-poem, "Mary's Dream," by the cleric John Lowe of Kenmore in Galloway (1750–1798), which tells much the same story as "Willy O!" though the two do not share any significant textual features in their respective traditions. (For an early Scots text of "Mary's Dream" see Buchan, *Gleanings of Scarce Old Ballads*, pp. 112–113. The original poem was remade at least once by Scottish hands themselves; see the headnote in Cox, *Fsgs South*, p. 435, and the two texts in the *Universal Songster*, III, 213. The song is in several North American traditional repertoires and is indexed in Laws, *American Balladry from British Broadsides*, as K20.) In short, "Willy O!" is not a version of 'The Grey Cock' or 'The Lover's Ghost' " (see Morton, *Come Day, Go Day, God Send Sunday*, p. 155) or of any of the other ballads in this group; the story and the motives of the dramatis personae (which resemble, apart from Laws K20, Child 78 more than anything else) are quite different from the others.

(5), "Here's a Health unto All True Lovers," has no supernatural inference whatsoever. Like the Child text of 248 and its related Story Type B texts in North America, it is simply a night-visit ballad of a lover to his mistress. But it bears no textual relationship to 248 and thus should not, in my opinion, be referenced as a version of that ballad, as it is for instance in *MWF*, 1963, 145, and elsewhere. The crowing of the cock as a signal for the lover to leave, on which Barry placed so much importance in *Brit Blds Me*, p. 313, cannot be given the same kind of significance in this ballad because the whole milieu in which the action takes place is entirely different: in the MacColl, *Folk Songs and Ballads of Scotland*, text, for instance, from bothy tradition I suspect, the protagonists are farm servants and the cock crow means nothing more than that the work day is about to begin. As the lover himself puts it, "Remember, lass, I'm a ploughman laddie / And the fairmer I must obey." It does occasionally share a line or two with (4), "Willy O!," in which the lovers kiss and shake hands before parting at dawn. The reasons some editors have had for considering copies of this ballad to be versions of 248 will be taken up shortly.

(6), "O Once I Loved a Lass," was advanced as a version of 248 by Friedman in his 1954 article on a text of this song found in a seventeenth-century drollery (see *BTBNA*, p. 140). By showing certain textual similarities to American and Irish versions of 248 which Child did not have at his command and in which the ghostly nature of the lover is clear, Friedman suggested not only that "O Once I Loved a Lass" was a direct relative of 248, but also that both ballads were originally revenant rather than mortal night-visiting ballads. The textual evidence that Friedman presents linking his drollery ballad with 248 and the supernatural is slender, as he himself recognizes, and relies perhaps overmuch on ballad cliches; the closest textual resemblance is in the lines in which the cock crows too soon and thus the lover departs before he needs to. But evidence that argues more convincingly against Friedman's thesis is that this ballad has been collected from at least two informants in twentieth-century England, apparently descended from a long oral tradition which one doubts would be indebted to the drollery text; the opposite would be the more likely case. In any event, the traditional texts are so close to the Restoration copy which predates them by some 250 years that it seems probable the drollery version is little changed from its own original, that the song was always what it is today: about a nocturnal assignment between a mortal man and a mortal maid, much like (5), "Here's a Health unto All True Lovers," and that it never had a major textual or thematic connection with the tradition of the overtly revenant versions of 248, since resemblances between the two go little further than minor verbal cliches and the common subject matter of lovers' secret meetings.

To summarize, Story Types A and C of Child 248 in North American tradition feature revenants, as do some Irish versions of the same ballad. All North American examples of these two story types come from Nova Scotia and Newfoundland—and those Canadian versions themselves probably came from Ireland. The Type B story, in which both lovers are clearly mortal, is epitomized in the single text in Child (from Scotland), in the southern and southwestern U.S. versions, and in the Maine version cited in *BTBNA* as Type A. Texts of 248, British and American, exhibit little more than casual thematic and textual relationships with the five other traditional ballads that have sometimes been hypothesized as being genetically linked as variants; all six ballads of the complex are for the most part distinct in their histories and more than likely in their origins.

What may be the most significant association within this complex has been suggested by Hugh Shields in a very thorough, wide-ranging article, "Une ALBA dans le poésie populaire anglaise?" *Revue des langues romanes*, 79 (1971), 461–475. His thesis also answers the question of whether the supernatural Story Type A is older than the nonsupernatural Type B: he thinks, with Child, that the original ballad was an aube and, further, that the revenant element was added in Ireland from Child 77. He suspects also that the ghost in "Willy O!" has the same source, though whether one may say that that Irish broadside and 77 are related to the extent that " 'Sweet William's Ghost' . . . is re-constituted in 'Willy-O' " (Hugh Shields, "Old British Ballads in Ireland," *Folk Life*, 10 [1972], 80) is questionable. See also his article referenced in the discussion to 77 in this Supplement, as well as Purslow's notes to an English version of "Here's a Health unto All True Lovers" in *The Wanton Seed*, p. 138. On the general topic of the archaism or modernism of supernatural elements in ballad tradition, see the discussion to 84 and references cited there.

There still remains the question of why so many scholars have cited various texts of "Willy O!," "Here's a Health unto All True Lovers," and "O Once I Loved a Lass" as versions of Child 248. In almost all instances, their reasons for doing so can be traced to the existence of a most unusual ballad sung by an Irishwoman, Cecilia Costello, living in England. Mrs. Costello's song is a unique amalgamation of four stanzas from "Here's a Health unto All True Lovers," one stanza shared by both "Here's a Health" and "Willy O!," two stanzas unique to the "Willy O!" textual tradition, two stanzas from 248, "The Grey Cock," and one stanza shared by 248 and "O Once I Loved a Lass"—a total of ten stanzas in all. Mrs. Costello's song indeed is so interesting in its obvious relationships to other ballads yet its equally obvious unusualness that the original collectors were moved to declare it "the greatest find in the whole set" (*JEFDSS*, 7 [1953], 98). Fully half of her text is the "Here's a Health" ballad, but the stanzas from "Willy O!" make the male lover a ghost, while the stanzas from 248 deal with the attempt to bribe the cock into keeping silent and his subsequent ignoring of the plea. This unique text has led to the assumption that it was an early form that kept together what had later, in tradition, split apart.

That all other recoveries of these ballads keep their respective identities, however, argues against this assumption. Moreover, the Costello text does not fuse the parts of these separate ballads into an organic whole but is organized on the principle of addition: the various parts are clearly distinguishable, especially since they are constrained by the formal unit of the stanza. Clearly what we see in her version is a unique integration made by a thoroughly competent and creative bearer of tradition, and not a prototype that became fragmented elsewhere.

The discussion to 248 in *BTBNA*, p. 140, notes that this ballad often shares a stanza or two with 4, which may be in part a result of their sharing an episode in which a maiden tries to bribe a bird. The association between these two is carried even further in the Burton & Manning, *E Tenn State U Coll Flklre: Fsgs II*, Type B text of 248: after her lover has departed at cock-crow the girl saddles two horses and rides away much in the manner of Lady Isabel both to and from her near fatal confrontation with the elf-knight. The same stanza has been noted in a version of 243 above; these crossings may be either a faint implication of a common supernatural element in the three ballads or, more simply, an illustration of the principle that secretive—if not illicit—love affairs involve similar journey motifs.

250. HENRY MARTYN

This ballad has been treated under "Sir Andrew Barton" (Child 167).

272. THE SUFFOLK MIRACLE

Local Titles: Lady Lady Lady Fair, The Lady Near New York Town, There Was an Old and Wealthy Man, The Unquiet Grave.

Texts: Story Type A: Emrich, *Am Flk Ptry*, 335–337 (A, B) / Gainer, *Flk Sgs West Va Hills*, 84–85 / Moore & Moore, *Blds & Flk Sgs SW*, 118–119 / Peacock, *Sgs Newfdld Outpts*, II, 407–408.

Fragments & Title Lists: Bronson, IV, 85 (#1b) / Brown, *NC Flklre*, IV, 102 / Rosenberg, *Fsgs Va*, 120.

Discussion: The narrative of 272 is extremely stable in North American tradition; only a single story type can be discerned among the several versions found in all the major ballad regions of the U.S. and Canada. Nor does the story differ much from that of the Child text, though it is in a condensed form. Seldom are any two texts enough alike to suggest the same immediate source for both, however, which suggests a vigorous traditional life for this song-story with a supernatural theme.

The Moore & Moore, *Blds & Flk Sgs SW*, text is unusual in that it does not have the episode in which the grave is opened and the corpse found with a handkerchief bound round its head, surely the dramatic core of the tale. Another of its unusual features (for North American tradition) is that it includes the girl's death, paralleled only in the British version.

The Peacock, *Sgs Newfdld Outpts*, text names the maid as "Esther," and also unusual is its concluding moral: like the Flanders, *Ancient Blds*, (B) text it is directed to young girls and admonishes them never to forsake their true lovers, whereas most other texts, British as well as North American, communicate their morals to parents and urge that they let young lovers have their own way.

For some thoughts on the European traditions of this theme in song and story and on the origins of the British version, see K. Mitsakis, "Greek Sources of an English Ballad: 'The Return of the Dead Brother' and 'The Suffolk Miracle,'" *Comparative Literature Studies*, 3 (1966), 47–52.

273. KING EDWARD THE FOURTH AND THE TANNER OF TAMWORTH

Local Titles: The King and the Tinker.

Fragments & Title Lists: *JAF*, 1966, 469.

Discussion: The somewhat confused single stanza and chorus collected in Ontario and cited above is from a broadside remake of a familiar theme. Child says that "next to adventures of Robin Hood and his men, the most favorite topic in English popular poetry is the chance-encounter of a king, unrecognized as such, with one of his humbler subjects" (V, 69). He admitted one of this thematic cluster to his canon but thought "King James and the Tinker" not worthy of inclusion in even the appendix of ballads related to 273. The Ontario fragment is of this secondary ballad and thus is not a trace of the "King Edward the Fourth and the Tanner of Tamworth" ballad as such.

274. OUR GOODMAN

Local Titles: Came Home the Other Night, Drunkard Blues, Drunkard's Special, The Drunken Fool, The Drunk Husband, Five Nights' Experience or The Three Good Nights, Five (Six) Nights Drunk, Home Came a Goodman, Johnny Came Home the Other Night, Mr. Goody Goody, Mustache on a Cabbage Head, Old Man Brown (Crip), Saddle on a Milk Cow, This Old Man, Three Drunken Nights, Three Nights Drunk (Out), You Old Fool.

Texts: *Story Type* A: Bronson, IV, 103–105 (#10, #12), 107 (#18), 109 (#23) / Burton & Manning, *E Tenn State U Coll Flklre: Fsgs II*, 11–12

/ Carey, *Md Flk Lgds & Flk Sgs*, 109 / Cray, *Erotic Muse*, 6–9 (A, B) / Gainer, *Flk Sgs West Va Hills*, 86–87 / Jackson, *Flklre & Society*, 56–57, 127–128 / Moore & Moore, *Blds & Flk Sgs SW*, 120–122 / Parler, *Ark Ballet Bk*, 17 / Roberts, *Sang Branch Settlers*, 97–99.

B: Bronson, IV, 126 (#52).

C: Abrahams & Foss, *Anglo-Am Fsg Style*, 108–110 / Bronson, IV, 103 (#9), 109–110 (#25), 114–121 (#31–#38, #42) / Burton & Manning, *E Tenn State U Coll Flklre: Fsgs II*, 65–66 / Emrich, *Am Flk Ptry*, 338–339 / Jackson, *Flklre & Society*, 122–123, 124–126 / *Miss Flklre Reg*, 1973, 131–132.

Fragments & Title Lists: Boette, *Singa Hipsy Doodle*, 14 / Bronson, IV, 105 (#14) / Brown, *NC Flklre*, IV, 103–111 / Brunvand, *Guide for Collectors of Folklore*, 72 / Combs, *Fsgs So US*, 207 (Story Types A and B) / *JEMF Quarterly*, IX, 2 (1973), 60–61 / *Ky Flklre Record*, 1965, 65 / *MWF*, 1963, 136 / Rosenberg, *Fsgs Va*, 100.

Discussion: At least one of the objects that strikes the drunken husband's eye has been modernized in contemporary hillbilly and Cajun recorded tradition: see Bronson, IV, #23, #32, and #34, where he spies a motor car parked on his property (#34 is most specific—it is a Ford). The wife's ingenuity is not set back by these modernizations, however. The automobiles may be explained as wheelbarrows, baby carriages, or even as a " 'bacco truck." In Bronson #34 he spies a horse the first night, a car on the fifth.

Constraints have been relaxed somewhat over the past decade to allow the publishing of bawdy versions hinted at so often in the past (see references in *BTBNA*, pp. 144–145, and in Cray, *Erotic Muse*, pp. 189–190). The Cray, *Erotic Muse*, pp. 6–7, and Jackson, *Flklre & Society*, pp. 56–57, texts (both Type A) are of this kind.

Carey's version from Maryland, in *Md Flk Lgds & Flk Sgs* (Type A), is unusual in that it is in Dutch/German dialect English. Philip S. Kuhn, "The Mustachioed Cabbage as Motif," *Miss Flklre Reg*, 8 (1974), 210–214, gives the text of a local "coon" song, with no discernible narrative thread, which has a final stanza taken from this ballad (p. 214).

275. GET UP AND BAR THE DOOR

Local Titles: Bar the Door O.

Texts: Story Type A: Boette, *Singa Hipsy Doodle*, 8 / Combs, *Fsgs So US*, 128–129 / Gainer, *Flk Sgs West Va Hills*, 88–89 / Moore & Moore, *Blds & Flk Sgs SW*, 122–124.

B: Peacock, *Sgs Newfdld Outpts*, I, 239–240.

Fragments & Title Lists: Bronson, IV, 139 (#19) / Brown, *NC Flklre*, IV, 112 (B).

Discussion: Most of the recently published North American versions of this ballad that comprise the references above follow the Child A and B textual tradition (Story Type A). The exception is the Peacock, *Sgs Newfdld Outpts*, I, Type B version, which is clearly related to the textual tradition of Child C. It is almost a repeat, with the addition of one stanza, of the only previous North American text of this type in Green-leaf & Mansfield, *Blds Sea Sgs Newfdld*, and may be from the same highly local tradition, since both were collected in the outport village of Rocky Harbour, though thirty-one years apart. The earliest version of this textual type is the one in Johnson's *Musical Museum* (the Child C text), which may have been a Burns refinement of a traditional text of the Child A and B (Story Type A) sort. This Type B strain has also been found in English country tradition (see Purslow, *Marrow Bones*, p. 47).

The Moore & Moore, *Blds & Flk Sgs SW*, Type A text is from a Scots-born informant who emigrated to the U.S. in 1929 (see the discussion to 199 in this Supplement).

277. THE WIFE WRAPT IN WETHER'S SKIN

Local Titles: (As, While) The Dew Flies Over the Green Valley, Dan Doo, The Farmer's Curst Wife (see Bronson, IV, 150 [#11], note), Geely Don Mac Kling Go, Gentle Fair Jenny, Gentle Jinny Fair Rosemary, The Green Valley, Hucklety Smuklety, Jennifer Jenny, Jenny Go Gentle, Lazy Woman, Nickity Nackity Now, Old Wetherskin, There Was an Old Man Who Lived Out West, The Wife in Wether's Skin—Dandoo!, Wife Wrapped in Weather's Skin, The Wife Wrapped (up) in the Wether's Skin.

Texts: *Story Type* A: Abrahams & Foss, *Anglo-Am Fsg Style*, 167–169 / Boette, *Singa Hipsy Doodle*, 18–20 / Bronson, IV, 146 (#4), 152 (#18), 156–157 (#29), 163–169 (#42a, #46, #49, #52, #55) / Burton & Manning, *E Tenn State U Coll Flklre: Fsgs*, 56 / Fowke, *Penguin Bk Can Flk Sgs*, 182–183 / Gainer, *Flk Sgs West Va Hills*, 90–91 / Grover, *Hrtge Sgs*, 68–69 / Moore & Moore, *Blds & Flk Sgs SW*, 125–126 / *NC Flklre*, XI, 1 (1963), 26–27; XIV, 2 (1966), 16 / Parler, *Ark Ballet Bk*, 10–11 / *Tenn FLS Bull*, 1971, 12–13.

B: Bush, *Flk Sgs Cntrl West Va*, I, 80–81.

C: Bronson, IV, 154 (#22), 156–159 (#27, #28, #30, #32) / *Green Mt Whittlin's*, IV (n.d.), 2 / Ritchie, *Flk Sgs So Aplchns*, 76.

Fragments & Title Lists: Abrahams, *Sngr & Her Sgs*, 182 / Bronson, IV, 150 (#11, #12), 152 (#19a, #19b), 168–169 (#53, #54) / Brown, *NC*

Flklre, IV, 113–116 / Combs, *Fsgs So US*, 207 (Story Type A) / *MWF*, 1963, 136 / *NYFQ*, 1966, 62 / Rosenberg, *Fsgs Va*, 138.

Discussion: The Type C story does not feature the sheepskin device in the beating. In these texts, it is usually a hickory stick that is applied directly to the recalcitrant wife's back.

The *NYFQ*, 1966, fragment is a single stanza collected from the same informant who furnished the Flanders, *Ancient Blds*, IV, A text, but which was not given at the time of the Flanders collecting.

Two "lazy wife" lyrics which show some textual but slight narrative resemblance to 277, not referenced above, may be found in Bush, *Flk Sgs Cntrl West Va*, I, 21, and Brown, *NC Flklre*, IV, 345–346.

278. THE FARMER'S CURST WIFE

Local Titles: Battle-Axe and the Devil, Devil Doings, The Devil Out of Hell, The Devil Song, The Evil Woman, The Farmer (and His Son, and the Devil), Farmer Jones's Wife, the Farmer's Old Curst Wife, The Farmer's Wife and the Devil, The Little Devils, The Old Devil, (The) Old Lady and the Devil, Old Lady Grant, The Old Man That Lived under the Hill, Old Woman under the Hill, There Was an Old Woman Lived under the Hill, Worse Than Men.

Texts: *Story Type* A: Abrahams & Foss, *Anglo-Am Fsg Style*, 99–101 / Boette, *Singa Hipsy Doodle*, 5–7 (A, B) / Bronson, IV, 180–181 (#8), 186 (#19), 188–193 (#26, #29, #30, #32–#34), 195–197 (#39, #40), 199–200 (#45, #49), 202–205 (#55, #57–#59), 207 (#62), 210–212 (#67, #70), 510 (#42.1) / Brown, *NC Flklre*, IV, 116–117, 118 (#2) / Burton & Manning, *E Tenn State U Coll Flklre: Fsgs*, 36–37 / Burton & Manning, *E Tenn State U Coll Flklre: Fsgs II*, 72–73 / Bush, *Flk Sgs Cntrl West Va*, I, 82–85 (A, B) / Carey, *Md Flk Lgds & Flk Sgs*, 105 / Dunson & Raim, *Anth Am Flk Music*, 26–27 / Emrich, *Am Flk Ptry*, 341–342 / Fowke, *Penguin Bk Can Flk Sgs*, 174–175 / Gainer, *Flk Sgs West Va Hills*, 92–93 / Jackson, *Flklre & Society*, 118–119 / *JAF*, 1970, 458–459 / Leach & Glassie, *Guide for Collectors of Oral Traditions*, 28–29 / Lomax, *Penguin Bk Am Flk Sgs*, 43 / Moore & Moore, *Blds & Flk Sgs SW*, 127–128 / Peacock, *Sgs Newfdld Outpts*, I, 265–268 (A–C) / Ritchie, *Flk Sgs So Aplchns*, 31 / Roberts, *Sang Branch Settlers*, 99–100 / Scott, *Bld of Am*, 152–153 / Shellans, *Flk Sgs Blue Ridge Mts*, 18–19.

D: *NYFQ*, 1967, 18–21.

H: The Type A story is told with this ending: when the farmer spies the devil returning with his wife he runs away so that the devil will not get him instead. "If he hasn't stopped he's running still." Bronson, IV, 185 (#17).

I: This story type begins like A and continues to the point where the devil reaches hell with his difficult passenger. When he gets to hell's gates, however, it is "all too late," and so the husband has to keep his wife for the rest of his life. Combs, *Fsgs So US*, 208 (C).

Fragments & Title Lists: Bronson, IV, 199–200 (#47), 510 (#43.1) / Brown, *NC Flklre*, IV, 117, 119 / Combs, *Fsgs So US*, 207 (Story Type A) / *JEMF Quarterly*, IX, 2 (1973), 61 / *MWF*, 1963, 136 / Rosenberg, *Fsgs Va*, 34–35.

Discussion: The new Type H story appears to have been created by a combination of the logical idea that the devil would want a replacement for the unacceptable wife—he must have his due—and a change in wording from the common "if the devil won't have her I'm damned if I will" to "he thinks he'll get me but I'll be damned if he will." The textual changes may be small, but they help effect a significant variation in the narrative.

The text that furnishes the sole example of Story Type I is one recently published from the Combs collection. The unusual episode has no parallel elsewhere, although the text itself is nothing out of the ordinary. It was contributed by a fieldworker who supplied many unusual versions of Child ballads to the Combs archives. See the discussion to 2 in this Supplement.

In the Bronson, IV, #39 (Type A), text there is an unusual switch during the goings-on in hell in that it is the devil who, at one point, grabs a poker and beats the wife's brains out, though this does not impair her usual vigor; she continues without setback in her customary aggressive manner.

Several texts (e.g., Bronson, IV, #29, #49, #55) end abruptly with the wife still creating havoc in hell, though there may be the final philosophical stanza. I have cited all these as Type A. Bronson #55 has several unusual elements of phrasing and content, and the editor remarks, "One surmises that Capt. Nye compensated for a faulty memory with a ready but reckless improvisation" (p. 203, note). Captain Nye, the informant, has already been pointed to in the discussion to 112 in this Supplement as one of the more creative bearers of traditional song.

The *JAF*, 1970, version is very unusual in that the story is told in the first person by the farmer. Another unusual feature is that it names the wife as "old Lady Grant" in the final stanza. Thomas J. Rountree, who presents the text in a note, speculates that it may possibly have been a southern satire on Mrs. Ulysses S. Grant but thinks it more probable that it was a dig at some local lady, now unknown. There may be a hint of another localization in the Moore & Moore, *Blds & Flk Sgs SW*, Type A version, the title of which is "Farmer Jones's Wife." The name does not appear in the text, however.

The Brown, *NC Flklre*, 118 (Type A), text is fragmented and has taken on a lyrical refrain from the "hard times" song complex.

279. THE JOLLY BEGGAR

Local Titles: The Jolly Beggar, The Wee Wee Man.

Texts: Story Type A: Moore & Moore, *Blds & Flk Sgs SW*, 129–131.

Fragments & Title Lists: Bronson, IV, 247 (#47).

Discussion: The Cox, *Trd Blds W Va*, text remains the only full version of Child 279 recovered from a North American singing repertoire; the reference above to the recent Moore & Moore copy is, like all other full texts from oral tradition cited in *BTBNA*, a version of "The Gaberlunyie-Man," which Child presents in the appendix to 279 (V, 115–116) as a sophisticated derivative of the traditional ballad. The Moore & Moore informant was born in Scotland and emigrated to the New World as a child; her version contains neither obvious traces of Scottish dialect nor any noticeable Americanisms. See the discussion to 199 in this Supplement.

283. THE CRAFTY FARMER

There are no published texts from North American tradition other than those already cited in *BTBNA* that are textually related to Child 283. Additional references to versions of the thematically similar "The Yorkshire Bite" (Laws L1) are Bronson, IV, 293 (#18); Combs, *Fsgs So US*, 130–132; Emrich, *Am Flk Ptry*, 343–345; Gainer, *Flk Sgs West Va Hills*, 94–95; Moore & Moore, *Blds & Flk Sgs SW*, 131–133; Peacock, *Sgs Newfdld Outpts*, I, 33–38.

285. THE GEORGE ALOE AND THE SWEEPSTAKE

Add to the references to "High Barbary" (Laws K33) texts: Bronson, IV, 308–310 (#7, #10); Emrich, *Am Flk Ptry*, 512–514; Grover, *Hrtge Sgs*, 133–134.

286. THE SWEET TRINITY (THE GOLDEN VANITY)

Local Titles: He Had a Little Tool, The Lonesome Sea Ballad, Sailing on the Lowland Low, A Ship Set Sail for North America, Sinking in the Lonesome Sea, There Was a Bold Captain, There Was a Little Ship, (The) Turkish Rebilee (Reveille).

Texts: Story Type A: Abrahams, *Sngr & Her Sgs*, 143–144 / Abrahams & Foss, *Anglo-Am Fsg Style*, 79–80 / Bronson, IV, 329 (#41), 332–333 (#49), 337–338 (#61), 340 (#67), 342–345 (#70, #73, #74), 347–351

(#81, #84, #86, #89), 353–354 (#95, #96), 356–359 (#101–#103, #105 / Burton & Manning, *E Tenn State U Coll Flklre: Fsgs*, 37–38 / Burton & Manning, *E Tenn State U Coll Flklre: Fsgs II*, 86–87 / Bush, *Flk Sgs Cntrl West Va*, I, 88–90 / *Colorado Fsg Bull*, 1964, 18–19 / Creighton, *Fsgs So NB*, 17–18 (A) / Emrich, *Am Flk Ptry*, 345–347 / Fowke, *Penguin Bk Can Flk Sgs*, 188–189 / Fowke, *Trd Sngrs & Sgs Ont*, 156–157 / Gainer, *Flk Sgs West Va Hills*, 96–97 / Grover, *Hrtge Sgs*, 138 / Moore & Moore, *Blds & Flk Sgs SW*, 134–135 / *NC Flklre*, 1974, 147–148 / Parler, *Ark Ballet Bk*, 24–25 / Ritchie, *Flk Sgs So Aplchns*, 80–81 / Scott, *Bld of Am*, 138–139 / Shellans, *Flk Sgs Blue Ridge Mts*, 62–63 / Warner, *Flk Sgs & Blds Estn Sbrd*, 51–52.

B: Jameson, *Sweet Rivers Sg*, 52–53.

G: Creighton, *Fsgs So NB*, 19–20 (B) / Fowke, *Trd Sngrs & Sgs Ont*, 20–21.

Fragments & Title Lists: Bronson, IV, 317 (#7), 321 (#20), 328–329 (#40, #42), 336–337 (#59), 339 (#65), 345–346 (#76), 350–351 (#87, #88) / Brown, *NC Flklre*, IV, 120–124 / Fowke, *Trd Sngrs & Sgs Ont*, 100 / *JEMF Quarterly*, IX, 2 (1973), 61 / Karpeles, *Flk Sgs Newfdld* (1971), 107 / *Ky Flklre Record*, 1965, 65 / *MWF*, 1963, 136 / Rosenberg, *Fsgs Va*, 122.

Discussion: The Story Types F and G, which feature retribution on the captain at the hands of the boy's spirit, do not originate in Canada as Coffin (*BTBNA*, p. 155) and Fowke (*Canada's Story in Sg*, p. 38, and *Trd Sngrs & Sgs Ont*, p. 164) suggest, but evidently in Ireland, as several unpublished versions in the Irish Folklore Commission's archives have this episode. See also Abrahams, *Sngr & Her Sgs*, p. 142, where Almeda Riddle gives two stanzas of another version she learned from an Irishman in which retribution also occurs, but at the hands of a pirate ship. (For other Irish additions of supernatural elements to nonsupernatural ballads see the discussion to 248 in this Supplement and further references there.)

Other unusual features in Canadian texts are in the Fowke, *Penguin Bk Can Flk Sgs* and *Trd Sngrs & Sgs Ont*, Type A version, where the boy is wrapped in a bull's skin in order to make his way through the water to the enemy ship, either as a disguise or as an aid in floating. This is not found in any other North American versions, and in very few British (Child B; *JFSS*, II, 9 [1906], 244; Ford, *Vagabond Songs & Ballads of Scotland*, I, 105–108. In Child C he is buried in a "cow's-hide"). In the Creighton, *Fsgs So NB*, Type G text the captain is killed in the retribution scene, but the crewmen are saved, which might be related to Story Type F in which the mate is singled out for survival. In Bronson, IV, #95 (Type A), from North Carolina, it is the boy's love for the captain's daughter rather than his affection for the rest of the crew that keeps him from sinking the "Golden Vanity" immediately.

287. CAPTAIN WARD AND THE RAINBOW

Texts: *Story Type* A: Carey, *Md Flk Lgds & Flk Sgs*, 99.

C: Peacock, *Sgs Newfdld Outpts*, III, 840–841.

Discussion: The Peacock Type C text is directly indebted to the *Forget-me-not Songster* text that Barry reprints in *Brit Blds Me* (D), missing only a couple of minor stanzas in the middle and the three at the end in which the king laments the loss of his property and his best sea lords.

289. THE MERMAID

Local Titles: "Merrimac" at Sea, The Raging Sea How It Roars, The Ship a-Raging, The Waves on the Sea.

Texts: *Story Type* A: Bronson, IV, 377–378 (#18), 381–384 (#26, #27, #29, #30, #32) / Emrich, *Am Flk Ptry*, 349 / Gainer, *Flk Sgs West Va Hills*, 98–99 / *SFQ*, 1972, 24–25.

C: Abrahams, *Sngr & Her Sgs*, 83–85 / Bronson, IV, 373–374 (#7), 378 (#20) / Jackson, *Flklre & Society*, 120–121 / Moore & Moore, *Blds & Flk Sgs SW*, 136–137.

D: A short, lyrical rendering of the tragedy: the captain laments that he will see his family no more, a crew member laments that he will never see his grieving love again, and a girl laments that her lover was drowned when the ship went down. *Flklre Forum*, 1974, 45.

Fragments & Title Lists: Bronson, IV, 374–377 (#8, #10, #13), 382 (#28) / Brown, *NC Flklre*, IV, 124–125 / *JEMF Quarterly*, IX, 2 (1973), 61 / Rosenberg, *Fsgs Va*, 81.

Discussion: The new Story Type D is from recorded hillbilly tradition. It bears some resemblance to the *JAF*, 1957, text in that it features a lamenting girl as an on-stage figure, though in this hillbilly version she is not on shipboard and is not among those about to die (see discussion to 289 in *BTBNA*, p. 158).

Most of the examples of the C story type are not localized (cf. the story description in *BTBNA*, p. 157). They are in the textual tradition of Child D (which, perhaps coincidentally, does specify Greenland as the locale) in that there is no mermaid; the captain and crew lament their imminent deaths and loss of their loved ones until the ship sinks. Only the Abrahams, *Sngr & Her Sgs*, version of this story type is localized, and that to New Orleans. It has an additional feature that is unique in the 289 tradition: the ship shares the name of the famous vessel of the Confederacy, the "Merrimac," though the text shows no recognizable debt to two of the better known native American ballads in which that famous warship appears (Laws A18, A26).

293. JOHN OF HAZELGREEN

Local Titles: Jock o' Hazeldean, Johnny from Hazelgreen.

Texts: Story Type A: Abrahams & Foss, *Anglo-Am Fsg Style*, 95–96 /
Bronson, IV, 393–395 (#5b, #9, #11).

B: Bronson, IV, 395–396 (#12) / Moore & Moore, *Blds & Flk Sgs SW*,
138–139 (B) / Peacock, *Sgs Newfdld Outpts*, II, 537–538.

Fragments & Title Lists: Bronson, IV, 392–396 (#4, #6, #10, #14) /
Moore & Moore, *Blds & Flk Sgs SW*, 137–138 (A).

Discussion: Several texts hint at an association with the common Anglo-
American "returned unrecognized lover" theme, but this element is too
covert to recognize as a new story type. In these texts it appears as if the
father and son figures have been merged into one, and that it is actually
the lover himself, unrecognized as such, who initially encounters the
forlorn maiden and tries to tempt her into marriage with another. She
refuses, asserting her fidelity to Hazelgreen, upon which that young man
himself takes her into his arms and so forth. All the texts which feature
this seeming crossing are impressionistic and in most cases obviously
fragmentary; none have taken on verses which would settle the matter
unambiguously—the producing of a token, for instance. The narrative
similarity between the usual "John of Hazelgreen" Type A story and the
"returned unrecognized lover" theme is obvious, but an even further
link in the association might be the opening two stanzas in several versions of 293 which resemble, both in phrasing and in story, the formulaic
openings of many ballads of disguised lovers: the walking by the woods
or river, the spying of a maid lamenting her absent lover, and the step-
ping up to her side and addressing her as to the cause of her distress. This
potential crossing—for that is as much as it is in the texts available—is
best seen in Bronson, IV, 395–396 (#12).

The Peacock, *Sgs Newfdld Outpts*, Type B text lacks the father's attempt to persuade the girl to accept his son in place of her absent lover.
After she has described her plight, they simply ride off together to his
castle where Johnny waits.

The Moore & Moore, *Blds & Flk Sgs SW*, (A) fragment is textually the
two stanzas of Child E, combining the usual Scott "Jock o' Hazeldean"
opening stanza with a second one from the traditional "John of Hazelgreen" ballad. The tune is the usual Scott air as well. There is no discernible narrative (cf. the Barry, *BFSSNE*, text discussed in *BTBNA*, p.
159). The informant was born in Scotland and emigrated to the U.S. in
1907 (see the discussion to 199 in this Supplement).

Charles G. Zug III, "Scott's 'Jock of Hazeldean': The Re-Creation of
a Traditional Ballad," *JAF*, 86 (1973), 152–160, takes a fresh look at the
relationship between Scott's song and the traditional ballad. He thinks
that Scott was indeed responsible for the whole of the song but composed

it in a manner far closer to the traditional style than that which had characterized his earlier compositions, thus "re-creation." (Cf. references to related scholarship in *BTBNA*, p. 159.)

295. THE BROWN GIRL

Note: At the time of the last edition of *BTBNA* in 1963, there were no reported versions of Child 295 in North American tradition. Quite common, however, was—and is—the thematically related "A Rich Irish Lady" (Laws P9), which was treated under the 295 heading as a derivative of the older ballad. A version from West Virginia which is a direct textual relative of 295 has recently been published, and so I have separated this from the Laws P9 texts and labeled it *Primary Version*, while maintaining recognition of the closely related Laws ballad under the designation *Secondary Version*. (Cf. Child 56 in this Supplement.)

Secondary Version: *Local Titles*: Pretty Sally (Sarah), A Proud Irish Lady, Queen Sally, The Rich Lady from Dublin, Rose of Ardee, Sally Dover, Sally the (Yo') Queen.

Texts: *Story Type* A: Bronson, IV, 403–404 (#2), 407–408 (#12), 410–411 (#20, #21), 413–415 (#29, #32a, #32b, #34), 417–418 (#38a), 421 (#47) / Burton & Manning, *E Tenn State U Coll Flklre: Fsgs*, 34–35 / Emrich, *Am Flk Ptry*, 133–134 / Grover, *Hrtge Sgs*, 35 / Huntington, *Sgs Whalemen Sang*, 111–112 / Karpeles, *Flk Sgs Newfdld* (1971), 108–110 (A, B) / Moore & Moore, *Blds & Flk Sgs SW*, 140–141 / *NC Flklre*, 1973, 145–146, 179–180; 1974, 152.

B: Jameson, *Sweet Rivers Sg*, 61.

C: Boette, *Singa Hipsy Doodle*, 42–43.

I: A short version, more homiletic lyric than narrative, goes like this: a rich, beautiful, and proud lady comes to London. She will have no one, and it is prophesied that her finery will fade as she "dances on." She dies and her beauty decays in the grave, while some other fine lady wears her clothes. Bronson, IV, 407 (#11).

J: The story is as Type A, but the roles are reversed throughout, as in the Child ballad and Primary Version Story Type A. Gainer, *Flk Sgs West Va Hills*, 100–101.

Fragments & Title Lists: Bronson, IV, 413 (#27, #28, #30), 418–419 (#39, #40, #43), 422 (#48) / Brown, *NC Flklre*, IV, 166–168 / Rosenberg, *Fsgs Va*, 13.

Primary Version: *Local Titles*: The Bonny Brown Girl.

Texts: *Story Type* A: A young man, plighted to a brown girl, is attracted to another woman. He breaks off his relationship with the former by letter, saying that he no longer loves her, because she is so brown. She replies with a letter of her own, saying that she does not value his love anyway. Six months later he falls ill, sends for a doctor, and then for his former love. She comes to his sickbed, but laughs at his condition, returns his troth so that his soul may rest peacefully, and promises to sing and dance on his grave. Boette, *Singa Hipsy Doodle*, 4.

Discussion: The new Story Type I of the Secondary Version preserves the tart "dancing on the grave" and other less memorable lines, but has a last stanza unique in the textual tradition of the ballad which nicely rounds out the homiletic tone of the whole piece. It is from the singing of Bascom Lamar Lunsford who performs many quite original re-creations of traditional ballads.

The single example of the new Story Type J bears some resemblance to Types E and F in its role reversal, which harks back to the Child version (cf. *BTBNA*, p. 161); but this text carries the resemblance even further than Types E and F in that the roles are consistent throughout. It also has another, more striking resemblance to Child 295 Primary Version in that he rejects her on the grounds (the sole ones, in the text) that she is "too brown" for him, a feature not paralleled in any of the other British or North American texts of "A Rich Irish Lady." Despite these similarities, it is textually the broadside ballad of Laws P9 and not a variant of the Child piece.

The only known recovery of the Primary Version ballad from American tradition, said to have been long in the family repertoire (Boette, *Singa Hipsy Doodle*, p. 4), is unique enough that the editor of the volume was led to classify it as Child 73, no doubt misdirected by its title, "The Bonny Brown Girl." Textually, the first seven stanzas are extremely close replicas of stanzas 1, 2, 3, 4, 5, 7, and 8 of the Child B copy, while the remaining three are direct textual relatives of the last three of Child A, though in the first rather than third person. Both Child texts A and B were reprinted in the Sargent & Kittredge edition of *English and Scottish Popular Ballads*, and that work cannot be discounted as a source of many twentieth-century versions of ballads in North American tradition. See 74 and 77 for textual as well as thematic parallels to the episode in this ballad in which the lover's troth is returned, and 78 for similarities to the final stanza.

299. THE TROOPER AND THE MAID

Local Titles: The Soldier and the Maid, Soldier from the North, The Soldier's Farewell.

Texts: *Story Type* A: Gainer, *Flk Sgs West Va Hills*, 102–103 / Moore & Moore, *Blds & Flk Sgs SW*, 142–143.

Fragments & Title Lists: Brown, *NC Flklre*, IV, 125–126 / Rosenberg, *Fsgs Va*, 127.

Discussion: Like most American versions of Story Type A, the texts cited above do not contain the sequence in which she follows him as he returns to his regiment, but end with the circumlocution for "never" which he delivers in response to her inquiry about marriage as he is dressing to depart. The Gainer, *Flk Sgs West Va Hills*, version resembles Child's A text in that he first promises to return, but when pressed to be more specific gives the "never" reply.

BIBLIOGRAPHY AND DISCOGRAPHY

Bibliography

BOOKS AND DISSERTATIONS

Abrahams, Roger D., ed. *A Singer and Her Songs: Almeda Riddle's Book of Ballads*. Baton Rouge: Louisiana State University Press, 1970.

Abrahams, Roger D., and George Foss. *Anglo-American Folksong Style*. Englewood Cliffs, N.J.: Prentice-Hall, 1968.

Barbeau, Marius. *Jongleur Songs of Old Quebec*. New Brunswick, N.J.: Rutgers University Press, 1962.

Baring-Gould, William S., and Ceil Baring-Gould, eds. *The Annotated Mother Goose: Nursery Rhymes Old and New*. New York: Bramhall House, 1962.

Barry, Phillips; Fannie Hardy Eckstorm; and Mary Winslow Smythe. *British Ballads from Maine: The Development of Popular Songs with Texts and Airs*. New Haven: Yale University Press, 1929.

Boatright, Mody C.; Wilson M. Hudson; and Allen Maxwell, eds. *A Good Tale and a Bonnie Tune*. Publications of the Texas Folklore Society, no. 32. Dallas: Southern Methodist University Press, 1964.

Boette, Marie, ed. *Singa Hipsy Doodle and Other Folk Songs of West Virginia*. Parsons, W.Va.: McClain Printing Co., 1971.

Brewster, Paul G., ed. *Ballads and Songs of Indiana*. Indiana University Publications, Folklore Series, no. 1. Bloomington: Indiana University, 1940.

Brocklebank, Joan, and Biddie Kindersley, eds. *A Dorset Book of Folk Songs*. N.p., 1948; rpt., London: English Folk Dance and Song Society, 1966.

Bronson, Bertrand Harris. *The Ballad as Song*. Berkeley: University of California Press, 1969.

Bronson, Bertrand Harris. *The Traditional Tunes of the Child Ballads with Their Texts, According to the Extant Records of Great Britain and America*. 4 vols. Princeton: Princeton University Press, 1959–1972.

Brown, Frank C. *The Frank C. Brown Collection of North Carolina Folklore*. 7 vols. Durham, N.C.: Duke University Press, 1952–1964. Vol. 2, *Folk Ballads from North Carolina*, ed. Henry M. Belden and Arthur Palmer Hudson (1952); Vol. 3, *Folk Songs from North Carolina*, ed. Henry M. Belden and Arthur Palmer Hudson (1952); Vol. 4, *The Music of the Ballads*, ed. Jan Philip Schinhan (1957).

Brunvand, Jan Harold. *A Guide for Collectors of Folklore in Utah*. Salt Lake City: University of Utah Press, 1971.

Buchan, David. *The Ballad and the Folk*. London: Routledge and Kegan Paul, 1972.

Buchan, Peter. *Gleanings of Scarce Old Ballads*. N.p., 1825; rpt., Aberdeen: D. Wyllie and Sons, 1891; rpt., Norwood, Pa.: Norwood Editions, n.d.

Burton, Thomas G., and Ambrose N. Manning, eds. *The East Tennessee State University Collection of Folklore: Folksongs.* Monograph no. 4. Johnson City: Institute of Regional Studies, East Tennessee State University, 1967.

Burton, Thomas G., and Ambrose N. Manning, eds. *The East Tennessee State University Collection of Folklore: Folksongs II.* Johnson City: Research Advisory Council of East Tennessee State University, 1969.

Bush, Michael E. *Folk Songs of Central West Virginia.* 2 vols. Ravenswood, W.Va.: Custom Printing Co., 1969–1970.

Carey, George G. *Maryland Folk Legends and Folk Songs.* Cambridge, Md.: Tidewater Publishers, 1971.

Carey, George G. *Maryland Folklore and Folklife.* Cambridge, Md.: Tidewater Publishers, 1970.

Cheney, Thomas E., ed. *Mormon Songs from the Rocky Mountains: A Compilation of Mormon Folksong.* Publications of the American Folklore Society, Memoir Series, vol. 53. Austin: University of Texas Press, 1968.

Child, Francis James. *The English and Scottish Popular Ballads.* 5 vols. N.p., 1882–1898; rpt., New York: Dover Publications, 1965.

Coffin, Mark Tristram. "American Narrative Obituary Verse and Native American Balladry." Doctoral dissertation, University of Pennsylvania, 1975.

Coffin, Tristram Potter. *The British Traditional Ballad in North America.* Rev. ed. Publications of the American Folklore Society, Bibliographical and Special Series, vol. 2. Philadelphia: American Folklore Society, 1963.

Coffin, Tristram Potter, and Hennig Cohen. *Folklore: From the Working Folk of America.* Garden City, N.Y.: Anchor Press, 1973.

Cohen, Anne B. *Poor Pearl, Poor Girl! The Murdered-Girl Stereotype in Ballad and Newspaper.* Publications of the American Folklore Society, Memoir Series, vol. 58. Austin: University of Texas Press, 1973.

Cohen, John, and Mike Seeger, eds. *The New Lost City Ramblers Song Book.* New York: Oak Publications, 1964.

Combs, Josiah H. *Folk-Songs of the Southern United States (Folk-Songs du Midi des États-Unis).* Ed. D. K. Wilgus. Publications of the American Folklore Society, Bibliographical and Special Series, vol. 19. Austin: University of Texas Press, 1967.

Cox, John Harrington. *Traditional Ballads and Folk-Songs Mainly from West Virginia.* Ed. George Herzog, Herbert Halpert, and George W. Boswell. Publications of the American Folklore Society, Bibliographical and Special Series, vol. 15. Philadelphia: American Folklore Society, 1964.

Cox, John Harrington, ed. *Folk-Songs of the South: Collected under the Auspices of the West Virginia Folk-Lore Society.* Cambridge, Mass.: Harvard University Press, 1925; rpt., Gloucester, Me.: Peter Smith Publisher, n.d.; rpt., New York: Dover Publications, 1967.

Cray, Ed, ed. *The Erotic Muse.* New York: Oak Publications, 1968.

Creighton, Helen. *Folklore of Lunenburg County, Nova Scotia.* National Museum of Canada Bulletin, no. 117, Anthropological Series, no. 29. Ottawa: National Museum of Canada, 1950.

Creighton, Helen. *Maritime Folk Songs*. Toronto: Ryerson Press, 1962.

Creighton, Helen. *Songs and Ballads from Nova Scotia*. Toronto: J. M. Dent and Sons, 1933; rpt., New York: Dover Publications, 1966.

Creighton, Helen, ed. *Folksongs from Southern New Brunswick*. National Museum of Man Publications in Folk Culture, no. 1. Ottawa: National Museum of Canada, 1971.

Davis, Arthur Kyle, Jr., ed. *More Traditional Ballads of Virginia: Collected with the Cooperation of Members of the Virginia Folklore Society*. Chapel Hill: University of North Carolina Press, 1960.

Davis, Arthur Kyle, Jr., ed. *Traditional Ballads of Virginia: Collected under the Auspices of the Virginia Folk-Lore Society*. Cambridge, Mass.: Harvard University Press, 1929; rpt., Charlottesville: University Press of Virginia, 1969.

Dunson, Josh, and Ethel Raim, eds. *Anthology of American Folk Music*. New York: Oak Publications, 1972.

Emrich, Duncan. *American Folk Poetry: An Anthology*. Boston: Little, Brown and Company, 1974.

Emrich, Duncan. *Folklore on the American Land*. Boston: Little, Brown and Company, 1972.

Fauset, Arthur Huff. *Folklore from Nova Scotia*. Memoirs of the American Folklore Society, vol. 24. New York: American Folklore Society, 1931; rpt., Millwood, N.Y.: Kraus Reprint Co., n.d.

Flanders, Helen Hartness. *Country Songs of Vermont*. Schirmer's American Folk-Song Series, set 9. New York: G. Schirmer, 1937.

Flanders, Helen Hartness, ed. *Ancient Ballads Traditionally Sung in New England*. 4 vols. Rev. ed. Philadelphia: University of Pennsylvania Press, 1960–1965.

Ford, Robert, ed. *Vagabond Songs and Ballads of Scotland: With Many Old and Familiar Melodies*. 2 vols. Paisley: Alexander Gardner, 1899–1901; rpt., Norwood, Pa.: Norwood Editions, 1975.

Fowke, Edith, ed. *The Penguin Book of Canadian Folk Songs*. Harmondsworth, Eng.: Penguin Books, 1973.

Fowke, Edith, ed. *Traditional Singers and Songs from Ontario.* Hatboro, Pa.: Folklore Associates, 1965; rpt., Detroit: Gale Research Co., n.d.

Fowke, Edith, and Richard Johnston. *Folk Songs of Canada*. Waterloo, Ont.: Waterloo Music Company, 1954.

Fowke, Edith, and Richard Johnston. *More Folk Songs of Canada*. Waterloo, Ont.: Waterloo Music Company, 1967.

Fowke, Edith; Alan Mills; and Helmut Blume. *Canada's Story in Song*. Toronto: W. J. Gage, n.d.

Fowler, David C. *A Literary History of the Popular Ballad*. Durham, N.C.: Duke University Press, 1968.

Gainer, Patrick W. *Folk Songs from the West Virginia Hills*. Grantsville, W.Va.: Seneca Books, 1975.

Glassie, Henry; Edward D. Ives; and John F. Szwed. *Folksongs and Their Makers*. Bowling Green, Ohio: Bowling Green University Popular Press, 1971.

Greenleaf, Elisabeth Bristol, and Grace Yarrow Mansfield. *Ballads and Sea Songs of Newfoundland.* Cambridge, Mass.: Harvard University Press, 1933; rpt., Detroit: Gale Research Co., n.d.

Greig, Gavin. *Last Leaves of Traditional Ballads and Ballad Airs.* Ed. Alexander Keith. Aberdeen: Buchan Club, 1925.

Grover, Carrie B. *A Heritage of Songs.* Ed. Anne L. Griggs. Bethel, Me.: Privately printed by Gould Academy, n.d.; rpt., Norwood, Pa.: Norwood Editions, n.d.

Henderson, W., ed. *Victorian Street Ballads: A Selection of Popular Ballads Sold in the Street in the Nineteenth Century.* New York: Charles Scribner's Sons, 1938.

Hudson, Wilson M. *Hunters and Healers: Folklore Types and Topics.* Publications of the Texas Folklore Society, no. 35. Austin, Tx.: Encino Press, 1971.

Huntington, Gale. *Songs the Whalemen Sang.* Barre, Mass.: Barre Publishers, 1964; rpt., New York: Dover Publications, 1968.

Jackson, Bruce, ed. *Folklore & Society: Essays in Honor of Benj. A. Botkin.* Hatboro, Pa.: Folklore Associates, 1966; rpt., Norwood, Pa.: Norwood Editions, n.d.

Jameson, Gladys V., ed. *Sweet Rivers of Song: Authentic Ballads, Hymns, Folksongs from the Appalachian Region.* Berea, Ky.: Berea College, 1967.

Joyner, Charles W. *Folk Song in South Carolina.* Tricentennial Booklet, no. 9. Columbia: University of South Carolina Press, 1971.

Justus, May T. *The Complete Peddler's Pack: Games, Songs, Rhymes, and Riddles from Mountain Folklore.* Rev. ed. Knoxville: University of Tennessee Press, 1967.

Karpeles, Maud, ed. *Folk Songs from Newfoundland.* London: Faber and Faber, 1971; Hamden, Ct.: Shoe String Press, 1971.

Killion, Ronald G., and Charles T. Waller. *A Treasury of Georgia Folklore.* Atlanta: Cherokee Publishing Company, 1972.

Laws, G. Malcolm, Jr. *American Balladry from British Broadsides: A Guide for Students and Collectors of Traditional Song.* Publications of the American Folklore Society, Bibliographical and Special Series, vol. 8. Philadelphia: American Folklore Society, 1957.

Laws, G. Malcolm, Jr., *Native American Balladry: A Descriptive Study and a Bibliographical Syllabus.* Rev. ed. Publications of the American Folklore Society, Bibliographical and Special Series, vol. 1. Philadelphia: American Folklore Society, 1964; rpt., Austin: University of Texas Press, 1975.

Leach, MacEdward, ed. *The Ballad Book.* New York: Harper and Brothers, 1955; rpt., Cranbury, N.J.: A. S. Barnes, n.d.

Leach, MacEdward. *Folk Ballads and Songs of the Lower Labrador Coast.* National Museum of Canada Bulletin, no. 201, Anthropological Series, no. 68. Ottawa: National Museum of Canada, 1965. (Cited in MS form in *BTBNA* as *Fsgs Labr Cst.*)

Leach, MacEdward, and Tristram P. Coffin, eds. *The Critics and the Ballad.* Carbondale: Southern Illinois University Press, 1961.

Leach, MacEdward, and Henry Glassie. *A Guide for Collectors of Oral Tradi-*

tions and Folk Cultural Materials in Pennsylvania. Harrisburg: Pennsylvania Historical and Museum Commission, 1968.

Lloyd, A. L. *Folk Song in England.* London: Lawrence and Wishart, 1967; rpt., New York: Beekman Publishers, 1975.

Lloyd, A. L., and Isabel Aretz de Ramón y Rivera, eds. *Folk Songs of the Americas.* Prepared under the Auspices of the International Music Council with the Assistance of the United Nations Educational, Scientific and Cultural Organization (UNESCO). New York: Oak Publications, 1965.

Lomax, Alan, ed. *The Penguin Book of American Folk Songs.* Baltimore: Penguin Books, 1964.

Long, Eleanor. *"The Maid" and "The Hangman": Myth and Tradition in a Popular Ballad.* Folklore Studies, no. 21. Berkeley: University of California Press, 1971.

MacColl, Ewan, ed. *Folk Songs and Ballads of Scotland.* New York: Oak Publications, 1965.

McIntosh, David S. *Folk Songs and Singing Games of the Illinois Ozarks.* Ed. Dale Whiteside. Carbondale: Southern Illinois University Press, 1974.

Mackey, Julie Reich. "Medieval Metrical Saints' Lives and the Origin of the Ballad." Doctoral dissertation, University of Pennsylvania, 1968.

Manny, Louise, and James Reginald Wilson. *Songs of Miramichi.* Fredericton, N.B.: Brunswick Press, 1968.

Moore, Ethel, and Chauncey O. Moore. *Ballads and Folk Songs of the Southwest: More Than 600 Titles, Melodies, and Texts Collected in Oklahoma.* Norman: University of Oklahoma Press, 1964.

Morton, Robin, ed. *Come Day, Go Day, God Send Sunday: The Songs and Life Story, Told in His Own Words, of John Maguire, Traditional Singer and Farmer from Co. Fermanagh.* London: Routledge and Kegan Paul, 1973.

Nygard, Holger Olof. *The Ballad of "Heer Halewijn," Its Forms and Variations in Western Europe: A Study of the History and Nature of a Ballad Tradition.* Knoxville: University of Tennessee Press, 1958.

Parler, Mary Celestia. *An Arkansas Ballet Book.* N.p., 1963; rpt., Norwood, Pa.: Norwood Editions, 1975.

Peacock, Kenneth. *Songs of the Doukhobors.* National Museum of Canada Bulletin, no. 231, Folklore Series, no. 7. Ottawa: National Museum of Canada, 1970.

Peacock, Kenneth, ed. *Songs of the Newfoundland Outports.* 3 vols. National Museum of Canada Bulletin, no. 197, Anthropological Series, no. 65. Ottawa: National Museum of Canada, 1965.

Pittman, J.; Colin Brown; and Charles MacKay, eds. *The Songs of Scotland: A Collection of One Hundred and Ninety Songs.* London: Boosey and Hawkes, [1877].

Purslow, Frank, ed. *Marrow Bones: English Folk Songs from the Hammond and Gardiner Mss.* London: E.F.D.S. Publications, n.d.; rpt., Norwood, Pa.: Norwood Editions, 1965.

Purslow, Frank, ed. *The Wanton Seed: More English Folk Songs from the Ham-*

mond & Gardiner Mss. London: E.F.D.S. Publications, n.d.; rpt., Norwood, Pa.: Norwood Editions, 1968.

Raim, Ethel, and Josh Dunson, eds. *Grass Roots Harmony.* New York: Oak Publications, 1968.

Reeves, James, ed. *The Everlasting Circle: English Traditional Verse Edited with an Introduction and Notes from the Manuscripts of S. Baring-Gould, H. E. D. Hammond and George B. Gardiner.* London: Heinemann, 1960.

Ritchie, Jean. *Folk Songs of the Southern Appalachians as sung by Jean Ritchie.* New York: Oak Publications, 1965.

Roberts, Leonard. *Sang Branch Settlers: Folksongs and Tales of a Kentucky Mountain Family.* Publications of the American Folklore Society, Memoir Series, vol. 61. Austin: University of Texas Press, 1974.

Rocky Mountain Collection. Salt Lake City: Intermountain Folkmusic Council, 1962.

Rosenberg, Bruce A. *The Folksongs of Virginia: A Checklist of the WPA Holdings at Alderman Library, University of Virginia.* Charlottesville: University Press of Virginia, 1969.

Sargent, Helen Child, and George Lyman Kittredge, eds. *English and Scottish Popular Ballads Edited from the Collection of Francis James Child.* Boston: Houghton Mifflin, 1904.

Scarborough, Dorothy. *A Song Catcher in Southern Mountains: American Folk Songs of British Ancestry.* New York: Columbia University Press, 1937.

Scott, John Anthony. *The Ballad of America: The History of the United States in Song and Story.* New York: Grosset and Dunlap, 1967; rpt., New York: Bantam Books, 1972.

Scott, John Anthony, ed. *Living Documents in American History.* 2 vols. New York: Washington Square Press, 1963–1968.

Scott, John Anthony, ed. *Settlers on the Eastern Shore, 1607–1750.* New York: Alfred A. Knopf, 1967.

Seeger, Peggy, and Ewan MacColl, eds. *The Singing Island: A Collection of English and Scots Folksongs.* London: Mills Music, 1960.

Shellans, Herbert. *Folk Songs of the Blue Ridge Mountains.* New York: Oak Publications, 1968.

Sweeney, Margaret. *Fact, Fiction and Folklore of Southern Indiana.* New York: Vantage Press, 1967.

The Universal Songster. 3 vols. London: Jones & Co., 1832.

Vargyas, Lajos. *Researches into the Mediaeval History of Folk Ballad.* Budapest: Akadémiai Kiadó, 1967.

Walker, William E., and Robert L. Welker. *Reality and Myth: Essays in American Literature in Memory of Richmond Croom Beatty.* Nashville: Vanderbilt University Press, 1964.

Warner, Frank M. *Folk Songs and Ballads of the Eastern Seaboard from a Collector's Notebook.* Eugenia Dorothy Blount Lamar Lectures Delivered at Wesleyan College on April 22 and 23, 1963. Macon: Southern Press, 1963.

Watson, Doc. *The Songs of Doc Watson.* New York: Oak Publications, 1971.

Wells, Evelyn Kendrick. *The Ballad Tree: A Study of British and American*

Ballads, Their Folklore, Verse, and Music. New York: Ronald Press Company, 1950.

Wilgus, D. K., and Carol Sommer, eds. *Folklore International: Essays in Traditional Literature, Belief, and Custom in Honor of Wayland Debs Hand*. Hatboro, Pa.: Folklore Associates, 1967; rpt., Detroit: Gale Research Co., n.d.

William, R. Vaughan, and A. L. Lloyd, eds. *The Penguin Book of English Folk Songs: From the Journal of the Folk Song Society and the Journal of the English Folk Dance and Song Society*. Harmondsworth, Eng.: Penguin Books, 1959.

PERIODICALS

Ball State University Forum (formerly *Ball State Teachers College Forum*), Muncie, Ind.
Bulletin of the Folk-Song Society of the Northeast, Cambridge, Mass. (*BFSSNE*)
Colorado Folksong Bulletin, Boulder, Col. (*Colorado Fsg Bull*)
Comparative Literature Studies, College Park, Md.
Folk Life, Cardiff, Wales.
Folklore Forum, Bloomington, Ind. (*Flklre Forum*)
Folkways Monthly, State College, Pa.
Green Mountain Whittlin's, Burlington, Vt., et al. (*Green Mt Whittlin's*)
Hermathena, Dublin.
Indiana Folklore, Bloomington, Ind. (*Ind Flklre*)
Jahrbuch für Volksliedforschung, Berlin.
JEMF Quarterly (formerly *JEMF Newsletter*), Los Angeles, Cal.
Journal of American Folklore, Washington, D.C. (*JAF*)
Journal of the English Folk Dance and Song Society, London. (*JEFDSS*)
Journal of the Folklore Institute, Bloomington, Ind.
Journal of the Folk-Song Society, London. (*JFSS*)
Journal of the Irish Folk Song Society, London. (*JIFSS*)
Kentucky Folklore Record, Murray, Ky. (*Ky Flklre Record*)
Keystone Folklore (formerly *Keystone Folklore Quarterly*), Philadelphia, Pa.
McNeese Review, Lake Charles, La.
Midwest Folklore, Bloomington, Ind. (*MWF*)
Mississippi Folklore Register, Columbus, Miss. (*Miss Flklre Reg*)
Modern Philology, Chicago, Ill. (*Mod Phil*)
Mountain Life and Work, Berea, Ky. (*Mt Life & Work*)
New York Folklore Quarterly, Cooperstown, N.Y. (*NYFQ*)
North Carolina Folklore Journal (formerly *North Carolina Folklore*), Chapel Hill, N.C. (*NC Flklre*)
Northeast Folklore, Orono, Me. (*NE Flklre*)
Philological Papers, Morgantown, W.Va. (*Phil Papers*)
Revue des Langues Romanes, Montpellier, France.
Selected Reports, Los Angeles, Cal.

Sing Out!, New York, N.Y.
Southern Folklore Quarterly, Gainesvilla, Fla. (*SFQ*)
Studies in the Literary Imagination, Atlanta, Ga. (*Studies Literary Imagination*)
Tennessee Folklore Society Bulletin, Nashville, Tenn. (*Tenn FLS Bull*)
Tennessee Studies in Literature, Knoxville, Tenn.
Traditional Topics, Leeds, England.
Western Folklore, Berkeley, Cal. (*WF*)

DISCOGRAPHY

FH 5723. "Harry Jackson, the Cowboy: His Songs, Ballads & Brag Talk." Harry Jackson. Folkways Records.
INT 25016. "Folksongs & Music from the Berryfields of Blair." Ed. Hamish Henderson. Prestige/International Records.
LEA 4055. "Folk Ballads from Donegal and Derry." Ed. Hugh Shields. Leader Records.

INDEX TO STANDARD TITLES
OF BALLADS AND SONGS

Archie o Cawfield (188), 253

Babylon (14), 219
The Baffled Knight (112), 204, 246–247
The Bailiff's Daughter of Islington (105), 245–246
The Battle of Otterburn (161), 250
The Bent Sae Brown (71), 231
Bessy Bell and Mary Gray (201), 252, 256–257
The Bitter Withy, 249
The Bold Pedlar and Robin Hood (132), 248
The Bold Princess Royal (Laws K29), 251
The Bold Soldier (Laws M27), 213
The Bonnie House o Airlie (199), 253–254
Bonnie James Campbell (210), 258
Bonny Barbara Allen (84), 200, 239–241, 270
Bonny Bee Hom (92), 242
The Bonny Earl of Murray (181), 252
The Braes of Yarrow (214), 195, 219, 258–260
The Bramble Briar (Laws M32), 219
The Broom of Cowdenknowes (217), 260–261
The Broomfield Hill (43), 223
The Brown Girl (295), 196, 198, 204, 233, 281–282
The Butcher Boy (Laws P24), 235

Captain Ward and the Rainbow (287), 279
Captain Wedderburn's Courtship (46), 200, 209, 210, 211, 223–224, 236
The Cherry-Tree Carol (54), 227–228
Clerk Saunders (69), 231
The Crafty Farmer (283), 277
The Cruel Brother (11), 216
The Cruel Mother (20), 198, 204, 221–222
The Cumberland (Laws A26), 279
The Cumberland's Crew (Laws A18), 279

The Daemon Lover (James Harris) (243), 196, 201, 263–267, 271
The Death of Queen Jane (170), 251
Dives and Lazarus (56), 228–229
Down in the Green Wood's Valley, 204, 221–222
The Dying Hobo (Laws H3), 241

Earl Brand (7), 213
Edward (13), 196, 198, 217–219
The Elfin Knight (2), 198, 200, 209–210, 211, 236
Erlinton (8), 213

Fair Annie (62), 229
Fair Margaret and Sweet William (74), 198, 232–233, 236, 282
The False Knight upon the Road (3), 200, 202, 210–211
The False Lover Won Back (218), 261
The Famous Flower of Serving-Men (106), 196, 246
Far Fannil Town, 234

The Farmer's Curst Wife (278), 200, 204, 210, 275–276

The Gaberlunyie-Man, 277
Geordie (209), 199, 257–258
The George Aloe and the Sweepstake (285), 277
Get Up and Bar the Door (275), 273–274
Glasgow Peggie (228), 196, 203, 262–263
The Golden Vanity (The Sweet Trinity) (286), 200, 277–278
The Green Bushes (Laws P2), 199
The Grey Cock (Saw You My Father?) (248), 200, 236, 240, 267–271, 278
The Gypsy Laddie (200), 199, 254–256

The Half-Hitch (Laws N23), 223
Henry Martyn (250), 204, 250–251, 271
Here's a Health unto All True Lovers, 267–271
High Barbary (Laws K33), 251, 277
Hind Horn (17), 219–220
The Hunting of the Cheviot (162), 249–250

I Gave My Love A Cherry, 224

James Harris (The Daemon Lover) (243), 196, 201, 263–267, 271
Jamie Douglas (204), 257
The Jew's Daughter (Sir Hugh) (155), 197, 248–249
John of Hazelgreen (293), 199, 280–281
Johnie Cock (114), 247–248
Johnie Scott (99), 244–245
The Jolly Beggar (279), 277
Judas (23), 222

Katharine Jaffray (221), 189, 261–262
Katie Morey (Laws N24), 247
The Keyhole in the Door, 223
King Edward the Fourth and the Tanner of Tamworth (273), 272
King James and the Tinker, 272
King John and the Bishop (45), 223

The King's Dochter Lady Jean (52), 226
The Kitchie-Boy (252), 204
The Knight and the Shepherd's Daughter (110), 246

Lady Alice (85), 199, 240, 241
Lady Isabel and the Elf-Knight (4), 203, 211–212, 230, 240, 265, 271
Lady Maisry (65), 196, 229–230, 234
Lamkin (93), 204, 242–243
The Lass of Roch Royal (76), 195, 196, 198, 234–235
Little Musgrave and Lady Barnard (81), 203, 237–238, 249
Lizie Lindsay (226), 262
Lizie Wan (51), 198
The Long Peggin' Awl, 210
Lord Derwentwater (208), 234, 257
Lord Lovel (75), 233–234, 240
Lord Randal (12), 216–217
Lord Thomas and Fair Annet (73), 198, 230, 231–232, 249, 265
Lovely Joan, 247
The Lowlands of Holland, 242

The Maid and the Horse, 247
The Maid Freed from the Gallows (95), 202, 243–244
The Maid on the Shore (Laws K27), 223
The Marriage of Sir Gawain (31), 223
Mary Hamilton (173), 198, 251–252
Mary's Dream (Laws K20), 268
The Mermaid (289), 265, 279
Mines of Coal Creek, 266

Nancy of Yarmouth (Laws M38), 204

O Once I Loved a Lass, 268–271
Oh No, Not I, 266
Our Goodman (274), 272–273

Pearl Bryan (Laws F1, F2, F3, dF51), 199
Pretty Fair Miss (Laws N42), 199
Prince Robert (87), 242
Proud Lady Margaret (47), 209

Raise a Ruckus Tonight, 231

The Rantin Laddie (240), 263
Rare Willie Drowned in Yarrow (The Water o Gamrie) (215), 196, 260
A Rich Irish Lady (Laws P9), 204, 281–282
Riddles Wisely Expounded (1), 200, 209, 210, 211, 224
Riley's Farewell (Laws M8), 235
Robin Hood and Little John (125), 248
Robin Hood Rescuing Three Squires (140), 248

Sailor's Tragedy (Laws P34A), 235
Saw You My Father? (The Grey Cock) (248), 200, 236, 240, 267–271, 278
Scarboro Sand (Laws K18), 246
Seventeen Come Sunday (Laws O17), 199
Sir Andrew Barton (167), 204, 250–251
Sir Hugh (The Jew's Daughter) (155), 197, 248–249
Sir James the Rose (213), 258
Sir Lionel (18), 220–221
Sir Patrick Spens (58), 229
The Suffolk Miracle (272), 271–272
The Sweet Trinity (The Golden Vanity (286), 200, 277–278
Sweet William's Ghost (77), 233, 235–236, 267–270, 282

Ten Thousand Miles, 264
Thirty Pieces of Silver, 222
The Three Ravens (The Twa Corbies) (26), 222

The Trooper and the Maid (299), 282–283
True Lover's Farewell, 264–265
The Turkish Lady (Laws O26), 227
The Twa Brothers (49), 198, 225
The Twa Corbies (The Three Ravens) (26), 222
The Twa Sisters (10), 198, 199, 213–216

The Unquiet Grave (78), 236, 268, 282

Waly, Waly, 257
The Water o Gamrie (Rare Willie Drowned in Yarrow) (215), 196, 260
The Whummil Bore (27), 223
The Wife of Usher's Well (79), 236–237
The Wife Wrapt in Wether's Skin (277), 274–275
Willie and Earl Richard's Daughter (102), 245
Willie and Lady Maisry (70), 231
Willie Macintosh (183), 252
Willie o Winsbury (100), 245
Willie's Fatal Visit (255), 267–268
Willy O!, 267–271

The Yorkshire Bite (Laws L1), 277
Young Andrew (48), 224–225
Young Beichan (53), 197, 226–227
Young Hunting (68), 198, 201, 230–231